WINSTANLEY THE DIGGER

Dürer's depiction of the *sol iustitiae* or Sun of Righteousness, from Malachi 4:2, the main image in Winstanley's works. *The Metropolitan Museum of Art, Fletcher Fund, 1919*

WINSTANLEY

THE

DIGGER

A Literary Analysis of
Radical Ideas in the
English Revolution

T. Wilson Hayes

HARVARD UNIVERSITY PRESS

CAMBRIDGE, MASSACHUSETTS

AND LONDON, ENGLAND

1979

Publication of this volume has
been aided by a grant from
the Andrew W. Mellon Foundation

Library of Congress Cataloging in Publication Data

Hayes, Thomas Wilson, 1940-
    Winstanley the Digger.

    Includes bibliographical references and index.
    1. Winstanley, Gerrard, b. 1609. I. Title.
DA429.W5H39   320.5'312'0924   [B]   79-695
ISBN 0-674-95368-1

To Heather and Claire

PREFACE

IN THE FOLLOWING study I view the works of the seventeenth-century pamphleteer Gerrard Winstanley from a literary perspective. Such an approach enables me to bridge the gap previous commentators have seen between the ecstatic millenarian of the early pamphlets and the later communist theoretician. By trying to do justice to the man and his works, I hope to promote a better understanding of the connection between literature and politics. A careful look at Winstanley's evolving symbolism, which embodies the development of his thought, shows that he defies categorization as a mystic or a materialist and is best seen as an immensely talented poet-prophet in the tradition of Langland and Blake. Placing Winstanley in the intellectual landscape of the English Revolution and analyzing the typological method of biblical exegesis in his early pamphlets allows me to explain the dialectic of his alchemical metaphors and clarify his relationship to other seventeenth-century writers. A consideration of the political implications of Winstanley's epistemology and an exploration of the rhetorical structure of the Digger pamphlets points up his espousal of moderation as a check against libertinism and shows how Winstanley grounds his view of natural and historical change in hermeneutics and bases his idea of civil society on the utopian family.

It is a pleasure to acknowledge my great debt to Christopher Hill for his warm reception of my original proposal to write a literary study of Winstanley. Without his encouragement over the last three years, I would not have completed this book. And without the guidance of J. Max Patrick, who introduced me to the serious study of seventeenth-century literature and history, I would not have been capable of writing it. C. H. George and Olivier Lutaud graciously answered queries concerning their work on Winstanley. In addition, Ted-Larry Pebworth, Claude Summers, Frank L. Huntley, John F. Huntley, Florence Sandler, and especially John T. Shawcross aided my work by the generous reception they accorded my paper "Gerrard Winstanley as a Literary Craftsman" at the Second Biennial Renaissance Conference at the University of Michigan-Dearborn in October 1976. Don Beecher, Patrick Cruttwell, and George Hibbard provided a similar stimulus by their remarks on my presentation of "Gerrard Winstanley and the Utopian Family" at the North Central Conference of the Renaissance Society of America at Carleton University in April 1978. I tested my ideas in discussions with Robert Fallon, Warren Cherniak, Stanley E. Fish, Carole Kaske, Lindsay Mann, and my colleagues at Baruch College granted me many kindnesses.

I especially want to thank Douglas Bush, who meticulously read the entire typescript, provided invaluable suggestions, and saved me from many blunders. Remaining errors are, of course, my own. The Baruch College Scholars Assistance Program granted funds for microfilming tracts from the British Library and from Jesus College Library, Oxford, where I was aided by Hilary Carr. The librarians of Cambridge University Library, Dr. Williams' Library, Lambeth Palace Library, the New York Public Library, New York University Library, and the McAlpin Collection at Union Theological Seminary let me use their resources. A portion of Chapter One appeared in *Notes and Queries*, and I thank the Oxford University Press for permission to use the material here. Occasional sentences appeared in articles and reviews in *Clio*, *Ambix*, *Seventeenth-Century News*, and *Bucknell Review*. My greatest debt is to Joanne Hayes, who, as a professional journalist, insists that her husband's prose be intelligible.

I have not modernized or "corrected" seventeenth-century sources, nor have I used the notation [*sic*]. Winstanley's unedited pamphlets are quoted from the copies in The British Library. All other Winstanley quotations, unless otherwise specified, are from George H. Sabine's edition of *The Works of Gerrard Winstanley* (1941, Cornell University Press; used by permission of the publisher). Abbreviations in the notes follow the master list in the annual *MLA International Bibliography*. Dates are English Old Style, but the year is taken to begin on 1 January.

CONTENTS

I
THE RISING SUN
1

II
THE DARKENING CLOUD
46

III
OIL IN HIS OWN LAMP
88

IV
THE SEED OF LIFE
128

V
THE IMPRISONED EARTH
174

NOTES
221

BIBLIOGRAPHICAL NOTE
247

INDEX
249

. . . and as for England, almost the last significant scrap of news from that quarter was the revolution of 1649.

Thoreau, *Walden*

I

THE RISING SUN

Today Gerrard Winstanley stands with his more famous contemporaries, John Lilburne, Thomas Hobbes, and James Harrington, as one of the important political theorists produced by the English Revolution. His rise from obscurity dates from Thomas Carlyle's brief admiration of him in his collection of Cromwell's papers.[1] And although interest in him has accelerated since the rediscovery of his works at the end of the nineteenth century, little attention has been paid to the way he expresses himself.[2] No attempt has been made to understand his symbolism or to analyze his prose style. And commentators tend to describe Winstanley's exposition as impenetrably obscure,[3] or dismiss it as a peculiar characteristic of the age.[4] In my book I set out to refute this view, for as J. Max Patrick indicates, Winstanley's works "constitute a literature which is . . . striking in its power of phrase and image, potent in its iconoclasm, suggestive of Traherne in its mysticism and pantheism, and indicative of the seventeenth-century trend toward secularism and materialism." Patrick points out that "a knowledge of Winstanley's early religious tracts is essential to an understanding of the development of his ideas, and that they contain most of the seeds of his later teachings," and he notes that "Winstanley's ideas were in advance of his vocabulary" and he therefore "was often forced into allegorical language or symbolism."[5]

Christopher Hill has written, "we should read Winstanley as we read a poet, as we read William Blake, and as Winstanley himself read the Bible."[6] My study attempts such a reading and tries to show that while Winstanley, like other radical pamphleteers and preachers of his day, naturally conveys his thoughts in religious terms, his special use of those terms ranks him among the important poet-prophets of the English language. Viewing his works in a literary perspective minimizes the sterile debate about whether he is a political materialist or a religious mystic and clarifies his position in the history of revolutionary utopianism. Winstanley was an extraordinary man. Neither an original theologian nor a profound political philosopher, he was primarily a self-taught mechanic preacher, a rhetorician, a craftsman in prose, and occasionally

1

a true poet in the Miltonic and Blakean sense. Like Milton's Samson, he saw himself as a leader of people, a prophet come to guide those who would follow the directions of the inner light. This doctrine, handed down from St. Paul to Augustine to Nicholas of Cusa, was alternately taken up by the Zwickau prophets, the Wittenberg radicals, and the Anabaptists and Familists.[7] Like other mechanic preachers, Winstanley used the idea of the light within, a metaphor with powerful political implications, to counter the notion that people have no choice but to sin and do evil. But more than that, he saw that the inner light enabled working people to challenge the widespread notion that men and women cannot control what happens to them and are the instruments of "God's will," which usually turns out to be the will of the rich and the powerful.[8]

Another important idea Winstanley molded to his purpose is that people are perfectible. Using Philo of Alexandria's interpretation of the prophetic books of the Bible, the twelfth-century monk Joachim of Fiore concluded that history falls into three overlapping stages, corresponding to the parts of the Trinity. The Age of the Father was the Kingdom of Law; the Age of the Son was the Kingdom of Grace; and the Age of the Spirit, yet to come, is the Kingdom of Grace Abounding when all will be saved. Thus Joachim was perhaps the first to suggest "dynamic processes inherent in human history itself," which would lead to perfection.[9] If people are perfectible, the next important question is how and when this perfection might be obtained. Such an idea inevitably has radical if not outright revolutionary implications, which, in times of economic stress, may be seized upon by those whose expectations are thwarted by material necessity. When John Wycliffe argued for a return to an imagined form of early Christianity, Protestantism became a reality. His "evidence," of course, was the Bible itself. His "extreme reliance upon scriptural authority in preference to the accumulated wisdom of the church" paved the way for the radical doctrine of the priesthood of all believers, a doctrine adopted by radical sects from the Lollards in fourteenth-century England to the Anabaptists of sixteenth-century Münster.[10] Following Wycliffe, and infused with Calvinistic fervor, John Foxe, in his *Actes and Monuments* (popularly known as "The Book of Martyrs"), forged the doctrines of predestination and the elect nation into a potent nationalistic faith that appealed directly to the poor and the disenfranchised.[11] In his turn, bringing together Foxe's notion of a chosen nation waiting upon the Lord and Thomas More's idea of humanistic communism, Winstanley called for the creation of a collectivist state. Undoubtedly he would understand why his ideas remain controversial more than three hundred years after he articulated them. He would also acknowledge that the power and influence of those ideas are directly related to the way they are expressed and that this is not a superficial matter of articulating disputed doctrines in an interesting way, but a matter of ethics. For he knew he was not merely dressing insurgent thoughts in clever language or imposing an arbitrary order on chaotic experience. He repeatedly insisted that people would do well to recognize that there is a pattern in nature and history. And, as Stanley Edgar Hyman explains in another context, "that this vision of order and form is primarily metaphoric makes it no less real."[12]

IN SEVENTEENTH-CENTURY Lancashire, private property and biblical prophecy sustained the hard-working men and women of the clothmaking industry. Nourished by such physical and spiritual fare, the Winstanleys of Wigan enjoyed a degree of social prominence and political importance. Like most local gentry they opposed the official state church as administered by the bishops under the Archbishop of Canterbury. In 1605 Edward Winstanley, a cloth merchant, and his wife were called before the courts and probably fined for holding conventicles, meetings of dissident churchmembers. However, on 10 October 1609 they dutifully had their son Gerrard baptized in the parish church.[13] Growing up in an environment where local conservatism was national rebelliousness, Winstanley had the close connection between God and the people keenly impressed upon him. By the time he finished grammar school, his father had become a burgess, one possessing full municipal rights as a citizen and freeman of the borough. But despite this prosperity, his family's staunch sectarianism prevented him from attending the university.[14] This was but the most glaring example of what a quick-witted young man must have seen as the inviolable relationship between word and deed. On 10 April 1630 he was apprenticed to Sarah Gater of Cornhill, the widow of a Merchant Taylor, and seven years later, on 21 February 1637, at the age of twenty-seven, he was received into the Merchant Taylors Company and became a citizen of London.[15]

In Lancashire, large-scale enclosure of common land had just begun. Industrial and agrarian growth proceeded side by side, and new farms were taking the place of old grazing rights on the commons. As a boy Winstanley witnessed the setting up of many small farms by families who enclosed and leased part of the open fields. He also saw the entry of large-scale land speculators into the open land market with "the break-up of large feudal estates through the decay and impoverishment of their owners."[16] A typical small freeholder like Edward Winstanley probably owned less than thirty acres. Much of the land was not under tillage and was used to graze a few cows, horses, and sheep. He might have grown a few acres of oats. Clothmaking was carried out in the home, where the linen was spun, wound, warped, and woven with the help of women and children. The elder Winstanley sent the finished cloth, usually fustian, to London to be sold by his son. But this arrangement ended abruptly with the father's death in 1639. Perhaps Winstanley attended the funeral in Wigan on 27 December, but he did not stay home. He returned to London and on 28 September 1640 married Susan King at St. Martin's Outwhich.[17] Nothing is known of Susan King or her family, and Winstanley never mentions her in his writings.

Four days before the marriage Charles I announced he would convene a new parliament, and when the Long Parliament opened on 3 November it resembled the sudden eruption of a volcano that had smoldered for a century. Historians trace the evolution of public opposition to the Anglican hierarchy from the previous century. As far back as 1570 efforts had been made to keep down what William Haller aptly calls "the wind of Lollardry." Puritan ministers "supplied popular discontent on the religious plane with such leadership as had never been before. They were intellectuals devoted to circumventing the law and outwitting the constituted authorities. In language designed to be intelligible and exciting to everybody they set forth a religious doctrine which exalted the individual soul and urged it to expression and activity in all walks of life." The sole check upon individualism that circumstances would permit them to acknowledge was the individual conscience.

Many Puritan intellectuals went over to the popular (independent or separatist) side where they inspired many small tradesmen to take up the preaching of the word. Winstanley by this time was certainly familiar with the enthusiasts of the conventicle who, in fantastic and often grotesque imagery, expressed "the insurgent democracy of common men who had hearkened to the pulpit." Older and respectable ministers in the 1630s repeatedly assured their listeners that common people have "all the wit and knowledge necessary to understand and believe the gospel." They insisted that formal academic training should not be obtrusive in sermons. Chief among these influential ministers was John Everard (c. 1575-1650) of Clare College, Cambridge, who was well versed in the Neoplatonism espoused by the humanists Nicholas of Cusa (1401-1464) and Marsilio Ficino (1433-1499). Along with his chief associate, Giles Randall (c. 1605-1650), he studied Plotinus, Dionysius the Areopagite, and German reformers such as Johannes Tauler (c. 1300-1361), Hans Denck (1495-1527), Sebastian Franck (c. 1499-1542), and Sebastian Castellio (1515-1563), all of whom disavowed innate human depravity.[18]

During these years unemployed workers became a potent political force, and Puritan ministers actively sought their support. "When the Long Parliament began its work," Haller notes, "this meant to the respectable Puritan reformer the early establishment of the presbyterian Utopia; to the saints of the separation, it meant the millennium."[19] For justification of these dreams the ministers turned, inevitably it now seems, to the books of Daniel and Revelation. The tradition of applying these enigmatic prophecies to contemporary events is long and varied. John Bale published what is probably the first analysis of Revelation in English in 1548, with new editions in 1550 and 1570. Henry Bullinger wrote another in 1561 that was reprinted in 1573, and Arthur Golding published a translation of Revelation in 1574, reprinted around 1592. But in England the most popular interpretation was found in Foxe's *Actes and Monuments*, which involved a periodization of history, based on marginal glosses of Daniel and Revelation, anticipating the Puritan notion of national identity. Winstanley, like Lilburne and many other apprentices, studied Foxe intensely. To each of five eras from the time of Christ to his own age Foxe assigned three hundred years, beginning with the persecution under Roman power and progressing through the growth of the church, its spiritual decline, the reign of Antichrist, and the final age of reform and restoration. Like other commentators, Foxe had difficulty in working out the exact dates of events to fit his millennial scheme and, at his death, left an incomplete exposition of Revelation. But his design, perhaps because of its indefiniteness, provided a framework that allowed others to see Protestant martyrdom as more than fortuitous suffering. Suffering, in fact, signified that salvation was near.

To Foxe, Revelation was primarily a metaphor for English history. His book gave meaning to Protestant radicalism and enabled men like Winstanley and Lilburne to see themselves as actors in a cosmic drama of history. Archbishop Laud refused to license the book's republication in 1637, but this only increased its popularity. During these years the presses could hardly keep up with the demand for explications of the heavenly kingdom on earth, which appealed to all classes but had a special meaning to those who felt powerless and disappointed. A brief sample would include John Napier's *A Plaine Discovery of the Whole Revelation of Saint John* (1593, 1611, 1645) and Thomas Brightman's *Apocalypsis Apocalypseos* (1609), which was translated in 1615 as *A Revelation of the Revelation*. (The 1616 edition, which ran to 1143 pages, was extracted in 1641 as *Brightman's Predictions and Prophecies*.) Johann Heinrich Alsted's *Diatribe de mille annis apocalypticis* (1627, 1630) was translated in 1643 by William Burton as *The Beloved City, or the Saints reign on earth a thousand yeares*, and Joseph Mede's *Clavis Apocalyptica* (1627) was translated in 1643 by Richard More as *The Key to Revelation*.

On the eve of the revolution, such visions articulated the aspirations of many oppressed workers. One popular example was John Archer's *The Personall Raigne of Christ upon Earth* (1641), a technical exposition of Daniel 2 and 7 and Revelation 10, 12, and 17. A more exciting version, and one containing many images Winstanley reworks, is *A Glimpse of Syons Glory*, brought out the same year by the Baptist William Larner, Lilburne's publisher, with an epistle by his friend William Kiffin, a successful wool merchant. The author, Thomas Goodwin, usually associated with businessmen and university graduates, but he was not hostile to the "common people" and frequently encouraged them to come to his church. The pamphlet was originally a sermon delivered in Holland and taken down by a scribe; it therefore is someone's report of what he thought he heard Goodwin say, not Goodwin's revised notes of what he intended to say.[20] Yet *A Glimpse of Syons Glory* eloquently expresses the utopian longings of common people and, in spite of a somewhat condescending attitude, Goodwin touches a genuinely radical nerve. He declares quite bluntly that Revelation 20, "where it is said, *The Saints shall reign with him a thousand years* . . . cannot be meant reigning with him in heaven . . . that could not be; and therefore it must be meant of Jesus Christ coming and reigning here gloriously for a thousand years. And although this may seem to be strange, yet heretofore it hath not been accounted so. It hath been a truth received in the primitive times."[21]

Goodwin understands the power of literal interpretation and uses it to exploit the utopian myth of primitivism; he looks at the past as a Golden Age, a more innocent and clear-sighted time when figures of speech were understood literally. He knows the psychology of the oppressed and legitimizes their natural longings for vengeance, and by adeptly exploiting their hopes and fears he establishes a rapport with those on the lower end of the social and economic ladder. After the creation of the heavenly kingdom on earth, "it is questionable whether there shall be need of ordinances, at least in that way that now there is," for "the presence of Christ shall be there and supply all kind of ordinances." Finally, the pamphlet promises there shall be perfect unity among all sects and, based on Revelation 21:7, material abundance for all. When Christ comes again "mountains shall be made plain, and he shall come skipping over mountains and over difficulties." All this will begin, as Brightman's interpretation of Daniel 12:11 had shown, in 1650, but "it shall be 45 years before it comes to full head." The "saints" will suffer during the next few years, but they are assured of eventual success. Ominously, poor people are warned at the end to "take heed that you lose not this opportunity," for increasing divisions among them will only increase their woes and "do more hurt to hinder this glorious work than all the persecutors could do."[22]

Perhaps Winstanley himself took part in the actions of tumultuous workers in the early days of the civil wars, for his business was failing. As Alfred P. Wadsworth and Julia DeLacy Mann explain, wealthy merchants and clothiers began driving out tradesmen who resented their control. "Their aim was to maintain a monopoly against country dealers who came into the town to sell, and to restrain townsmen to the use of their own branch of trade." From 1631 to 1641 "the atmosphere was more favourable to fiscal and commercial monopoly than it was ever again to be. The activity of Charles's Privy Council and Committee on Trade was reflected in that of corporations, companies, patentees, and groups of traders, who alike sought to reestablish privilege and prerogative, as Strafford and Laud sought to establish those of State and Church."[23] A further "cause" of Winstanley's bankruptcy was his revulsion to the world of getting and spending. Small masters and shopkeepers, forced to the back streets, dealt less with individual customers and became dependent on the larger merchants. As rents increased in London, minor traders moved out. Small masters like Winstanley were subject to strict regulation but had inferior status in the City companies and no direct representation. Some time in 1643, "when the late unhappie wars in England were violent," he "left off his trading . . . by reason of the badness of the tymes." His debts, even in failure, were meager. When sued in 1660 for the recovery of £114, he reported in a bill of complaint that "about the beginning of April 1641, your oratour being then a citizen of London had some trading with one Richard Aldworth late citizen . . . of London, deceased, for fustian, dimities, and lynnin cloth and such like commodities which trading continued for the part of two or three years." In a period of thirty months his transactions totaled £331.1s.[24] Instead of returning to Wigan, Winstanley took up residence with friends in the vicinity of Cobham in Surrey. He herded cows as a hired laborer. Turning his back on his business associates, training, and background, he now had time to think and reflect. Searching for solace and peace of mind during this period of intense social, political, and economic strife, he remembered, no doubt, the quiet of his boyhood days on the small farm in Lancashire; perhaps this led him to want to live a simple uncluttered life close to the soil.

By the beginning of the second Civil War in January 1648, Winstanley recognized that something should be done about opening up the possibilities for human betterment. In the seven years since his bankruptcy, he had seen the hope for a new society badly shattered. One by one the Presbyterians, the Independents, and, in the last year, even the Levellers seemed to renege on their promise to carry out full-scale reform of society based on a widening of the franchise. There were rumors that some Levellers "negotiated with the royalists, regarding them as a lesser evil than Oliver Cromwell."[25] To Winstanley, the various political groups must have seemed a sordid lot, indecisive, timeserving, corrupt. What was needed was a vision that would unite poor people into a significant political force. All the existing political groups, from royalists to Levellers, represented less than one fifth of the population.[26] No one knew this better than Winstanley. He was in an excellent position to see that the poor needed neither tears nor crumbs; what they required was a faith, a hope, a belief in themselves and their potential to change the world for the better. He found a degree of solace among these people in the five years he shared their life. He realized how peaceful life could be away from the worries of buying and selling. He saw neighbors sharing food, clothing, and shelter; he witnessed the inner peace these country people enjoyed. It reminded him of his native Lancashire and of the people he had known there as a boy.

Winstanley saw, as the Baptist preachers and the chaplains of the New Model Army saw, that to break the bondage of the sense of damnation among the people he must provide the means by which they could undergo the spiritual experience of conversion. For belief in salvation gave people self-confidence and a feeling of group solidarity, which, in turn, infused the sectaries with energy. If poor men and women felt free from hell, priests, worldly authorities, magic, and the blind forces of nature, they would gain the power to win political freedom. Instead of patiently enduring their suffering, the poor would rise up and claim their birthright. Before the beginning of the civil wars the ruling class contentedly rested on the theory that only a few well-to-do, educated, and well-behaved souls could properly be discerned as being among the elect. There was no point in being chosen for eternal salvation if everyone enjoyed the same right. Puritans had sympathy for the poor as long as they were diligent, meek, upright, and lawful. But all agreed that "there was no salvation in idleness or in vagabondage."[27] "Nobody," writes Hill, "denied the wickedness of the multitude until the multitude began to speak for itself—and then the propertied were all the more convinced of the need for repression."[28] Even Thomas Goodwin called his congregation the "vulgar multitude," and believed it was "a certain sign of an unregenerate estate, to be carried thus along with the stream, and to be moulded to the same principles the generality of most men are."[29]

Winstanley differed from these men not because he was nobler or had greater sympathy for the poor, but because he lived with and shared the problems of working people. Yet he was also the son of a successful merchant, a freeman, a master clothier, a citizen of the City of London. This put him in an ambivalent position. He saw more clearly than most that the clergy had lost control of the common people; they could no longer frighten the uneducated with eternal damnation. As long as the controversy took place within a stable state church, a workable patronage system, and an efficient censorship, the ministers and their parliamentary allies were secure. But by 1648 all these had broken down; the common people had tasted the forbidden delights of liberty, and now the Army, not Parliament, still less the Presbyterian clergy, decided who should rule. To attack the idea of inherited sin Winstanley had to attack the vehicle of its dissemination, the biblical account of the Fall. He decided to pick up where his predecessors had left off. He would interpret the story of the Fall in a way that would make clear that all mankind was to be saved. He would contribute to the building of Jerusalem by providing his adopted brethren with a liberating creed.

He entitled his first work *THE MYSTERIE OF GOD, Concerning the whole Creation*, Mankinde. *TO BE Made known to every man and woman, after seven Dispensations and Seasons of Time are passed over. According to the Counsell of God, Revealed to his* Servants.[30] The title page cites Psalms 145:13, "Thy kingdome is an everlasting kingdome, and thy dominion endureth throughout all generations," and Romans 11:26, "And so all Israel shall be saved, as it is written, There shall come out of Sion, the Deliverer, that shall turne away ungodlinesse from Jacob." The opening epistle is addressed, appropriately, "To my Beloved Country men, of the Countie of LANCASTER," to whom Winstanley feels he must apologize. "Deare country men," he explains, "when some of you sees my name subscribed to this ensuing Discourse, you may wonder at it, and it may be dispise me in your heart, as Davids Brethren dispised him, and told him it was the pride of his heart to come into the battell." Having cast himself in the role of a youthful slayer of giants, an underdog, he proceeds to define himself as the humble instrument of God, for "Gods works are not like mens, he doth not alwayes take the wise, the learned, the rich of the world to manifest himself in, and through them to others, but he chuses the dispised, the unlearned, the poor, the nothings of the world, and fills them with the good things of himself, when as he sends the other emptie away." From the first words he wrote, then, Winstanley sided with the poor. He is their spokesman, their prophet. "I have writ nothing," he says, "but what was given me of my Father; and at the first beholding of this mysterie, it appeared to be so high above my reach, that I was confounded and lost in my spirit, but God, whom I believe, is my teacher, for I have joy and rest in him, left me not in bondage, but set me at libertie, and caused me to see much glory in these following truths; and when God works none can hinder." Conventional as this is, Winstanley clearly sees his failure in the cloth trade as liberation from his "bondage," his own fortunate fall. God's ways are mysterious, and even the most destructive experience can be transformed into an opportunity for spiritual renewal and rebirth.

Aware of the heterodoxy of what he is about to do, he does not naively plunge into theological waters. He makes no attempt to draw the cloak of innocence over his heresy: "It may be somethings herein may seeme very strange at the first reading, and you may crie out, an error, an error, for this is usuall, when the flesh cannot apprehend and beare a truth of God, it brands it for an error, and rejects it as a wicked thing." He was once in such a situation, but he escaped from envy and hardheartedness toward his neighbors. His message is simple but should not be discounted: "You shall finde that I call the whole power of darknesse by the name Serpent, which dwells in, and hath taken every man and woman captive, and that God through his Son Christ will redeeme his own workmanship, man-kinde, from it, and destroy the Serpent only." Everything Winstanley will write during the next four years elaborates and explains this state-ment. Every word counts—the frank use of metaphor not merely to ex-cite his readers but to help them understand complex ideas typifies his method of exposition. Swiftly he states the primary qualification of all conversionary experience; to apprehend his message readers must be prepared to die in order to be reborn:

> for when God lets you see into the mysterie of this iniquitie, in the least degree of it, it will prove too hard for you, and you will be nothing but death, curse, and miserie. Therefore, as you desire that God would manifest love to you, and make you free, be not of-fended to heare, that God, who is love it self, hath a season to mani-fest his love to others that are lost, and quicken them that were killed, while you were made alive, and that fell further under death, when you that were lost are redeemed an houre or two before them.

The primary effect of oppression is envy, which must be cast out if read-ers are to receive his message. Working against the grain of his readers' sensibilities, he refuses to condescend, to simply tell them what they want to hear. His point is not that only the poor and humble will be saved but that everyone will be saved in due time. Christ, he reminds them, died for all, and St. Paul himself was once "their bitter persecu-tor." He warns his readers not to be offended and miserable "if your persecutors and enemies should in Gods time be delivered from under the curse, and partake of the glorie of the Citie, together with you." The "Citie," of course, is the City of God, or Zion, the New Jerusalem ex-plained in Augustine's great work, which Puritan preachers refer to as often as to Calvin's *Institutes*.[31]

Winstanley tells his fellow saints not to be unhappy that even evil people will be saved, "for as he is honored in saving you of the Citie that were lost, so he will be honored in redeeming these that lie under the power of the second death, and that entred not into the Citie, seeing there was no difference between you and them, till the will of God made the difference, in taking you at the first, and leaving them till the last houre." His opening epistle concludes with the hope that "if any of you be unsatisfied with what I have writ, that you will speake to me" so they can discuss differences openly and discover the truth together. He assures readers his ideas may be confirmed with scripture and his opinions are not a "private fancie" but are "agreeable to the written Word." He therefore wishes to dissociate himself from fanatics who advance subjective opinions as gospel truths. Neither a demagogue nor a charlatan, he enters the fray not to put forth the word, not to provide answers to unanswerable questions, but to contribute whatever talents he may possess to the betterment of mankind. To do this he returns to the ancient theory of biblical prophecy.

As Erich Auerbach has shown, at the start of the Christian era an opposition developed between Tertullian's historical interpretation of scripture and Origen's allegorical approach. And while Tertullian's wish to preserve the full historicity of the scriptures along with the deeper meaning prevailed, Augustine kept Origen's purely "spiritual" method alive in his attempted compromise. For though he favored a figurative reading and rejected the purely abstract "spiritual" interpretation, his idealism removed the concrete event from history and transposed it to a "perspective of eternity." In the Middle Ages farfetched figural interpretations were often mixed with purely abstract, ethical allegory. Although the basic method of interpreting the scriptures as a concrete historical prefiguration remained strong, the opposition between literal and metaphorical truth, between an actual event and its literary expression, became blurred; the figurative meaning of a text was often taken to be its literal significance. The concrete meaning of the words was obscured in an attempt to make the text fit the interpreter's idea. Figurative interpretation became an intellectual exercise containing little of its original poetic significance. The Old Testament was stripped of its normative character to show that it was merely an allegory. Literal and metaphorical meanings diverged, reflecting the widening gap between the physical and spiritual worlds, the order of nature and the order of grace. Increasingly the Old Testament was interpreted *only* abstractly and allegorically, and Christianity was in danger of losing its conception of "providential history, its intrinsic concreteness."[32]

With the Reformation this began to change, and Europeans started to read the Old Testament as Jewish history and Jewish law. In England Foxe led the way in reestablishing the notion that the two poles of a figure are separate, but both, being real events, are within history and time. In comparing the biblical nation of Israel to contemporary England, he understood that he was dealing with concrete historical events, not vague abstractions. And, as William M. Lamont has shown, the rejection of Foxe by Puritan ministers after 1641 indicates that there is a fundamental difference between "orthodox" and "radical" Independency.[33] Orthodox Independents such as Thomas Goodwin, John Goodwin, and Stephen Marshall, following the prophecies of Brightman, Mede, and Archer, look for an apocalyptic millennium when Christ will literally appear again to lead the saints into the New Jerusalem. Radical Independents such as John Everard, Giles Randall, and John Saltmarsh, following Foxe, foresee a political, social, and economic revolution, demanding great sacrifice, that will gradually progress toward a more ideal state. Further evidence of contemporary awareness of this difference may be seen in a brief tract by Everard's future editor, Rapha Harford, entitled *Reverend Mr. Brightmans Iudgement, or Prophesies what shall befall Germany, Scotland, Holland and the churches adhering to them*, which was first published around 1640 and reissued in 1643 and 1650, and also in Thomas Hayne's devastating attack on the literalists in *Christs Kingdome on Earth, Opened according to Scriptures*, published on 10 April 1645, which declares that "herein is examined, What Mr. *Th. Brightman*, Dr. *J. Alstede*, Mr. *I. Mede*, Mr. *H. Archer*, *The Glympse of Sions Glory*, and such as concurre in opinion with them, hold concerning the thousand years of the Saints Reign with Christ, And of Sectaries binding: Herein also their Arguments are answered." Orthodox Independents mangle typology by interpreting concrete images literally. But radical Independents insist on the concreteness of the sign and the thing signified, thus bringing together the orders of nature and grace. By reading something of the original meaning back into biblical prophecy, this small group of poetic thinkers tried to restore the historicity of biblical events and apply the meaning of those events directly to the present. Their method may justifiably be termed typological, while that of the orthodox Independents is more accurately called allegorical.[34]

Orthodox Independents such as Joseph Caryl and William Strong use the interpretations of Revelation by Alsted, Brightman, and Mede to advance the fantasy of a literal Second Coming, but Winstanley agrees with John Everard, who said people would not "so much trouble themselves about a personal Reign of Christ here upon earth, if they saw that the Chief and Real fulfilling of Scriptures were within them; And that whatever is externally done in the world, and expressed in the Scriptures,

is but Typical and Representative."[35] He heeds Giles Randall's preaching
that "there are many that think that Christ will come and reigne a thou-
sand yeares here on earth personally, but they will be deceived, for they
look and judge of the Scripture after the outward appearance."[36] And he
builds upon John Saltmarsh's idea that "the true Personal Raign of
Christ . . . is Spiritual . . . The Lord Jesus reigns already . . . in
Spirit," for his kingdom will not be fleshly, political, or monarchical.[37]
Winstanley supports what the Baptist New Model chaplain Thomas
Collier said at Putney on 29 September 1647: "Some apprehend that
Christ shall come and reign personally . . . But this is not my apprehension; but that Christ will come in the Spirit and have a glorious kingdom
in the spirits of his people, and they shall . . . reign over the world."[38]
Like these radical Independents, Winstanley wrests the apocalyptic rhetoric from the literalists and turns it to his purpose of building a base
among working people. Since such rhetoric denigrates Charles as the
accepted ruler, monarchy as a political system, and parliament as an
effective governing body, it provides him with a way of discussing the
establishment of a more humane social system, a way of negating the
negation. For unlike the literalists, he firmly believes in the gradual transformation of society.

In *The Mysterie of God* Winstanley establishes the basis of his exegesis
of the Fall by use of the typological method whereby the four levels of
meaning correspond to literal, moral, allegorical, and anagogical truths.
First, the Garden of Eden, the world before the Fall, represents the perfection possible on earth once people accept the spirit of Christ. Second,
Adam represents all men; his story typifies the struggle of each individual
to overcome temptation, sin, and suffering. Third, the serpent represents
covetous evil and is not part of God. Fourth, this serpent will be crushed
by the heel of the righteous men and women who spring from the seed of
mankind. This fourfold outline indicates Winstanley's full awareness that
the origin of sin, more than any other topic, drew the attention of Puritan ministers such as William Perkins, John Downame, William Gouge,
Thomas Taylor, Richard Sibbes, and John Preston, who reiterated the
battle between the two Adams within each man. But their interpretation
stressed that only a small minority could be saved. Their more or less
official exposition of Calvinism held that once man had broken the
divine law he was condemned. The universal depravity of the carnal or
natural man, Adam, was present in everyone. Since to err was human,
all sinners were alike in God's eyes. As Haller notes, "since no sinner, no
matter how righteous, wise, learned, powerful or rich, could hope to
satisfy the law, the least righteous and the humblest, weakest and poorest
had as good a chance to be saved as any. For God saved whom he would,

not whom sinners deemed he ought." God's grace was free, so all men were born free as well as equal—free, that is, to share as absolutely in his favor as they had in the original Adam's depravity. Christ, the second Adam, withstood the tempter as completely as the old Adam gave in to him, and he too might be present in each man. The new Adam was unceasingly opposed to the old. Any man might be helped, "but this help came only from God and worked only through a man's own self. He must become a new man, must acknowledge the law of his nature, fight his own weakness, blame none but himself for his troubles and failures, endeavor to be strong, believe that providence was with him, persevere, and trust that all would be well in the end." Through the ordeal of the flesh, the spirit triumphed. As long as sin troubled him, he knew God was with him.[39]

The Mysterie of God tells this story with significant differences. After God made Adam there were two distinctly different beings, but "though Adam was pure and spotlesse, yet he had no other wisdom, beauty, and power, but what God had Created. God himself, who is the infinite and endlesse beeing, did not dwell bodily in *Adam*, as he did dwell bodily in the Humane Nature, Jesus Christ, the second *Adam* in aftertimes; but a pure Created wisdom, beauty, and power did rule, dwell, and act in that Created Humanity." By creating Adam and Eden, "God declares, That *Adam* himself, or that living flesh, Mankinde, is a Garden which God hath made for his own delight, to dwell, and walk in, wherein he had planted varietie of Hearbs, and pleasant Plants, as love, joy, peace, humility, knowledge, obedience, delight, and purity of life." Thus Adam is not only representative of man, but man himself is a "type" or metaphor for God.[40] He is the concrete symbol of God's love. This indicates the way Winstanley's mind works and is an important clue to his method. He possesses, from the start, a poetic understanding of the relationship between the actual experience and the metaphorical representation of it in scripture. This enables him to interpret biblical images as "shadows" of literal truths. He understands that images appealing to the sensory imagination are the most dramatic representations of reality.

Like Andrew Marvell and John Milton, Winstanley stresses that though Eden was created for pleasure and delight, everything in it was made for use, not luxurious waste or idleness.[41] Yet in his Eden Eve does not appear, for, to him, Adam represents all mankind, not just masculinity. Instead he simply insists that Adam deliberately chose to do evil when he ate the forbidden fruit, which was like a weed, "an inclinable principle, or spirit of self love, aspiring up in the midst of this Created, living Garden," which is "an aspiring to be as God, or to be a beeing of it self, equall to, and yet distinct from God." This desire appears in all living creatures, even animals, as "an inclinable disposition to promote it self, or its own beeing," but "God did not make it." Adam himself brought "forth fruit to maintain his Created beeing equall with God; and God would bring forth fruit to maintain his uncreated beeing, and to swallow up all other beeings into himself, and he to become all in all in every creature that he made." So it wasn't Adam's eating in and of itself that was sinful; it was "a secret tickling delight arising in him, to be a more knowing man then God made him." After he ate he began to reject God, and was not content with being as God made him. Thus "the ground of *Adams* fall" rose up first in his own heart "as fruit growing up from a Created beeing," for "it was in his heart to do evill." Selfishness, therefore, is the forbidden fruit called "the Serpent, because it windes it self into every creature, and into every Created facultie & twists it self round about the Tree, Mankinde." After he ate, Adam "did begin to delight in that inward fruit of wickednesse" and, taking the fruit from the Tree of Knowledge, "delighted his outward senses therewith." This is the first statement of Winstanley's dialectic, his method of explaining the cause of things by reference to a convergence of inner and outer motivation. To him no human act is caused by a mere inner compulsion or a simple outer force. He combines references to internal and external forces whenever he gives causal explanations, and he holds to this dialectic throughout his writing career.

After eating the apple, Adam, who was a "Garden of pleasant plants," becomes "a stinking dunghill of weeds." He now "brings forth nothing but pride, envy, discontent, disobedience, and the whole actings of the spirit, and power of darkness." But of course all is not lost, for "the work of God shall be restored from this lost, dead, weedy, and enslaved condition, and the fruit of the Created beeing shall utterly perish and be ashamed." The mystery of God is that "he will destroy and subdue this power of darknesse, under the feet of the whole Creation, Mankinde, and every particular branch, man and woman, deliver them from this bondage and prison, and dwell in his own house, or Garden, himself." People will, by allowing the goodness within them to emerge, become more truly godlike. Christ, the first to destroy the power of darkness and allow true human nature to shine forth in his person, is "the first manifestation of this great mysterie of God," and "when his work is compleated, he will dwell in the whole Creation, that is, [in] every man and woman, without exception." God did not curse man to lasting death; he only cursed "the serpent, or mans worke, which was the fruit that sprung up in, and was acted both inwardly and outwardly by the creation, or created beeing, in rebellion against the beeing of God, therefore sin is properly mans own act."

Winstanley bases his idea of universal salvation on God's curse to the serpent in Genesis 3:15—"I will put enmitie betweene thee and the woman, and betweene thy seed, and her seed, it shall bruise thy head, and thou shalt bruise his heele, so that the serpent must be killed"—and this is the most frequently cited biblical text in his works. The serpent-seed image serves as a dialectical metaphor of the unity of good and evil, and, like a leitmotif in a symphony, it is repeated with modulations, elaborations, and explanations. Here, in its initial appearance, the image "proves" that the curse against Adam (mankind) is temporary while the curse against the serpent (evil) is permanent, for "God will destroy death, and quicken *Adam*, or mankinde again." This, again, is the mystery of God: "God will bruise this serpents head, and cast that murderer out of heaven, the humane nature, wherein it dwels in part, as in the man Christ Jesus; And he will dwell in the whole creation in time, and so deliver whole mankind out of that bondage." Winstanley knows this is true because his experience of it is supported by scriptural evidence. He becomes the one in whose breast the war between good and evil is waged. The formulas are familiar to those acquainted with spiritual autobiography, but instead of reducing biblical metaphors to dogmatic "truths," Winstanley revitalizes these figures of speech by internalizing them and making them conform to his individualized dramatization of the inner conquest of evil. The pattern of spiritual autobiography provides him with a form that he invests with new meaning:

> I lay dead in sin, weltring in blood and death, was a prisner to my lusts . . . I was ashamed men should know it . . . I delighted in the savour of these weeds . . . those things wherein I did take pleasure, were my death, my shame, and the very power of darkness, wherein I was held as in a prison . . . yet I could not deny selfe; and the more I used moanes to beat him downe, as I thought, the more did this power of darknesse appeare in me, like an overflowing wave of wickednesse, drowning me in slaverie, and I saw I was a wretched man, wraped in miserie . . . & I mourned to see I had no power to get out of that bondage of selfishnes . . . I was a stranger to God, though among men, I was a professor, as I thought, of God. (A "professor" was one who affirmed publicly).

Having reached the nadir of despair, a kind of spiritual death, he begins to trace his gradual restoration. Following the mythical birth-death-rebirth pattern of all "twice-born" heroes—Christ, St. Paul, Augustine, Luther, and later John Bunyan—he recounts the process of turning from a worldly self of socially derived norms and standards to an internally created ideal of himself. As a "fallen" man who was once "religious" in the orthodox sense, he forsakes comfortable and sanctimonious piety for a radical doctrine of universal salvation and social cooperation. He becomes his own hero by "killing" his previous self. "Now," he says, "God hath set me free from that bondage, so that it rules not, though sometimes it seems to face me, like a daring conquered enemie, that cannot hurt." Confronting his old self, his shadow, he now examines the face in the mirror that his new self stares down; he projects his inner sinful self, the serpent, out into the external world. This former self, the Winstanley of conventional piety and middle-class respectability, the London cloth merchant and master tradesman, is fully rejected. He now sees that God's purpose was not to destroy him but only the serpent of evil that was in him. "I see and feele," he says, "that God hath set me free from the dominion and over-ruling power of that bodie of sin." Having freed himself from his former status as a money-grubbing tradesman by becoming aware of the conditions that determine his existence, he is able to transcend his former circumstances. He refuses to internalize a value system that legitimizes the selfish pursuit of profits. His growing awareness of this slavery he was in makes him want to cast aside the prevailing social conditions. Having objectified the evil that was within him, he now rebels against the social, economic, and political norms supporting the conditions in which that evil flourished. Therefore his dramatization of the Fall recapitulates the growth of his consciousness. Out of his awareness of class conflict, he begins forging a new ideology. His experience is typical of many middle-class tradesmen. But no others understand the meaning of that experience so profoundly or express it so vividly.

Laying aside his tradesman's burden, Winstanley prepares to enter the kingdom of heaven. God's purpose, he declares, "was not to destroy me, nor any of his owne creation; but onely the serpent," selfishness; he realizes God has promised salvation to all. His own liberation, he believes, is somehow linked to his refusal to conform to the prevailing social norm, the so-called Protestant ethic, which says his job is to work for his own selfish pleasure, to accumulate profits for the greater glory of God. Winstanley's failure as a tradesman starts him on the pilgrim's path of revolutionary politics where his awareness will quickly perceive private property as the root of all social evil. Yet, as G. E. Aylmer cautions, "to say that Winstanley became a communist because he had failed as a businessman may not be untrue, but it is simply inadequate as an explanation of his writing and his career."[42] Inadequate because it is a narrow, mechanistic explanation that neglects the sense of liberation Winstanley expresses in *The Mysterie of God*, where, released from the Calvinistic sense of sin, he exalts in his newly discovered freedom and stands ready to act:

I rejoyce in perfect hope and assurance in God, that although this serpent, or murderer doe begin, by reason of any temptation, or outward troubles, to arise, or endeavour to act in rash anger, in pride, discontent or the like, as sometimes it does, yet every appearance of this wicked one in me becomes his further ruine, and shall never rise to rule and enslave me as formerly . . . every day more and more I am not still a captive, in a beeing of darkness distinct from God, but God hath freed me therefrom, and taken me up into his own beeing; so that now his wisdome, his love, life, his power, his joy and peace, is mine glorie here, I can glorie no where else. And here I wait upon God with a sweet peace under reproaches, under losses, under troubles of the world.

These are not the words of a failure; they are not the thoughts of a despondent man; this is not the psychology of a loser. "This mysterie of God," he says "is not to be done all at once, but in several dispensations, some whereof are past, some are in beeing, and some are yet to come." God's work shall be redeemed and all corruption, bondage, death, and pain shall perish "and be cast into the lake." But this will not take place at once and Winstanley never promises that it will.

Like mechanic preachers such as Paul Hobson, he is primarily concerned with the alleviation of physical and psychological suffering, not with rhetorical revolutionary posturing. When he cites 1 Corinthians 3:13: "Every mans work shall be made manifest, for the day shall declare it, because it shall be revealed by fire: and the fire shall trie every mans work, of what sort it is," he shows his desire to bridge the gap between ideas and acts. For ultimately God's work and man's work are oriented toward the same end—the preservation of creation. Citing Revelation 20:10-14, 21:24, 22:1-2, and 2 Corinthians 5:4, he clarifies his belief that all will eventually be saved. The elect will be saved first, and as others repent their sins and ask for God's forgiveness, they too will achieve salvation. Adam, of course, exemplifies this process. He is the truly archetypal man. After his fall from purity into ignorance, enviousness, pride, disobedience, and lust, he became unclean: "he fell to be a childe of wrath; and of a pure garden, he became a stinking dunghill, and this is the death or mortality, which not only *Adam* in particular, but all the branches of *Adam*, men and women, lie under. Even under a corrupt beeing." But the final typological fulfillment of Adam's role is yet to be. For the paradoxical meaning of the tragedy of the fortunate fall is Adam's promised salvation. The keystone of the belief in universal salvation is Romans 8:19-26, of which verses 21-22 are the most important, for they promise "the Creation it self also shall be delivered . . . from the bondage of corruption, into the glorious liberty of the children of God." "God hath determined," Winstanley says, "to finish this great designe, to make his garden man, a garden of pleasure to himself, when he hath plucked up all the weeds, and so husbanded the ground, that weeds shall never grow again."

Since God delights only in spiritual things, all material things are made for man: "these outward creatures were made for pleasure, profit, and use of man, while he is carnall, and stands in a beeing distinct from God." After man is purified there will be no more lust after material things, for the New Jerusalem will not require them—he cites Revelation 21, 23, and John 14:20. "Some may say," he writes in anticipation of a rebuttal, "if this be true, that God will save every one, then I will live, and take my pleasure in sin, and eat, drink, and be merry, and take all delights while I live, for I am Gods workmanship, and he will not lose his own work, I shall be saved." Winstanley simply says that while this hedonistic argument may be true, it is also futile, for if people devote themselves to lives of pleasure their "work shall perish." Sensing the inherent rebelliousness in the refusal to conform to the moral strictures of the Protestant ethic, he implies that a life of sensual pleasure is better than a life of drudgery. But who can afford such a life? Only the rich. For them perhaps a life of debauchery is better than a life of tyranny and oppression. Sin, a form of enslavement, is not punished by eternal torment in an afterlife but by bad conscience in this life, "a paine more intollerable, then the plucking out of the right eye, or the cutting off the right hand." Why are people tempted to sin, he asks rhetorically, if they suffer for committing sinful acts? Temptation comes not from God, but from the selfish desire to be like God, to escape from God, to refuse God's love and cut oneself off from God's protection and salvation.

As an emblem of this conflict Winstanley sees the spirit of light, an angel, contending with the spirit of darkness, the serpent, within creation. God makes the outcome clear in diverse dispensations explained in the second half of *The Mysterie of God*. The first dispensation is God's law given to Adam not to eat of the Tree of Knowledge, the punishment being death of the flesh. This disobedience and death made humanity create its own law, which is the first of two murderers. For when one creature began to obey another instead of God, his own law killed him: "it is not the King, but the Kings Law that hangs an offender." As long as this law stands in force, no one can be saved because it makes every one selfish and sinful; "therefore the condemning power of the Law is to be taken away." The second murderer is aspiring to be God. This kills people because it makes them want to act and be acknowledged as gods. "There is no other righteous beeing, to be acknowledged, but only God." In an oblique attack on divine right, Winstanley notes that people cannot obey both God and king, for their laws are opposed. The king's law leads to selfishness; God's law leads to communal sharing and cooperation. This, of course, is dangerously close to what was called antinomianism, the belief Saltmarsh was often accused of advancing that no law is binding on the "saints." But Winstanley checks this impulse by saying there is no purely righteous being but God, and therefore one cannot invent his own laws; people cannot decide moral problems on the basis of convenience. Yet people's basic conception of God as a judge saying "do this, and live; do not this, and die, must be cast out." For if God were to abide only by this harsh justice no one would be saved. If God redeems anyone at all, he must be a "God of love" acting under a "Law of love." "Secondly, the other murderer, which is worse than this, must be cast out of heaven too, or else the creature cannot live, and that is the Serpent, or this aspiring spirit in him to promote self." Here the imitation of Christ provides the answer, for he was the first to cast out the serpent of selfishness. The spirit of sin within, which enslaves humanity, is easily defeated by the angel of light.

Citing another of his favorite biblical passages, Revelation 12:7-10, which he joins with Genesis 3:15, 2 Corinthians 5:19, and John 5:21, Winstanley embellishes his theory of universal salvation with the vivid imagery of battle between the forces of good and evil taking place within each heart. Since the social function of sin is oppression, people must be relieved of demoralizing guilt if they are to liberate themselves and assert their rights. He therefore encourages them with the assurance that "the time is drawing neer that they shall be delivered, and the wicked one himself, the Serpent, shall be cast into the Lake, and perish for ever." Basing his idea of universal salvation on a dialectic of inner and outer freedom, he shows that by destroying the oppressive law of the king and the selfish antinomian impulse within, people can liberate themselves from bondage. Genesis 3:15 is the key to this utopian plan, for this prophecy holds out the promise of a heavenly kingdom on earth, the city of Zion. Since this will be brought about "in length of time, by degrees," God has seen fit to provide "dispensations or discoveries of himself more, which he will have the creatures passe through before he finish his work, cast the Serpent, death and hell into the lake, and before he himself appeare to us, the tree of Life on each side, and in the middle of the pure river of the water of Life: which I conceive is the whole creation man, perfectly redeemed" (see Revelation 22:1-2). The second dispensation is the carrying out of Genesis 3:15 from Adam to Abraham. The third, which continued from Abraham to Moses, based on Genesis 18:18, is the promise given to Abraham that all nations of the earth shall be blessed. The fourth dispensation, from Moses to Christ, "is more then the former, for God, by types, figures, ceremonies, and shadowes, did more manifestly set forth his love to his creature, and his wrath to the Serpent; when the sacrifice was slaine and offered, God received an attonement, it being a tipe of Gods in-dwelling in flesh, or a shadow of Christ, the Lamb, the substance of all those sacrifices."

Continuing his typological analysis of the story of mankind's Fall and gradual restoration to Edenic purity, Winstanley suggests that Hosea 2:15—"he will give the valley of Achor for a doore of hope"—indicates that God's anger is assuaged and Christ "was the sustance of all those types and shadowes of the Mosaicall Law." The fifth dispensation, from the time of Christ's birth to his appearance to the Apostles after his crucifixion, is foreshadowed throughout the Old Testament and in Revelation 5:9. The sixth dispensation, from Christ's appearance to the Apostles to Judgment Day, is prophesied by John the Baptist and John the Apostle. Thus "whosoever preaches from his book, and not from the anointing . . . is no Minister sent of God, but a hireling, that runs before he be sent, only to get a temporall living; therefore O *England*, minde what thou dost, leave off to embrace hirelings." Sounding a note he will play with many variations during the next four years, anticlericalism, Winstanley contrasts "the strict professors of the Law" who killed Christ with the "Saints of God," who should "be patient, wait upon God, this troubled sea, the Serpent, shall not overwhelme ye, for stronger is he that is in you, then he that is in the world; rejoyce, the time of your redemption drawes neere." The foretaste of this victory so excites him that his imagination leaps forward and his pen races to keep up. His words suddenly exhibit a vitality and ebullience characteristic of his style in the months ahead:

> And againe, thinke it not strange to see many of the Saints of God at a stand in a wildernesse, and at a losse, and so waiting upon God to discover himself to them; many are like the tide at full sea, stands a little before the water run either way; and assure your selves, I know what I speake, you must be dead to your customes before you can run in the sea of truth, or the river of the water of life; some walk still according to example, and have either seene nothing, or very little of the anointing in them; and some walke more in spirit and truth, as the same anointing of the Father, which dwells bodily in Christ, teacheth them, and leadeth them into all truth.

In the time of the sixth dispensation the elect "are to be gathered into one City, and perfected." This is the city of Zion, documented in "the Lambs book," Revelation. The sea-tide-river image continues in a flourish of figurative language: "All those that were not found writ in the

Lambs book of life, were cast into the lake of fire . . . all the time of this dispensation, or till the day of Judgement be ended, that the serpent, death, and hell are cast into the lake of fire, and that there shall be no more curse lie upon the creature . . . the whole creation being redeemed, shall flow forth a pure river of the water of life." Revelation 12:5 documents the idea that the beast has all the advantages ("riches, outward libertie, worldly power, and generally humane Authoritie"). The saints have no weapon but faith "to fight against the reproaches, slanders, oppressions, poverties, weaknes, prisons, and the multitude of temptations, which the Beast through her wit, malice and power casts upon the Saints, like a flood of water to drown them." Using one of the oldest themes of transformation, Winstanley tells his saints that the time of the beast grows near because things are getting worse: "the rage of the Serpent increases, because his time growes short, and his violence, wrath, reproach, oppression, provocations and murders against the Saints are multiplied, and times grow very bad, for now iniquity abounds, and the love of many in whom the Serpent dwels, waxes cold, and extreamly bitter and mad against the Saints." This misery, he warns, continues until the end of the sixth dispensation. But the saints' patience under their trials is not in vain; "the Saints are tried to some purpose, while the beast thus rages, and swels with malice against them."

Having laid the basis of his revolutionary theory in a typological vision of the future, Winstanley returns to the present. "I believe," he writes, "it will appear more generally visible in time, to me it appears very plain, that the great bitternesse, envy, reproachfull language, and expressions of malicious wrath in; and among men and women in these dayes, against others whom they brand Sectaries, by severall names, will prove part of the smoak of her torment, and part of the restlesnesse of her Spirit, day and night, which is the beginnings of her sorrowes, for this is the raging sea that casts out its own shame." Salvation cannot be obtained by wit, learning, study, meritorious acts, or selfish powers, "yet every man shall be saved in the end." God saves "some at one hour, and some at another, both when he will, and whom he will." "The elect are gathered as wheat into Gods store-house." The seventh dispensation is Judgment Day itself when all will be liberated from death out of the dust where God has "reserved them all the time of the battel between the anointing and the Serpent, as a man would keep his jewels in a box for an appointed time." Then all will be rewarded; the elect will be taken up to God's kingdom; the serpent will die, and the disobedient and wicked will be "cast into the everlasting fire." But this is not the end.

The salvation of the elect on Judgment Day is not a mere allegory; it is the promise of the future. Referring, no doubt, to small tradesmen such as himself ruined by the wars, Winstanley notes that some people say "they would be content to suffer the misery of a new war in England, so that such as they mentioned, might suffer as wel as they; this is the spirit of the serpent." He calls instead for a time of healing. Punish the wicked, he says, but spare the nation: "as the tree of life brought forth fruit every change of time, and age of the world, to heale the elect, the lost ship, or City; so in this last and great day it brings forth leaves to heale the nations, or such as were not of the City; their turne to receive mercie comes, though it be at the last houre." For the pure river proceeding from the throne in Revelation 22:1-3 is the whole creation delivered from death. Interpreting Revelation 14:14ff, Winstanley constructs a vision of the city of Zion, the fulfilling prophecy of Genesis 3:15. He mentions three "scruples." First, only the serpent shall burn everlastingly, for the word "everlasting" is a figure of speech. Second, no scripture says there is no redemption. Hell is merely death, "or a condition below life," a state of mind "far below the comfort and joyes of God." The third scruple is that Judgment Day is not just twenty-four hours of "the twinkling of an eye," but a short time in comparison to the past history of mankind. The Sabbath is not just one day out of seven but "the constant raigne of Christ in, and over the Saints," for Christ reigns "every day constantly." The elect will be taken up to the city of Zion immediately on Judgment Day, but unrepentant sinners will burn until the dispensation changes and the whole of creation is set free. Precisely when this will happen is, again, the mystery of God. Concluding with another apology for his presumptuousness, he says he writes because he knows by experience that "it quiets the heart under what condition soever." He asks his readers to "waite patiently . . . waite with an humble quiet spirit" for deliverance. "Waite with an humble, thankfull heart still upon God . . . for his freedome is a freedome indeed . . . And this is all I have to say concerning this truth. And I have done." But he has not; he has just begun.

THE BREAKING OF THE DAY OF GOD. Wherein, Four things are manifested was published before 20 May 1648 by Giles Calvert, whose bookshop at the sign of the black spread eagle at the west end of St. Paul's was an important meeting place for dissidents. All Winstanley's pamphlets, possibly excepting the first impression of *The Mysterie of God* and *Englands Spirit Unfoulded*, appeared under Calvert's aegis. This indicates the respect his writings invoked in radical circles. A. L. Morton says Calvert's name on a title page was itself "almost a political manifesto."[43] He published William Dell's sermons and all of Saltmarsh's works after 1645. He was Lilburne's friend and also knew Laurence Clarkson, the Ranter, who became Winstanley's nemesis. "Giles Calvert's shop," Hill writes, "came nearest to uniting the radicals in spite of themselves."[44] In the late 1640s Calvert published translations of Jacob Boehme, the mystic, and Henrick Niclaes, the Familist. And it seems likely that Winstanley knew of these works and may have read them, but, as Petegorsky points out, he owed his religious doctrines to "the environment of the age rather than to any individual thinker or sect."[45]

The Breaking of the Day applies the fourfold method of biblical exegesis to promote understanding of comtemporary events. The four manifestations mentioned in the title are, first, "That the two Witnesses [of Revelation 11:3] are not in killing: but in rising from death"; second, "The three daies and half: or 42 months of the Saints captivity under the Beast [Revelation 11:2], very near expired"; third, "Christ hath begun to reign in his Saints, and to tread their corrupt flesh under his feet"; and fourth, "Christs dominion over the Nations of the world, near the approach."[46] The opening epistle is addressed "To *The despised Sons and Daughters of* Zion, *scattered up and down the Kingdome of* England," who are "the object of the worlds hatred and reproach . . . because the light and beautie of our Father shines forth of you; which they cannot behold; therfore they brand you for wicked ones, and your principles to be errour. And under that name of deceivers and troublers (though indeed they themselves are the only deceivers and troublers) they threaten your ruine and death." Extending this classical inversion of values he explains, "you are the object of every ones laughter and reproach; you are the men that they would plunder, you are the men, that are sentenced to be put to death in these uproar risings, under the name of roundheads, That the name of *Israel* might be no more known in the Land." Seeing the poor as beleaguered victims, Winstanley identifies his personal longings for radical social and political change with the longings of those who, for whatever reason, have not prospered in middle-class society. The saints, to him, are not the well-to-do gentry composed of merchants, traders, landlords, lawyers, and ministers. Nor are his saints confined to the New Model Army; they are found among the dispossessed, the disenfranchised, the common wage-earning people whom even the Levellers seemed to think not worth including in their proposed widening of the franchise.[47] "You are the men," he tells them, "preached against, writ against, and petitioned against to the higher Power, to bring you under their footsteps: you are the men that are counted the troublers of Kingdoms and Parishes where you dwell, though the truth is, you are the only peaceable men in the Kingdom." The dark world fights them because they are "children of light"; their sufferings and apprehensions will "be but for a little time," for he brings them "glad tydings that your redemption draws neer." The beast's reign is nearly over; the time "may be very hot, yet it wil be short," for the cold, rainy clouds of men's lusts are being dispersed. The summer season, full of light, heat, and fruit-fulness, is about to begin.

With prophetic excitement, Winstanley assures his readers that the defeat of the corrupt power in commonwealths and churches is at hand. "This thing, God ere long will doe; for he is judging the serpent. And if *England, Scotland,* and *Ireland;* this three-fold Kingdome, united under one head or State Government, be the tenth part of the City *Babilon,* that must fall off from the Beast first, as I have no doubtings but daily con-firmations in me, that it shall be," then the people will be free. All envy and bitterness shall die and be swallowed up in love: "you shal see these great nationall divisions, to be swallowed up into brotherly one-nesse, you shall see oppressing injustice, to bee swallowed up." No anarchist, he looks for the day when "Magistrates shall love the people, and be nursing Fathers to them . . . and the people shall love and cheerfully obey the commands of Magistrates." This hope was not, in the summer of 1648, unique. The second Civil War was coming to an end. Perhaps the Levellers and the New Model Army would, with the Independents, triumph over the conservatives in parliament. Winstanley wants what many others want—an end to monarchical tyranny, the dismantling of the state church, complete religious toleration, and the preservation of a reformed, more democratic, parliament. Even Cromwell appeared more radical after he spoke against monarchy. Babylon was indeed falling, but Winstanley enjoins the people to cast out fear: "Well, all that I have to say is this, rejoyce in the midst of this cloud of Nationall troubles, for your redemption drawes near, God is working out, an inward, and an outward peace, and liberty for you all."

Picking up where *The Mysterie of God* left off, *The Breaking of the Day* proceeds with a full-scale typological interpretation of Daniel and Revelation. "The great Mystery of God" is that "Hee will cast the Serpent out of man; and subdue that corrupt flesh under his feet, and dwell in man himself." In *The Mysterie of God* water imagery is a guiding symbol of life-baptism-salvation; in *The Breaking of the Day* seed imagery con-veys the dominant theme of potency-fruitfulness-posterity. From Genesis 3:15, "the seed of the woman shall bruise the serpents head," to Galatians 3:16, which tells of the promise to Abraham and his seed, Winstanley sees the fulfillment of the prophecy that "in thy seed shall all the Nations of the earth be blessed." "This was Gods sowing time, and all our mer-cies, graces, pardon, life, salvation, are in that seed of his love, Jesus Christ whom the Father hath sent and cast into the world: even as the fruitfull crop of corn, lies in the small seed, which the husband-man throws into the earth." Such imagery is not mere rhetorical ornamenta-tion to people who gain their livelihood from the soil.

Undoubtedly the prophetic books, where concrete metaphors stand for actual events, hold immense attraction for Winstanley, just as they do for Milton and Blake. The idea that "God did make knowne his Sonne, under types, figures, shadows and ceremonies of the Law," appeals to his need to find a comprehensive pattern in history that will give meaning to experience and purpose to suffering. Moses is therefore viewed as a "Type of Christ," a mediator between God and the people who, like "a teaching Schoolmaster," set up laws and ceremonies to lead the people. These laws increased until "the seed came: For it was impossible that the bloud of Buls and Goats should take away sins." But instead of observing Moses's covenant of types only till Christ came, the ancient Jews rejected Christ when he appeared and kept to the types. They kept the letter of the law instead of the spirit or, in literary terms, they observed God metaphorically but refused to accept him literally.

The logic of this is essential for understanding Winstanley's career, which may be looked upon as an attempt to put into practice what others had preached, to transform words into deeds, to make the abstract concrete. Like most profound ideas it is extremely simple. He self-consciously and deliberately sets out to change biblical figures of speech into specific acts because he actually wants to bring about the heavenly kingdom on earth. Repeatedly he insists that words must mean what they say; that is, a figure of speech must have some logical application to everyday reality. This is not simple naivete about figurative language. Winstanley understands what a metaphor is; he knows how to speak of one thing in terms of another, but he wants the correspondence between the signifier and the thing signified, between vehicle and tenor, to be explicit and particular, not abstract as in the thoughtless figuralism of contemporary pietists. To him, imagery should rest upon actual sense experience, things one can see, hear, taste, touch, and smell. Since language itself is an abstraction, he does his best to close the gap between the experience spoken of and the words used to represent it. Because he constantly struggles to reverse the movement of scholarly prose into deeper abstraction and obfuscation, writing, for him, is a politically rebellious act. He employs biblical prose defiantly, as a way of insisting upon his right to use words with something approaching their tangible meanings.

A grasp of Winstanley's theory of typological transformation is essential because, when he makes the connection between the Jews of the Old Testament and Anglican ministers of his own day who "keep to the bare letter of the Apostles," he points out that they worship but figuratively, through forms and ceremonies. The signal for Israel to be delivered from the Babylonian captivity was God's revelation " to *Daniel* in a Vision, his counsell and purpose," which was, first, "the nature and power of this misticall Enemy"; second, how "the house-hold of Faith . . . shall lie under that antichristian power"; and third, that the saints shall be delivered "from this Captivity; and the ruine of that tyrannicall Beast." Christ, "the seed of the woman," knows the right meaning of all those visions sealed to the former prophets, but since people are "not able to bear all truths at once," revelation must be progressive. Now the time "growes very near, if not begun already," when the saints shall see clearly into the mystery of God. The two witnesses are neither the law and the gospel nor Christian magistrates and ministers nor faithful men and women. Their testimony is that "the seed of the Woman should bruise the Serpents head; and that this seed is Jesus Christ . . . or . . . A perfect man in the unity of faith with all his Saints . . . this is called the Branch, and the Vine. Now a Branch or Vine, doth not consist of one sprig or rod; but of divers: and so the seed of Woman . . . doth not consist of one man." All saints "make up but one seed of the Woman" who shall inherit Zion "because Christs mistical body springs from the first *Adam*, which is from the earth." If, according to Isaiah 60:21, "thy people also *shall* be all righteous: they shall inherit the land for ever, the branch of my planting, the work of my hands, that I may be glorified," then the land will be purified, and "this seed of the Woman shall break the Serpents head: for . . . the feet of Saints, as well as . . . the feet of Christ [are] . . . but . . . one branch, one vine."

The seed-serpent-heel-head image recurs so often that it becomes a litany and has the effect of a chant. Nothing could show more explicitly Winstanley's fascination with images, with the liturgical power of words to transfix the listener or reader so that even when, or especially when, the literal meaning evaporates, the mere repetition of the words in the reader's mind creates an atmosphere, an ambiance of oneness. Winstanley's communication of personal experience through familiar biblical imagery enables the reader to feel a closeness to him that would otherwise be difficult to attain. Genesis 3:15 is used throughout to assure "the poorest members that lives alone among the scoffing sons of bondage" that they are "part of that seed, which the Father hath said shall break the Serpents head; so that the Serpent shall only bruise the heel, by his temptings; but he shall never blot out one name that is writ in the Lambs Book of life; for this compleat man, or seed of the Woman, shall break the Serpents head."

Ceaselessly reiterating this text, Winstanley encourages his readers to accept "that the seed of the Woman should break the Serpents head; was declared as soon as the devil, or red Dragon had deceived the whole world in *Adam*. And this councell of God is held forth to the world in all the promises; in all the Mosayecall types, and in all the prophesies of old." For those who will not accept scriptural authority, witnesses "can and will prove their testimony, not from the writings and words of others: but from their own experienced knowledge, of what they have seen and heard." Winstanley's anti-intellectualism stems from his desire to strike out anew. Like a true poet he turns to sense experience not as a basis for generalizing about human nature but as a way of obtaining authenticity, of returning to point zero. He starts with the obvious: everyone is a product of heredity and environment, but he also believes that the combination of those forces can produce new insights. He usually expresses these perceptions in a simile or metaphor. And just as scientists from Galileo to Watson and Crick have thought they had something new to tell the world, utopian thinkers from Plato to B. F. Skinner have thought they had a "new vision" of what society might be like.[48]

The world has become so skeptical of accepting experience in preference to intellectual and traditional authority "that when Christ appeared as a man in the flesh; they reproached him, under the name of a Mecannick tradsman, a Carpenter; and never rested till they had killed him and cast him out." Winstanley is not much concerned that Christ was not universally recognized as the Son of God or that he was crucified. What disturbs him is that he was "reproached" because of his humble social and intellectual status. "This descended world, or corrupt flesh of man," he says, "endeavours to make lawes and establish them with all possible policy and power, to bring the Anointed into bondage, and will not allow him a liberty too worke where and upon whom he pleaseth, but would restrain him to their scanty measure, . . . yet they will act these offices themselves, both over him, and over his body the Church." This probably refers to the stringent act against heresy and blasphemy passed by the Presbyterian majority in parliament on 2 May 1648, which classed as felonies, punishable by death, the publishing or maintaining of any heresy concerning the Trinity or the Incarnation. Ironically, only two witnesses were needed for conviction. This Blasphemy Ordinance condemned anyone who propagated universal salvation to life imprisonment.[49]

The two witnesses of Revelation 11:3 are the historical "Christ in flesh" and "Christ in Spirit," those in whom the spirit dwells.[50] Heaven is "the Church or the City Zion, in whom the anointing dwels," not some far off place in the hereafter. People bear witness to this through their sense experience. The earth is mankind, all sects and nations considered one flesh, to which God sends water, blood, and spirit in the form of Christ, the seed, a perfect man to whom the spirit descended like a dove when he was baptized. As "proof" that Christ was a real man, Winstanley cites the water and blood that came out when the soldier pierced his side:

"Now Phisitians say, and it is a truth, that the heart of man hath ad-
joyning to it a bladder or skin of water, which cools the heat of the
bloud; which they call the perecardium. And the speare piercing Christ
to the heart did breake that skin of water, and so there came out that
water and bloud that was in his heart; this shewes he was a man, the seed
of the woman." However this strikes modern minds, it shows how much
Winstanley respects the rational and empirical. His radicalism, like that
of Chaucer's Wife of Bath, rests upon experience as the basis for judging
truth. And while his ingenuousness may invoke smiles, the impulse behind his naive attempts at scientific explanations for supernatural events
is not trivial. For his unsophisticated efforts to apply his knowledge of
physiology to biblical incidents display the habit of mind which will, in a
few brief months, lead to the Digger experiment. His sometimes cleverly
contrived explanations of scripture result from his struggle to overcome
irrational superstition and dogmatic authority. He wants to know and
understand the world and how it works so that it may be put to use for
the material improvement of humanity. He knows this desire for empirical knowledge must be nurtured among the poor, for the well-to-do are
enmeshed in an authoritarian value system they can never forsake because of their desire to maintain things as they are.

The truth "is not to be restrained to Magistrates, Ministers, particular
Men, or Women: but to all the body, consisting of learned, unlearned,
poor and rich, men and women, in whom the spirit of the Son dwels."
Recalling 1 Corinthians 1:27 where God chooses the foolish to confound
the wise, Winstanley asserts, "these Saints are not onely learned Schol-
lers in humane wisdome; but such as the world counts fools." Like the
Shakespearean fool who, in John Danby's words, embodies "the consciousness of a split society," Winstanley's fool "sees rich man and poor
man, head and heart, sympathizes with neither, yet cannot dissociate
himself from the conditions of the strife. Harsh as the . . . world of corrupt society is, there is no escape from it."[51] As proof of working people's
ability to govern themselves, Winstanley traces through the seed of
Christ and the water and blood he shed, the history of "the whole body
of Saints, both Jewes and Gentiles," who were "given power to prophesie
in sack-cloth, one thousand two hundred and sixty daies." Of course this
"history" is typological and is explained by a symbolic interpretation of
such things as the two candlesticks and the two olive trees in Zechariah
4:11 and Revelation 11:4, and Zerubbabel, a descendent of David cred-
ited with beginning the rebuilding of the temple, as one who "tipes out
Jesus Christ."[52]

This history also shows that sin should not be punished "by an earthly
power, of prisons," but by the Lord, for the great battle of Revelation

"when Christ and his Saints Fought with the Beast and the Kings of the earth" foreshadows England's civil war between the "saints" and the "wisdome of the flesh strengthened by Humane Authority." And the defeat of this kingly beast is foreshadowed in Revelation 16:10: "they were Plunged into a deep Vexation of Spirit, so that they gnawed their tongues with anger." This may seem like mild punishment for King Charles and the royalists, but Winstanley understands that this "is as terrible to that proud Spirit, as a fire of Brim-stone to tender flesh." By the remnant slain by the sword "is meant the Common people, that were deceived by the learned wisdome of the Beast." After the beast's destruction the people will be undeceived and convinced by the word of Christ, which "is a sharp two Edged sword; and when that appeares, no Policy or strength of flesh, can stand before it." Therefore, anyone who tries to injure the common people, anyone who denies them, lies to them, or turns them to wantonness, will be destroyed, "not by prisons whips, or punishments of men; not by any *Carnall* weapons. But by the Spirit of truth, that proceedeth out of their mouth." Anyone who denies that Christ came in the flesh, that Christ's spirit is in the flesh of the saints, or that the people have the right to testify to their birthright, their stake in the "common treasury," is Antichrist.

The seed of the woman that will bruise the serpent's head, Christ's blood and water, suggests Revelation 11:6: "these [the witnesses] have power to shut heaven, that it rain not in the days of their prophesy: and have power over waters to turn them to blood, and to smite the earth with plagues, as often as they will." Heaven is the Church; the rain is Christ's appearance in everyone: "And so the Church . . . shall sweep away the City Babylon, with all her beastly practises and fleshly inventions . . . Now by this Raine, the earth or flesh of man, is filled with fruits of righteousness and truth . . . And these manifestations of love and justice, shall appear like a shower of raine, sweeping away the refuge of lyes before it." The power to turn water into blood is the power to prove hypocrisy false, for "when the Angel powres out his Viall into the Sea, fountains and waters of Babylon; that is, upon the very spirit of subtil enmity it self, and upon all the carnal wisdome and appearances that have flowed therefrom; and caused them to become like the bloud of a dead man: that is, to corrupt and die for ever . . . every living soul within the Sea dyed . . . All the strength, glory, and being of the Beast, dyed." But before its death a "spirituall fornication" took place between the beast, the whore of Babylon, and "Kings of the Earth," which brought forth the notion of the divine right of kings.

Concerned to clarify his new-found role, Winstanley pauses midway to give a three-part definition of prophecy. "First, to Prophesie, is to foretel, either in plain or dark language, what hereafter shal come to passe," for example the promise of Genesis 3:15. Second, "to Prophesie is to make such things plaine and easie to the understanding of others, which appeared dark and hidden before," as when Christ made the mysteries of the heavenly kingdom understandable to his disciples. Third, "to Prophesie, is to give testimony or proofe of such things to be true by experimental discoveries," for example when Christ "did experimentally prove himself to bee the seed of the Woman that broke the Serpents head" by spilling his blood and water. Like Frazer's image of the three threads in the fabric of civilization—the black thread of magic, the red thread of religion, and the white thread of science—Winstanley's definition recapitulates the history of epistemology from primitive soothsaying to authoritarian instruction to experimental science. The "sackcloth" in which the saints shall prophesy are Christ's sufferings and the agonies of his saints. The 1260 days are literally the time from Christ's baptism until his crucifixion and figuratively "the time of the Battel; that was fought, between *Michaell* our Prince, The seed of the Woman, And the Dragon; or the power of darknes ruling in the corrupt Posterity of *Adam.*" This battle also is both a figurative war in heaven and a literal struggle taking place "in every believer." Indeed, Winstanley testifies that he experienced such a battle within his breast: "the Prince of darknes, and powers of my flesh, that fought in me against the Anointing, or Spirit of truth, is now cast out; for God hath pardoned all my disobediences; and taken me into his owne rest."

This transformation takes place in eremitic seclusion: "the soul by the wisdome and love of God, is carried into a condition of sensible Barrennes, both in itself and in others, in which condition the soul is under Gods protection from the face of the Serpent, so that this wildernes spoke of, is a very safe condition or a hiding place from the Serpent, wherein the soul is fed and nourished by God, and not by any creature." This wilderness will not be found through conceited wisdom, learning, and strength nor through customs, prayers, and forms of worship; "this is to prefer the broken Cisternes before the Fountaines." To Winstanley, what John Saltmarsh calls the "Wildernesse condition" is found "wherein a Man is dead, to all his own wisdom, memory, strength, Learning, actings, and looks upon all as Priviledges of no gain . . . without the Anointing, he cannot meditate, nor understand."[53] He cannot speak and feels his heart barren of understanding, love, and peace; he only thirsts after God. Once the soul reaches this nadir of barrenness and death within itself, "she [the soul is feminine to Winstanley] findes no comfort or strength from any man or creature; preaching, praying, and all outward formes are barren actions . . . therefore she cries, saw ye not my beloved[,] him whose enjoyment I long after." The seeker waits "with tears in his eyes till God come, longing to see him; mourning in his absence; for the soul hath no sensible manifestation as yet . . . she waits, she sighs, and Breathes after him, O when shall I see my God, when shall I be satisfied with . . . the sweet enjoyment of the Anointed." God is now engaged to take care of this soul, which is in a safe condition, "because the soul is now in a way of nourishment before God . . . God never manifests himself to a soul, till he hath first emptied her of her self, and drawn her off for sucking Milk from the teats of creatures," for God says, "whom shall I give understanding to? And to whom shall I teach doctrin, but to them that are drawn from the Milk, and are weaned from the teats of a mans own self conceit and from sucking contentment from Mens Learning or inventions."[54] Fully aware of the psychological implications in this, Winstanley knows that to be reborn one has to return to the mental and emotional dependence of an infant, to go back to one's origins and begin to construct a new man. The obstacle to returning to this infantile state is fear, fear of vulnerability to social ridicule and personal insecurity. To the objection that Revelation 12:15-16 says "the earth helped the woman," he answers that "the Magistrates, or the common people be this earth," and they will help, "for God makes use of Magistrates and common people to help his Church and Saints against the serpents flood of malicious temptations."

The beast, in addition to being the external oppressor, is also in everyone's heart. Look within and then look "into the world," Winstanley advises, "and you shall see the same confusion of ignorance, pride, self love, oppression and vain conversation acted, against Christ, in States, in assemblies, and in some Churches in the world." But he has no doubt the beast will be destroyed both within and without and the heavenly kingdom will become a reality. He cites "the day of *Nero*, when Magistrates and people were all deceived," but even then Satan found "he could not do mischief enough," so he changed himself into an angel of light and became the "Universall Bishop that should rule successively," the pope. After he was discovered to be very "Hipocriticall and full of abominations," the beast became "reformed Episcopacy and, appears by faire shews, of pretending peace, even more closely hipocriticall." This, of course, is Anglicanism, "she that will not suffer Christ to choose his owne Church." Neither will she allow him "to call, to gift and to send forth, his owne Ministers and servants." The people "must either be content, with such ministers as she ordains, and counts able schollars and Orthodox Divines," or else they shall have none. "Shepards and Fishermen or Trads-men that are unlearned in mens writings, she will not allow to Preach the Gospell though Christ give them Anointing, and bid them speake the things which they have seen and heard."

Now Winstanley angrily hurls his thunderbolts. The first he aims at religious coercion and intolerance, the second at the opposite extreme, pious sectarianism and arrogance. And, to conclude, he follows Saltmarsh's admonition in *Free Grace* (December 1645) and introduces his favorite biblical pun.[55]

> Now doth the Sonne of righteousness, rise higher in the bright manifestations of himself upon the souls of his Saints, And the day of Christ begins to shine more clear . . . this day of Christ . . . began to dawne upon the seaventh day in course after the creation of all things; for *Adam* sinned upon the sixth day towards the close of the day . . . but the Sonne of our righteousnes rises presently and love appeared in this promise that the seed of woman should bruise the serpents head . . . therefore I say: This one day of Christ; did dawn upon the seaventh day from the creation: and the Sonne of righteousnes hath rose higher and higher.

This restatement of the Fall rests upon a frequently repeated pattern of organic imagery that begins with the God-created sun, moves to the fruit Adam eats and the seed of Eve that will bruise the serpent's head, continues with the baptismal water that fertilizes that seed, and culminates in the sun-son pun with Christ rising to bring forth the fruit of the seed that will restore the garden to its primal state. Sun-fruit-seed-water-son-fruit: with this, his restatement of the birth-death-rebirth monomyth, Winstanley sets out to construct an ideology based on communal sharing and mutual self-respect. As the Song of Solomon promises, winter is nearly past, summer is coming in, "the flowers appears in the earth . . . The time of the singing of Birds is come . . . And the voice of the Turtle is heard in our land . . . these Saints . . . will raise up like drops in a shoure of raine . . . Al the opression, injustice, false shewes and formes of Gods Worship, shal all be destroyed in the world; and judgement shal runne downe our streets like a Stream, and righteousnesse like a River."

Moving to first-person narrative, Winstanley returns to conventional spiritual autobiography. But, as with Bunyan's *Grace Abounding* (1666), his soul-history does not tell much about his secular life. That is not its purpose. The account of his awakening is written to encourage fellow saints of weakened faith and to show that he has undergone fierce temptations. The "rules" for such works did not allow for much ingenuity or individuality. A spiritual autobiography records God's dealings with man, not man's personal traits or habits. To introduce mundane events would be a sign of arrogance and would reduce the magnitude of the spiritual struggle, for the fundamental experience depicted in such works is conversion.[56] But at one point Winstanley temporarily breaks the bounds of commonplace piety and becomes genuinely impassioned: "Formerly," he says, "my life and joy was bound up in creatures, in riches, in friends, in self satisfaction, in my pride, covetousnesse, and contents of the flesh. Ah but now my life is the enjoyment of my God; His wisdome I glory in; His will, His love, His Spirit of truth I glory in. Not only to heare of these without by the voice of others, but to feel these working, dwelling and ruling in mee." This seems more personal than most other renunciatiors of worldly existence because it touches on the concrete, specific experience of people in his situation. He forsook his middle-class life of material gain and comfort to accept the Spartan, ascetic life of the evangelical mechanic preacher. In deliberately stripping himself of his respectable values and "creating" new standards based on his recently acquired status as a social pariah, he became a symbolic figure. For just as he sees Moses and Zerubbabel as types of Christ, he represents the new hero of his new class: the wage-earning pre-industrial proletariat. The process Winstanley passes through—from the son of a freeholder to an apprentice in London to a self-employed cloth merchant to a tender of someone else's cows on the heath—typifies the plight of thousands of men during the 1640s.

No wonder he, a man of words, says words escape him. He cannot relate the intensity of his experience with mere words; instead he is reduced to reciting biblical catchphrases and repeating the shibboleths of Puritan spiritual autobiography. Unlike Lilburne, Winstanley had no flair for self-dramatization, and unlike Luther or Bunyan, he does not appear to have suffered from any deep neurosis or psychopathic trauma. Thus he is not a very interesting subject for psychobiography. To the dismay of his critics, everything known about him indicates that he was a well-balanced, healthy, moderate man. Seventeenth-century England surely had its share of mentally unbalanced people, and they have much to tell us about the relation between social and psychological pathology. But Winstanley was not, like Lodowick Muggleton, John Reeve, John Robins, Roger Crab, Abiezer Coppe, and Laurence Clarkson, and unstable and deeply troubled neurotic who sought release from his anxieties by acting the wild-eyed prophet. Another lesson drawn from Winstanley's relatively quiet inner life is that the relationship between mental instability and radical politics is neither causal nor essential. The myth of the mentally unbalanced revolutionary, like the myth of the suffering eccentric artist, is largely a sentimental creation of romantic fantasy. Winstanley turns all internal contradictions out into the external world. His dialectical habit of mind is just that, a strong tendency to see all problems and contradictions as a combination of internal and external forces. He therefore does not look for happiness until the world's problems are solved. People will only be at peace with themselves when the world is transformed into a kingdom of peace and love. Like St. Paul he says: "I have obtained mercy, and by the grace of God am made to preach, to acknowledge and practise, that faith of God which once I endeavoured to destroy." The bottomless pit of Revelation 11:7 is the corrupt heart and flesh of man, but "no Man can search the bottome of his heart."

Winstanley's psychology is thus quite simple: evil is in people and in the external world, but it is neither eternal nor invulnerable. Its elimination is therefore social. An apocalyptic transformation of man and society is neither possible nor desirable. Instead social ills should be gradually ameliorated through the reformation of existing political institutions. In the same sense that Joachim's millennial scheme is less radical than Augustine's solemn quietism, Winstanley's goal of an acceptable social state is less apocalyptic than that of many supposedly more "orthodox" reformers. Augustine's City of God is so idealized that it cannot exist on earth. His concession that all earthly states are corrupt makes it useless to expect happiness. But while this nondialectical separation of celestial and temporal worlds effectively lessens earthly expectations, it raises spiritual (psychological) aspirations. For though earthly perfection is unobtainable, heavenly perfection is infinite. By resigning himself to secular corruption, Augustine, with his infinite striving for spiritual perfection, creates the perfect formula for existential despair. And since his followers, Luther for example, do not believe in human progress or human perfection, they may safely ignore political schemes for social betterment and tend to their individual souls while awaiting the apocalyptic Second Coming.

To challenge this Manichaean conception, Joachim divides history into three progressive stages corresponding to the three persons of the Trinity. In his scheme, as Frank E. Manuel notes, "the world is no longer an Augustinian struggle between two cities only one of which is capable of perfection, but a rising ladder of goodness and love."[57] Joachim secularizes providential history and makes possible doctrines of political reformation. In contradiction to Augustine, he raises humanity's temporal aspirations and lessens its spiritual expectations. And since his worldly desires for progress are linked to practical reality, anyone seriously wanting to improve the human lot must have a realistic plan, a plan to illuminate mankind's spiritual intelligence. Winstanley's unspectacular spiritual autobiography testifies to his awareness that such a plan is necessary. Causal interaction between inner and outer worlds renders prolonged introspection unnecessary and unprofitable. This does not mean he was shallow, but early in life he developed an extraordinary capacity for externalizing problems instead of locking them up inside. His spiritual autobiography remains free of the cant often found in such works because he sees that he is neither better nor worse than anyone else. He believes everyone has the same moral potential; this is implicit in everything he wrote and did.

The tendency to self-absorption is the smoke that rises from the bottomless pit to hide "the Sonne of righteousnesse" from mankind, the obfuscation of vain counselors "Which drowns the souls of men under ignorance" by coercing them to seek material gain. The church of Jews and Gentiles must suffer this tyranny of the beast for 2300 years after the 70 years of captivity in Babylon. Then the two witnesses will rise again even though they are killed by envy on the part of scholars, by hypocrisy and subtle policy on the part of officials, and by the spirit of cruelty on the part of legislators. Winstanley's awareness of the way the ruling class manipulates language is evident in his protestation that "now the beast makes directories, and Church Governments, not according to scripture, but by her conclusions and inferrences, from scripture that agrees (not with the Mystery of God) but with her owne being and maintenance." Anyone, he implies, can do what the ministers do, but they have the power to enforce their interpretations by what he earlier called "an illegal law." For "by this Ecclesiasticall bastardly power, which was got in fornication with the Kings of the Earth, The Beast hath reigned and lived in pomp like a delicate whore, first killed, and then trod the witnesses under her feet, for now she doth what she will, she sits like a Queen, and knowes no sorrow; for she hath a power from the Kings of the earth, and this power is permitted and limited by our God." Therefore the beast "envies Gods two witnesses; and uses all her policie to kill them," not through any particular man or office but through advancement of the ideology of selfishness. The slaying of the witnesses is not just a physical torture of the flesh but "a slaying of their actions and testimonies, by reproaches, oppression and Ecclesiasticall Lawes: not suffering them to act like themselves." To accomplish this exquisite torture the ruling class "turns the scriptures that testifies of Christ, upside down."

With this analogy of inversion, Winstanley is making much the same point illustrated by Marx's famous remark in the afterword to the second German edition of *Capital* (1873) that "the mystification which dialectic suffers in Hegel's hands, by no means prevents him from being the first to present its general form of working in a comprehensive and conscious manner. With him it is standing on its head. It must be turned right side up again, if you would discover the rational kernel within the mystical shell."[58] Winstanley attacks royalism and its immediate antecedents on the same basis. By turning the scriptures upside down the rulers are playing God and using their own subjective interpretations as a basis for governing. He wants them to stop "advancing the misterie of iniquitie";

that is, to stop obscuring the objective truth everyone is capable of recognizing for himself. Hegel, like the royalists, believed people could play God; therefore he converted his own longings into a grandiose theory of history and the state. Marx wanted philosophers to stop obscuring what he was convinced was the objective truth—that history was the struggle of one class against another and that the state simply represented the interest of those in power.[59] What Hegel and the royalists have in common is a desire to justify things as they are by referring to God as their ultimate protector. The ruling class wants to carry sinners back to a ceremonial, legalistic form of worship. They believe "we must be taught by men," and call "the teachings of God, without mens teaching, a delusion." They "will suffer none to preach . . . unlesse they come out of her Schools of Learning first, and so speak what they have seen and heard from Comentaries, books, and ancient Authors." They pretend to love God but kill and oppress "peaceable men" who will not conform to their principles and practices. They speak evil of the people and subject them to prisons, whips, and murder. Finally, they usurp the power of God and appoint "directories, ordinances and Ecclesiasticall Governments, to inforce every one upon paine of prisons, and death not to deny these, but to owne them and submit to them, as Gods directories, ordinances, and Government . . . when the plain truth is, they are but the thresholds of the Beast." But though the two witnesses "are lying in the street of the great City like dead bodies," they will rise again, but Winstanley does not presume to say when. That would be to usurp God's judgment. "Yet," he declares, "I have perswasions in me from experimentall, grounds of Gods owne working, that ere long within a few years, God will make this visible to the world." The beast strives mightily to keep its power and fights "like a dying hog for life at the last gaspe," but murdering the saints "under the name of Erronious round heads" is malice, not zeal. The beast, like the Euphrates, overflows but will dry up. In the river are four evil angels: subtlety, hypocricy, malice, and cruelty. They fight against the saints "that are branded sectaries, *Schismaticks, Anabaptists,* Round-heads" and kill not only bodies but "the very mindes and consciences of men." But no more than a third of the people will join with them against the "round-heads, *Anabaptists,* or *Independents.*" These four angels, the four horsemen of the Apocalypse, may be compared to the Cavalier army, which, by fire, smoke, and brimstone, kill a third of their enemies, fire being hanging and murder, smoke being false doctrines, threats, reproaches, scoffs, oppressions, and bitter provocations, and brimstone being persecution, whips, plundering, and prison.

Winstanley describes all this vividly, and recounts the horrible events of the civil wars in specific detail. He is careful not to attack civil magistrates and only says they are sometimes deceived by the royalists. The Cavaliers are portrayed as corrupt and despicable enemies. Using every rhetorical device at his command, he depicts them as inhuman monsters, violent, destructive, and pitiless. The "roundheads" can do no wrong. Christ is the only king, priest, and prophet; yet the beast has usurped these three offices and declares he can discern "what is truth and what is errour." The beast presumes to punish errors by "plundering, prisons and death," and thereby declares himself "to be as God in knowledge knowing good and evil." Only someone wishing to play God would punish everyone opposing him, "and so he declares himself to be an absolute infallible prophet to teach men, A King to rule and punish men, And a Priest to save men from death by his skil and operation." But this too will pass. The three days and a half during which the two bodies of Revelation 11:9 lie dead are the three ages and a half of the beast.

The first, the age of the Dragon, was "Magistracy out of joynt," when Christ and his saints were persecuted by open violence. The second, the age of the Leopard, is what "we call grosse popery . . . before there was any Church reformation." Third, the "age of the Beast with two horns like a Lamb," is what "we call reformed Episcopacy," which is like the previous age only "a little more hypocriticall; for it came in sheeps cloathing; but it spake like a Dragon; for it devoured the sheep by his common Laws, ecclesiasticall power, and high-commission Courts." This Joachite conception of the three and a half ages culminates with the final half-day, "the age of the Beast, under which *England, Scotland* and *Ireland,* does now groan, and it may be a very hot time, for the length of it; but it will be but short." This is the dividing of time because people are neither under absolute bondage nor have they obtained absolute freedom. Magistrates, common people, and ministers, especially "outside professing Presbyters" and Independents, have been corrupted; "but this will not last long," first because the scriptures say so and second because, as Winstanley's own changing class-consciousness illustrates, the fulfillment of Ezekiel's prophecy draws near. Even though the saints "cannot acknowledge Christ and his testimony publiquely for fear or by restraint of those laws . . . yet they will acknowledge and remember Christ among themselves."

Winstanley sees his defense of prophecy as a revolutionary act. Blake wrote on the back of the title page of Bishop Watson's *An Apology for the Bible:* "To defend the Bible in this year 1798 would cost a man his life / The Beast & the Whore rule without control . . . Who dare defend either the Acts of Christ or the Bible Unperverted?"[60] Winstanley writes of the civil wars: "in all this determinate time," the Beast walks up and down at liberty (as a man walks up and down in a street of a City where there is no stop) and knows no sorrow . . . God hath suffered the Beast to walk at liberty up and down . . . when the Dragon: (that is, Magistracy out of joint) And the Leopard: (that is, a spirit of whoredome pretending love to God, but intending to advance itself above God,) had committed fornication together; then they begat this Beast (or Ecclesiasticall power) to kill and suppresse, not men and women simply, but the manifest appearance of God in them.

The purity of the scriptures is corrupted, "and the practise of it quite altered: And the invention of learned self seeking flesh set up in the roome of it; and sharp punishing Lawes were made, to forbid fishermen, shepherds, husbandmen, and tradsmen, for ever preaching of God any more; but Schollars bred up in humane letters should only doe that work." Everard, Randall, and Saltmarsh express similar sentiments, and even so confirmed an intellectual as Milton believed that not only were the Anglican ministers corrupt but that the scriptures as well were an incomplete guide to truth and must be reinforced with human experience. Milton and Winstanley agree that the scripture engraved upon the heart is the primary source of knowledge.[61]

Throughout these early pamphlets Winstanley is sharply aware of how a feeling of clandestine suffering binds a group of people together and cements their revolutionary ardor. No better testimony to this can be found than the final pages of *The Breaking of the Day*. Not the least of the objections to reformed episcopacy is that it is too easy an answer to the church's problems. It is a "lazie" way to worship. Like many other Puritans, Winstanley protests against a relaxation of moral restraint as well as the oppression of the ecclesiastical laws. To him the state church is too harsh in its external forms and ceremonies and too lax in the spiritual demands it makes on its adherents. He wants fewer legal restraints on religion and more moral restraint in religion. He does not deny that there are "precious Saints" among "such as they call round heads," but also "some that are so called are meerly carnall, and are but the chaffe among the wheat, or weeds among good corn. For it is the bright appearing of God, in the Saints; casting down all forms and customs of the Beast; which doth torment the world at this very day, as the bright shining of the Sunne doth mightily offend a weak sighted eye." Winstanley wants religious freedom so that he may secure righteousness; above all he desires a sense of participation in saving his own soul. The formal, customary, and "tyth oppressing way of pretended Divine worship" no longer gave people of his station a feeling of belonging to a religious community. To them, episcopacy "nurses up pride, covetousnes, ignorance, opression, and is the mother or harlot rather of all abominations; And if men might be freely taught, that they shall go to Heaven, though they but seek it, not by faith only, but as it were by the works of the Law: that is, by bidding them doe what they are able," Christ will do the rest. His merits and men's works would then be joined and "it would be a merry world, and we should have good times again." That potent final word speaks worlds, for Winstanley's postulation of the previous existence of a lost Golden Age lends historical validity to his desire to restore it. What happened once can happen again.

Whether such an age ever actually existed is a moot point; what counts is that Winstanley believes it did, and to make the possibility of regaining it seem real he has but to "translate" the Bible typologically, to interpret the striking images, tropes, and allusions of the scriptures themselves. With minimal theological import but with awesome literary ingenuity, he spins out his prophecy, endlessly embroidering his themes and figures. His adaptation of the fourfold method amounts to a kind of "layering" or stratification of the text. Taking a single scriptural passage, often no more than a line such as Revelation 11:12—"and they ascended up to the heaven in a cloud"—he expounds for four pages, multiplying meanings, themes, applications, interpretations, and allusions. Or he quotes a passage in answer to a hypothetical question: How do we know the two witnesses will be saved? because the four ways the text may be interpreted—literally, morally, allegorically, and anagogically—all point to this conclusion: "by cloud, Note four things. First, what the cloud is. Secondly, it darkens the Sunne from our sight. Thirdly, it sends down rain. Fourthly, the effects that follows." He then expands, one by one, each of these levels by referring to related scriptures or personal experience. A cloud reminds him of rain showers, which remind him of shelter, which reminds him of a flood, which suggests drowning. This process continues until he exhausts the image or passes to another. He may have read William Perkins' influential *Arte of Prophecying* (1592), which says the preacher's duty is "to apply (if he have the gift) the doctrines rightly collected [out of text] to the life and manners of men in simple and plain speech."[62] But he learned to link organic imagery so consistently and to construct metaphors so powerfully from the Bible itself, and he draws most of his images from the scriptures; yet occasionally an unforgettable original phrase—"a dark vail is drawn over the mindes of men"—flashes across the page, reminding the reader of Winstanley's poetic gift.

The cloud-rain-shelter-flood-drowning series of organic metaphors culminates with images of an earthquake and a hailstorm. The earthquake has an internal and an external meaning. Internally it "shakes down" the city of Babylon so that a new city, the New Jerusalem, may be built. "God shakes down all the corrupt flesh in a Saint, and treads it under his feet." He destroys the old Adam's building so he may set up his new building. The shaking of the earthquake is also the emotional trembling of the saints in religious ecstasy, "that which unbelievers scoffs and makes a laughing stock at, in these daies." But never mind them, for they "can doe no otherwise, for they are slaves to the Serpent, and he makes them doe so." The earthquake also indicates "when God shakes down corruption in Magistracy . . . And when he shakes down all false shews, forms and customs of pretended divine worship . . . God shakes, and will yet shake, Kings, Parliaments, Armies, Counties, Kin[g]doms, Universities, humane learnings, studies, yea, shake rich men and poor men, and throws downe every thing that stands in his way." While the earthquake destroys "the outward abominations and unjust practises, in Church and State," it also restores "the tenth part of the City *Babilon*" whose leaders "shal appear so bright, and the Government in their hands becometh more righteous, more peaceable and more safe, for the well being of men, then the former customs, lawes, and directories were" that their enemies will submit to their leadership.

Winstanley greatly desires "that this Land may be the tenth part." But it is up to the saints to provide the moral leadership so others may follow. This does not mean that "Kingly Authority, or Parliamentory Authority" should be completely destroyed, "for these two Authorities are Gods Ordinances . . . which God hath ordained for to preserve peace in the World." But "Cleargicall, Ecclesiasticall, Classicall" powers must be totally wiped out, for they "are stoln by craft from those Kings of the earth, on purpose to make war with the Saints." All ministers, bishops, and scholars need not be killed; some will give up their power when they "see that inferiour people, even fools of the world . . . are raised up to speak the deep things of God, which those Masters of Art understand not." Others, Prospero-like, "shall even burn their books, forsake their private chambers and colledges, and deny their Ecclesiasticall trade, which their fathers and friends for worldly living sake have bred them too, and shall come in and joyn with the Saints." The remnant, the "common people, that have been deceived by the false prophet," will then reign, for when ministers "see that husband-men, and trads-men in every corner are able to speak in experience of things and truths which they have heard and seen," they will "be sleighted in their office, and be ashamed in their own visions."

Again guarding against the charge of sanctioning anarchy, Winstanley turns the tables on his opponents by declaring: "why now the ignorant common people are afraid, that all Laws and Governments shall be thrown aside, nay, the Beast doth buz them in the head with such a conceit." Ministers try to create the impression that people cannot help themselves, that they are sunk in ignorance and error, but actually ministers fear being overthrown. They conduct a propaganda war against those who want reform by portraying them as fanatics, cranks, and fools, but this will not work, for the civil magistrates will be restored "to the beauty and purity of justice and tendernesse." The troubles of the age are caused by "the usurped Ecclesiasticall power, which God never made," which in turn, causes men to be "so mad and ignorant (as the Beast hath deceived them) that they will throw down the Lawfull Power too, even Magistracie, which is the higher power God hath ordained, and commands every man to be obedient too." Some "count Magistracie no Government," but they must not be allowed to triumph, "for Magistracie in the Common-wealth must stand, its Gods Ordinance. But this Ecclesiasticall beastly stoln power in and over the Saints shall fall."

As evidence of how ecclesiastical power corrupts conscientious magistrates, Winstanley refers to a book he obviously read and studied intently—Foxe's *Actes and Monuments*. This passage, unnoticed by previous commentators, exemplifies how expertly he combines historical and typological evidence to support his controversial ideas. In his explanation of how it is a grief and a burden to "tender hearted Magistrates" to exercise ecclesiastical power and judge people's religious practices and convictions he writes: "witnesse Queen *Maries* dayes, as in the book of Martyrs, To imprison, banish, fine, and sometimes put to death, peaceable quiet men; that have no offence laid to their charge, but about the matters of their God; as *Darius* bad councellers troubled *Daniel*, who indeed were a type of this Ecclesiasticall troubler." It is not the men who corrupt the system of reformed episcopacy and ecclesiastical courts; the system corrupts the men who fill its positions. "It hath been observed, that when some Bishops have first been made Bishops, they were tender hearted and zealous, but after a little time, by mannaging this Ecclesiasticall beast, which their Office tyed them too, they grew hard hearted and great oppressors of peaceable men . . . I wish this were seriously minded in these our dayes."[63]

Clearly, Winstanley recognizes that he is in the mainstream of the radical Protestant tradition handed down since Wycliffe and the Lollards. As Haller shows, Puritan apologists looked upon the New Testament as both an inspirational and a historical work. To explain the church's failure to avoid corruption, they had to construct an account of its historical development down to their own day. This account was based on the premise, laid down by Foxe, that the true church had been corrupted by a coalition of priests, prelates, and popes who conspired with secular rulers to persecute the saints, suppress the gospel, and promote idolatry, ignorance, and superstition to fool the people into supporting them. Foxe's *Actes and Monuments* provided complete documentation for this idea. The enlarged edition of some 2314 pages, containing a dedication to Queen Elizabeth, was ordered to be made available in churches and other public places. By the end of the seventeenth century approximately 10,000 copies were in circulation—more than any other book except the Bible. Winstanley therefore had easy access to this influential work. He knew that during Mary's brief reign (1553-1558) at least 275 men and women were executed for heresy. But more than that, Winstanley's graphic depiction of his own struggle indicates that Foxe's method of presenting evidence greatly impressed him. Haller remarks, "every examination, as Foxe reports it, tended to wind up in a dramatic scene in which an honest believer was shown pitting the plain truth of the Word against the super-subtle sophistries of hypocritical churchmen and a loyal subject of the Crown was shown asserting his rights as an Englishman against a popish prelate."[64]

Foxe directed his appeal to people of Winstanley's class and station. His subjects were either young men who had barely begun their careers as ministers when they were caught up in the tide of reaction and dragged before public prosecutors, or they were people of little formal education, many of them workers in the cloth trade, who, captivated by the Bible, felt compelled to tell what happened to them and what it meant, undeterred by doubt as to their understanding of the truth revealed in the Word. Many, women as well as men, were working people who incurred the suspicion of neighbors and local officials by talking too freely, by absenting themselves from church, or by other impudent behavior. The stories of George Marsh, Rawlins White, and especially William Hunter must have strongly affected Winstanley, for, like him, they were lower-middle-class tradesmen made to suffer emotionally and economically for their beliefs.

The millenarian conception of England that Foxe brought back from exile after Mary's death gave immediate expression to individual experience and restored a historical dimension to the Joachite prophecy of establishing the heavenly kingdom on earth. "The example of martyrs, the lessons of history, and the teachings of the pulpit led men to suppose that they might expect the coming of a great change which would set them free from the weakness and uncertainty which flesh is heir to."[65] In attacking the confluence of governmental and ecclesiastical powers ruling in God's name, Winstanley sees himself challenging the same evil Foxe had attacked a century earlier. He insists the magistrates take back their legitimate power from the church and let "the Government of the Church-work lie only upon the shoulders of our Lord Christ . . . Indeed, the main cause of all our nationall troubles is the discontent of the whorish spirit in men that wonders after this beast, but when once it is faln really, in common-wealths, as it is faln in some Saints, then men will be freed from bitternesse; and rejoice because the Lord God omnipotent reigneth." If magistrates would abandon the ecclesiastical courts and permit religious freedom, "they would Govern Common-wealths in justice, love, and righteousnesse, more peaceably." The impassioned conclusion to *The Breaking of the Day* reads like a close paraphrase of Foxe's final words in the 1570 edition of *Actes and Monuments*. Winstanley also pleads with his countrymen to "Wait patiently upon the Lord, let every man that loves God, endeavour, by the spirit of wisdom, meeknesse, and love to drie up *Euphrates* . . . that like a great River hath over-flowed the earth . . . For it is not revenge, prisons, fines, fightings, that will subdue a tumultuous spirit: but a soft answer, love, and meeknesse, tendernesse and justice, to doe as wee would be done unto, this will appease wrath." And, relying on the powerful image he will refine and develop throughout his works, he promises that "When this Sun of righteousnesse and love arises in Magistrates and people, one to another, then these tumultuous national storms will cease; and not till then. This Sunne is risen in some, or else these tumultuous storms would have made it a cold and uncomfortable season before this time, this Sun will rise higher and must rise higher, and the bright shining of it will be *Englands* liberty."[66]

Winstanley's encounter with Foxe's book, together with his altered perception of the rapidly changing political climate, gave vitality to the idea of an inner spiritual transformation leading to a new way of life. Like many others, he believed naturally enough that the lively apprehension of the Word in his own familiar speech was the key to "a knowledge which would settle everything once and for all."[67] Moreover, Winstanley's reference to Foxe stands out all the more when we remember that left-wing Puritans did not agree with the Anglican practice of larding prose works with references to other writers. For while orthodox ministers thought it was a sign of sophistication and erudition to cite the church fathers and Latin and Greek classics, Puritans who advocated the so-called plain style rejected this display as pretentious and relied exclusively on the scriptures and their own ingenuity in interpreting them. This, they believed, made for a more honest and straightforward approach. Winstanley knew his citation of Foxe in the midst of the controversy surrounding millenarian interpretations of Revelation would remind his readers of the popular analogy between biblical Israel and contemporary England. Even more important, he knew no reference to Foxe in May 1648 could be taken fortuitously, for since 1641 Foxe had come to stand for a moderate approach to change, and many Puritan ministers had rejected his tutelage in favor of an apocalyptic view.[68]

Therefore, Winstanley's careful avoidance of attacking the magistrates arises not from timidity but from his strong disagreement with the Puritan mainstream. His adherence to Foxe is a political act signifying his conviction that society should be changed gradually, not apocalyptically. Since there will be no literal Second Coming, he looks forward to a third historical age initiated by spiritual transformation. God does not need man's work or his gifts. Those who best bear his mild yoke serve him best. Since his is the only true kingly state, they also serve who only stand and wait.

II

THE DARKENING CLOUD

AT THE END of *The Breaking of the Day* Winstanley looks forward to a new dawn when the sun will rise higher "and the bright shining of it will be *Englands* liberty." Confidently, he expects "within a short time" the saints, "scattered up and down like a few drops of hayle before the showre fall in force," will "sweep away all the refuge of lyes" and peace will reign. But they will not accomplish this by violent military action. A concluding ode challenges the Puritan notion of individual heroism by declaring the "Commander in Chief, is God himself,/ who rules the Spirits of men." Poor people should stand together and "Wait then on him, uproars to quell,/ and settle peace again." Those who "rise, for fleshy ends" will "undoe themselves,/ and vanish like a buble." Now God is "trying man, and changing times and customs,/ Ruining the Beast, and saving men,/ a midst these great cumbustions." Accordingly the poor should not be led to destroy one another, for "God will avenge, him that's opprest,/ by Christ our elder brother." Once he takes the realm, "Beast and Devil, Pope and Sin,/ shall never reign again." A transformation of human relations and human nature must accompany a change in political leadership.

> But yet mens hearts, disquiet are,
> and bitter as we see,
> Hot times have been, hot times yet are:
> but hotter yet may be.
> For now the Image of the Beast,
> appears to act his part,
> But hee's a falling, And Saints shall sing,
> Haleluja with joy of heart.

Hotter times did indeed await. And *THE SAINTS PARADISE: OR, The Fathers Teaching the only satisfaction to waiting SOULS. WHEREIN Many Experiences are Recorded, for the comfort of such as are under spirituall BURNING*, published late in 1648 by Giles Calvert, catalogues Winstanley's spiritual sufferings and outlines his attack on the corrupt clergy. Like Blake's *Marriage of Heaven and Hell*, this handbook of

46

radical psychology contains a comprehensive assessment of the effects of triumphant capitalism on the minds and hearts of the poorer classes. Far from describing a utopian vision of the future, *The Saints Paradise* exposes the insidious attitudes that keep working people from becoming aware of the corruption inherent in the dominant ethos. As Karl Mannheim notes, political discussion during times of crisis often takes the form of "the tearing off of disguises—the unmasking of those unconscious motives which bind the group existence to its cultural aspirations and its theoretical arguments."[1] And Winstanley opens with a metaphorical summation of such a condition: "it hath been the universall condition of the Earth (Mankinde) to be overspread with a black Cloud of darknesse; and the knowledge of the King of righteousnesse hath been manifested but in some few scattered ones, which as they have had the spring in themselves, so they have been as lights in the dark world."[2]

Living in a world of upheaval where new values are created and old ones destroyed, Winstanley was once blinded by his ignorance; he knew "nothing but what I received by tradition from the mouths and pen of others: I worshipped a God, but I neither knew who he was, nor where he was, so that I lived in the dark, being blinded by the imagination of my flesh, and by the imagination of such as stand up to teach the people to know the Lord, and yet have no knowledge of the Lord themselves." Worship of this traditional God, this lord of established authority, brought only pain and sorrow: "my comforts were often shaken to pieces, and at last it was shewed to me, That while I built upon any words or writings of other men, or while I looked after a God without me, I did but build upon the sand, and as yet I knew not the Rock." But now he has objectified the "ideology," the beliefs and values, of the ruling class, and in this newly acquired state of recognition he knows his readers will be offended at him for saying they do not know God. In order to cope with this resentment, he assures them that he does not write as an authoritative teacher and tells them they have a guide within them who will show them everything they need to know and help them remember all they need to recall. Once their eyes are opened, they will see the sun of righteousness within them.

Now, as the just man raging in the wilds, Winstanley unmasks the intellectual establishment so that working people may see how they are being misled. He wants to help build confidence and self-sufficiency. This "radical unmasking" is, in Mannheim's words, "the process of exposing the problematic elements in thought which had been latent since the collapse of the Middle Ages." For with the rise of capitalism "there is nothing accidental but rather more of the inevitable in the fact that more and more people took flight into scepticism or irrationalism."[3] Two things happened during the civil wars that made such flight all but inevitable: first, a unitary intellectual world with fixed norms disappeared; second, the hitherto hidden motives of the ruling class came to light. By 1648 Winstanley had become conscious of his thought patterns, had distanced himself from them, and even freed himself from the prevailing values of the ruling class. Still he could not create, out of whole cloth, an entirely new set of values without resorting to what would now be called utopian thinking—thinking that transcends reality and at the same time "breaks the bonds of the existing order." Again in Mannheim's words, "as long as the clerically and feudally organized medieval order was able to locate its paradise outside of society, in some otherworldly sphere which transcended history and dulled its revolutionary edge, the idea of paradise was still an integral part of medieval society."[4]

However, *The Saints Paradise* decidedly locates the utopian dream within society and within history; its place and time are here and now. Of course Winstanley was not the first utopian thinker in England. Thomas More and Francis Bacon, to name but two of the most obvious predecessors, suggested ideal societies, but they did not attempt to put their dreams into operation, to make them functional in time and space. Winstanley did, and his only real predecessors were the Hussites and the Anabaptists of Münzer who, building upon the ideas of Joachim of Fiore, joined with the demands of the oppressed. Mannheim explains: "the fact that modern socialism often dates its origins from the time of the Anabaptists is in part evidence that the movement led by Thomas Münzer is to be regarded as a step in the direction of modern revolutionary movements."[5] Münzer's contribution to revolutionary politics is "Chiliasm," the desire for immediate and total revolutionary transcendence based on the transformation of an inner mystical experience into an outer social reality. Originally, chiliasm was synonymous with the millenarian belief that Christ would physically come again and reign on earth for a thousand years. But literalists such as the Presbyterian Robert Baillie branded as "Chiliasts" those who denied Christ would come again and who believed Christ was in them.[6] Such Chiliasts—John Everard, Giles Randall, John Saltmarsh, and Winstanley himself—wanted to set about building Christ's kingdom on earth without waiting for a Second Coming. To them, Christ had already risen in their hearts, and that was enough. Thomas Edwards had already overtly linked William Dell to Münzer and John Lilburne to John of Leyden.[7] And he undoubtedly saw Winstanley's appeal to the poor in similar light. But, for Winstanley, Münzer's literary significance is as important as his political ancestry.

Like Münzer before him, with *The Saints Paradise* Winstanley begins the arduous process of trying to realize his inner dream in concrete, objective reality. He sets up a dialectic based on the ancient dichotomy of the few versus the many, the inner way of experiencing truth versus the outer way of following the dictates of authorities. He establishes this complex issue in the minds of his readers by dissociating his imagery from his own private experience.[8] The logic of this imagery goes beyond the platitude that some people are ignorant and others are enlightened. He challenges, even chastizes, those who have seen the light to act on their insight. For he insists that all true prophets must recreate the process of transformation in the real world. It is not enough simply to understand the cause and consequence of oppression. Those who sincerely wish to change things for the better have to be willing to work hard under strict self-discipline. This is an important advance in Winstanley's thinking. Previously he saw his main task as one of reaching his potential followers and gathering them to his cause. Both *The Mysterie of God* and *The Breaking of the Day* seek to instill courage in believers to resist the common foe of reformed episcopacy. *The Saints Paradise* goes beyond this. No longer content merely to argue and explain his position, Winstanley, following Münzer and in agreement with Foxe, Everard, Randall, and Saltmarsh, sees that personal suffering has a purpose in God's providential plan and is necessary for those who wish to create a heavenly kingdom on earth.

Münzer assured his followers that Christ was in them, not a thousand miles away.[9] "To have Christ born in the soul means also to 'do the deeds of Christ,' " Everard preached, "to grow and increase toward perfection . . . to be able to say as we read of divine events, 'this day is this Scripture fulfilled in me.' "[10] Randall wrote: "We must not imagine the powerfull and mighty Godhead to be any Idea, Image, or likenesse of any thing, but what he hath declared himself to be to us; for it is said, that Christ is in us."[11] Any conception of Christ's reign or personal kingdom, Saltmarsh specified, "was occasioned by 'the *Allegories,* and *Allusions,* and *Parables* the *Spirit* speaks; which they that are weak and carnal . . . take more in the *Letter* then in the Spirit.'"[12] "The Spirit, or Father, which as he made the Globe, and every creature," Winstanley writes, "dwels in every creature, but supreamly in Man . . . and there is no man or woman can say that the Father doth not dwell in him, for he is every where . . . but disobedient man knows him not . . . his covetous flesh hath deceived him, for he either looks abroad for a God, and so doth imagine and fancie a God to be in some particular place of glory, beyond the skies, or some where he knows not, or in some place of glory that cannot be known till the body be laid in the dust."

Such statements place Winstanley squarely in the radical Protestant tradition handed down from the time of Wycliffe and the Lollards. Like them he reaches a point where he sees that the poor, who are potentially the elect, must be filled with the desire to build a New Jerusalem. But first they too must renounce lustful desires, selfish yearnings, and frivolous pastimes so that they may have the courage, self-discipline, and motivation to sustain them in a protracted struggle. Winstanley tells his readers not to be afraid of intellectual hypocrites; they must have faith in themselves, believe in their own experience. It makes no difference in the eyes of God whether they know Latin or Greek. Priests do not know as much as they pretend; formal education is a sham. Professors just parrot words they learn from books; they know nothing about God based on their own inner experience; formal religion is a hoax; priests merely threaten people with damnation to frighten them into giving money to the church. This tradition of popular anticlericalism, which goes back to the mendicant preachers epitomized by John Ball, had immense appeal in mid-seventeenth-century England.

The church was the instrument of local administration and taxation; everyone had to pay a tithe, one tenth of his produce or profits, to a clergyman whom he had no say in choosing and of whom he might heartily disapprove.[13] Winstanley is one of the more articulate of several people who, in the years 1647-1649, stumbled upon what is now called a class split. He perceives a gap in the social fabric between what the common people want and need from their religious and educational institutions and what these institutions are prepared to give them. Men trained in these institutions are unprepared to serve the people because they are not taught to recognize their needs. Instead they are taught to serve their own needs by promoting their careers through the system of patronage, favoritism, and timeserving. The needs of these two groups—the common people and the clergy—so diverged as to be nearly incompatible. Dell, Milton, Samuel Hartlib, and others saw that the entire educational system required drastic reforms. Relatively few orthodox clergymen, such as Robert Herrick whose *Hesperides* was published in 1648, attempted to enter into the lives of poor parishioners and bridge the division of class interest.

Since God dwells in everyone, no one has an excuse not to know or serve him. The indwelling of God has both a democratic and a coercive impetus. Like its kindred notion, the priesthood of all believers, it imposes a freedom as well as a responsibility. "If you would have the peace of God (as you call it)," Winstanley warns, "you must know what God it is you serve, which is not a God without you, visible among bodies, but the spirit within you, invisible in every body to the eye of flesh, yet discernable to the eye of the spirit." These are hardly words of consolation. By late 1648 Winstanley has passed beyond that; instead of pitying the poor, he encourages them to take control of their destinies, to assume responsibility for their welfare. Here he surpasses other radical pamphleteers of the day. He advocates meekness and humility before God, but encourages submission only to the God within: "if you subject your flesh to this mighty governour, the spirit of righteousness within your selves . . . you shall not need to run after others, to learn of them what God is, for as you are a perfect creation, every one of himself; so you shall see, and feel that this spirit is the great governour in you." The practical effect of this admonishment was the charge of antinomianism Saltmarsh drew from his critics when he advocated similar steps in *Free-Grace* (1645),[14] but this freedom from outer governors did not mean people were free to indulge in licentiousness. Quite the contrary, it demanded a commitment from the saints more strict than any external law could demand. Freedom from sin did not mean freedom to sin.

The saints must raise themselves above selfish worldly and fleshly interests, must disengage themselves from the love of power, riches, and self-aggrandizement. "When you come thus to know the truth," Winstanley says, "the truth shall make you free from the bondage of covetous, and proud flesh, the Serpent that held you under slavery all your life time." The imagery of light and darkness reinforces this dramatic inversion of values:

> as darkness hath overspread the Earth (Mankinde) so now is the time come, that knowledge shall abound, and cover the earth (Mankinde) light begins to arise, the spirit begins to appear in flesh, he spreads himself in his sons and daughters, so that as the Sun shines from East to West, so shall the appearing of this Son of righteousness be; he comes not now in corners, but openly; the poor receive the Gospel, (which is this everlasting spirit) wise men in the flesh are made fools, fools are made wise, scholars are declared to be ignorant, the ignorant ones in mens learning, become abundantly learned in the experimentall knowledge of Christ.

This statement perfectly encapsulates what Winstanley is trying to accomplish. The carrying out of such a program would indeed turn the world upside down.

Encouraged, no doubt, by his recent perception of a society of saints, Winstanley achieves a new clarity and forcefulness: "I do not write to teach," he says, "I only declare what I know, you may teach me, for you have the fountain of life in you as well as I, and therefore he is called the Lord, because he rules not in one, but in everyone through the globe, and so we being many, are knit together into one body, & are to be made all of one heart, and one minde, by that one spirit that enlightens every man." The antinomian tendency to fragmentary individualism indicated by the fountain image, where every man is a law unto himself, submits to the wholeness indicated by the knitting image. The inversion of values—spiritual enlightenment, communal unity, and prophetic insight vanquishing material gain, selfishness, and intellectual authority—is accomplished by another self-consuming inversion: the leader becomes follower; the teacher becomes the silent pupil of his disciples. Having emptied himself of his spiritual insight, Winstanley becomes a student of his own writings. "I see more clearly into these secrets then before I writ them," he notes. He looks forward to the time when no one will be recognized as an authority but everyone will gladly teach each other: "I shall be as ready to hear as to speak."

Characteristically, *The Saints Paradise* opens with a dialectic between the teachings of schools, represented by moonlight, and the teachings of God, represented by sunlight. The moon "shines not of it self, but by the means, and through the help of the sun." People teach in two ways, by "natural industry," in studying books and the thoughts of others, and by "their own experience." True teaching should be done freely, for "if any man take up this trade of teaching, to get a living by (for preaching is now adayes become a trade) and speaks not from God by experience . . . they are clouds without rain." But this kind of teaching will soon vanish, "for this moon light . . . is to be swallowed up into the light of the sun." Ministers not only preach for profit, they also preach insincerely and have no genuine experience of God. Since they merely uphold things as they are, they do not help people but merely help themselves. Winstanley advises readers not to be concerned with them. "Let them alone," he says, "and wait upon God." The imagery of Revelation 21:23, where the City of God needs neither sunlight nor moonlight, summarizes the thought that the time has begun when "God himself will be the light," for, as St. Paul said (1 Corinthians 13:8), "knowledge (or rather this way of conveying verbal knowledge . . .) shall cease." But words are tricky, for they may deceive as well as enlighten. "I have been proud envious and discontent, and I have heard words from men against these, yet in those dayes I thought I was good, and I knew not those evils; but when God came, and wrought humility, love, and contentedness in me, he then taught me to see, and know by experience what the strength of God in me is."

Experience is the great teacher, for words are easily forgotten. Winstanley grounds his anti-intellectualism in his staunch belief that "there are so many Hypocrites amongst Professors, they know much in the letter, as men teaches them; but they know nothing in spiritual power." And those lacking spiritual power cannot resist temptation. It is one thing to read and agree that injustice, covetousness, rash anger, hard-heartedness, and lust are evil and that justice, faith, humility, tenderness, and charity are good, but it is quite another to know by experience why these things are evil and good. Unless people have this experience they cannot be free. Reliance on experience builds self-confidence, for those who feel free act autonomously.[15] Of course people may think they are free and yet not be. But the test is simple; if people flaunt their knowledge, which only "puffs up" and deceives them into arrogance and licentiousness, they clearly are not free but bound to fleshly desires. Pompousness and pretentiousness are the intellectual equivalents of lechery and gluttony. Liberated people have the strength to resist temptation. "I can hardly hear a sin named," Winstanley writes, "but I have been tempted to it." He speaks so much of fleshy sins because he knows by experience that they are "the most subtil, most ensnaring, and most dangerous."

Weak, lazy, incompetent ministers are irrelevant. "The most glorious" literalists are "the subtilest hypocrites." The most able ministers are the most corrupt. Having seen how the ecclesiastical court system corrupts even the best-intentioned magistrates, Winstanley now sees that the educational system corrupts the most conscientious man. He wants the church as a national, governmental institution destroyed. To show why this must be so, he sets out to prove that even though "a man may attain to the literal knowledge of the Scriptures . . . and raise many uses for the present support of a troubled soul, or for the restraining of lewd practises, or for the direction of a civill conversation, and yet both they that speake, and that they hear, may be not only unacquainted with, but enemies to that Spirit of truth, by which the Prophets and Apostles writ." Following the prophetic tradition of Jeremiah, Ezekiel, and Isaiah, Winstanley sees himself as one who speaks from what he sees and feels, and warns against applying scripture literally to another age: "Now if any man speak, and assure others of victory, when God purposes destruction, or speaks of destruction, when God purposes a victory; these men speak at random, and though they speak the very words of the scriptures, yet they speak not the minde of him that gives life, or destroys, and so having seene nothing from him, they are to be reckoned among false Prophets." Eloquence may be a sign of deception, for "a man may know the scriptures as they are written, & yet be a stranger, yea an opposing enemie to the God of the Scriptures." This, again, is part of Winstanley's inversion of values, for just as he previously said that poor people, by their experience of poverty, have a greater understanding of goodness than the rich, he now says that those who have responded to the spirit within have a greater knowledge of God than the learned: the test for this is also simple; if peace and comfort "only remain with you while you are either hearing, or reading Scriptures, or while you have the society of such as can speak or discourse thereof, and then finde again that your comfort and peace is gone, when you are deprived by any occasion of that society of Saints; truly let me tell you, that though you prize and know the Scriptures, yet there is a great strangenesse between you and the God of the Scriptures."

By inverting middle-class values, Winstanley intends to undermine smugness and apathy. This becomes apparent when he reflects upon the spiritual complacency of middle-class life. Those who enjoy superficial physical comfort believe "they are in peace, and they live in heaven as they conceive, and it is a sweet life, but it is not The life." Those who practice orthodox piety are locked into selfish fleshly pleasures and material joys. They will forsake God the moment the going gets tough. With a striking baroque image, Winstanley invests the Puritan spiritual autobiography with new meaning. He tells his readers not to despair if they have lost opportunities to forsake selfishness; instead they should look at them as times when "we sucked refreshment from the creatures breasts, but not from God." But if they have such opportunities and still mourn "like a fruitlesse Fig-tree, or ruinous Wildernesse . . . when there is no Cows in the Stalls, nor blossomes on the Vine, when no creature speaks peace . . . then God will make his people to suck life from him." God let him see that he had rested upon outward helps and means "though I thought not so, but was offended at any that told me I rested thereupon." He was rescued from middle-class comforts—maternal paps from which he was denied sweetness—by "a beam of light" in which he rested until he had the power to speak and act. This let him recognize the desirability of experiencing the wilderness condition, the nadir of despair, renunciation, and dejection by which seventeenth-century autobiographers associate themselves with biblical Israel. Winstanley compares it to being in prison; it is a kind of moral emptiness or necessary withdrawal from worldly pursuits before returning to active life.

But he injects this commonplace pattern of spiritual introspection associated with the "conquest of self" meditative tradition with what would now be called class-consciousness. That is, instead of using the Puritan notion of spiritual combat as a way of defeating temptation and despair and achieving self-assurance within the existing social order, he inverts the reconciliation of self and society that usually takes place at the end of the meditative experience and concludes with a total renunciation of things as they are. The instrument of this inversion is metaphorical distancing. Whereas the conventional seventeenth-century meditation concludes with a tension, held in abeyance, between spirit and flesh, nature and grace, the individual and society, Winstanley projects these conflicts out into the world. He ends, in other words, with the necessity for social action. Like the contentment offered from metaphysical poetry that, followers of T. S. Eliot emphasize, is a power of detachment enabling the speaker to analyze a problem while participating in the dramatic action of holding the experience at arm's length, inspecting it, exploring it, judging it, the contentment Winstanley seeks is active, not passive. Once one obtains this inner peace, God may "seem to withdraw" so "he may teach you more experiences; for that soul that God purposes to give plentifull experiences unto, it is his will to cast that soul often into straits." If "in the midst of these Nationall hurly burlies" people are without riches, food, clothing, or "communion of good people" they may still "rest quiet" knowing their suffering has purpose and meaning.

The Saints Paradise details that meaning: "In these dayes the bottomlesse pit is opened, and the mysterie of iniquity is begun to be made manifest to men." The corruption hidden before the civil wars is now laid open to view. Because of the spread of hypocrisy, envy, cruelty, fear, shame, and violence, good people are attacked by slanders, lies, threats, and outright murder. No wonder they are troubled. "Indeed I believe God may suffer some few of his Saints to endure wasting in their estates, and may give up the liberty and lives of their bodies into the hands of wicked men." With such words Winstanley speaks directly to those like himself, middle-class people gradually impoverished during the civil war era. As in Foxe's *Actes and Monuments*, the biblical nation of Israel typologically foreshadows England and exemplifies how poor people must endure suffering and trials to achieve their place in the world.[16] God suffered Pharaoh to live, but he did not allow him to cross the Red Sea, "then God appeared to preserve his son, even to deliver Israel, and drowned *Pharaoh* . . . and when this storm was over, God set Israel in a condition of greater liberty and freedom, from the oppression of enemies than ever he was in before," and when "the uncircumcised Nations" tried to destroy Israel, God protected it. So even though "Canon Laws, Whips, Prisons, and death" destroy the saints, "as in the time of Martyrdom, not all, but some were slain." Just as it was then, "in these dayes . . . it is the generall language of all the scoffing sons of bondage, they will destroy all the free born *Isaacs* under those reproachfull names of Roundheads, Anabaptists, Independents." Rising to new heights of political openness, Winstanley strikes out: "nay, there were some that were not ashamed to say, that when the Countries rise against the Parliaments Army, they would destroy men, women, and children of the Independent party, and root them all out."

Growing ever more indignant, he addresses his enemies with ironic superiority: "Alas poor creatures, God may suffer you to do something in this kinde, but you shall finde that God will hide his people under the shadow of his wings, and when you have killed all, yet those that you would kill shall be left alive." This will happen because Laudians kill Presbyterians and Presbyterians kill hypocritical Independents "and so make the seed of the Serpent to sheath their swords in one anothers bowels." If it is scripture these "hot spirited men" want, he too can cite chapter and verse to support his case. He chooses the text of Ezekiel 38:14ff concerning the fate of Gog and Magog, the Turkish tyrants who tried to destroy God's people, and in so doing absolves himself of the charge of literal scriptural typology. For he does not say that Israel is England or even that Israel represents England. He simply says that the plight of Israel may be used to illustrate the sufferings of contemporary saints. Like Milton, he understands that "it is essential to the whole doctrine of typology that the type be different from as well as similar to the antitype."[17]

Adherence to typological theory specifically excluded literal application of scripture. William G. Madsen remarks, "someone has wittily observed that the trouble with Satan is that he cannot recognize a metaphor,"[18] a sentiment with which Winstanley would heartily agree. In fact, precisely on this ground he earlier explained the Jews' failure to recognize Christ. Likewise, the hot-spirited of his own day cannot "root out" the saints for the same reason that "the Nations of old could not root out *Israel* after the flesh . . . for now the Saints doe not live all in one Nation, but are scattered through all Nations, kindreds, tongues, and People; The appearance of God among them is not altogether in out ward formall worship, and Temple service, as it was to the Jews, visible to the eye of the world." Winstanley's vision of the saints swimming among the people like fish in the sea, then, is primarily metaphorical, as is his interpretation of scripture. Just as Herod could not kill Christ even though he "killed all the children about two yeres old," the hot-spirited men cannot kill all the saints. For in seeking the ruin of the saints, "they will pull their own ruine speedily upon themselves." If the saints stand and wait, they will be delivered. "The number of bloody minded men shall decrease." But hypocrisy still reigns and sincerity is scorned. Peace and liberty are mere pretenses, for secretly most people "intend either to inrich themselves with the kingdomes monies & ruins, or else by their secret underhand working, endeavour to vent their malice upon the king-domes friends, even the Saints."

Having already forsaken orthodox piety, Winstanley now goes further and breaks with the Manichaean dualism most mystics embrace. The law of righteousness is not in the ten commandments; it is "the manifestations of God in all," which, like the alchemical operation, burns up "all the dross of the flesh, that the creature may appear pure gold." The spiritual combat within each person between the forces of good and evil fills one with horror and torment, but it is an "error" to think that evil is a power distinct from God; it is simply "the power of my proud flesh." Winstanley has learned from experience that a man only thinks he "cannot live without money, lands, help of men and creatures," but this is the devil's work. True life begins when one is stripped of these things. "When riches fayle, friends frowne, men withdraw help, and begin to speak evil, and to hate." Relying on his inner resources, such a man rationalizes his predicament and wallows in self-pity. The typical bankrupt middle-class tradesman thinks:

> I have no riches, no certain dwelling place, no way to get a subsistence, I am crossed in all, I have no cordiall friend, no succour from men; if any seem to succour me, it is for their owne ends, and when they have got what they can from me, they leave me, and turne enemies; so that the heart sees he is left alone, and in this low estate, feare & distrust, two strong divels buffets the poor creature, and squizes his spirit flat, for he sees nothing fulfilled to him, he feeles no power from God, and his spirit droops. So that here is depth of misery in the hearts apprehension, it is hedged in with sorrows on every side.
>
> Let him look to men and creatures, and there is no help, all hath forsaken him, and stands aloofe off; let him look within himselfe, and he sees nothing but slavish feare, and unbelief, questioning the truth and power of God, how can such things be?

Surely Winstanley could not have written this passage if he had not undergone such an experience. And he could not have assumed this highly detached manner if he had not overcome the restrictive thought process here depicted and been able to step back from his experience, to analyze it and obtain a rare perspective. He coolly examines the life of the middle-class tradesman, casts a cold eye on it, and passes by. This raised consciousness, this lucid objectification of middle-class ideology, is his chief intellectual accomplishment.

In the Garden of Eden, "that which we call Devill . . . is but the declaration of the rigour of the righteous law of God, laying hold upon the corruption that is in the creature, which the sinner cannot look upon, and live." But the law of love, as opposed to the law of works, allows for imperfection so man may "behold God, and live." When God drove Adam out of Eden he "placed at the East of the garden of *Eden*, Cherubins, and a flaming sword which turned every way, to keep the way of the tree of life" (Genesis 3:24). The tree of life is "God himself, in whom

Adam dwelt; and *Adam* himself, was that living garden in whom God delighted; But since *Adam* began to delight in himself, he went out of God, and God sent this flaming sword to slash against *Adam*, that so he might come into God again, and taste, and eat, and delight himselfe in that tree of life, till it was the good pleasure of God to take him in again." Adam's story "teaches every one to waite upon the Father for pure teaching, and to covet after no more knowledge, then what is freely given them." Adam cannot be saved until he is changed. Then he will be admitted "into the most fruitfull garden of *Eden*." God's flaming sword "is the enmity of natures . . . which is set in our hearts since the fall." Relating this to his personal experience, Winstanley describes his spiritual transformation, his metanoia, which was preceeded by what Erik Erikson calls an "integrity crisis."[19] As long as he "looked upon God as an angry God," he says, "I could not look upon him and live." Alone "in any dark room, or in the night," he was afraid. He thought the devil kept him from God, but now he sees that his own hardheartedness alienated him from spiritual rebirth. Once he recognized this he found peace, joy, love, and liberty. After attaining this solace he may stoically face "afflictions, crosses, prisons, frownes of friends, sickness, death, any thing."

Convinced that his suffering has purpose and meaning, and with the examples of Adam and Job before him, he justifies what he once perceived as gratuitous anguish. Freed from guilt and hypocrisy, he may return to Edenic joy: "Now *Adam* is come into the garden again, and finds rest in God, and there is none to keep him out of this enjoyment any longer." An early seed of the Digger experiment lies buried in this statement. The image of the Garden of Eden, like the middle-class value system, is in the process of being inverted, of being placed in the future in addition to being seen as a literal, historical place. Obviously Winstanley views the story of Genesis as a "myth," a metaphor of the process taking place within each person: "while these enmities are in force, there is great flashings one against the other, and sometimes there is troubles within a man, horror and trembling, and secret burning; and sometimes frightings, and apparitions of wrath without a man." But these dreadful neurotic symptoms of psychic distress disappear when man recognizes this spiritual conflict for what it is—God's attempt to awaken man to his love. The "whisperings of flesh" that rose up in Adam represent "the serpent that inticed him to disobey." He had "a tickling desire to be more wise and honourable then God at present had set him in, to which *Adam* gave consent, and so eat of the tree of knowledge of good and evill, even his owne selfe and imagination." This last phrase, which at first seems extraneous, resounds and echoes throughout Winstanley's work. For, in agreement with Milton, he sees that Adam's disobedience stems from an egotistical desire to remake God in his own image and so flatter the carnal self. Winstanley emphasizes what Stanley E. Fish points out in a similar context, that "spiritual apprehension . . . is achieved only when the self acknowledges its own powerlessness and unworthiness."[20]

Anticipating Milton's *Paradise Regained*, he explains how Christ himself experienced "the same whisperings of flesh" Adam was subject to, "for he was thereby inticed to dislike that condition his father had put him in." First, he merely murmured against the Father's carelessness for letting him fast for forty days. This was Christ's flesh rebelling against the spirit within, and he "rejected that inticement." Next "the flesh begins to move him to presume upon his fathers protection, that is, to cast himselfe down from the pinacle of the Temple, upon this conceit, that he was the son of God." Christ also rejects this unreasonable presumption of the wisdom of the flesh. "Then the flesh intices him to Covetousness, and vaine glory, after the things of the world." The flesh "told him, that if he would cease waiting upon the fathers providence, and follow the imaginations of the flesh, all the glory of the world should be his; for the imagination of the flesh thinks it can compasse any thing by its own wit and policy." But, naturally, Christ turned this down because "he delighted to obey, and to wait upon his father, and was content with his condition." Therefore Christ rejects unbelief, pride, covetousness, and vainglory—all "fruits of the flesh."

Setting the example of Christ beside that of Adam shows how the fleshly imagination may be rejected. And, correspondingly, it points out another "truth" frequently associated with spiritual autobiography, that "conversion," in G. A. Starr's words, "brings no immunity to further spiritual vicissitudes, but it does supply a new orientation from which to face them, and a new strength with which to endure or overcome them."[21] "Till such time," Winstanley writes, "as Christ hath finished this great mysterie, there is, & will be troublers in this flesh, our bodies; for the risings up of a mans own concupiscence will trouble him, and the flaming sword, the dispensations of the righteous law, laying hold thereupon, will affright and terrifie the enslaved creature, and raise mountains of miserie against him." Employing the second person to intensify his appeal, he takes his reader by the hand and speaks confidentially: "Well, in all your troubles, I could wish you could look upon the hand of God that smites, and not upon the Devill at a distance from God, as I have done, and I know you do." Reinforcing this congeniality he warns: "when God is pleased to open your eyes, as to see that it is he that smites, affrights, torments, shakes kingdoms, families, estates, & persons . . . then that which you call devill will appeare to be in you, & his power wil appeare to your sight, & you will see that by the . . . law of love (and by

no other power) you will & must be set free from the devil in short time."
This inner sight enables people to understand St. Paul's dictum that "it is
the letter that kils, but the Spirit gives life," which means that after "all
the clouds and storms are blown over . . . the love of the father shines
bright and hot upon the soul, making it fruitfull in love, joy, and peace."

A full assault on the problems of the ego further objectifies and universalizes his experience as a middle-class tradesman and householder.
Abandoning the metaphysical style of the Puritan preacher, Winstanley
adopts the clear, straightforward prose of the middle-class tradesman
and speaks now in the voice Defoe will use to such great effect. Concerning problems of inarticulateness, he notes that a troubled soul mis-
places his words," or finds "he cannot understand, nor speak what is in
his heart, and when he findes himself able to speake, then memory fayles
him." Business problems also plague the troubled soul: "in his course of
trading in the world, if he ask sometimes too little, or sometimes too
much for his wares, then he is troubled, and do what he can, his heart is
troubled, because he thinks he might have done better; when business
goes cross to his minde, he is troubled; whether it be fair weather or fowl,
if it be not just to his minde, he is troubled." In this and in similar passages, by merely stating how the typical businessman thinks, by giving a
transcription of his day-to-day mundane consciousness, Winstanley
dramatizes, simply and accurately, the stultifying limitation of such
thoughts. His ordinary tradesman is a seventeenth-century Willy Loman,
a pitifully tragic figure who, stripped of humane and aesthetically pleas-
ing thoughts, is intellectually bankrupt—his very existence becomes
problematic: "if he cannot speak for God, when others speak against
him, as he thinks, then he is troubled; if he do speak of the things of God,
then his heart tels him he is an hypocrite, or self-lover, and then he is
trobled; so that there arises not a thought in his heart, but there is some
fretting, or trouble tyed to it." Winstanley announces knowingly, "I call
it a hell, for it is a condition of darkness, below the life, comfort, and
peace of God." Rejection of "the righteous Law" brings on all these
troubles:

> for the creature strives to be wise, and the Law proves him a fool; he
> would fain be righteous, and the light of the Law shews him he is a
> wicked hypocrite; he would fain have faith and holiness in him, and
> the Law shews him he is an unbelieving sinner; he would fain enjoy
> the peace of God, and yet enjoy himself too, the Law tels him, he
> must deny himself, and take up his cross daily if he would enjoy
> God; he would fain be counted some body for wisdom, faith,
> prayer, preaching, the Law tels him, all is as good as nothing, be-

cause he goes forth in his own strength, and the power of the father is absent.

Even though he himself has passed beyond the small tradesmen, he understands and sympathizes with their predicament. Far from berating them for their tawdry existence, he finds their conduct explicable and even pardonable. He knows what their lives are like; he knows they are not the cause of social misery and injustice because they expect no more than a trivial share of the social rewards and because their existence is insecure at best. Thus he objectifies their demoralization and despair. He knows how they have suffered economically and psychologically during the civil war period. He sees the small tradesman as a "poor prisoner" of the system that oppresses him. In fact he recognizes that the system thrives on such people and the fear, envy, and failure they generate: "and while the soul is thus tormented by the dispensation of wrath, the envious spirit of darkness that rules in other men, delights to see this poor creature thus under bondage, and so casts jeers, slanders, reproaches, and hard usage upon him: Envy rejoyces in others misery, even as Love rejoyceth in the liberty and life of others."

While he assures readers that there is a way out of their predicament, he continues to document their sufferings, to give them shape and structure. Just as the inner miseries of the poor prisoner of the system keep him in bondage, outer sufferings also further ensnare him. Such things as "sicknesse, frowns of friends, hatred of men, losses of his estate by fire, water, being cheated by false spirited men, death of his cattle, or many such like casualties," produce poverty and hunger, which lead to demoralization, imprisonment, and "abundance of such provocations in the world." These, in turn, produce "fearfull Apparisions" and "terrors in the night" that break out "in bitter words and speeches, through oppression of the spirit, to the disturbance of others, and this is called madness, or distraction, which grows upon a man." Yet, at just this point of the soul's despair, of madness, Winstanley breaks into lyrical approbation: "when Christ comes and sets him free, then he comes to see, that whatsoever did befall him, must befall him, it was the will of the father, for the burning up of his dross, and pride of flesh, and shall be made to say, Father, thy will be done."

Ironically, perhaps, the figure he most resembles in passages like this is that most conservative of metaphysical poets, George Herbert. The pastor of Bemerton has a way of "drawing out" his soul's affliction, intensifying and objectifying it until he wraps his reader in a cocoon of self-identifying misery; he then bursts into a cathartic release centered on an acceptance of God's mercy. Similar to Winstanley's catalogue of misery springing into wholehearted acceptance of Christ's mercy is "The Collar," with its build-up of protest and suffering to the concluding acquiescence:

> But as I rav'd and grew more fierce and wilde
>   At every word,
> Me thoughts I heard one calling, *Child!*
> And I reply'd *My Lord.*[22]

By itself this similarity means only that, like Herbert, Winstanley takes advantage of an effective convention to dramatize the poignancy of spiritual conversion. But, seen in context, the culmination of his spiritual conflict in acceptance of providence attains a larger perspective. For whereas Donne's shorter poems often achieve witty detachment through cynicism, self-mockery, or fideistic belief, Herbert's best lyrics show his engagement with the harsh facts of social reality. "Jordan (I)," for example, is a political as well as a poetic manifesto:

> Must all be vail'd, while he that reades, divines,
>   Catching the sense at two removes?

> Shepherds are honest people; let them sing:
> Riddle who list, for me, and pull for Prime:
> I envie no mans nightingale or spring;
> Nor let them punish me with losse of rime,
>   Who plainly say, *My God, My King.*[23]

Furthermore, Herbert's rejection of "quaint words, and trim invention" in "Jordan (II)," where key words in each stanza—sell, rich, expense—point to the middle-class world of getting and spending, indicates a discontentment Winstanley would have applauded. And Herbert's disciple, Henry Vaughan, who experienced a metanoia about the same time as Winstanley,[24] opens his *Silex Scintillans*, Part Two (1655), with a renunciation of "those ingenious persons, which in the late notion are termed *Wits*," who have "cast away all their fair portion of time, in no better imployments, then a deliberate search, or excogitation of *idle words*, and a most vain, insatiable desire to be reputed *Poets*." And lest he be thought only to condemn the style and not the content, he adds that he would not object if their vanities "could defile no *spirits*, but their own; but the *case* is far worse. These *Vipers* survive their *Parents*, and for many ages after (like *Epidemic* diseases) infect whole Generations, corrupting always and unhallowing the best-gifted *Souls*, and the most capable *Vessels*."[25] Vaughan is not referring to humble writers; he means "persons of honor." "I my self," he notes, "have for many years together, languished of this very *sickness*; and it is no long time since I have recovered." Nor is he simply describing innocuously erotic literature written by hacks. "An idle or sensual *subject* is not all the *poyson* in these Pamphlets," he says. "Certain Authors have been so irreverendly bold, as to dash *Scriptures* . . . with their impious conceits; And . . . some . . . reckoned amongst the principal or most learned Writers of *English verse*."[26]

In addition to the experience of spiritual conversion, Herbert, Vaughan, and Winstanley share a perception of how moral reformation is linked to the reformation of language. But whereas Herbert and Vaughan stop there, Winstanley unites moral and linguistic reclamation with political reformation. If a "poor troubled soul is offended at my words, and thinks, and saies, this cannot be, it is impossible that any man should have such a frame of spirit," Winstanley writes, "alas poor man, I have been as thou art." But he hastens to add, in a potent alchemical image: "this wrath, bitternesse, and discontent that appears generally in mens spirits in *England*, one against another, upon the breakings forth of the truths of God, doth whisper in my spirit, that the Father hath cast *England* into the fire, and is purging the drosse from the gold, that liberty is not far off." He feels that England, Ireland, and Scotland will be set free "from the bondage of the serpent within, and the dispensation of wrath without." His transformation engenders this optimism, for if he has found peace and tranquility, he argues, everyone can. This is more likely than that everyone should be "of a smooth, close, fawning, hypocriticall, self seeking, fearefull spirit, that playes of all sides, for self-ends sake." After all, "God received persecuting and bitter spirited *Paul* to mercy, when as he let hypocriticall, self-seeking *Simon Magus* go by." Just as the devil is a power within everyone and the life of a middle-class tradesman is hell, so too "every particular Saint is a true heaven, or place of glory." Therefore, if everyone were to become a saint they would constitute the whole city of Zion "and this is heaven in the largest sence, which every particular son and daughter of the father shall enjoy hereafter." Echoing the title of Saltmarsh's famous work, Winstanley indicates that "the particular sparks of glory, or heavenly principles in man, which the father hath set as lights, to make known himselfe in his Saints . . . are Angels, and Angels of glory too; because they are sparks of glory issued out of the father, into earthen vessels, and makes them to become the salt of the earth, and light of the world" (compare Matthew 5:13–14). Those wholly "taken up into God, are called Angels" because they know God abstractly through love, humility, sincerity, and contentment and concretely through their sense experience.

This radicalization of Christian mysticism is one of the hallmarks of Winstanley's thought. He has an extremely metaphorical imagination and insists on translating all abstractions into specific, sensuous images. This stems, no doubt, from his insistence on the primacy of personal experience as the basis for all knowledge. Here again the similarity to Vaughan is unmistakable, for Vaughan also owes his largest aesthetic debt to the Bible, but he synthesizes alchemical elements "so integrally into the common language of Christian tradition that they do not disconcert the reader; they are not resented as the technical terms of an unfamiliar philosophy, but are accepted as the poet's way of expressing his conviction of the 'commerse' between earth and heaven."[27] Both writers draw heavily upon nature for their images; references to the sun, moon, stars, fire, light, darkness, seed, garden, and water dominate their work. In a typical Vaughan poem the controlling image is a source of light, the sun outnumbering all others, which contrasts with either darkness or firelight, forming a link between heaven and earth. Many of his poems, such as "The Retreat," reflect Winstanley's point that sainthood is a state of innocence whereby the original angelic nature of man, represented by a spark of light, expresses itself. And such poems indicate that Vaughan shares Winstanley's fascination with the ontological Joachite belief that the growth and maturation of each person recapitulates that of the entire species, that the " 'early days' of the individual's childhood become one with the 'early days' of the human race, as related in the Old Testament."[28] "Cock-Crowing," for example, epitomizes, through its exquisite integration of hermetical and biblical imagery, Winstanley's idea of the relationship between heavenly and earthly perfection. After explaining how the "Father of lights" has planted a "Sunnie seed" in the cock, which expels night and indicates that the bird knows the way to the "house of light," the poem asks if "the breath of God" shall not prevail in man:

> O thou immortall light and heat!
> Whose hand so shines through all this frame,
> That by the beauty of the seat,
> We plainly see, who made the same.
>   Seeing thy seed abides in me,
>   Dwell thou in it, and I in thee.[29]

Winstanley too is fond of contrasts of light and darkness, and he is especially attracted to alchemical imagery identifying the sun with the seed of all life, relating it to the earth as the "womb of creation."[30] *The Saints Paradise* also mixes alchemical imagery and biblical paraphrases, but whereas the function of Vaughan's connection between heaven and earth is to raise fleshly man to the spiritual level and back to his original perfection, Winstanley's imagery serves to lower heavenly perfection to earthly attainment and move man forward to surpass his present state.

This inversion of traditional theology is nowhere more apparent than in his description of angels. First, there are "the particular sparks of glory . . . the father hath set as lights to make known himselfe in his Saints." Second, there are those "wholly taken up into God," as in Vaughan's "They are all gone into the world of light!"; the prime example is Christ, who "was called an Angel . . . for he was the glorious sparke, and light of the father . . . the severall measures of his spirit are sparks of his glory . . . which the father sends down into humane flesh." Some who have been made perfect "have the sparks of glory, or Angels of light within them; which are the severall measures of the fathers spirit poured into them, which remaines for ever; and they themselves are Angels of light, sent from the father, to do his will here in this low condition of weak flesh."[31] But those who are angels, in the sense that everyone has a divine spark of glory planted within, "are faln from their excellency, and are become Devils, or evill Angels, or spirituall powers of darknesse . . . they were those glorious lights, and sparks of glory, shining Angels of light . . . which God had placed in the humane nature, *Adam*, before his fall." When Adam listened to the selfish whisperings of the serpent, which Winstanley ingeniously conceives as twisting itself around him, the serpent blinded the glorious spark in him, so when anyone delights in selfish aspiration the angel of light within becomes an angel of darkness, a devil "reserved in chaines of darknesse."

Seldom content to let a metaphor speak for itself, Winstanley explains that "these chains are the dispensations of Gods wrath through his righteous Law; for upon every one . . . the righteous sparks . . . like a flame of fire . . . meets with them, bindes them, keeps them in, and restrains them within bonds." Pride, self-love, envy, hypocrisy, subtlety, cruelty all act by God's leave, and when he allows them to act the righteous law follows "their heels like fire, burning up the stubble." Winstanley's antinomianism, like Saltmarsh's before him, dictates that "while these Angels lived in God, they had no restraint, for love God, and thou art at liberty . . . But when thou lovest self and flesh . . . then the flaming sword, which is the righteous spirit of burning, doth flame upon thee . . . and restrains thee." Finally, on Judgment Day, the serpent will be cast into the lake of fire and the "chains of darkness" will be broken. But man now lives in a "poysoned estate" where "masculine powers"—envy, hypocrisy, pride, anger, self-seeking, and subtlety—rule his heart. Here Winstanley again reaches a point where his mind seems to race ahead of his pen. He has gradually led up to the notion of the progressive restoration of mankind; upon arriving at its description, his prose takes on new vigor and urgency. The imagery suddenly becomes more complex and he adds metaphor after metaphor, straining at the bonds of language itself in attempting to express his thoughts.

An understanding of how alchemical imagery infuses seventeenth-century culture provides a key to understanding Winstanley's train of thought. As Keith Thomas explains, before the civil wars knowledge of alchemical lore was the province of learned men. But in the 1640s England saw the "democratisation of this magical tradition . . . There was a spate of translations into English of the major continental works on magic, hitherto couched in the learned obscurity of Latin or a foreign language. They included the writings of Agrippa, della Porta, 'Hermes,' Naudé and Paracelsus; and they coincided with the publication or republication of the native compositions of Roger Bacon, John Dee, Elias Ashmole" and the two leading hermeticists of the day, Thomas Vaughan and John Everard.[32] But unlike these intellectuals, Vaughan and Winstanley made no searching study of alchemical lore, nor do they, like Donne or Ben Jonson, demonstrate familiarity with Paracelsian texts. Instead they adopt and assimilate several key alchemical symbols into a Christian context as heuristic devices. Chief among these is the ancient concept associating the sun with the masculine powers of procreation and the earth with the feminine function of generation and birth. In the alchemical tradition the beams of the sun were frequently associated with the notion of a spermlike seed or germ which, when planted in the earth, produced new life. Closely allied with this idea was the Neoplatonic concept of the macrocosm-microcosm where each individual is seen as a "perfect world." Hermeticists transformed this idea into the concept, justified by biblical texts such as Romans 8:21-39, 9:7-8, John 12:36, and 1 Thessalonians 5:5, that infancy and childhood correspond to the early development of the human race, and this state of moral innocence and spiritual purity can be regained here on earth. Seventeenth-century writers infinitely vary the application of this complex construct of ideas and symbols.[33]

The alchemical idea of the sun as God the Father engendering new life in Mother Earth to produce a "new man" Winstanley finds especially attractive. "The spirit of truth," he notes, "who is the Father, by whom the creation, man doth live, move, and hath his beeing, doth lie buried under that unrighteous fleshie power. But now in the restored estate which the Father hath begun to work . . . All the powers of the soul, as his love, delight, and peace, &c. run Godward again, and is centured in the Father again." Here the two key verbs—"buried under" and "centered in"—retain much of their alchemical significance. True to the hermetic tradition, rejuvenation requires purification and self-sacrifice. The alchemist believed he must first reduce his materials to their lowest form before he could produce the magic elixir, and just as he must purge his life of extraneous matters before setting to work, so too must Winstanley and his saints cast off their "fleshie" longings and reach the bottom of sorrow in the wilderness condition. To move from the idea of individual to universal salvation is to pass from the microcosmic image of personal redemption to the macrocosmic image of the heavenly kingdom on earth.

Thus, on the Day of Judgment everything will once again be reduced to that primal state of chaos from which the Father created the universe. According to ancient legend, in this archetypal union the Father relinquished part of his power to Mother Earth to engender life. From this grew the belief that procreation required sacrifice on the part of the male and suffering on the part of the female. Early metallurgists, ancestors of the alchemists, adopted this cosmology in the form of ritual union and blood sacrifices, ensuring microcosmic identity with the macrocosm. Anthropology was often presented in terms of ontogeny. The alchemist's aim was never simply the making of gold; smelting, after all, was a well-known process. Rather the alchemist saw goldmaking as a purgative process linking knowledge of the material and spiritual worlds, and as the alchemist tried to perfect nature's work he tried to perfect himself. Above all, he wanted to understand the cause, principle, and meaning of change; so any process of change, be it chemical, biological, psychological, or historical, had special significance. Christian alchemists saw a connection between sexuality and death in the mythical birth, death, and rebirth of the sacrificial hero, Christ. The earliest extant Graeco-Egyptian alchemical text (a pseudo-Democritean fragment of the second to first century B.C. preserved by Zosimos) indicates that the process of initiation into the mysteries of alchemy consisted of participation in the passion, death, and resurrection of a god. The transmutation of man, in other words, accompanied the transmutation of matter.

The alchemist also had to undergo the birth, death, and rebirth he projected onto matter; in so doing he believed he must go back to the origin of life and repeat the cosmogony; after his rebirth he must return to the innocence of childhood. Everard's translation of *The Divine Pymander of Hermes Mercurius Trismegistus*, published in 1649, contains mystical ideas much like those of Jacob Boehme, whose works were brought out by Winstanley's publisher, Giles Calvert, beginning in 1648.[34] Both Everard and Boehme knew the *Theologia Germanica*, and although Winstanley cannot be supposed to have studied such works closely, he no doubt found hermeticism's adaptation of Neo-Stoic material pantheism persuasive; and he agreed with the hermetic belief that a rational intelligence governs the universe. Moreover, hermetic texts emphasize the symbolism of light and darkness and frequently use images of snakes, seeds, fires, and eyes to symbolize man's potential perfectibility. Evil, to the hermeticist, is like rust or dirt. Man can be purified by forsaking irascibility and concupiscence and embracing justice. Regeneration is achieved by spiritual transformation, which requires psychological death and rebirth and, once accomplished, is sustained by intuitive knowledge rather than good works or discursive thought. But in the final analysis, while Winstanley was receptive to ideas from all sources and while he shared with the traditional mystics and hermeticists a profound distrust of accepted hierarchical authority, the most important thing he learned from them was how to read biblical metaphors back into the real world. His relationship to mystics like Boehme approximates Blake's to Swedenborg. That is, in the same way that Swedenborg's mysticism leads Blake to see the one-sidedness of Newton's physics, Boehme's alchemical symbolism enables Winstanley to avoid the sterility of the deism espoused by Lord Herbert of Cherbery. Although they believe the five senses to be clouded by selfish desires, at no time does either Winstanley or Blake adopt the mystical idea that sense perception is an untrustworthy basis for knowledge.[35] Instead they transmute hermetic ideas for their poetic and prophetic purposes and adapt such imagery to political ends.

Following the passage from John 3:19, "Light is come into the world, and men love darknesse rather then light, because their deeds are evill," Winstanley develops the macrocosm-microcosm analogy. "The *world* is mankinde, and every particular man and woman is a perfect creation of himself, a perfect created world." So that if a person wants "to know what the nature of other men and women are, let him not look abroad but into his own heart." The importance of this concept cannot be overestimated, for here Winstanley flies into the teeth of the Calvinistic notion that people are divided as to their natures, that there is something fundamentally different about a person who is elected to be saved by God. Of course early Puritans used the idea that some people were morally superior to challenge the aristocratic notion that some people were inherently superior by birth, but Winstanley completes the Calvinistic inversion of the aristocratic claim to natural superiority by, in Hegelian terms, negating the negation, by saying that no one is superior to anyone else by birth or by election. By understanding themselves, all people will come to understand others and, eventually, the world. This typifies Winstanley's inner-outer dialectic, his tendency to invert all conventional wisdom, and it also represents his tendency to stress internal similarities rather than external differences. This "perfect created world" has been corrupted internally and externally through "the lust of the eye, the lust of the flesh, and the pride of life," which did not come from God. The light that has come into the world is "the spirit of right understanding . . . dwelling in this flesh." This makes man "a reasonable creature," distinguishing him from beasts. If men would submit to reason "they would act righteousness continually . . . *But men love darkness rather then light;* men here spoken of, are the evill masculine powers of created man in his poysoned estate." Over this poisoned estate rules "King imagination," creator of paranoid fantasies and self-delusions. These are masculine powers "because they rule over the created flesh, which is the feminine part," and will not allow it to obey the sun of righteousness, which is called conscience. The masculine side of human nature corrupts the feminine side and holds it in bondage. Of course, mankind's original androgynous nature was an old hermetic doctrine,[36] but Winstanley takes this notion a step further and links masculinity with traits necessary for success in a capitalistic society—aggressiveness, selfishness, egocentricity, belligerence, acquisitiveness, tough-mindedness, and ruthlessness. The feminine or uncorrupted side of human nature represents sharing, loving, giving, yielding, helping, caring, and nurturing. Again, this is a dialectic, an interpenetration of opposites. No one is completely masculine or totally feminine. "For I say, every particular man and woman is a perfect creation, or a world of him, or her self."

Men and women who follow the masculine powers will not submit to righteousness. They deliberately choose evil deeds and follow socially accepted evil ways. "Indeed covetousness is an evill man, and pride and envy are evill men, and all the rest of their imaginary companions in the soul, they are evill men, yea, the wicked man, and all their actions are evill like themselves, and they will not submit themselves to righteousness." But the "mightie man of truth" dwells in these evil ones just as he dwells in the righteous ones. The difference is that the evil ones "smother his smitings within themselves, and will not submit." This, in turn, causes a host of psychological terrors that appear socially as neurotic and psychotic tendencies. Since these masculine powers will perish, but not the people who practice them, "no man or woman needs to be trobled at this, for let every man cleanse himself of these wicked masculine powers that rule in him, and there will speedily be a harmony of love in the great creation, even among all creatures."

Therefore Winstanley countenances no one who whines that others "will not obey this light." He advises such people to look within their own hearts, for there they will find those impulses for which they chastise others. If the "light of reason" is within each person, what of the angels sent from God to do particular work? These good angels "are inward discoveries of God," not outward appearances or apparitions. Sometimes, as in the story of Elijah (1 Kings 19:5), angels speak inwardly; other times, as in the tales of Samson, Abraham, and Lot, angels are material men who are "taken up into the spirit of the Father, and sent by him to do such a work." Even Satan, who is often called an evil angel, "did the will of God, in troubling *Job,* for the end of that trouble was good to him, his last dayes being his best dayes." So even these so-called evil angels are instruments of God's will. Here, of course, Winstanley, like his Augustinian predecessors, wants to avoid saying good and evil, God and Satan, are equal powers. Yet, at the same time, he feels the need to justify the ways of God to man by explaining how, in a universe governed by a just and omnipotent deity, evil will be transformed into goodness. Evil angels purge man and allow him to see the path of goodness. They take three forms: first, the hardness of heart that struck Pharaoh; second, pestilence and famine that destroy a rebellious people; and third, "King envy, King covetousnesse, or King pride, that uncleane spirit that rules in the children of disobedience." This last obviously concerns Winstanley most, for his use of personification here, so anticipatory of Bunyan, enables him to construct a concrete universal out of an abstract particular.

He sees the widespread evils of envy, covetousness, and pride as three kings. This, in turn, allows him to objectify these internal qualities so that people may rid themselves of them by projecting them into the social world. And the figure of a king, of course, exemplifies the idea of dominance, superiority, and authority he wants to expose. For without directly challenging the doctrine of divine right, which he finds absurd and pernicious, he merely turns it against itself. Through his manipulation of language and images he transforms what were believed to be static qualities of human nature (envy, covetousness, and pride) into changeable external properties of the state. He sees Charles I, the coercive, legalistic ruler, as a retributive angel of God. His "mighty powers" (as in Isaiah 10) become "Angels sent by God, either to waste and destroy, or else to be a terrible warning to a sleepie people, to awake them, as the King of *Assyria* was sent to do a worke in that kinde, that is, to whip the Nations, but to brighten *Israel.*" Moving back from Isaiah's justification of suffering to the triumph of virtue in Judges 6-7, he assures his reader that when the work of the destructive angel is done, God will send another powerful angel to destroy the cruel and unrighteous one sent to purge the nation of Israel and awaken the remnant to its task. For if, following Foxe, the fate of biblical Israel stands for the destiny of contemporary England, then the New Model Army under Fairfax and Cromwell represents Gideon's victorious army. In fact, Winstanley juggles biblical history to make it seem as if Gideon's army was responsible for destroying the King of Assyria. In this way he makes his allusions to Charles I and the New Model Army fit. But he withholds total support from the Army. The Israelites, he reminds his reader, did not need to destroy their enemies, for "the Lord sent an Angel, which was no other but a mighty spirit of feare and confusion of minde among the *Midianites, Israels* enemies; which made them to destroy one another, while *Israel* had the liberty to looke on." Thus those who only stand and wait, the neglected common men and women of England, are the real nation of Israel.

Hurling defiance at the ruling classes, Winstanley asks "the Powers, Governours, and Armies of the land" to "learne to worship the Lord in righteousnesse, lest while the Lord hath made them Angels to destroy some, and to warne others; the Lord do not give out a Commission to others, to destroy and confound them, and so bring about his work by another power." In the same way that Saltmarsh, a few days before his death, cautioned that the New Model Army had departed from God, he threatens: "Assure your selves, you Kingly, Parliamentarie, and Army power, and know this, that all unrighteous powers and actings must be destroyed."[37] Christ is now rising from the dead, not as a single person to be exalted but as a spirit "in every man and woman." He is not coming "to answer the types of *Moses* law," nor will he come as a military or political "Saviour." Christ's power is spiritual and universal rather than fleshly and individual: "The flesh was as the woman to the man, or the box that carryed that precious oyntment in." Returning to his favorite alchemical metaphor, Winstanley explains that just as the body of Christ, "in his Ascension, so called, went out of the Apostles sight, in a cloud of the Skies, so shall the same mighty man rise up out of the earth." This earth he interprets as "the earthy imaginations and lusts of the sons of men; for mankinde is the earth that containes him buried, and out of this earth he is to arise, and appear in the clouds." Lest his metaphors be misunderstood, he adds that Christ's appearance in the clouds means that "as he begins to shew himselfe in a man or a woman, the fleshy powers in those enslaved soules will, and do rise up to darken the light of that sun as he can, till he, the flesh who is the wicked man, or the cursed thing that dwels within (mankinde) be taken away."

Implicit in this earth-cloud-sun metaphorical pattern is the origin of the Digger experiment. In *The Saints Paradise* Winstanley is but one short dialectical leap away from the idea of cultivating the commons on St. George's Hill, of converting the land now shared through avarice and rapine into a communistic utopia. For nearly a year he has shown how the Bible should be interpreted metaphorically. The time quickly approaches when he will see that his biblical exegesis requires that the earth be transformed into a New Jerusalem. For if the despised and neglected people of England can become the saints of the heavenly kingdom on earth, then the earth itself, a common treasury, can sustain these saints once it is transformed from private property to a new Garden of Eden.

Winstanley tells his reader not to look for an external resurrection of Christ, for "the spirit within the flesh is the Jesus Christ, and you must see, feel, and know from himself his own resurrection within you, if you expect life and peace by him." The microcosmic image indicates that every son and daughter of the Father is "a perfect created world of them-selves, and need not to seek abroad after other creatures for teaching." This self-sufficiency merges with the essential Protestant notion of the inner light: "for every one hath the light of the father within himself, which is the mighty man, Christ Jesus." This inner light, this son-sun, "is now rising and spreading himself in these his sons and daughters, and so rising from one to many persons, till he enlighten the whole creation."

Knowing that all deities reside in the human breast, Winstanley con-verts this inner light into "the lightning that shall spread from East to West." This inner kingdom of heaven "is the wisdome and power of God . . . the light and life of every man and woman that is saved by him." Yet, as with Blake, just when he seems most conventional, Win-stanley bursts into a paean of heterodoxy. Jesus Christ's dual nature is indicated by his two names. Jesus was a "meek spirit," but Christ was "a man filled with the power of God." "Therefore you are not saved by believing there was such a man, that lived and died at *Jerusalem*." The historical Jesus is inconsequential; what matters is that his followers "feel the power of a meek spirit come into" them. The Jesus of orthodox re-ligion is merely a historical abstraction, a spirit-filled man who lived long ago. Christ is contemporary and empirical, a living creature of flesh and blood. He is not a disembodied presence, a specter or ghost, but "the power of the righteous spirit come into you." Winstanley does not con-demn the body; he does not wish to escape mortality. Instead he wishes to make the body "subject to the spirit of the father within it." Everyone is a potential Christ. "So," he enjoins, "do not look for a God now, as formerly you did, to be a place of glory beyond the Sun, Moon and Stars, nor imagine a divine beeing you know not where, but you see him ruling within you." And, guarding against pride in election, he insists that this spirit exists "not only in you, but you see and know him to be the spirit and power that dwels in every man and woman; yea, in every creature, according to his orbe, within the globe of the Creation."

If the doors of perception were cleansed, body and soul would be united and experience would guide man to infinite knowledge. Enlighten-ment comes from what people "see, and feel, and taste." Flesh, by itself, is an evil power: "If you live in the flesh, that is, if you be subject to the powers of the flesh within you, then you believe in the flesh, and bring forth the fruit of the flesh, which is self-conceit, covetousness, envy, pride, hypocrisie, and the like." But if the flesh is transformed by the spirit, it is preserved and allowed to "bring forth the fruit of the spirit, which is love, joy[,] peace, humilitie, obedience, sincerity, and the like." Thus truth, to Winstanley, is a matter of perception, of how one sees the world, not a matter of how social, intellectual, and ecclesiastical hierarchies define it. He escapes the doubts that drew university-educated, introspective Anglicans like Burton and Browne into their studies to contemplate. In their carefully contrived skepticism, the "thinking man's philosophy," they questioned the prevailing truths of the social, intellectual and ecclesiastical world. And even Milton, whose "hatred of priests, an established church, forms, ceremonies, and tithes was as fierce as that of any of the radicals," recognized that his privileged status as a leisure-class intellectual imposed special responsibilities upon him.[38] Therefore, no matter how skeptical or critical these men were of prevailing ideas and beliefs, their questioning was done from a protected position Winstanley did not share. This no doubt contributed to his view of the interrelatedness and interdependence of man and nature, since neither man nor nature, to Winstanley, is unchangeable.

The gradual transformation from hierarchical to experimental attitudes toward man and nature, reflected in the utopian ideas of More and Bacon, leads the preservation and observation of the divine reflected in what was deemed "natural" and toward the "artificial exploitation and manipulation of nature for material benefit.[39] Influenced by travelers' tales of the unspoiled, pure and "natural" life of the New World savages, More, following Erasmus, portrays a world where reason and nature combine to reflect the correct and divine order. Without private property gold is valueless except as ornament and an indication of low status, and laws are few because the people, uncorrupted, have little need of them. Since "all men have abundance of all things," favoritism and avarice, the vices of the new, probing Renaissance man of learning, have no place and all things are held in common.[40] But Marlowe's Renaissance man, Faustus, aspires to know and control the world. With knowledge of its secrets he can crown himself with glory. Paralleling Spenser's Redcross Knight and anticipating Marvell's Mower, the natural world of appearances succumbs to a devious world as double as his mind. "Be a Divine in shew," Faustus says, "Yet levell at the end of every Art."[41] More's *Utopia* looks back to a medieval world of timeless order, seen as nature's recommendation, while Faustus wants a Baconian mastery and turns to the new learning that will provide the impetus for progressive change.

The profound effect of the "new philosophy" on Donne's sensibility is a textbook cliché: yet perhaps not enough attention has been paid to the way his attitude toward nature does not encompass civil order, but discovers the individual in nature. He does not seek enlightenment outside nature and therefore does not become alienated from God and man as Faustus does. For although Donne did, like Faustus, glut himself "with learnings golden gifts" and surfeit himself "upon cursed Necromancie," the naked body is his script and, as he perhaps was aware, his ironic arguments lead to a facile libertinism.[42] Conversely, Marvell's Mower chronicles the woes done to nature by the advance of Renaissance man. The opening lines of "The Mower Against Gardens" epitomize this attitude:

> Luxurious Man, to bring his Vice in use,
> Did after him the World seduce.[43]

The poem speaks of corrupting perfect nature by enclosing gardens, making them into "dead and standing" pools of air, tainting roses with strange scents, changing the color of flowers, and adulterating plants to get strange, "unnatural" strains such as the pitless cherry. All these things the poem deplores and views as transgressions against nature:

> 'Tis all enforc'd; the Fountain and the Grot;
> While the sweet Fields do lye forgot:
> Where willing Nature does to all dispence
> A wild and fragrant Innocence.[44]

And in "Damon the Mower," "The Mower to the Glo-Worms," "The Mower's Song," and "Upon Appleton House," each leveling, metronomic sweep of the mower's scythe represents conflicting attitudes toward nature. The mown way is at once a religious one, the advance to a new freedom allowed by God, the path of the Israelites through the Red Sea, at once the sharp sweep of love's desire, and also the movement against the hierarchical ranks of society by the advance of political parties like the Levellers. Marvell also gives intimations of a mysticism that would find in nature a path to God. Faustus' flight is on a dragon's back, but Marvell's is one of Neoplatonic ascension:

> Casting the Bodies Vest aside,
> My Soul into the boughs does glide:
> There like a Bird it sits, and sings,
> Then whets, and combs its silver Wings;
> And, till prepar'd for longer flight,
> Waves in its Plumes the various Light.[45]

As an "easie Philosopher" of nature, in "Upon Appleton House," his fancy weaves "Strange *Prophecies*" out of "Natures mystick Book"; he is content to "move/ Like some great *Prelate of the Grove*, . . . languishing with ease" until "loose Nature" is benumbed by the beauty of young

Maria, whose father, the commander-in-chief of the New Model Army, Winstanley will soon confront.[46]

Maria's awesome beauty inspires a Brownean O *altitudo!* and the woodpecker who resurrects the diseased oak by feeding on the worm gnawing like cancerous sin within suggests agreement with Browne's observation: "*Natura nihil agit frustra,* is the only indisputable axiome in Philosophy; there are no *Grotesques* in nature . . . the most imperfect creatures . . . having their seeds and principles in the wombe of nature, are every-where where the power of the Sun is." Browne wants "to suck Divinity from the flowers of nature" and disdains the scholarly definition of nature as "the principle of motion and rest." He sees God as "an excellent Artist [who] hath so contrived his worke, that . . . he may effect his obscurest designes . . . Art is the perfection of Nature: Were the world now as it was the sixt day, there were yet a Chaos: Nature hath made one world, and Art another. In briefe, all things are artificiall, for nature is the Art of God."[47] Milton, in this context, is closer to Winstanley when he maintains "that indeed according to art is most eloquent, which returnes and approaches neerest to nature from whence it came; and they expresse nature best, who in their lives least wander from her safe leading, which may be call'd regenerate reason."[48]

To Vaughan, as to Winstanley, nature reflects divinity. Alchemically, miracles are still possible because

> . . . Religion is a Spring
> That from some secret, golden Mine
> Derives her birth . . .[49]

Nature, then, represents both the innocence necessary to commune with God and the clearest source for a renewed faith. Human nature, uncontaminated, is the child shining in "Angell-infancy" and meditating on nature:

> When on some *gilded Cloud,* or *flowre,*
> My gazing soul would dwell an houre,
> And in those weaker glories spy
> Some shadows of eternity.[50]

And whereas Douglas Bush warns that Vaughan's longing to escape the cares of worldly existence and return to his heavenly home is "not merely *contemptus mundi* or nostalgia for a lost Eden,"[51] there is no denying that in his near obscurantism, his romantic individualism, and his nature worship, "Vaughan's poetry is less social, more removed from the world of action than that of Donne or Herbert,"[52] and Traherne takes Vaughan's mystical withdrawal from the adult material world even further. In fact Vaughan and Traherne, though both conservative Anglicans, carry two radical modes of thought developed by the Puritans—continuous revelation and inner experience—to their logical extremes.[53] Traherne's shadows (the springwater's reflection) of himself mirror the divine scheme in which his body is but a shadowy reflection of his heavenly self. The "Seeds of Delights" God sowed in him "That might grow up to future Benefits" are the same sunny seeds Vaughan finds in the cock, the types and shadows of the seed Milton and Winstanley find in Genesis 3:15, which God promised would bruise the serpent's head.[54] The idea that the divine sun has separate illuminating rays in everyone sustains Milton's Samson, who is "With inward eyes illuminated,"[55] and in his "Virgin Youth" Traherne believes he had

> A Secret self . . . enclosd within,
> That was not bounded with my Clothes or Skin,
> Or terminated with my Sight, the Sphere
> Of which was bounded with the Heavens here.[56]

Nature, unquestioned in the literal medieval world where things were what they seemed, became a mirror of the progress of Renaissance man, serving as a source of civil instruction, of love's teaching, then of God's intimate individual grace. During the first half of the seventeenth century the Faustus figures prodded nature's secrets for use and profit. Bacon's *The New Atlantis* (1627) projects a vision of "natural harmony," of nature working hand in hand with man's "God-given" powers of transformation to create a new nature—one of towers, medicines, luxury, and technology, "a relation of the true state of Salomon's House."[57] *New Atlantis* exemplifies the artist cum scientist as prophet, a modern Moses transforming the deserts of vast eternity to reveal the fantastic springs of the future. But Bacon's optimism neglects the aspect of nature that transformed Donne—death. Lamenting the acceleration of transformation that alienates people from their bodies, Donne was aware that neuroses were setting in with the split between pristine nature and artificial nature:

> What hope have we to know our selves, when wee
> Know not the least things, which for our use bee?[58]

The popularity of Baconian science widened the Cartesian gulf between matter and spirit. "Whatever pious motives for the study of nature Bacon professed," James D. Simmonds points out, "his insistence inferences drawn from the study of material phenomena should be determined by the observations of the senses and not referred to first causes had the effect of driving yet another wedge between matter and spirit, the Creation and the Creator human morality and the temporal environment."

From Vaughan's point of view "this was idolatry of things, and Bacon's demand that mankind exploit its dominion over the natural world by applying knowledge to the amelioration of temporal existence, rather than to the glory of God, was a signal example of intellectual pride."[59] Thus Vaughan and Winstanley come to alchemy from different directions but with a common objective. Each sees in the ancient philosophy a way of forestalling the exploitative implications of Baconian science, of healing the breach between material and spiritual realities and accepting the universe as one God-created whole. Both use hermeticism in a Christian context as a metaphorical guide to truth, for seeing God in nature offers a way of resolving the opposition between a ruthless and arrogant exploitation of nature for selfish ends and a quietistic resignation before nature as an escape from worldly cares and responsibilities. But although they both internalize hermetic doctrines as a way of expressing their private yearnings for comfort and solace, Winstanley turns the theories of the Paracelsian philosophy into metaphors for the internal transformation of man and the external transformation of the public world. To Vaughan, a metaphor is a way of thinking about the world; to Winstanley it suggests a way of changing it.

From biblical images Winstanley constructs an elaborate alchemical metaphor by explaining that, when the spirit rules within, it checks and condemns "every unrighteous thought, as well as extravagant words, and loose actions, though no other man see and know your secret wickednesse." But when "King-flesh" rules within, "then you go on in secret and open wayes of unrighteousnesse with greediness and delight, and have no checks within at all." Comparing the body to a house inhabited by a "strong man of sin" where peace only seems to reign, Winstanley tells how the sun of righteousness will cast out the strong man of sin, the serpent, and bruise his head. Therefore, he warns, "assure your selves, you that glory in flesh, you shall not go scot-free, you shall be cast into the everlasting burnings as well as others, and tryed in that fire, as gold in the furnace." The book of Proverbs contains two references to the purgation of gold in a furnace (17:3, 27:21), but Winstanley cites neither. He gives a marginal gloss to Hebrews 12:29—"For our God is a consuming fire"—and extends his metaphor by comparing God to the purifying alchemical furnace "into whom, when any creature fals, he burns up the drosse in the creature, which is the curse that came in through unrighteousnesse, which is all the imaginary glory of the flesh." In purging and transforming each individual, the Father carries out his traditional role as the chief alchemist or super magus.

Another persistent alchemical idea, that if nothing impeded the process of gestation all ores would in time become gold, Winstanley sees as a metaphor for the transformation of poor working people into the saints who will turn England into the New Jerusalem. The function of the alchemist was to accelerate the growth of base metals into gold; similarly, Winstanley sees the power of the spirit within everyone as an alchemical agent, a homunculus. Jonson's *The Alchemist* cynically mocks this aspect of alchemical lore when, in Act I, Surly questions Subtle about his professed ability to "hatch gold in a fornace, sir,/As they doe egges, in *Egypt!*"[60] Certainly Winstanley did not believe in the supernatural hocus-pocus associated with alchemy any more than Jonson did. But he knew the power of a good metaphor. The association of gold with wealth, power, and nobility reminded poor people that they were "crude" in comparison to the nobility and the rising commercial class. By manipulating the alchemical metaphor of purgation Winstanley implies that the poor are merely "not ripe," that once they undergo the harsh process of purification they will inherit the earth. The alchemical analogy suggests that poor people must purify themselves by standing before the sun of righteousness: "you cannot burne away the drosse, but the gold must suffer the heat of the fire, the father cannot consume the serpent, the man of sin, out of my body, but I that have been incorporated into that nature of the serpent, must needs suffer paine; this drosse and gold in man is so mixed together, that nothing can separate them but the fiery orb."

This fiery orb, the *sol iustitiae*, identified as "the father himselfe," tries all things. Just as smelting was, in the alchemical tradition, a sinister operation requiring the sacrifice of a human life, so God, as the original alchemist or "master of fire" who created the universe out of primordial chaos and darkness, requires a sacrifice of the old self, a purification and cleansing through fire, so that a new self may be born. For, as God created man by an alchemical operation involving the collaboration of sun and earth, light and darkness, so now man himself, to be reborn, must repeat this cosmological operation, sacrifice his old self, interact with nature, and be tried by the fire of psychological torment. The image of God as a master of fire, an alchemist, is a metaphorical key to understanding Winstanley's conception of the deity. Fire, the transmuting agent controlling the passage of matter from one state to another, symbolizes science itself, for the "demiurgic enthusiasm" associated with its use by alchemists encouraged man to manipulate natural processes. It allowed for the possibility that man could, in Mircea Eliade's words, "interfere in the processes of the cosmic forces. Fire turned out to be the means by which man could 'execute' faster, but it could also do something other than what already existed in Nature. It was therefore the manifestation of a magico-religious power which could modify the world."[61]

An adaptation of alchemical tradition to Christianity easily accommodated the ancient myth of the master of fire, the first smith, to the Promethean notion that the son of the supreme being was sent by God to complete the creation and share the trade secrets with men. The sun-of-righteousness image, from Malachi 4:2, so prevalent among seventeenth-century poets and pamphleteers, has alchemical connotations.[62] In Vaughan's "Faith" the "blest beame" of the sun impregnates "his spouse," the church, whose feminine body, like nature, ceaselessly changes from darkness (forms and ceremonies) to light (the spirit of salvation):

> So when the Sun of righteousness
>   Did once appear,
> That Scene was chang'd, and a new dresse
>   Left for us here;
> Veiles became useles, Altars fel,
>   Fires smoking die;
> And all that sacred pomp, and shel
>   Of things did flie.[63]

Rejecting such sacred pomp, Vaughan's alchemical metaphors allow him to turn to nature for spiritual renewal. But what Eliade calls the "mythologized victory of *homo faber*," the man that both acts and knows, also "presages his supremacy in the industrial ages to come."[64] Combining respect for the spirit in nature with a progressive view of man's potential victory over nature, Winstanley attacks the conventional notion of the deity as abstract and subjective: "you call the father your God, and the word God is much in your mouths; but here you deceive your selves, for you know not the father to be your God." The flesh must be made subject to the spirit known by inner experience. "He that looks for a God without himself, and worships God at a distance, he worships he knows not what, but is led away, and deceived by the imaginations of his own heart, which is *Belzebub* the great Devill; but he that looks for a God within himself, and submits himselfe to the spirit of righteousnesse that shines within; this man knows whom he worships." As before, the test of fidelity to the spirit within is practical experience, "when a man can say, I see, feel, and know that my flesh is in part subject." All else is dross; "what I heare another man speak or write, it is nothing to me till I finde the same experience within my self."

Readers often put the story of the Gergesene demoniacs from Matthew 8:28 before Winstanley for clarification and interpretation, but he "knew not the meaning of it; if I went about to studie or imagine the meaning, I was lost presently, and trouble took hold upon me," but he persevered and learned to have faith in his ability to comprehend and so became "quiet within," at which point "not only this, but divers other truths was, and I can almost say, daily is given into me." The meaning of the two insane men confronting Christ is that the earth is full of "troublesome distempers of all sorts" and that the spirit of love can destroy this wickedness. For no matter how inflicted with sorrows and troubles, "every man and woman . . . are every one a perfect creation of themselves and the spirit of the father dwells supremely in every man, as in the whole globe." Returning to the alchemical image of God as the everlasting fire that tries all things and separates dross from gold, Winstanley explains that "this spirit, or father, is pure reason." And just as a fire never ceases burning as long as there is fuel, the fire of pure reason burns the devil with delight, "and works the restauration of mankinde with abundance of love and cheerfulness." Scripture is "but the declaration of a historicall truth, pointing out this higher mysterie"; therefore it should not be taken literally. The "holy Law" is not in the letter of the scriptures but in the spirit, where the struggle between the devil and the spirit of righteousness takes place. And man "looks upon these two as they fight." The watching of this battle objectifies it and enables man to witness his own psychological death and rebirth. In modern psychological terms, the distanced ego observes the conflict between the id (flesh) and the superego (spirit). The two struggle within man's own breast "as a murtherer of him, for hereby his earthly peace is killed." In such a condition a man may truly believe he will be destroyed before his time, but once the spirit triumphs "then all fightings within, and troublers in the flesh shall cease, and there shall be perfect peace." This is the ultimate meaning of the two men possessed by devils. The swine into whom Christ cast the devils represent a man who lives "in the imaginary delights and glory" of the flesh "snudling up his food from among the filth of the earth." The swine who run down the hill into the sea are "earthly minded men" who run down from Zion's hill.

Here Winstanley's secularization of religious enthusiasm draws a step nearer to the founding of the Digger colony on St. George's Hill. Those who run up Zion's hill, he explains, accept self-denial and love righteousness. Having attained, metaphorically and psychologically, the summit of the spiritual conquest of self, they can go no higher. This is the closest one can come to God: "Gods dwelling is not in any locall place above the skies, as men fancie, and say, God dwels above the heavens." He is said to live in heaven only in that his wisdom and power are "above" people's total comprehension. Heaven, like hell, is a metaphor. When people say God lives above the heavens they mean that "the spirit that is the life and peace of all things, which is reason, is incomprehensible." This is the nearest thing to a climactic sentence in *The Saints Paradise*. For a hundred pages the reader has looked for some vision of a utopia, expecting perhaps a commonplace *locus amoenus* evoking dreams of a restored Eden. Instead of a plain man's pathway to heaven, if he perseveres, the reader is led through a series of arguments designed to force him to a rigorous self-appraisal. By presenting a more or less objectified version of his self-development, Winstanley engages the reader in a comparative dialectic of self-awareness. Point by point readers are encouraged to match the psychological subtleties of their own lives against those in the text. But we never arrive at a comforting vision of the hereafter or even an idealized portrait of the future; on the contrary we meet repeated challenges to our innermost thoughts, ideals, and beliefs. Veil after veil of self-deception falls away, leaving the stark realization that the ideal life is simply one of pure rationality. Winstanley makes this austere vision attractive by sealing off all alternatives, not by describing its material pleasures. The saints' paradise is a place where those willing to renounce selfish desires work with others to make a better world.

Heaving Samsonlike against the pillars of scriptural literalism and solipsism, Winstanley insists that hell, heaven, and even God are metaphors. This widening gyre of symbolic thought results from social interaction; inability to think symbolically leads to self-worship.[65] Winstanley's expanding metaphorical meaning broadens perspective on the possibilities of human progress. By ceasing to want to rise in the middle-class world, the saints elevate themselves spiritually; by ceasing to worship a God outside themselves, they expand their love of humanity. The story of the Gergesene demoniacs is the key scriptural text of *The Saints Paradise* because it represents the ultimate sealing off of external salvation and the final authority for rational divinity on earth. After Christ cast the devils out of the men and into the swine, "the swine ran into the waters and perished there." This, of course, must be interpreted symbolically: "By waters, are pointed out to me the wisdom of poysoned flesh, which is branched forth into established doctrines of the flesh, into formes, customs, and governments of the flesh, which deceived men conform unto for fear, and shame of others." Here the conventional sea-of-faith topos is not identified with giving oneself over to universal piety but with a self-indulgent fantasy, which, in reality, turns out to be merely the external trappings and habitual motions of "governments of the flesh."

Furthermore, this process of "unmetaphoring," of extending figurative language to its breaking point, inverts the commonplace notion that one must submerge one's individuality in the sea of faith. To submit to the waters of faith is not a courageous renunciation of selfish individualism but a cowardly and hypocritical worship of mutual greed. Uncontent to end here, Winstanley draws out the ramifications of his sea of faith topos with a Shakespearean pun: "And so the doctrine and practises of Rome, being altogether after the flesh, is called the sea of *Rome*, & sometimes multitudes of people that are deceived by the flesh, and follow after the wisdom & lust thereof, are called seas, or great waters."[66] Allowing a metaphorical connection to carry his argument forward, he moves to Revelation 16:3-4 where the angels pour out the vials of God's wrath upon the sea. There are "the inhabitants of the earth, that live in the flesh, not in the spirit of the father, they are drowned, and they perish in this sea, into which they are run." They glory and delight in this sea of flesh "as a fish doth in the materiall water." So the passage from Matthew 8:31 and Mark 5:12 where the devils ask to be allowed to go into the swine foreshadows the promise in Revelation 12:9-10 that people shall one day be free of all distempers. Language itself becomes a purgative; the troubles are cast out of mankind into the serpent, which is "King flesh, a swinish nature, a herd of swine; for all . . . are like so many filthy swine snudling upon the earth, as covetousnesse snuddles upon the earth, pride licks the dust of the earth, envy lives in the filth of the earth, hypocrisie and self-conceit . . . do tumble, and dwell, and live in the mire of the earth, that is, delight in nothing but the filth of mankinde, like so many swine as they are."

This is Winstanley's version of what John Middleton Murry, in reference to Swift, calls "the Excremental Vision," which Norman O. Brown defines as Swift's "insight into the universal neurosis of mankind."[67] The distinction between those who follow the flesh and those who follow the spirit parallels Swift's contrast between Yahoos and Houyhnhnms. Those who follow the dictates of the flesh "represent the raw core of human bestiality" whose essence is filthiness.[68] The Yahoos' affinity for excrement is like the fleshly delight in filth. Further, Winstanley's excremental vision is truly psychoanalytic in that he sees this attraction to filth not as part of man's biological nature but as culturally determined and capable of alteration. What he and Swift despise is the reduction of man to his biological drives and, through repression, the sublimation of those drives into venality, greed, and selfishness. Winstanley anticipates Swift in suggesting that anality is an infantile stage in human development easily sublimated into the desire for private property and money. For through neither Swift nor Winstanley expressly articulates this connection, the steps in its equation are implicit in their symbolic use of language. Like Swift, Winstanley sees that the Puritan's fragmented sensibility leads to idealized religiosity and repressive sexuality, a willful divorce of flesh and spirit.

But whereas Swift, as William Empson says, was horrified at his discovery that "everything spiritual is really material,"[69] Winstanley welcomes this discovery and makes it the foundation of his philosophy. If, to Swift, Puritan religious enthusiasm constitutes "a lifting up of the Soul of its Faculties above Matter," which means that "the Corruption of the Senses is the Generation of the Spirit,"[70] then, to Winstanley, Swift's dialectic is standing on its head. Instead of closing the gap between the demonic and the sublime by retreating to a cynical embrace of misanthropy, he attempts to harmonize spirit and matter by, on the one hand, demystifying idealized notions of the deity and explaining away hypostatized concepts such as heaven and hell and, on the other, by encouraging people to renounce harmful aspects of materialism so that they may live more contentedly. Winstanley promises his followers neither pie in the sky when they die nor blood, sweat, and tears. The saints' paradise is nothing more or less than the full realization of human potential here on earth. For when the "corrupt power of darknesse" runs into the sea, man shall escape the "confusion of his own invention, and imagination"; people will then "sit down in peace." Though "King flesh" rules now, "yet he is but suffered so to do for a time . . . and this sufferance is for his destruction, and mans deliverance from the bondage of the flesh."

The Gergesene demoniacs did not cease to exist after Christ cured their insanity. Their fleshly existence did not cause their mania. Winstanley wants to unify body and mind; he wants the creation, mankind, and the righteous law, the spirit, to embrace while the filthy powers and wisdom of the flesh perish in the sea of their own inventions, forms, customs, governments, and imaginary glory. The powers of light and darkness contend within everyone. The devil is not a third power between God and man; "he is the curse in flesh," not flesh itself, who must die "under sorrow, beholding no way of comfort, but misery on every side." By the working of "the spirit within, not any outward means of preaching, &c. the Father kils, and destroyes the powers of disobedient flesh." For proof of this, Winstanley appeals "to the experience of any of you that have been sensible of your bondage." Anger caused by awareness of imperfection indicates a recognition of selfish desires, and frustration in wishing to overcome these desires is a positive thing. Driven by "self-seeking lusts" the murderer within each of us holds its victim under the apprehension of darkness and death and makes life miserable. The disobedient flesh coaxes people to take pleasure in pride, covetousness, uncleanness, envy, self-conceit, and hypocrisy. And people sometimes think it is liberty to have their "filthy wils satisfied," but "alas, this is your bondage, and it is that Devill that was a liar from the beginning, that never gave true peace to his children, though he promised much."

Following such desires leads to "a more powerfull bondage of the Law of the spirit within you . . . wherein you stick fast, as in mire and clay, or, as in a deep pit, and cannot get out." Then the sun of righteousness appears angry, "which is the greatest darknesse the poor creature can lie under: What greater darknesse can there be, then for a man never to see nor feel the light, heat, nor warmth of the sun, but alwaies to live in some dungeon, where the sun never appears."

With this ancient image of the quest for freedom—the escape from a dark dungeon into the light of day—Winstanley portrays the struggle between the "humble spirit" of love and the demon of self-conceit and secret envy. Resisting the Manichaean tendency to see the motivating principle of the cosmos as an eternal struggle between good (light) and evil (darkness), he blatantly insists again that the devil is not a power distinct from God but is, quite simply, guilt. To follow the powers of the flesh is to follow the individual impulse and set up the flesh as God, but since "the father of all things . . . is reason," there is no real division between flesh and spirit. People falsely make such divisions, and this also "makes one creature a tyrant over another . . . and so pulls the creation in pieces." While tormented by this divisive devil, people live in hell, but once they renounce him "the wisdom and power of the Father is come to open the prison doors, to pull you up out of the earth of covetousness, and self imagination, under which you have been, and are buried." The "corne of wheate," like the prisoner, "lies buried under clods of earth, till the warme, cherishing, meeke, and loving spirit in the earth cause it to sprout, and spring, and shoot out, and so bring forth fruit like himself in great abundance." The righteous law in the flesh is like "a seed buried under the weight of that cursed earth." Here Eve's seed that will bruise the serpent's head reappears as the agent that will destroy the evil within, enabling eternal peace to reign and a new Eden to be constructed. The saints' paradise will come into being when people renounce the irrational way of covetousness and live according to the dictates of pure reason.

Winstanley does not minimize the difficulties of asking anxious souls to forsake their lives of quiet desperation and create a totally new consciousness. When they first look within they see and feel no peace, "for the appearance of the spirit of righteousnesse is like the offended Law of a King, that speaks death to the offender which way soever he turn himself." And people who avoid confrontation with this inner law and look abroad are again greeted by the flaming sword of wrath. Warning against bewailing the loss of middle-class comforts, Winstanley enjoins his readers not to "sit down in sorrow" and declares that "this Devill, or murtherer, that takes away your peace is within you, it is your sin . . . expect no peace in earth, that is, in your flesh, till there be peace in heaven, that is, till your flesh be made subject to the spirit." Even if people temporarily find the strength to "rise up in rebellion against the spirit, by scoffing, hating, self-loving, despising, expression of bitter-nesse and discontent," and so seek to advance themselves, the spirit's flaming sword crosses them at every turn. To give purpose to suffering, those in torment must see the tumult of the civil wars as a sure sign that the millennium approaches: "for now the bottomlesse pit is opened, that is, The curse, or serpent in humane flesh is let loose, to act, and shew it self in his own likenesse." The recent turmoil exposes evil and corrup-tion. The disguise has been torn away, and things now appear as they really are: "the four evill Angels, that is, Subtilty, Hypocrisie, Envy, and Cruelty, backed and strengthened with all the power of Hell, or Curse, are let loose." But even though these apocalyptic horsemen now ravage the land, they will not triumph.

Searching for stability in an unstable world, Winstanley calls for an alternative to the middle-class values of orderliness, parsimony, and obstinacy. "When your eyes are opened," he counsels, "you shall see that it is the righeous Law, or rule of truth that thwarts, and crosses the sinfull and cursed principles that rule, and that still would rule a King in your flesh." The righteous law of human goodness, sharing, and generosity fights against the middle-class values that cause guilt and envy. "Some-times thou hast had vain glorious imaginations rising up within thee, puffing up thy mind with big thoughts of thy self, as if thou wert some great body for thy learning, riches, parts, prayers, fasting, preachings, to whom every man must give respect." Winstanley does not dismiss these goals for which he himself once longed. He understands the tempting thoughts of covetousness, injustice, and uncleanliness; he knows how people feel when others discover their lewdness and how thoughts of revenge contribute to their resolution to get power, which they mistake for zeal, to put envious desires into practice. However, most people fail in this hypocritical delusion because they lack the "opportunities of the earth." But people do not have to play this game leading to bad con-science, guilt, shame, and anger, nor should they charge its terrors to momentary lapses of heart or to the devil. Winstanley will not allow his reader to excuse such behavior by attributing it to unchangeable human nature. People can overcome vicious traits, can alter their characters for the better. The righteous law sends messengers as dispensers of wrath to make them look to the spirit of the scriptures, "to burne up thy drosse, to consume the curse out of thee, to refine thee, and make thee pure gold."

The conflict within each person is objectified through a series of brilliant metaphors. First, this inner battle is like "a man, upon whom two fierce band-dogs hath laid hold, tearing, and pulling to pieces."[71]

These dogs named Sin and Wrath gnaw at the heart, and only the spirit of Christ can free a person from their grasp by destroying the curse of sin and pulling away the selfishness that prefers the flesh over the spirit. Wrath then has nothing on which to fasten. The mind-forged manacles of envy, covetousness, discontent, pride, and hypocrisy are converted into patience, humility, and contentment. Since Christ "is not a single man at a distance from you; but . . . is the wisdom and power of the father, who spirits the whole creation, dwelling and ruling King of righteous-nesse in your very flesh," the individual conscience acting in accordance with the heart's dictates is the final arbiter. Few are now saved; yet this is but "comfort to the earth," for the sun of righteousness is coming to heal the earth, "he goes on mightily, conquering, and taking up sons and daughters out of their imaginary earth, under which they have lien buried, . . . so that ere long, the sweet song that is sung in private, shall be sung publickly upon the house tops." Then people "shall see that books are nothing, mens words and teachings, studies, and imaginary thoughts and conjectures are nothing." The desire to break the hold of restrictive conventional thinking, to shatter the oppression of allowing authorities to decide what are acceptable ideas, necessitates this fierce anti-intel-lectualism.[72] The mind, freed of fetters, can create a new consciousness to meet the needs of working people. Books and teachings, the church and the schools, are propaganda organs of the establishment. Requiring people to depend on "the Lord alone" challenges them to depend on no external authority. This creates a further problem: intellectual self-sufficiency contributes to the destruction of economic and political cohesiveness. How can people live in harmony and at the same time freely develop their own ideas? Winstanley asks his reader to follow the dictates of reason to ensure the victory of the spirit and in this way to re-define what is acceptable to the vast majority, "for though men esteem this word Reason to bee too mean a name to set forth the Father by, yet it is the highest name that can be given him."

What a revolution in thinking (quite literally) these words imply! Win-stanley wants people to give up superstitious belief and fearful reliance on experts and accept only what they can sense. He calls for a new value system, a new ideology, based on self-sufficiency, moderation, and sensuous knowledge. Since reason made all things and governs all cre-ation, if flesh were subject to the spirit of reason within, it would never act unrighteously, "for if rash, forward, and mad anger rise up in a man, and makes him walk according to the hasty violence of that Devill, now he is said truly to be an unreasonable man, or a man that is not subject to Reason. But if Reason be King in a man, then he moderates the man both within and without, so that he may be truly said to be a reasonable man, or a man subject to reason, and so a profitable man amongst his fellow creatures." "A profitable man" is one useful to society, one who contributes to the public good. "Reason tels him, is thy neighbour hungry, and naked to day, do thou feed him, and cloath him, it may be thy case to morrow, and then he will bee ready to helpe thee."

This is not the ethos of the middle class. It is, rather, the ethos of the poor, the dispossessed. In a world where tyranny and selfishness reign, the voice of moderation and reason is the most radical voice of all: "When the Curse in flesh moves a man to oppresse or deceive his neighbour, or to take away his rights, and liberties, to beat, or abuse him in any kinde, reason moderates this wicked flesh, and speaks within, Wouldest thou be dealt so by thy self? Wouldst thou have another to come and take away thy Goods, thy Liberties, thy Life? No, saith the flesh, that I would not." And since this spirit of reason is within everyone, people need not "run after others, to tell him, or teach him, for this spirit is his maker, he dwels in him, and if the flesh were subject to him, he should finde daily teaching therefrom, though he were alone, and saw the face of no man." Here, truly, Winstanley's teaching is, in Fish's apt phrase, "self-consuming." By casting out (the most frequent active verb in *The Saints Paradise*) envy, covetousness, and pride, the spirit of reason becomes the true God. "But if your flesh be subject to the spirit within it, which is Reason, and which made the flesh, then is the Father your God, and you may lawfully call him your God, for you know now what you speak, and that your words are words of experience; but if you act contrary to reason, you act like a beast, and not like a man." With this, his most controversial philosophical point, Winstanley enters the public arena.

III

OIL IN HIS LAMP

WINSTANLEY closed *The Saints Paradise* by defending his anti-Manichae-anism and his belief in universal salvation. He knew that these touch-stones distinguished him from sectarian mysticism on the one hand and Anglican orthodoxy on the other. Yet he sought no safe middle ground. After Presbyterians passed the savage act against heresy and blasphemy on 2 May 1648, and the disastrous rains continued into early autumn, the radical troops in Major Skippon's London militia alarmed the conservative Independents who said Skippon wanted "to put the power of the sword into the hands of servants and sectaries."[1] With the fall of Colchester on 27 August, the second Civil War ended, and a treaty between the King and the New Model Army was planned at Newport. Opposing the negotiations, the Levellers made their feelings known on 11 September in the *Humble Petition of Thousands of Well-affected Persons*, where for the first time they found it necessary to repudiate communism.[2]

In the midst of "these National hurly burlies," a dispute between some ministers and local insurgents broke out at Kingston-on-Thames. Winstanley defended William Everard, probably a former trooper and army agitator dismissed for his participation in the Ware mutiny in November 1647. As a man of action, Everard ideally complemented Winstanley's natural modesty. Publicity excited him, and like John Lilburne, he had a flair for self-dramatization. His unabashed mixture of radical theology and political activism indicates his familiarity with the ideas of such New Model Army chaplains as John Saltmarsh, William Dell, and Hugh Peters. On 19 April 1649 Captain John Gladman, sent to investigate the Diggers by order of General Fairfax and the Council of State, reported back that Everard was "no better than a mad man," and when Everard and Winstanley visited Fairfax at Whitehall the next day Everard said he was "of the race of the Jews" and refused to remove his hat. He forsook the Digger colony soon after its inception and joined a Familist community in Bradfield led by John Pordage, whom Richard Baxter called the chief student of Jacob Boehme's mysticism in England.[3]

But whatever Everard's failings, he successfully drew Winstanley into the public arena, where he was forced to confront those who held organized power. This helped him specify his charges against the establishment and enabled him to broaden his appeal to common people. And more important, Winstanley's association with the Digger colony affected his style, his method of presenting his ideas. For while his first three pamphlets are filled with brilliant metaphors and specific biblical allusions, they tend sometimes toward the abstruse; the language, too often vague and repetitive, makes the train of thought difficult to follow. This resulted from Winstanley's struggle to articulate unfamiliar ideas and from his tendency, perhaps in reaction to his meager formal education, to cloud his prose with verbose defenses and arguments.

For nearly a year Winstanley had spoken of working people; now it was time to speak for them. The title page of *Truth Lifting Up Its Head Above Scandals*, the first of many pamphlets he wrote quickly in response to a pressing situation, is dated 1649, but the opening epistle addressed TO THE SCHOLARS OF OXFORD AND CAMBRIDGE, AND TO ALL THAT CALL THEMSELVES MINISTERS OF THE GOSPEL, IN CITY AND COUNTRY is dated 16 October 1648.[4] Here Winstanley makes it appear that while his opponents are irrational, emotional, hypocritical, and excessive, he speaks from a position of reason, temperance, honesty, and commonsense. The behavior of the establishment during the civil-war era led the common people to mistrust fanaticism in word and deed, for what were Laud and Strafford in the popular imagination if not extremists? Like Wycliffe, Langland, and More before him, Winstanley believes his advocacy of moderation is the correct path to a more just and free society. He believes the scholars' and ministers' control of scriptural interpretation is the basis of their intimidating power. They determine whether an act is sinful or not, and the legal profession, with its lawyers, courts, judges, and precedents in common law, is built upon this clerical monopoly. Rebelling against this control, *Truth Lifting Up Its Head*, based on the conventional dialectic between idealistic and materialistic knowledge, maintains truth may be discovered only when the spirit speaks from within the flesh. Speaking from the flesh alone, ministers attempt to cover their hypocrisy by esoteric scriptural interpretations.

The opening epistle therefore attacks ministers as misleaders of common people: "You are the men that stand up, assuming the power to your selves to teach the People the mystery of the Spirit." Winstanley is especially incensed that they profess to be "the onely men sent of him for that office: therefore you are called spirituall men, or men that are all spirit." Pretending to be spiritual leaders, these men arrogantly espouse selfish doctrines, form political parties, and attack the very people they are supposed to help. They say they are fit to judge between spirit and flesh and use scripture to support their arguments. But this is unwarranted, "for the People having the Scriptures, may judge by them as well as you." Furthermore, if they say the people cannot judge "because they know not the originall: I answer, neither doe you know the originall." With autodidactic suspicion of formal education and healthy skepticism about what goes on inside the colleges, he strikes at the heart of the intellectual class. Ministers may say that by their learning they are able to translate Hebrew or Greek into English, but they cannot claim to translate from original texts, "for those very Copies which the Prophets and Apostles writ, are not to be seen in your Universities."

The fascinating question here is how someone like Winstanley knows what may or may not be seen in the universities? And what gives him the audacity to confront the learned establishment so boldly? Radical preachers provide an answer. Although a great scholar at Clare College, John Everard, after undergoing a spiritual conversion, counted his former academic training as "loss and dung."[5] He preached that "poor beggerly fellows, *Tinkers* and *Coblers*," not schismatical and conceited fellows, "would lead people out of the darkness imposed on them by the scholars and clergy."[6] And his associate Giles Randall wrote, "To the wise of this world, the wisdome is foolishnes, and they laugh it to scorne, and thinke it meer madnesse."[7] In *Sparkles of Glory* (1647), Saltmarsh says that all forms of ministry—Anglican, Presbyterian, Independent, Baptist—are equally misleading and that "the Scriptures or writings of the everlasting Gospel, are the true scriptures as they are the very Image and letter of the mystery of Salvation of Spiritual things or the mind of God, or as they are in that pure and spiritual Order and form of words to truth its self, not as they are meerly in their grammaticall construction and sense or common reading, which any that understand the Hebrew or Greek may receive."[8] Dell believed formal religious training worthless and thought a mechanic could work as effectively for Christ as a nobleman or king.[9] He saw clearly that "all divinity is wrapped up in human learning to deter the common people from the study and enquiry after it, and to cause them still to expect all divinity from the clergy, who by their education have attained to that human learning which the plain people are destitute of."[10]

Therefore Winstanley's attack on the ministers should be seen as part of a larger social and intellectual change taking place in English society. Milton, who shared many of the practical educational views of Samuel Hartlib, John Dury, and John Amos Comenius, notes in *Animadversions* (July 1641) that clerics spend their youth in "loitering, bezzling, and harlotting, their studies in unprofitable questions, and barbarous sophistry"; he says "a man shall commonly find more savoury knowledge in one Lay-man, then in a dozen of Cathedrall *Prelates.*" "A plaine unlearned man that lives well by that light which he has," he concludes, "is better, and wiser, and edifies others more towards a godly . . . life." And in *The Reason of Church Government* (1642) he says good men learn nothing in the universities "but the scragged and thorny lectures of monkish and miserable sophistry."[11] Hugh Kearney points out that "the universities' insistence upon Latin and the Latin classics, at a time when the Bible was available in English, seemed to many a sinister piece of popery." "The sect itself was the basis of a new status system, in which godliness and not gentlemanly style of life was the criterion."[12] Winstanley's anti-intellectualism signifies social discontent, not hebetude. Scholars know only what is told them by their teachers. Tradition, he says, is not a valid test of truth. Neither may scholars claim to translate according to the spirit of the original scriptures, for to do so requires the "same testimony of Spirit, as the pen-men of Scriptures had; for it is the Spirit within that must prove those copies to be true."

The many contradictory translations and interpretations only show the ministers themselves "are at losse." How then, he asks, can common people trust them and rely on their interpretations. Characteristically, Winstanley sums up his point with a striking concrete image: Presbyterians and Independents alike try to "leade the People like horses by the noses; & ride upon them at . . . pleasure from one forme and custome to another."[13] The ministers demand that people "maintain the Gospel," but what is the gospel? "How can these Scriptures be called the everlasting Gospel, seeing it is torne in peeces daily amongst your selves, by various translations, inferences and conclusions; one pressing this, another that; and the People are lost in the midst of your waters?" Pressing his point, Winstanley places his opponents in a double bind: if they say they can "judge by the Spirit," so may others, "for the Spirit is not confined to your Universities; but it spreads from East to West, and enlightens sons and daughters in all parts."[14] On the other hand, if the ministers say "that visions and revelations are ceased," then what is the point in interpreting them for the present? Why not "leave the Scriptures in their own genuine language, that People may read the very letter without alteration"?[15] Making the right to interpret scripture the central contention of his attack on the educational establishment shows Winstanley's awareness that literacy is the key to social persuasion and political manipulation. He declares the gospel is not synonymous with scripture, for the gospel is the spirit that inspired the prophets and apostles: "their writings is not the *Spirit*; but a report or declaration of that law and testimony which was within them."[16]

This distinction between gospel and scripture is essential to the democratization of learning. The spirit spreading itself "in sonnes and daughters, is everlasting," but since "the declaration of the *Spirit*" is "but words gon out of the mouth," it is "corrupted by the subtilty of imaginary flesh; it is the *Spirit* within every man that tries all things: words cannot try all things." The test of truth is experience. Winstanley does not for a moment deny the importance of words; quite the contrary, he is so struck by their power that he insists upon everyone's right to interpret them according to personal experience. His emphasis on the spirit is not, then, an abstruse point of theology, a mere Puritan shibboleth. For four centuries knowledge had been the province of the church, a hierarchy of doctrinal authority resting upon the Thomistic synthesis of theology and science, faith and reason. But when the discoveries of Galileo, Kepler, Harvey, and Gilbert began to take hold of the public imagination this synthesis was ignored.

Winstanley speaks of a "matter of the greatest concernment" to the people. Warning that such things "are to be judged with a wary and moderate spirit," he says, "I my selfe being branded by some of your mouthes, as guilty of horrid *blasphemy*, for denying" God and Christ, the scriptures and the gospel, prayer and sacriments, "was drawn forth by the Spirit to write what here followes; which I leave to the spirituall men all the world over to judge." For nearly a year he had written day and night in the privacy of his home, producing over 300 pages of printed text. With the turmoil of the second Civil War swirling around him, he had conducted his own psychoanalysis while living among poor farmers and peasants. Now he enters the public arena prepared to defend himself and attack those whom he perceives as his enemies. The quiet dignity of hard-won identity with working people gave him an unshakable self-confidence. Denying the charge against him, he leaves no doubt where he stands: "When the Apostolicall gifts ceased, which was to speak from an inward testimony of what they heard and saw . . . then began the false Christs and false Prophets to arise, that speak from tradition of what they had read in Books; expounding those writings from their imaginary thoughts; getting a power from the Magistrate to protect them; and to punish such as speak from the testimony of Christ within them."

A second introductory letter addressed TO THE GENTLE READER defends William Everard, imprisoned for a week by the bailiffs of Kingston for holding blasphemous opinions, and is set forth "as a vindication of the man and my selfe, being slandered as well as he (by some of the Ministers) having been in his company." How easy it would have been for him simply to have kept quiet; how prudent it would have been for him to have defended Everard from a safe, impersonal distance by writing an abstract attack on the university-trained clergy. Yet here is an open admission at the start that he intends to vindicate himself and his imprisoned friend, "that all the world may judge of his and my innocency in these particular scandals." The thesis is clearly stated: "the parish Ministers themselves, and every one that followes their way of worship; doth turn the Scriptures into a lye." By neglecting the original text and molding scripture to fit their language, by reading into scripture their inferences and conjectures, and by thus alienating God from man, ministers deny God, Christ, scriptures, and holy sacraments, "walking in the practise of their own invention, to which ignorant flesh closeth without examination: and so the greatest theeves cry, stop theefe first." This last exemplifies Winstanley's technique of inversion. He, a bankrupt tradesman, calls priests and professors thieves, and does so in a context that suggests he is able to interpret scripture quite as well as they! What if I do interpret scripture for myself, he implies, I do not take money for it or deliberately mislead people to support my own privileged position.

This is the negative part of his thesis; the positive assertion he will defend is his substitution of Reason for the name of God. Traditional definitions of God, he explains, are confused and confusing. Reason accurately describes that which makes, governs, and preserves all things. "Reason is that living power of light that is in all things . . . it is the fire that burns up drosse, and so restores what is corrupted; and preserves what is pure . . . It lies in the bottom of love, of justice, of wisdome; for if the Spirit Reason did not uphold and moderate these, they would be madnesse." But human reason, traditionally defined, is only, as the Cambridge Platonists explained, a candle "shining through flesh" that is "darkened by the imagination of flesh," for "many times men act contrary to reason, though they thinke they act according to reason." Reason is a light by which people "may see a sutablenesse in many things, but not in all things; for the reason that acts in another man, may see a weaknesse of reason that acts in me." But if people learn to follow "the Spirit Reason, which I call God," they may come to see the necessity of preserving not only themselves but the whole creation. The nearer human reasoning comes to this the more spiritual people become. Not wishing to make a fetish of a word, he says other words may be used as long as the unity of man and nature is maintained as the governing, controlling principle of the universe.

The identification of God with reason and reason with natural law is a key to Winstanley's philosophy, but it is neither unique nor miraculous. Although Winstanley's use of reason in this context exemplifies a shift from a metaphysical to a secular understanding of man's relationship to nature, his proximity to Milton and Richard Overton in this respect indicates that he is reflecting a trend of the times. In seventeenth-century England long-accepted notions of what was reasonable in economics, politics, and religion came into question. The issue was whether reason should be defined according to precedent, as Richard Hooker argued in *The Laws of Ecclesiastical Polity* (1594), or according to individual perception, as Bacon suggested in *The Advancement of Learning* (1605). Hooker appeals to reason to justify established power; Bacon uses reason to plead for change. The debate centered on the concept of *recta ratio*, right reason. From the time of Socrates this phrase denoted the congruence of knowledge and virtue. The Stoics made it a sacred formula, including both intellectual and moral truths, and Aquinas' conception of it was codified into religious dogma. When this concept came in for some hard times during the civil war era, people became confused. In the flux of changing values, word meanings also shifted. As Robert Hoopes puts it, "the intellectual history of the seventeenth century is marked by the gradual dissociation of knowledge and virtue as accepted and indivisible elements in the ideal structure of human reason, a shift from the tradition of right reason to the new tradition of scientific reasoning."[17] Christopher Hill says that "one could oversimplify the process by describing it as a transition from old to new reason via a phase of irrationalism."[18] The archetypal example is, of course, Galileo's trial in April 1633 where the key issue was not whether the scientist's observations were correct but whether he maintained that Copernicus' theories were opinions, in which case he had committed no heresy; or whether he said Copernicus' theories were matters of fact, in which case he was liable to punishment for asserting a "truth," which only the church had the right to decide. The idea that an insignificant craftsman working alone in his shop, puttering with mechanical devices and conducting so-called experiments with mere physical matter, could call his conclusions "rational truths" as well as "empirical facts" seemed preposterous to the Catholic hierarchy.

The same was true in seventeenth-century England. That a mechanic could, through perusal of scripture and observation of the world, decide what was true and therefore reasonable seemed outrageous to the Anglican hierarchy. If anyone had the right to decide rational truths for himself, conservative churchmen argued, mere anarchy would be loosed upon the world. And in a sense it was. While the Royal Society quickly learned to "tame" scientific reasoning for practical purposes by segregating it from other rational processes, especially theological ones, the ecclesiastic equivalent of the Society, the Anglican bishops, were older and less flexible.[19] After the failure of the *Root and Branch Petition* in 1640, Westminister Assembly gave ample testimony of the confusion. It required a full-scale cataclysm in church and state for the heads of the

Anglican church to loosen their ties on official reasoning in regard to scriptural interpretation.

Milton's published pamphlets from *Of Reformation* in May 1641 to *Colasterion* in March 1645 constitute a running commentary on the growing assertion of practical reason. The seed of the principle Milton refines and develops is his statement that "the people vilifi'd and rejected by them [the prelates], give over the earnest study of vertue, and godlinesse as a thing of greater purity then they need, and the search of divine knowledge as a mystery too high for their capacity's, and only for Churchmen to meddle with, which is that the Prelates desire, that when they have brought us back to Popish blindnesse we might commit to their dispose the whole managing of our salvation." In *Of Prelatical Episcopacy* he opposes tradition in the name of reason, and in *Animadversions* he boldly says "reason is the gift of God in one man, as well as in a thousand," and declares he would not accept Calvin's authority unless "convinc't with *Calvins* reason."[20]

The Reason of Church-Government, according to Stanley E. Fish, exhibits a thorough refusal to accept the established rules of systematic logic. Milton exchanges "one way of looking at the world for another, moving from a context in which rational processes have some place in the consideration of matters spiritual to another, in which reason and the assent of a reasoning mind are somehow superfluous."[21] Yet, while Milton's manipulation of Ramistic logic in *The Reason* amounts to an emperor's-new-clothes ploy by which the reader sees the "old reason" sanctioned by the church hierarchy as specious, vacuous, sterile, mechanical, tautological, and useless, he does not forsake rational processes but turns the tables on the prelates by making perception rather than deliberation the hallmark of reason. To unlink the chain of inferences held together by the "old reason" leading to "exaltation of the Pope,"[22] Milton entertains something approximating Baconian reason. "They expresse nature best," he writes in his next published work, "who in their lives least wander from her safe leading, which may be call'd regenerate reason."[23]

The Doctrine and Discipline of Divorce opens with a vociferous attack on "Custome" as the basis for rational judgment and characterizes discursive reasoning as a "swoln visage of counterfeit knowledge . . . which not onely in private marrs our education, but also in publick is the common climer into every chaire." Since error supports custom and custom error, these two would destroy all truth were it not that God supplied "free reasoning" by which people may push aside the obscurities wrought by custom and perceive truth. This reliance on "free reasoning" leads to the "law of nature" as the criterion of truth.[24] And when Milton asserts in *Areopagitica* that when God gave Adam reason, "he gave him freedom to choose, for reason is but choosing," he identifies himself, however tentatively, with the left wing of the Puritan movement.[25]

In *Man's Mortallitie* (1643-44), Richard Overton set out to prove "that whole Man (as a rational creature) is a compound wholly mortall, contrary to that common distinction of Soule and Body: And that the present going of the Soule into Heaven or Hell is a meer Fiction."[26] This pamphlet, linked with Milton's *Doctrine and Discipline of Divorce* and branded as heretical by the Stationers Company on 24 August 1644, clearly identifies God with reason. Combining the Neo-Stoic principles of William Walwyn with his continental Anabaptist training, Overton imbues the notion that God created nature and man to some rational purpose with a fiercely democratic spirit.[27] His quest is for a "rational philosophy of God and Man, a philosophy including the goodness, the wonder, the glory, at the heart of the material universe."[28] In *A Remonstrance of Many Thousand Citizens, and other Free-born People of England, to their owne House of Commons* (7 July 1646) he declares Magna Charta to be "but a beggerly thing, containing many markes of intollerable bondage," and, tracing English oppression under law to the Norman Conquest, he appeals to "common *equity,* and *right reason,* which ought to be the Forme and Life of every Government."[29] In *An Arrow Against All Tyrants and Tyrany,* published on Winstanley's thirty-seventh birthday (10 October 1646), Overton, imprisoned in Newgate, maintains that "it is natures instinct to preserve it selfe . . . and this in nature is granted of all to be most reasonable, equall and just . . . from this fountain or root, all just humain powers take their original; not immediatly from God . . . but mediatly by the hand of nature . . . Every man by nature being a King, Priest and Prophet in his owne naturall circuite." And "by the same rule of right reason," parliament may be justly opposed by the people, "for the safety of the people is the Soveraigne Law, to which all must become subject."[30] And in *An Appeale From the degenerate Representative Body the Commons of England assembled at Westminster* (17 July 1647), where "Reason is . . . [the] very life and spirit" of all just laws, Overton foreshadows Winstanley's conception of God as reason:

All Formes and Lawes and Governments may fall and passe away; but *right Reason* . . . shall and will *endure for ever* . . . for neither *Morality* nor *Divinity* amongst *Men* can or may transgresse the limits of *right reason,* for whatsoever is unreasonable cannot be *justly* tearmed *Morall* or *Divine,* and *right reason* is only commensurable and discernable by the rule of merciful *Justice* and just *mercy* . . . its *perfection* and fulnesse is *only* in *God,* and its several *Branches* and *Degrees* are only communicable, and derivated from *Him,* as severall *Beames* and *Degrees* of *heat* from the *Body* of the *Sunne,* yet all *heat;* so in *Reason* there are different degrees . . . all derivated and conveyed from the Creator (the originall Fountaine) to the creature.[31]

Because "God is not a God of irrationality," Overton concludes, "all his communications are reasonable and just, and what is so, is of God." "Nothing which is against reason is lawfull," he maintains, *"Reason* being the *very life* of the *Law of our land:* So that should the Law be taken away from its *Originall reason* and end, it would be made a shell without a kernill." If right reason is the basis of law, what is rational should be legal and what is legal should be rational. A following paragraph connects right reason to the "radicall principle in Nature engraven in the tables of the heart by the finger of God in creation for every living moving thing." Therefore, since reason and natural law are synonymous, Overton combines them in what he calls "this naturall radicall principle of reason."[32] Inverting the conservative application of right reason and natural law used by royalists and Presbyterians to uphold divine right and oligarchical government, he turns what was a justification for tyranny into a justification for democracy.[33]

Such precedents enabled Winstanley to cut through the bewildering array of theories surrounding right reason and natural law, and to establish a workable synthesis that cannot be labeled either mystical or materialistic. Asserting that God, reason, and natural law are virtually synonymous, he eschews all forms, customs, and dogmas, and adopts the mantle of the biblical prophets. Having shed the cloak of humanistic learning identified with the universities, he freely associates his teaching with his vatic ancestors: Elijah and Elisha, Isaiah and Jeremiah, Ezekiel and Daniel, John the Baptist and John the Apostle. This prophetic tradition, revived in the twelfth century by Joachim of Fiore, kept alive the possibility of establishing a heavenly kingdom on earth.[34]

Through the efforts of John Foxe, this tradition entered the mainstream of Protestant thought. But in times of crisis the radical potential of apocalyptic and millenarian schemes, never far beneath the surface of Protestantism, reasserted itself. As long as this potential appeared in obscure and confused forms, there was little the establishment had to fear; the vagueness and irrationality of most millenarian schemes allowed them to be dismissed as harmless visions and metaphysical meanderings; they were a kind of psychic safety valve for social and political malcontents.[35] But Winstanley's adaptation of Leveller ideas posed a graver threat to those who wanted the government to protect the rights of property and a free market economy, for by casting himself in the role of the prophets of the Old Testament he linked millenarian eloquence with political radicalism in a manner quite foreign to the Leveller imagination.

Like the prophets, Winstanley speaks against the prevailing state of things in the name of reason. Indeed if reason is man's ability to decide what is best for him by consulting the dictates of his conscience and the validity of his experience, then the Reformation may be called a "rational" movement away from external hierarchical authority toward internal personal authority. The Anglican church, as the guardian of truth, easily recognized scientific truths as long as they did not directly contradict Anglican dogma. And as long as scientists agreed to submit their learning to the service of the establishment there was little hostility between them. Each, after all, represented different aspects of a "given" external reality. The main Puritan complaint against the church hierarchy was its worldliness, its obsessive concern with material things. Puritanism arose to fill the vacuum of people's inner lives; only gradually did it come into conflict with external authority, and it only became antiestablishment because the Anglican church and its ally, the monarchy, were not content to control the material conditions of people's existences but insisted on attempting to dictate their spiritual lives. One consistency in Puritan thought, as A. S. P. Woodhouse points out, is its tendency to separate the order of grace, spiritual existence, from the order of nature, material existence.[36] As long as church and state were content to control what people could do, they remained invulnerable; when they tried to control what they could think, they became entangled in a net from which it took them twenty years to escape. Laud intervened and attempted to suppress Puritan thought at the point where it threatened to be put into action. No doubt most Puritans in 1641 would have conceeded the order of nature to the establishment if they could have continued to oversee the order of grace. In a sense that is what Presbyterians and conservative Independents wanted even after the first Civil War had ended.

The turning point came soon after Winstanley published *Truth Lifting Up Its Head*, for on 6 December 1648, while Cromwell was still in the north at Pontefract, Colonel Thomas Pride, probably under the direction of Henry Ireton, purged the Commons of more than 240 members not ready to see the revolution through to the end. This, in effect, put the New Model Army, under Fairfax and Cromwell, in control of the government.[37] Meanwhile, the Levellers, and radical Independents like Milton and Ireton, seriously tried to forge a revolutionary program out of the exigencies of practical necessity and the desire for spiritual regeneration. Winstanley, like Thomas More a century earlier, saw that before one could embark on a utopian communistic scheme for society, the order of nature had to be rationally united with the order of grace. Although several writers from Plato onward espoused communism, no one before More "achieved the sort of modern conception of society which manifests itself in Utopian communism."[38] St. Gregory and Milton agreed that primitive communism existed before the Fall, but they also held that after mankind's corruption and expulsion from Eden (after the fall of the Golden Age), private property became a necessary safeguard against man's "natural" selfishness. More found this view, like Marx found Hegel's dialectic, standing on its head and proceeded to turn it right side up.[39] Both More and Winstanley start with the premise that people are rational, that by analyzing their experiences they may decide what is best for them and put those decisions into action. Reason links the world of nature to the world of the spirit; it is the tool by which people mediate between their material needs and their psychological needs. Utopians are drawn, by natural virtue, toward decent pleasure and supreme good. They define virtue, More says, "as living according to nature since to this end we were created by God. That individual, they say, is following the guidance of nature who, in desiring one thing and avoiding another, obeys the dictates of reason."[40] Reason "dwels in every creature," Winstanley writes, "according to the nature and being of the creature, but supreamely in man. Therefore man is called a Rationall creature, and the well-beloved son of the Father, because by his creation, he is to live in the light of Reason." "Now reason first of all inflames men to a love and veneration of the divine majesty," More says, "to whom we owe both our existence and our capacity for happiness. Secondly, it admonishes and urges us to lead a life as free from care and as full of joy as possible and, because of our natural fellowship, to help all other men, too, to attain that end."[41] Drawing on his recent experience as a cowherd, Winstanley explains the connection between nature and spirit through reason:

> The clouds send downe raine, and there is great undeniable reason in it, for otherwise the earth could not bring forth grasse and fruit. The earth sends forth grasse, or else cattle could not be preserved. The cattle feed upon the grasse, and there is Reason in it, for else man could not be preserved. The Sunne gives his light and heate, or else the creation could not subsist. So that the mighty power, Reason, hath made these to give life and preservation one to another.

More carefully qualifies his hedonism. Nature prescribes a joyous life, but she also "calls all men to help one another to a merrier life. (This she certainly does with good reason, for no one is raised so far above the common lot of mankind as to have his sole person the object of nature's care, seeing that she equally favors all whom she endows with the same form.) Consequently nature surely bids you take constant care not so to

further your own advantages as to cause disadvantages to your fellows."[42] Similarly, Winstanley maintains that "Reason makes a man to
live moderately and peaceably with all; he makes a man just and righteous in all his actings; he kils forwardnesse, envy and pride in a man: and
why? where lyes the Reason? Because this man stands in need of others,
and others stand in need of him." Defining pleasure as "every movement
and state of body or mind in which, under the guidance of nature, man
delights to dwell," More insists that "just as the senses as well as right
reason aim at whatever is pleasant by nature . . . whatever things mor-
tals imagine . . . to be sweet to them in spite of being against nature . . .
are all so far from making for happiness that they are even a great hind-
rance to it."[43] "There is nothing but unreasonablenesse in all the powers
of the flesh," Winstanley maintains, "as in covetousnesse, pride, envy,
and the like; and hereby the flesh brings misery and ruine upon it self.
But pure and perfect Reason makes every thing sing and rejoice in righteousnesse: When this King reignes the City is glad." And More likewise
says that those who go against nature and reason "become deep-seated
with a false idea of pleasure so that no room is left anywhere for true and
genuine delights."[44] Free reason, not determinate nature, is the arbiter of
true happiness.

This comparison illuminates the dialectic inherent in Winstanley's
thought and shows there is no need to apologize for his reluctance to
embrace thoroughgoing empiricism. *Truth Lifting Up Its Head* contains a
fully articulated theory of human understanding. The basis of Winstanley's epistemology is an absolute monism. He sees the world as an inte-
grated totality, a unity of opposites. Orthodox theology, from the time
of Augustine, escaped the predicament of heretical Manichaeanism, of
seeing the cosmos as a war between good and evil, spirit and flesh, God
and the devil, by an all-embracing spiritualism. The City of God could
never exist on earth because all earthly things, all material reality, merely
reflected a higher spiritual reality. To challenge this idealistic monism
unorthodox thinkers, mystics, usually posited some sort of dualism.
They tended to see the world as fragmented into "evil" material qualities
and "good" spiritual qualities and looked to the day when materiality
would be transcended.[45] But Winstanley, like his famous utopian predecessor, seeks to unify materiality with spirituality. He does not want to
do away with materiality; he never talks about a spiritualized "essence"
above material reality. However, Winstanley's rationalism does not
confine knowledge to sense perception but points to what Hill calls "a
kind of materialist pantheism, in which God or abstract Reason can be
known only in man or nature."[46] He wants "to destroy the powers of the
flesh; which leades creatures into divers waies of opposition one against

another, and to bring all into pure experience of that sweet rest and peace that is in the unity of himselfe, the one spirit." The key phrase here is "pure experience," which is neither the product of mere sensualism nor the upshot of shallow introspection (nature or grace). It results, rather, from a process of rational reflection, including conception, judgment, and inference, where truth is arrived at by reconstructing the data of sense perception, discarding the dross and selecting the essential, eliminating the false and retaining the true, proceeding from the one to the other, from external to internal, to form a system of concepts and theories for understanding the real world.

Just as Blake believes that everything that lives is holy, Winstanley maintains that even a horse has reason that "carries him along to eate his meat." But only man is privileged "to see and know that Reason rules him . . . Therefore he is said to be the Lord of creatures, because he knowes how to govern them by reason that is within himselfe." Of course not all men are reasonable; their senses are clouded with pride, greed, and envy, but when this veil of bitterness is torn away they become perfect. To walk righteously in the sight of reason is to act in love to feed, clothe, and relieve the oppressed. For "whereas before he exercised outward senses to follow creatures; now he lives in the exercise of his spiritual senses, . . . for his soul now sees, feels, tasts, smels and hears the Father spiritually in all things." This idea of reason is quite distinct from what Cromwell, writing to Colonel Robert Hammond twelve days before Pride's Purge, calls "fleshly reason."[47] Winstanley means, rather, what John Everard, anticipating Milton, intimates when he says Eve represents "the sensitive, and fleshly and inferior part" of mankind, whereas Adam stands for "the rational and the higher part of man, viz. The Reasonable Soul."[48] He means also what Saltmarsh, following Aquinas, suggests when he writes that the "Law of Nature or right Reason, is the Law or principle for administration of Justice and Righteousnesse in all Societies."[49] Winstanley takes the further dialectical leap, not into Luther's *sola fides*, but into a harmonious vision where the flesh unites with the spirit, where nature becomes one with grace through the "use of all the spirituall senses." In his epistemology, objective reality is reflected through the filter of purified reason. With this dialectic internalized, he begins to turn his vision out into the objective world in an attempt to transform it into a rational community.

Freed from the tyranny of literal interpretation, Winstanley develops his theory of nature's physical restoration. Christ, the first to exercise his spiritual senses, the first rational man, did not save mankind by his fleshly death but by his spiritual life. As "the Seed that bruises the *Serpents* head . . . he is in every place, and in every creature."[50] His body "is where the Father is, in the earth, purifying the Earth; and his Spirit is entred into the whole creation." His ascension "was onely a declaration in vision to" the Apostles. When the time of the Beast expires, Christ "will spread himselfe in sons and daughters from East to West, from North to South." The flesh will then become subject to the spirit, not in the hereafter but on earth; elemental material creation will be transformed. Adam and Christ symbolize flesh and spirit, darkness and light. The idea of Christ's physical ascent into heaven is ludicrous, for scripture is "but a report of spirituall mysteries, held forth to the eye of flesh in words." The Apostles said they saw and touched Christ because "their very bodies and mindes were changed." Christ's spirit inhabited his body "as a bucket of water first taken out of the Sea, and standing alone for a time, is afterwards powred into the Sea again, and becomes one with the Sea."[51] Adam, like Blake's Albion (the fallen aboriginal giant who conquered Britain and named it for himself), is "that mighty power of flesh, that leades flesh to live upon it selfe." He brought into being an unholy Trinity—the King of darknesse, his beastly son, fallen man, and the uncleane spirit or bottomless pit. This Adam has three emanations: the first man, fallen men and women, and a second Adam (Christ). This second Adam also has three emanations: the well-beloved Son, the Lord from heaven, and a mighty man. Also called "a man anointed, or mankind living in the light and strength of pure Reason, the essentiall Father," he is "the whole bulke of mankinde, when they shall be drawne up to live in the unity of the one spirit." When this second man assumes control of the earth, "he wil change times and customs, & fil the earth with a new law." And just as the first man filled the earth by multiplying "with that graine," the second man "shal fill the earth with himself, as a corn of wheat multiplying every yeare, fils the earth with that graine." All his sons and daughters will then be the second man. "And this is the generation of the second man, or second Adam: mankinde living in and upon his maker from the power within himself." This second man declares the perfect Trinity: Father Reason, the Son, and the spirit of holy breathing. Amid the "rage of the world," the two witnesses, Justice and Judgment, teach people to know and do righteously. The word of God, the logos that animated Christ, will "be poured out upon sonnes and daughters; and shall spread in the earth like the shining of the Sun." All the Lord's people will be prophets.

Superbly controlling his metaphors, Winstanley explains how

the same spirit that hath layne hid under flesh, like a corne of wheat for an appointed time, under the clods of earth, is now sprung out, and begins to grow up a fruitfull vine, which shall never decay, but it shall encrease, till he hath filled the earth. This is the Kingdome of

God within man. This is the graine of mustard seed, which is little in the beginning, but shall become a mighty tree. This is the fire, that shall dry and burne up all the drosse of mans worke, and turne all things into his owne nature. This is that spirit which is broke out, that will bring mankinde into one heart, and one minde: For, assure your selves, I know what I speake. The Thorne bush is burning; but the Vine is flourishing. The Ashes of the Thorne bush is laid at the root and feet of the Vine, and it growes abundantly.

This 157-word passage contains nine images, moving in logical progression from the "corne of wheat" to "clods of earth" to "fruitfull vine"; the chain of images then bursts into a primary declaration: "This is the Kingdome of God within man." With increasing momentum the passage continues, linking "mustard seed" to "tree" to "fire" to "spirit"; then the chain again breaks with the bold secondary declaration: "For, assure your selves . . ." Reaching its climax, the passage telescopes the tree and fire images into one, the burning thorn bush. This climactic image evokes, as its prime referent, God's message to Moses, but it also looks backward, by typological analogy, to the Edenic Tree of Life and forward to Christ's crown of thorns. Simultaneously, the image suggests Winstanley's own relationship to the prophetic tradition. He is a modern Moses come to lead his people to the promised land. The flourishing vine at whose "root and feet" the ashes are laid reaches back to the "fruitfull vine" that introduces the primary declaration, here re-emphasized by the allusion to the abundantly growing vine, symbolic of the heavenly kingdom, the Garden of Eden, and Garden of Gethsemane. Seed, tree, bush, and vine are all "types," leading to the spirit growing within everyone. And the culminating image, like the popular medieval legend concerning the mysterious relationship between the cross and the Tree of Life, evokes the sacrificial relevance of the crucifixion. In addition, the passage would suggest to a seventeenth-century reader not only Genesis 3:15, the seed passage, but also the parable of the sower in Matthew 13:18-44 and Mark 4:1-20, illustrating that those who know the mystery of the heavenly kingdom must share it.

Having learned to distinguish "betweene the Report, and the thing Reported of," those "saved" eschew "various translations, interpretations and constructions" and announce the simple truth of their experience. Those who make exposition upon scripture from their imagination are "false Prophets, and their way of teaching is meer deceit both to your soules, and to your purses." People may speak their experiences, but they "must not speake thoughts." Not knowing who may be regarded as "a sincere hearted friend," they must wait for experience to inform them of the truth. People must not try "to have all knowledge, peace, and ex-

perience on a sudden." The true guide to action is first-hand experience of
the inner light, not the words and writings of others. Scripture cannot be
a guide to truth because it is merely a record of "the eyes of other men,
and the spirit is not so scanty, that a dozen or 20 pair of eyes shall serve
the whole world; but every sonne and daughter as they are called children of light, have light within." Neither reason nor scripture allows
anyone "to speake any words, but what he knowes positively to be
truth." To speak from the imagination, egocentrically, is to speak "from
the flesh and devill."[52]

When Winstanely says reason must triumph over imagination he does
not mean the intellect should take precedence over the emotions, thinking over feeling, but that since, in Hill's words, "imagination distorts
reality by looking at it through the eyes of covetousness or self-love,"[53]
people must learn to look at the world rationally because reason sees
reality through the eyes of cooperation and benevolence. The perceptive
faculty may only be cleansed from within. It is not the physical world
that is evil and corrupt but people's perception of it. When men and women clear their perceptive faculties they may declare, "by their particular
experiences," the truths of human existence. For "an imaginary perswasion grounded upon thoughts . . . is a sandy foundation, and deceiveth
all the world." But "an experimental perswasion, grounded upon sight
and feeling of the spirit of truth . . . is the rock that will never fayl." This
emphasis on inner experience also has political ramifications. One who
preaches to a settled parish marked out by a government that forces
people to pay and attend corrupts scripture. But one who speaks his
inner experience substantiates scriptural truth. "Lands and Kingdoms are
most commonly governed more by the wisdome of the flesh, then of the
spirit" because "it is an easier thing for magistrates" to oppress those
who speak from experience than those who speak from imagination, for
the former are uncorruptible and therefore arouse envy. A reasonable
government would protect those who speak from experience from the
"oppression of unreasonable men." A righteous government would not
force attendance at church, collect tithes, or punish heretics.

Finally, Winstanley reveals the working of his epistemology most
clearly in explaining the Trinity. "The spirit Reason; out of whom the
creation of heaven and earth, with every branch of it proceeded," makes
its presence manifest in the material world by what "is called the fiery
orbe, or spirit of burning," because it tries all men's works. In other
words the Father, the *petra genitrix* or master alchemist, unites with the
terra mater, the Mother Earth, which, according to the parable of the
sower, is a kind of purifying furnace, womb, or limbeck. "The Son is the
light and declaration of the Father, to the creation" (hence the son-sun

pun), and every creature living on earth likewise "is a son to the Father; because every single creature doe demonstrate his maker to the view of his fellow creature." But the light of ordinary people is a candlestick compared to the light of the sun, which "is the Father himself, and the Father shewes forth himself to the creation." Yet people "are but darke or weake shining Suns, Suns over which the clouds are much spread." Christ, the only perfect man, declared the Father "by all his senses, to the creation," thereby showing that when freed from the cloud of corruption, one "sees and heares, feels, smels and tastes, that he who is the spirit of gentlenesse, uniting all together in love, and sweet compliancie, doth governe the whole creation, and subjects all the flesh under him, and makes it serviceable." People must therefore liberate their senses from selfish arrogance clouding them like "a Sun under a dark eclipse," for an egocentrically clouded person has the physical "forme of the Son," the external body of a perfect being, but has "no brightnesse in him, he is not the well beloved Son."

The third part of the Trinity, the holy ghost, is anyone "in whom the Father dwels bodily." Unable to resist a pun, Winstanley explains that, like the soldiers of the New Model Army, one perfect man ruled by reason "is as an hoste of men, or a strong army, or a Go-host, going or travelling among enemies." Such punning may seem ingenuous, but puns are a way of speaking of several things at once and depend on literary sophistication for their invention and enjoyment. They show an awareness of the power of words for their own sake and derive, no doubt, from a playful intellectual impulse. Here again the comparison with *Piers Plowman* is apt, for as Morton W. Bloomfield indicates, Langland's constant punning shows "his desire to pass beyond the limitations of his medium" and, simultaneously, his belief "in the magic power, in a literal sense, of language."[54] To kill the serpent of evil within, the spirit too must suffer. Nothing worthwhile is easily won; success demands sacrifice. Selfishness and arrogance so possess people's bodies "that before the spirit hath parted them, thou shalt roar in bitternesse . . . the founder cannot burn away the drosse, but must burn the gold too in the fire."

This essential metaphor of purgation, of suffering to obtain purification and renewal, epitomizes the idea of transformation. The alchemist's fire and the farmer's seed have an immediate sensuous appeal to Winstanley's audience because fire and seed are essential parts of their daily lives. When he says the spirit will "rise up like seed of wheat, from under those darke and heavy clods of fleshy earth," he calls up a visual image, not an abstract allusion. His images, like his ideas, are based on experience, not speculation. Since man has no body distinct from his soul, he explains that to live in the spirit is not to live in solipsistic withdrawal

from the real world. It is, rather, a total liberation of the senses, a sensuous awakening to the realization that "whatsoever we see or hear, is but
the breathings forth or declaration of an infinite being." He therefore
does not want to debunk religious symbols; he wants to revitalize them,
to make them real again. He does not intend to "explain away" concrete
images like God and the devil, but to redefine them in an intelligible and
rational context. To him the devil is neither a cloudy, quasi-historical
figure of reproach nor the ludicrous character of medieval folklore; he is
"the flesh of man within, and the objects of the creation without." He is
an attitude, a perception, a way of looking at the world, made concrete
through the vivid metaphor of a "prisoner under the power of darknesse." Only the power of reason will set people "free from the bondage
of that darknes, burne up all those thornes and briars that flesh hath
brought to terrifie it self."

The fleshly appetites to be eschewed are not normal physical desires,
but immoderate and irrational longings that society promotes and that
lead man "away like a bear by the nose, by every object before his eyes,
which the flesh lusts after to enjoy, and places contentment in." To act
reasonably, sensibly, is to treat one's body well, to eat moderately and
avoid drunkenness and gluttony. For flesh "will destroy it selfe in a short
time" if not governed by reason. This, logically, leads to a restatement of
Montaigne's primitivistic doctrine that cannibals are "less barbarous"
than modern man "eu esgard aux regles de la raison," for "they are still at
the happy stage of desiring no more than their simple appetites demand . . . the undivided possession of their property, to be held in
common."[55] Winstanley feels that "English Christians are in a lower and
worser condition, then the heathens," and those "guided by principles of
fair dealing void of deceit, knowe not this day how to live, but they will
be cheated and cosoned."[56] Political application of primitivism may be
expected at this point, but the doctrine of primal innocence also leads
Winstanley to consider the corruption of language. The professors cover
their hypocrisy with a great torrent of meaningless words and merely
seek to delude people. The true man of reason is empty of words until
inspired by his experience. Those who speak from books spread confusion and dissension, but those who speak from experience articulate
carefully: "when thou comes before the Lord, let thy words be few and
faithfull." Such words "shall not die, they are sincere milke which once a
wearied soul did suck from the Fathers owne breasts of love."

Closing with a denial of antinomianism and a plea for toleration, Winstanley reaffirms that "the Clergie and professors of *England*, in their
publike worships doe practise their own inventions, which neither Reason, nor Scripture, doth warrant; and yet they call them Gods Ordinances; by which practise they are the men that deny God and Christ,

and turne the Scriptures into a lie." He observes the same eight ordinances outlined in the General Baptist creed Overton subscribed to: prayer, testimony, good works, readiness to help others, toleration, open communion, spiritual baptism, and the sabbath.[57] He does not recognize prayer by custom, preaching for money, prayer before and after sermons, preaching by exposition of words and texts, compulsory church attendance, settled parishes, forced sabbatarianism, closed communion, infant baptism, and clerical elitism. Ministers merely "persecute the Gospell" and tear it to pieces; they "trouble the children" and "throw durt upon their food." Moses, he reminds them, was a shepherd, Amos a fruit gatherer; the Apostles were fishermen and Christ a carpenter, and none of them had big purses. Ministers deny scripture by setting their inferences and constructions above it. They thus "deny God, and Christ, the one Spirit, from whence the Scriptures were breathed." A concluding poem sums up his message with the Traherne-like charm of simple authenticity:

> Leave of your trade, yee proud Priests then,
>   and trouble not the Spirit:
> By forcing sense, from the Saints words,
>   if ye would life inherit.
> Let every one speak what he knowes,
>   and utter what's received:
> And let not any soul by you,
>   hereafter be deceived.
> For you as traytors to our God,
>   have stood to justify:
> That your constructions are all truths,
>   and other lights a lie.
> Your fleshly learning yee have own'd,
>   as sound, divine, and good:
> Though you by that in ages still,
>   have shed the childrens blood.
> But know yee now, the time is come,
>   for truth to spread all over:
> And he will tread you down apace,
>   and all your lies discover.
> Leave off therefore I say, betimes,
>   and stoope unto our God:
> If yee would life, and peace enjoy,
>   with them that know the Lord.

Closing with a plea for clemency, justice, and peace for the poor, the poem looks for the restoration of "all to what hath beene" and asks why people so clamor against the spirit of reason within them.

Some, it seems, were already attempting to restore England to Edenic innocence. A pamphlet Winstanley did not write but certainly read, *Light Shining in Buckinghamshire*, published sometime before December 1648, declares unequivocally that since man was made in God's likeness by the word of God made flesh, the light of life is the "pure spirit in man which we call Reason." Man, this Buckinghamshire pamphleteer maintains, "was priviledged with being Lord over other inferior creatures, but not over his own kinde; for all men being a like priviledged by birth, so all men were to enjoy the creatures a like without proprietie one more than the other . . . no man was to Lord or command over his own kinde: neither to enclose the creatures to his own use, to the impoverishing of his neighbours." Anticipating Milton's argument in *The Tenure of Kings and Magistrates* (February 1649), the pamphlet says scripture and reason show "that Kings were not of Gods institution at first, but it arose from . . . those that lived after their own beastly lusts." Linking the Leveller theory of the Norman Yoke directly to the Book of Revelation, *Light Shining* articulates fundamental Digger principles that Winstanley himself will soon take up. It asks the "children of light" to "restore" what rightly belongs to them—the land of England. Calling for the downfall of the monarchy, the house of Lords, and the Anglican church, it demands "a just portion for each man to live . . . A just Rule for each man to go by, [and] . . . The government to be by Judges . . . chosen by the people." It suggests a new commonwealth should be based on the Israelite nation described in Genesis 1 and 9, where people looked upon themselves as a family that "had all things common."

THE EFFECT of such ideas is apparent in *The New Law of RIGHTEOUS-NES Budding forth, in restoring the whole Creation from the bondage of the curse*. In this unique pamphlet, published four days before Charles I was beheaded, a sense of simultaneity enables the reader to experience the central vision in much the same way it occurred. As Petegorsky points out, although Winstanley had previously described the continuous and dynamic inner conflict between the flesh and the spirit, his analysis of the social and political implications of that struggle was vague. In *The New Law* "the internal struggle in each individual is still fundamental for him; but he now realizes the independent and vital importance of its objectivication in the social conflict."[58] This work has an intensity generated by its cumulative embodiment of all the thoughts previously articulated, and the urgency of its prose bespeaks the desire to leap ahead to newly discovered ideas and positions. Its subtitle indicates that this is *A Glimpse of the new Heaven, and new Earth, wherein dwels Righteousnes*, and a title-page prolepsis warns that "Out of the despised poor people, which are the stones and dust of the earth, man-kind upon whom the children of the flesh treads, shall the blessing rise up, that shall restore all things . . . You learned and great men of the earth, take notice of this, and remember you have been told."[59]

As a literary genre *The New Law*, like *Piers Plowman* and Blake's prophetic books, takes the form of an apocalypse. Such works combine three literary genres: the allegorical dream narrative, the dialogue, and the encyclopedic or Menippean satire; these, in turn, are influenced by three religious genres: the complaint, the commentary, and the sermon. Apocalyptic literature often includes the "dream vision," which has its roots in "the divine oracle and revelation." To the writer such a vision is not a mere subjective happening caused by an overexcited imagination but "objective reality." In reporting the vision the writer believes he is "only fulfilling his traditional role as seer." In addition, the vision is "often associated not only with a higher truth but with actual descriptions of the next world." Such works are "markedly eschatological and frequently highly critical of this world. The vision could be and was used to portray social and religious finalities which directly or indirectly condemned this world."[60] Used self-consciously, such visions lead to extensive personification and allegorization and also make possible an emphatic telescoping of time and space. The first lets the writer create "characters" who move around the central figure and sets up a natural dialectic between the internal and external worlds, between thought and act, word and deed. The second allows the reader to enter the work, not as perspective invites him to enter a Renaissance painting, but rather as the clear line invites him to enter the world of the woodcut or the engraving. Here, because of the small size, the reader's sense of space is negligible; space in such cases is created inside the viewer's imagination; the actual picture, a mere series of black lines, is but a suggestion. Space and time stop at the frame. In the world of the woodcut or engraving it is always now. Everything happens immediately, at the time the viewer witnesses it. The story does not move through time and space; it happens simultaneously with the viewer's perception of it. And the reader-viewer is not confused by intricacies of plot or character, but is presented with a homiletic set-piece. What D. W. Robertson, Jr., says happens to time in spiritual exegesis is relevant here: "an action carried out in the Old Testament may be, spiritually understood, an action described in the New Testament, and the same action, considered tropologically, becomes a potential action in the life of any man. Thus allegory has the effect of reducing the events of the Old Testament, the New Testament, and one's own actions, together with those of contemporaries, to a kind of continuous present."[61]

The opening epistle sets the stage for the events about to take place.

Like the arguments at the beginning of each book of *Paradise Lost*, the epistle shifts the emphasis away from narrative content toward literary form, away from history toward myth. The action portrayed is of psychological and political torment, not physical and personal suffering. The metaphor-packed address "TO THE TWELVE TRIBES OF ISRAEL THAT ARE CIRCUMCISED IN HEART, AND SCATTERED THROUGH ALL THE NATIONS OF THE EARTH" condenses "real" time to a continuous present so that the mythical material may reassert itself. The "circumcised in heart," as Thomas Goodwin noted in *A Glimpse of Syons Glory*, are "the despised ones of the world" represented by a "field wherein the treasure hath lien hide; all the dark and cloudy dayes of the Beasts time." This parable of the sower, which both John Ball and Thomas Münzer used to show how the poor are bound together by common suffering,[62] has alchemical implications that Winstanley transmutes into radical political significance. For he sees the rising sun of righteousness as a purifying agent transforming common people into golden saints in the womb of Mother Earth: "yet you are the firmament, in whom the Son of righteousnesse will rise up, and from you will declare himself to the whole Creation; for you are *Sion* whom no man regards, out of whom salvation shall come." Experience had taught him that if every man must be a phoenix the stronger birds survive only at the expense of the weaker. But if the common people collectively are the arch of the heavens in which the sun will rise, microcosmic alienation is superceded by macrocosmic identity. Each individual succeeds only by seeing his own needs as identical with those of the group.

In these opening paragraphs Winstanley announces his theme of inversion, establishes his method of typological presentation and metaphorical interpretation, dispenses with chronological time and sets up a telescoped mythical time scheme, puts forth his dialectic of inner and outer causes, introduces, if only subliminally, his political subversiveness, and, through the field-seed-sun image, moves the reader into a symbolic way of looking at history. Before the reader knows the subject, he is immersed in a sea of language where his mind, held fast by concrete images, ceases to function impassively and is presented with a world of symbolic actions where metaphoric analogy replaces discursive reason. Winstanley assures his readers the seed of Abraham lies within each of them, the sole "Saviour and joy of all men, from inward and outward bondage, and the restorer of the whole Creation from the curse it groans under." Now "hated, persecuted and despised," this hidden inner seed, like the biblical Jacob, is a servant to Esau. "But though this Jacob be very low, yet his time is now come, that he must rise, and he will rise up in you that are trod under foot like dust of the earth; he will glorifie him-

self both in you and from you, to the shame and downfall of *Esau* . . .
this blessed *promised seed*, shall go through the Earth in this ministration
of the Spirit that is now rising up." Drawing his readers together in a
sense of shared destiny, Winstanley says the time has come when the
flesh will serve the promised seed; elder sons will serve younger sons;
"this is the fall of *Esau*, and the rising of *Jacob*." The Abrahamite now
lives not "in the *type*, but enjoyes the *substance* of circumcision; For he is
not a Jew, that is one outward in the flesh; but he is a Jew, that is one
inward, whose circumcision is of the heart." (William Everard said he
was a Jew.) Whether one is born of "the Nation of the *Jews* extant in the
world" or not, "it is *Abrahams* promised seed that makes a Jew." Combining the spiritual with the material, the seed planted in the earth and
the spirit planted within the heart, a new Tree of Life will rise in a new
Eden that will save all people and all nations. For Abraham, who carried
the seed of the new law of righteousness, "was a type of the Man Christ
Jesus." Christ "hath the honour above his brethren, to be called the
spreading power, because he fils all with himself." In this metaphorical
and typological construct, time is cyclical.

In cyclic time, things return to their original state, but the restoration
requires patience and effort. "Those in whom the first fruits of restauration appears, do see darknesse, nay thick darknesse do cover man-kind."
Yet the hidden seed within "now is breaking forth. And the Nations shall
know, That salvation or restauration rather, is of the *Jews*." And this
restoration is not just psychological; the physical world too will be re-
juvenated. The seed "will fill the earth, both man-kind, and the whole
Creation, Fire, Water, Earth and Air." Likewise, it will transform social
relations: "though the seed of the flesh [the accident of birth] have cast
you out for evil . . . and the children of the flesh refuses to buy and sell
with you, yet now your glory is rising." There will be no second coming
except this, the appearance of a spirit within men and women. Thomas
Goodwin said in 1641 that Christ would literally level mountains. But
Winstanley says "He will throw down the mountaines of the flesh, fill up
the low valleys of the spirit, he will make rough wayes smooth, and
crooked wayes strait, he will make the earth fruitfull, and the winds and
the weather seasonable." With the "powers of the earth" (scientific technology), at their feet and the spirit as their "governour and teacher,"
people will build the New Jerusalem, which "may be the praise of the
whole earth."

Inverting Puritan hermenutics, Winstanley "translates" the Bible typologically in the light of his own reason, relying on images to convey an
emotional appeal. By turning common abstractions back into their
original metaphors, he revitalizes language so that it may truly become a

guide to action. If anyone says the New Jerusalem is only "to be seen hereafter, after the body is laid in the dust; it matters not to me what they say, they speak their imagination, they know not what. I know that the glory of the Lord shall be seen and known within the Creation, and the blessing shall spread in all Nations." Lest anyone mistake his meaning he declares emphatically that "the glory and riches of men shall be brought low." Reworking another image quoted by Goodwin (Isaiah 60:8), he enjoins the poor to watch for the doves to "flock to the windows (not to your Church-windows) but to the teachings of the Father, for his discoveries are the windows that lets the light of the Father shine into the soul"; emphasizing his radical epistemology he signifies that these discoveries are "dreams, voices and revelations *immediately from the Father himself, his own inward teaching, without which the soul is* hungry." A closing crescendo promises that when the poor "see or hear" themselves rising up, they will rejoice and know their "redemption draws near." Winstanley signs himself in the Foxean manner as "A waiter for the consolation of Israel."

An apocalypse, as a literary subgenre, has three identifiable characteristics. First, it is based on a singular, personal, visionary experience. It is not therefore merely a general impression of things or a statement of social, political, or economic disenchantment. Second, it is prophetic in the sense that it involves a specific comparison of a negative present with an ideal future, with the added impetus that the writer is speaking for a persecuted group. And third, it is teleological in that it assumes present suffering is justified because history has a purpose and is moving toward a more perfect future. The civil war millenarian prophesies were extremely popular, especially among Puritan sectaries. Brightman, Alstead, and Mede, along with Jeremiah Burroughs and Thomas Goodwin, popularized apocalyptic interpretations, but their works are either diffuse, vaguely-ordered interpretations of other prophesies or moralistic sermons drawn from predictable biblical passages. An apocalypse requires both an intense conviction that one's vision is real and a supreme control of one's craft. Perhaps no other genre makes such demands on its creator, for if the writer experiences the necessary vision but lacks the skill to order it into art he produces little more than the ravings of an unsettled mind, and if he possesses the craft but lacks the vision he creates nothing but the crabbed reflections of the pedant. Moreover, since the apocalyptic vision is almost totally metaphorical, the writer must have a precise visual sense.

In all these respects Winstanley's *New Law* stands out from contemporary interpretations of the millennium the way Dürer's *Apocalypse* (1498) dwarfs all previous attempts to illustrate the Book of Revelation.

Indeed, the comparison between Winstanley and Dürer is pertinent because Dürer portrayed contemporary sociological conditions in a timeless religious context at a time and in a place of acute political and theological conflict. Just as the original Book of Revelation has as its source the gradual disintegration of the Roman Empire among the Christian-Jewish communities of Asia Minor in the second half of the first century and reflects the hopes and frustrations of people who endured centuries of oppression, Dürer's *Apocalypse* is clearly a call to arms against the established powers of church and state. Dürer's book may in fact be looked upon as the earliest illustrations of a class war. Scenes such as *The Whore of Babylon, The Four Horsemen, The Day of Wrath,* and *The Warring Angels* depict high-born and well-to-do civil and ecclesiastical authorities as figures of corruption and contempt well-deserving of the scourges they receive. Like Winstanley, Dürer read his view of contemporary events into the story of Revelation, rejuvenating the scripture with his personal vision. In fact Dürer's *Apocalypse* is a kind of Reformation *Life* magazine where contemporary events are visually compressed, dramatized, and presented in a format meant not for public viewing, as with paintings, but for private contemplation. This destroys the "mystery" of the unique painting and allows the viewer to analyze the work when and where he chooses. Once the woodblocks were cut, an almost infinite number of copies could be made, each as clear and as sharp as the one before. Moreover, the woodblock prints themselves, with their dynamic interplay of light and dark, their crisp outlining and their ability to convey a sense of lifelike detail, create a verisimilitude that, as Kenneth Clark says, enabled many people to accept them as a correct record of the scenes they represented.[63]

Erwin Panofsky points out that the content of Dürer's woodcuts is imaginary, but the form is naturalistic. By stressing the "plane surface" of the composition, Dürer transplants "the miraculous event from the level of factuality to that of an imaginary experience." To emphasize the contrast between naturalistic things and imaginary visions, Dürer simultaneously stresses and denies the three-dimensionality of space by manipulating perspective. And St. John, included only where he directly participates in the action, invites us to share the visionary experience.[64] Whether or not Winstanley knew Dürer's *Apocalypse* is a moot question, but he was familiar with the excellent woodcuts in the Geneva Bible, and the woodcuts he saw in Foxe's *Actes and Monuments* brilliantly depict scenes from English history. Moreover, the point of comparing *The New Law* to Dürer's *Apocalypse* is not to establish a source but to draw a parallel. In his woodcuts Dürer demonstrated the sensibility of the middle-class Protestant craftsman, which meant that even, or perhaps especially, a work of art based on a visionary biblical text had to have immediate application in the real world. In other words, the topical and secular application of visionary experience in Dürer's *Apocalypse* and Winstanley's *New Law* represents a distinct advance from the idealized and purified monasticism espoused in *Piers Plowman*.[65]

The new law of righteousness is, quite simply, the unification of flesh and spirit, for when the flesh is made subject to the spirit it "walks uprightly . . . in the light of that spirit, then it lies down in rest." Citing the first epistle of St. John, whom he believed to be the author of Revelation, Winstanley declares that he speaks "as the Light is pleased to manifest himself in me." Assuming this visionary role, he recapitulates his account of the Fall. "In the beginning of time the whole Creation lived in man, and man lived in his Maker." During this Golden Age "there was no opposition between him and the beast, fowls, fishes, or any creature in the earth." In this idyllic age every creature gladly contributed to mankind's well being. But as man became selfish and covetous "he lost his dominion, and the creature fell out of him, and became enemies and apposers of him, and then rise up mountaines, and valleys, and hils, and all unevenness, both in mans heart, and in mans actions." Nature too fell, and all the beasts became selfish; they began to devour each other "to preserve self" so that all were in a "rest-lesse condition, groaning under bondage, waiting for a restauration."

Humanity now lives under the curse of reification—the worship of material things. So obsessive is people's desire to possess material things that they have rejected the spirit to "live upon objects. But now the time is come, that the Spirit will draw all things into man againe, to live and be at rest in him, as their Governour . . . and all bondage, curse and tears shall be done away." Having "received a taste" of the perfection awaiting mankind, Winstanley believes the present world is a moral and social inversion of the original Golden Age. "In times past and times present, the branches of man-kind have acted like the beast or swine; And though they have called one another, men and women, yet they have been but the shadows of men and women." Following John Everard he notes that "the Moone is the shadow of the Sun, in regard they have been led by the powers of the curse in flesh, which is the *Feminine* part; not by the power of the righteous Spirit which is Christ, the *Masculine* power."[66] This reigning fleshly power, the first Adam who worships the beast of Revelation 13:4, "seeks to compasse all the creatures of the earth into his own covetous hands, to make himself a Lord, and all other his slaves." He therefore is "the chief Rebell," who, by getting riches and government in his hands, tries to lift himself up and suppress universal liberty, personified as Christ.

Perversely, the old Adam preaches and prays for peace to honor his own fleshly procurements more strongly. But earthly power itself tends to corrupt those who possess it so that "every one that gets an authority into his hands, tyrannizes over others; as many husbands, parents, masters, magistrates, that lives after the flesh, doe carry themselves like oppressing Lords over such as are under them; not knowing that their wives, children, servants, subjects are their fellow creatures, and hath an equall priviledge to share with them in the blessing of liberty." Inwardly the first Adam causes "covetousnesse after objects," pride, envy, self-aggrandizement, revenge-seeking, hypocrisy, subtilty, lying. Outwardly he provokes tyranny, "particular interest, buying and selling the earth from one particular hand to another, saying, *This is mine,* upholding this particular propriety by a law of government of his own making, and thereby restraining other fellow creatures from seeking nourishment from their mother earth. So that though a man was bred up in a Land, yet he must not worke for himself where he would sit down."

The point could not be made stronger or clearer. Here Winstanley's prose attains a sureness and pithiness it previously lacked. The first Adam either bought the land or inherited it "So that he that had no Land, was to work for those for small wages, that called the Land theirs; and thereby some are lifted up into the chair of tyranny, and others trod under the foot-stool of misery, as if the earth were made for a few, not for all men." The chair-footstool image vividly conveys the relationship between those who "are lifted up," not raised by their own efforts, to tyranny and those "trod under," not lying down, to misery. The next paragraph emphasizes that "the common-people by their labours, from the first rise of *Adam* . . . have lifted up their Land-lords and others to rule in tyranny and oppression over them. And let all men say what they will, so long as such are Rulers as cals the Land theirs . . . the common-people shall never have their liberty." Condensing a pun he will develop later, Winstanley declares this unrighteous Adam "that dammed up the water springs of universall liberty" will be killed by the king of righteousness so that "a man shall have meat, and drinke and clothes by his labour in freedome, and what can be desired more in earth." With the earth as a "common treasury" everyone will be a perfect creation of himself. The second Adam, Christ, "stops or dammes up the runnings of those stinking waters of self-interest, and causes the waters of life and liberty to run plentifully in and through the Creation, making the earth one storehouse, and every man and woman to live in the law of Righteousnesse and peace as members of one household." The storehouse and the household, those two bastions of middle-class society, would be universalized for the good of all. The earth is, metaphorically, a storehouse, a treasury of common bounty, and everyone should partake of the mutual selfhelp implicit in the ideal family.

The personified Spirit of Reason makes people "see, loath and forsake this *Adam*, this fleshly man," who leads them into misery, pain, and death—"which is hell, a condition of uncomfortable darknesse." He also makes people see reason, "which is the law of Righteousnesse, that made them." For when flesh is subject to Reason, the light of truth illuminates the world. Winstanley knows this by "three methods" of understanding: first, by a typological interpretation of Moses' covenant; second, by apostolical testimony as exhibited in Acts 3:22; and third, as indicated in Ephesians 4:6 and Romans 8:22-23, by the testimony of the spirit within each human being, as each single body is a type of Christ. And, as Christ "far exceeded the Doctrine of *Moses*; the one being the substance of the other," when the spirit rules over the flesh in everyone the world will be transformed into a more perfect society. The Second Coming is nothing more or less than "the rising up of Christ in sons and daughters." This is the dividing of time in Revelation in which the Beast is to reign, when "every ministration pleads his priviledge" and "many false forms, customs and observations of Divine worship are raised up," all of which misunderstand scripture and plead privileges. Those most zealous in their claims are the bitterest enemies of truth. Eschewing all forms of sectarianism, the common people now rising up to claim their rightful inheritance will destroy "self-seeking oppressing government" and make the earth "a common treasury for all."

Winstanley warns those in high places that all their enmity will not uphold their forms; all their imprisonings and laws will not successfully thwart the common people. The most frequently cited biblical text in *The New Law* is Acts 4:32: "And the multitude of them that believed were of one heart and of one soul: neither said any *of them* that ought of the things which he possessed was his own; but they had all things common." With this as his guide Winstanley challenges "Teachers" who say he denies scripture to judge him according to the words of the prophets and Apostles. Those scriptures which they "seeme to preserve with such love and zealous tendernesse, shall cast the first stone at you, to stone you out of your Pulpits; for you doe not professe those Scriptures in love of them, but in zealous covetousnesse to uphold your trade." Now common men and women honor scripture and prove true prophesies, promises, visions, and revelations; the teachers "deny their testimony, and cry out Visions and Revelations are ceased." "Well," Winstanley concludes in a blend of colloquial and biblical paraphrase, "he is at worke that will discover your shame; *Wickedness shall slay the wicked, though no mans hand be upon him.*"

There are three ways people may see the light and make it "shine in its excellency." The first is through nature—"Sunne, Moon, Stars, Earth, Grasse, Plants, Cattle, Fish, Fowl, and Man"—for all these are "sweetly conjoyned to preserve each other." Therefore people may know the spirit is in them and in the world through their own "clear sighted experience . . . by seeing, hearing, tasting, smelling, feeling." But to have this experience one must "see Christ within himself, before hee can see him in other creatures." The second way people come to know the spirit is through "The Scripture in their severall declaration, types, prophecies, visions, voyces, revelations, [and] actings of men," for scripture is the letter "lying under the experimentall words of those Pen-men." Yet though some have seen the light in nature and in scripture, they have not seen the light within themselves and so know truth only from a distance. Here again Winstanley skillfully introduces the sun of righteousness motif: "As the pleasant beames . . . of the Sun, which refreshes the outward man, may be lost, for when the Clouds come between, the beames returne into the Sun again, which is their proper seat, and men loseth, the refreshing, warmth and heat," so "the spreading power of light," who "is drawing the knowledge of himself . . . into the clear experience of man . . . he the Sonne of Righteousnesse will not only shine into, but fix himself in every one. So that perfect man shall be no other but *God manifest in flesh.*"

The implications of this image are immense, for as we have seen, not only is the sun of righteousness an essential motif of all typological and millenarian interpretations and a fundamental alchemical symbol, it also establishes a link between classical antiquity, medieval mysticism, and the Renaissance. Here again Durer's *Apocalypse* provides the representative example. As Panofsky shows, "the religious experience of late antiquity was so closely allied to astral mysticism, and so thoroughly imbued with the belief in the omnipotence of the sun-god, that no new religious idea could gain acceptance unless it was either invested with solar connotations from the outset—as was the case with Mithras worship—or else acquired such solar connotations *ex post facto*—as was the case with Christianity."[67] Traditionally, Christ defeated Mithras, but in so doing he absorbed vital features of sun worship, such as the date of Mithras' birth (25 December) and his glorious appearance as described in Revelation 1:14: "His head and *his* hairs *were* white like wool, as white as snow; and his eyes *were* as a flame of fire." The church originally sanctioned this union between Christ and the sun but substituted for the cosmological sun-god a moral one: *sol invictus* became *sol iustitiae.* This substitution was facilitated by the fact that paganism itself tended to spiritualize the physical sun into an "intelligible Helios," and the sun-god was often seen as a judge. Furthermore, the words of Malachi 4:2: "But unto you that fear my name shall the Sun of righteousness arise with healing in his wings," seemed to justify a connection between the last Old Testament prophet and the concluding book of the New. What is more, in Panofsky's words, the image

> had a perfectly literal meaning. The 'sun of righteousness' represented not so much the impersonal idea of justice as a personal sungod—or solar daemon—in his capacity as judge. St. Augustine had to warn vigorously against carrying the identification of Christ with Sol so far as to relapse into paganism. But these very pagan implications of the *Sol Iustitiae* formula endowed it with an irresistible emotional impact; from the third century on it was one of the most popular and effective metaphors in ecclesiastical rhetoric; it played a large role in sermons and hymns; and it has its place in the liturgy up to this day; to the early adherents of Christianity it was 'a triumphant invocation' by which they 'were moved to almost drunken ecstasy.'[68]

Just as Dürer transforms the Apollonian sun-god into the ecstatic *sol iustitiae*, then into Adam, and finally into the resurrected Christ, Winstanley reworks the visual images of Revelation into a political concept of regeneration much as Blake reworks the Apollonian sun-god into the ecstatic image of liberation in *The Sun at His Eastern Gate* to illustrate Milton's "L'Allegro" and again in *Glad Day*. And like his great German predecessor and his humble English descendent, Winstanley could do this because "he had the courage to be literal within the framework of a style aspiring to the sublime."[69] Dürer's engraving fuses the grandeur of the apocalyptic judge with the strength of the mightiest natural force; Winstanley, by reading back into the metaphor something of its original concrete meaning, transforms Dürer's image of the judge of nature into a universal and democratic life force:

> The light, and heat, and Spirit of the Sunne, shall be declared by the Sonne of Righteousnesse in man: The sweet compliance of love in one creature towards another; as the clouds to water the earth, the earth to send forth the fruits to preserve the living creatures, that feeds thereupon, shall be declared by that living power, Love and Righteousnesse, that is seated in man towards any creature.
>
>   So that, though this one Almighty power be spread in the whole Creation, yet it will appear to have his chief residence in man.

This ruling life force will make everyone grow toward perfection. "Even as wee see any tree, corn or cattell, grows up in the eye of man by degrees; for as these creatures doe not attaine to perfection on a sudden;

neither doth the spirit of Righteousnesse rise up on a sudden perfection, but by degrees." Winstanley takes pains to affirm his moderation because this identifies him with Foxe's regenerative notion of human history, distinguishes him from the pessimism of Anglican orthodoxy, and shows his desire to escape the label of fanaticism.

Through the development of such contraries, Winstanley advances his argument. For example, he introduces the conventional notion of Christ as a mighty king who shall come to reign forever, but no sooner does he put forth the idea than he inverts it by telling his reader, "And this is he you would call God; but indeed the *power of darknesse* is the god that rules in most men and women, both professours and others: and they will subject to this their god of darknesse, till the power of light Christ take him away." This ploy heightens the reader's awareness of the conventionality of his own ideas and reinforces the point that to achieve a better life he must give up his idealistic notions and join in "destroying all opposing powers," beginning with those within the reader himself, so that he "who is the divine, may grow up, flourish, remaine and bring forth aboundance of fruit in you, when your created flesh is purged from bondage, and made subject to him." Yet while the metaphoric sun of righteousness is spread democratically within everyone, he retains the alchemical and judicial characteristics of Dürer's *sol iustitiae*, for as Zion is the promised kingdom of the spirit, *"Sinai* is the mountaine of flesh, that is to be burned with fire, that is, the Spirit of Righteousnesse is the fire, that will burn up all unrighteous powers." To see this happening "is to see him you would call God, with open face." But Winstanley realizes there is ambiguity here, for the powers of alchemy (science) and magistracy (legality) are easily perverted to unscrupulous and unjust ends when people presume to play God. Therefore priests and "zealous professors" should learn "to know what power it is you call God: for the word God, signifies a Governour, and it may as well be attributed to the devil, as to the law of Righteousnesse; for assure your selves, if covetousnesse, pride and bitter envy doe rule you, as it is apparent this dark power rules most of you, then the devil is that god you worship."[70]

The exposition of the sun of righteousness motif continues with an explanation of how this power was, is, and will be spread throughout creation. Again the inner and outer dialectic comes into play, for with humanity's restoration comes nature's restoration. People will live at one with nature, and they will "see, feel, taste, smell and hear, the power of the whole Creation." And of course the instrument of this transformation is the poor, for "it is yet hid from the *learned ones,* the teachers and rulers of the world." When the earth is made into a new garden "the distinction . . . in one single person over all, shall cease, and no distinction shall be owned" because the sun of righteousness will dwell in everyone. Returning to the text of Revelation 5:13, Winstanley raises his prophetic voice to chastize established ministers for their hypocritical spiritualism: "O ye hear-say Preachers, deceive not the people any longer, by telling them that this glory shal not be known and seen, til the body is laid in the dust. I tel you, this great mystery is begun to appear, and it must be seen by the material eyes of the flesh: And those five senses that is in man, shall partake of this glory."

Becoming increasingly personal as he settles into his stride, he explains that pride and humility cannot "dwel quietly in one heart together." Turning his key metaphor, the act of seeing inwardly, he again lashes out at preachers and professors: "if you have eyes look within your selves, and see what power rules within the bodies of your flesh." If they find there "envy, rash anger, covetousnesse, self-honouring, secret pride . . . and the like," they will know "that that power is your self, your very self, a devil, the serpent, the subtil, and yet strong power of darknesse, that would fain be counted an Angel of Light." Men and women possessed of such powers must be purged by "the spirit of burning" till they are made mentally and physically into "a temple for the Father himself to dwell in, a garden wherein he himself will take delight." Winstanley now recognizes that "you that would be Angels of light and are not, will count this which I speak madnesse, but you shall find these words true." (Langland, we recall, says he is "a lunatik" and Blake celebrates his "madness" in a song.) Drawing a parallel between his own sufferings and those of Christ, he implies that just as the scribes and pharisees persecuted Jesus in biblical times, contemporary preachers and professors call his power blasphemy because he crosses them. Yet he cannot blame them, for if his message triumphs, if Christ does "rise in flesh," the preachers and professors must fall: "If he be King, as he must be, you must be his footstool."

In the role of the long-suffering humble man whom others think mad, Winstanley explains how to see and know the difference between the two powers that strive to govern him. Turning to the stock figures of the first and second Adams, he puts forth his persona as typical of how these two powers battle within everyone. Only one assured of his self-consciousness would dare use himself as an example of how the covetous Adam within causes one to seek "after creature enjoyment or riches; to have peace from them." Only one having undergone intense self-analysis could use himself as an illustration of how "Pride looks abroad for honour; Envy seeks the revenge of such as crosses his fleshly ends, by reproch, oppression, or murder. Unclean lusts seeks to embrace strange flesh. Imagination flies abroad, to devise wayes to satisfie the flesh in these desires: Hypocrisie turns himself into divers shapes; yea, sometimes into an Angel of light, a zealous Professour to compasse these ends." These six devils are guided by a seventh, self-love, and together they comprise "one Devil." Such passages show the impossibility of divorcing Winstanley's personal life from his persona, for the "I" that speaks of his sufferings and successes is at once the tradesman turned cowherd and everyman. Winstanley is so bound up with events that self-revelation is the best means of pointing out that the answer to the question of how humanity may find perfection requires the forging of new consciousness and new ways of expressing that consciousness. As a craftsman he knows he is only as good as the materials he works with, and this is as true of language as it is of human personality. Molding that personality, Winstanley renounces the beast within himself and allows the sun of righteousness to anoint him. Thus he arrives at contentedness even in poverty. For just as humility and meekness kills pride and loftiness, "Love to enemies . . . kils envy and rash anger."

The external proponents of the power of darkness advocate scriptural literalism. They represent "this first man . . . *by whose disobedience many are made sinners,* or by whom the whole Creation is corrupted; Therefore you Preachers, do not you tell the people any more, That a man called *Adam*, that disobeyed about 6000 years ago . . . filled every man with sin and filth, by eating an apple." This is patent nonsense because "*Adam* is within every man and woman." The apple is a symbol, "not a single fruit," representing "the objects of the Creation; which is the fruit that came out of the Seed, which is the Spirit himself that made all things: As riches, honours, pleasures, upon which the powers of the flesh feeds to delight himself." This is the "messe of pottage" Esau sold to Jacob in exchange for his birthright. "Therefore when a man fals, let him not blame a man that died 6000 years ago, but blame himself." "Therefore" indeed! With a stroke Winstanley discards the incremental tradition of discursive reason, where history is seen as a continuous roadway along which humanity travels into the future, and substitutes a dialectical interaction of forces: "day and night, the light and darknesse, Winter and Summer, heat and cold, Moon and Sun, that is typed out by the Fabrick of the great world; for within these two powers is the mystery of all divine workings wrapped up." Instead of a roadway, history now becomes a stream on which humanity navigates until "*in the fulnesse of time;* that is, When the first man hath filled the Creation full of his filthinesse, and all places stinks with unrighteousnesse, as it doth at this day," a storm of righteousness comes to "take the Kingdome out of the others hand, and restore all things."

But while the power of darkness, Adam, the son of disobedience, rules, everyone must wait patiently for the sun of righteousness to arise. For these two powers "are typed out by *Iacob* and *Esau; Iacob* put forth his arm first, and it is marked by the midwife, and then he draws it in again: then *Esau* comes fully forth, and is called the elder brother." This nonbiblical story of the twins' birth justifies Jacob's purchase of Esau's birthright for a mess of pottage. Jacob is Christ, the elect or chosen one, whereas Esau is the rejected one, the reprobate, who "steps before (by permission) and gets the government" of mankind first. Esau rules until Jacob supplants him "and takes both birth-right and blessing from him," which are his by "equity and reason" since he was cheated "by a violence" in the womb. Jacob, who typifies Christ, "is the spirituall man, that judges all things according to the law of equity and reason, in moderation and love to all, he is not a talker, but an actour of Right-eousnesse." But Esau, the type of the first Adam, "the man of the flesh, which would be counted an Angel of light, cannot judge of any thing in righteousnesse; for all his judgement and justice is selfish, and confined to particular ends, not to the publick safety and preservation." As usual this conflict between Esau and Jacob simultaneously takes place within each man and woman and in the external world, and the internal conflict influences and is influenced by the external one. The internal conflict between Esau and Jacob, between the old Adam and Christ, appears in the external world as the conflict between the hunter and the hunted, the warlike and the peaceful, those who ruthlessly grab all for themselves and those who share evenly with their neighbors.

With the link between his inner and outer dialectic clearly established, Winstanley attacks the Esaus of the world who judge it a "righteous thing" that some rich men, whether honest or not, "should be Magis-trates to rule over the poor; and that the poor should be servants nay rather slaves to the rich." But the Jacobs of the world, who judge accord-ing to "the light of equity and reason," believe there should be "free-dome, to live upon earth; and that there shal be no bond-man nor begger in all his holy mountaine." Since "Man-kind was made to live in the free-dome of the spirit, not under the bondage of the flesh," God wants people free so they may glorify him, for surely imprisoning, whipping, and hanging of fellow creatures cannot please him. Again the emphasis is on seeing: "let mens eyes be opened, and it appears clear enough, That the punishers have and doe break the law of equity and reason." This is why "every body wee see is filled with sorrow and complainings." Even though the earth has been "mowed" into the hands of a few covetous men, "the spreading power of wisdome and truth . . . wil take off that bondage, and give a universall liberty, and there shal be no more com-plainings against oppression, poverty, or injustice. When every son and

daughter shall be made comfortable . . . according to their measure."
Oppression will cease, destroyed by universal love. "But this is not done
by the hands of a few, or by unrighteous men" who merely wish to pull
tyrannical government out of other's hands and keep it in their own.
According to Revelation 18:19, Babylon will be destroyed in one hour;
tyrannical government will fall, and the lands and riches covetous men
have hoarded will be given to the poor "so there may be no complainings, no burdens, nor no poor in *Canaan*, but that it may be a *Land flow-
ing with milke and honey*, plenty of all things . . . as it was in the beginning." For surely the threat of James 5:1-3, that rich men will howl and
weep for their riches, will be materially fulfilled when the poor inherit the
earth.

With uncanny cognizance of the way reason is socially determined
Winstanley declares: "The rich man tels the poor, that they ofend Reasons law, if they take from the rich; I am sure it is a breach in that Law in
the rich to have plenty by them, and yet wil see their fellow creatures
men and women to starve for want; Reason requires that every man
should live upon the increase of the earth comfortably." But since covetousness fights against reason, "the rich doth lock up the treasures of the
earth, and hardens their hearts against the poor." Yet the poor will survive because they share the "gifts of love and tendernesse one to preserve
another." Reason is on the side of the poor because people were not made
to by tyrants and slaves. Esau's usurpation of Jacob's birthright typifies
the origin of tyranny. At first "every man had an equall freedom given
him of his Maker to till the earth," and although this freedom was destroyed by covetousness, it will be restored, not by "Selfish Councellours,
Selfish Governours, Selfish Souldiers," but by "The Lord himself . . .
without either sword or weapon" acting through poor men and women.
Animals have already established a social contract: "The beast of the
field; though they break over hedges, and eat in any pasture . . . do not
imprison and hang one another, the earth is a common livelyhood for
them." Likewise, men hold land "not by right of blessing, but by
permission." Still, this does not permit confiscation: "I do not speak that
any particular men shall go and take their neighbours goods by violence,
or robbery (I abhor it)." Everyone must wait until the spirit rises within
him. Then, as prophesied in Revelation 11:15, Esau will be defeated.
The universal power of righteousness will be written so plainly "in every
ones heart, that none shall desire to have more then another." The phrase
"Mine and Thine shall be swallowed up in the law of righteous actions."
All will "live as brethren, every one doing as they would be done by; and
he that sees his brother in wants, and doth not help, shall smart for his
iniquity, from the hand of the Lord, the righteous Judge that will sit upon

the throne in every mans heart." Then "there shall be no need of Lawyers, prisons, or engines of punishment . . . and there shall be no beggar,
nor cause of complaining." Therefore Winstanley again counsels patience
until more people see the need to live in communal harmony. Soon, he
assures his readers, the "prisoners of hope" will be set free. Like More,
whose Utopians transferred their sun worship to Christianity when they
learned that Christ's disciples practiced a "common way of life,"[71] he
declares that "every one shall put to their hands to till the earth, and
bring up cattle, and the blessing of the earth shall be common to all."
And also like More's Utopians he believes in the doctrine of sufficiency:
"When a man hath meat, and drink, and cloathes he hath enough." Everyone will work to make these necessities. No one will be "over others," but
everyone will be responsible for his own behavior. People will see and
tell of new feelings of love, and a "universall freedom," which never before existed, will fill the earth. A New Jerusalem will be built, as foretold
in Revelation 12:9, with the sun of righteousness within each individual
as its only ruler.

Always wary of "the scoffer," Winstanley does not mean "mens wives
shall be common . . . For when man was made, he was made male and
female, one man and one woman conjoyned together by the law of love,
makes the Creation of humane flesh perfect in that particular . . . Reason
did not make one man and many women, or one woman and many men
to joyn together, to make the Creation perfect, but male and female in
the singular number." Anyone who breaks this rule "shall then become
servant to others" until the sun of righteousness rises in him. Those in
whom this sun rises are known by their deeds, not their words. They are
not interested in creating a fantasyland for frustrated sensualists or a
haven for loquacious egoists. Such are "filled with confusion" and are
slaves to their lusts. Yet many "of the lowest and despised sort of people,
that are counted the dust of the earth . . . that are trod under foot" will
come forth. The sun of righteousness will "break forth first" in them, for
"the waters of the learned and great men of the world, begins to dry up
like the brooks in Summer." When the poor become active the sun of
righteousness will rise, the elements will be purified, and there will be "no
barrennesse in the earth or cattle . . . Unseasonable storms . . . shall
cease." But the doubting Thomas Dydimus cries out, "When will these
things be? not in our time? I cannot believe such things till I see them?"
Such questions are always raised by those not wishing to change or be
changed. Some think revolutionary change comes through "flesh wit,
policy or strength." But to those willing to change and be changed the
transformation will come "speedily." People see that the whole earth is
corrupt and cry out, but "the more they strive, the more they entangle
themselves in the mud" because they want riches and respectability.

Writing now at the top of his form, Winstanley launches a tirade against the church hierarchy. The following outline exemplifies his skill in building emotional force, piling phrase upon phrase, until the crescendo angrily ends:

first, they that stand up to teach others, they teach for gain, and preach for hire, and fils people with division and confusion, through their pride and envy, and they do this by the Authority of the governing power, by which they have ingrossed the earth into their hands. A man must not take a wife, but the Priest must give her him. If he have a child, the Priest must give the name. If any die, the Priest must see it laid in the earth. If any man want knowledge or comfort, they teach him to go to the Priest for it; and what is the end of all this, but to get money.

Soaring to new heights of indignation, he strikes out at tithe-gatherers. And if the tithe is not paid willingly "some oppressing impropriatour" takes it and shares it with the priests. First, this law of tithes "was brought in by the Pope," and shames those who still live by it and call themselves Christian Protestants. This is "high treason." Because of such practices "the earth stinks" with the "fruit of imagination" under the bondage of "a compulsive binding power." Second, as to buying and selling, Winstanley sounds a personal note in his outcry that "though I was bred a tradesmen, yet it is so hard a thing to pick out a poor living, that a man shall sooner be cheated of his bread, then get bread by trading among men, if by plain dealing he put trust in any." The whole business of trading, he laments, "is generally become the neat art of thieving and oppressing fellow-creatures." Third, the "Justices and Officers of State . . . multiply wrongs, and many, if not most times oppresses the poor, and lets the offending rich go free." By treating the law as the priests treat the scriptures, they act "by subtil covetousnesse and smooth words to get money, or else ruling by their own wills, through envy to imprison and oppresse others, letting poor people lie in prison half a year many times, and never bring them to trial at all." Rallying his forces, Winstanley calls upon "you *Tribes of Israel*, that are now in sackcloth, every man with his hands upon his loins, like a woman in travel, stand stil and see the salvation of *David* your King." During this time of Jacob's trouble, people will try to persecute him and rob him of his livelihood, forcing him to move about under poverty, but this is a sign for him to give up covetousness and "forsake the forms and customs of the National worship." And if any scoff and laugh and cry, "O when shal this be! . . . *it is impossible*, for it is madnesse thus to speak; wel, such may live to see it, but shal not enjoye the blessing." For when Jacob rises, Esau will be his servant. The poor, like the dust and stones, are trod upon by the rich, but these dust and stones will rise up and be made the blessing of the earth.

Having prepared the reader, now, at the very heart of the work, the mathematical center, Winstanley describes his revelation:

> As I was in a trance not long since, divers matters were present to my sight, which here must not be related. Likewise I heard these words, *Worke together. Eat bread together;* declare this all abroad. Likewise I heard these words. *Whosoever it is that labours in the earth, for any person or persons, that lifts up themselves as Lords & Rulers over others, and that doth not look upon themselves equal to others in the Creation, The hand of the Lord shall be upon that labourer: I the Lord have spoke it and I will do it;* Declare all this abroad.

When he awakened from this trance, he vividly remembered what he saw and heard. He told those with him of his vision and was "filled with abundance of quiet peace and secret joy. And since that time those words have been like very fruitfull seed." With these seeds he sets out to cultivate his garden.

The prophecy of Genesis 3:15 now takes on new urgency. The vision clarifies the meaning of the metaphorical battle between the spirit and the flesh, the sun and the serpent:

> It is not for one creature called man to kill another, for this is abominable to the Spirit, and it is the curse which hath made the Creation to groan under bondage; for if I kill you I am a murderer, if a third come, and hang or kill me for murdering you, he is a murderer of me; and so by the government of the first *Adam,* murder hath been called Justice when it is but the curse.

Those who profess to kill for love are hypocrites. Since only acting in love will relieve the oppressed, the prisons, banks, and barns should be opened so the treasures of the earth may be enjoyed by all. The rejection of both sensual indulgence and mystical asceticism is the revolutionary consequence of Winstanley's revelation, the real negation of the negation.

Those who profess to be lovers of humanity and yet do no labor in the earth are egoists and enemies of reason. And if they wait for some single embodied spirit to appear upon earth, the wait for what will never be. Poor people must throw off despair: "You dust of the earth, that are trod under foot, you poor people, that makes both schollars and rich men your oppressours by your labours, Take notice of your priviledge." Believing, as he must, that his vision was the voice of the Lord, Winstanley says that those who refuse to work and eat bread together deny the scripture because the symbolic meaning of the Last Supper is the communal sharing of the fruits of the earth (cf. 2 Thessalonians 3:10). Undeterred by self-doubt or desire for personal gain, he will translate his words into deeds. For just as the ancient Pharaoh was told to "let Israel goe free," modern rulers must allow poor people their freedom. "Be not you more proud and hardhearted, then *Pharaoh* your type," Winstanley cautions them, "for the anti-type oft times is more powerfull then the type."

Weaving the analogy between ancient Israel and contemporary England ever tighter, he warns modern Pharaohs that they will perish. By withholding their labor, common people can force landowners to work. Under these conditions Winstanley is quite willing to see who shall inherit the earth: "Whether they that hold a civil propriety . . . or those that hold a common right." Here the results of the epistemological premises laid down in *Truth Lifting Up Its Head* come into view. The law written in everyone's heart, reason itself, arises out of the clear perception of the need to shape reality for constructive ends. For just as Milton felt that truth would become plain if we would "but purge with sovrain eyesalve that intellectual ray which *God* hath planted in us,"[72] and just as Traherne asks the sun of righteousness to "let the Ey of our Mind enter into thine,"[73] Winstanley wants to clarify reality and expose false consciousness. Everyone may, as Marvell implored, make their destiny their choice.

IV

THE SEED OF LIFE

THE SECOND half of *The New Law* encourages others to join in setting up a utopian community. Persuasive rhetorical questions bring the issue into focus: "Was the earth made for to preserve a few covetous, proud men, to live at ease, and for them to bag and barn up the treasures of the earth from others, that they might beg or starve in a fruitful Land, or was it made to preserve all her children?" Who can be offended at the poor for withholding their labor from the landowners and cultivating the commons? Why should some work while others live idle? Reason did not make the law that if one man must borrow from another, "that he that did lend should imprison the other, and starve his body in a close room." "Did the light of Reason," he asks, "make this law, that some part of man kinde should kil and hang another part . . . that could not walk in their steps?" He warns the leaders of the New Model Army against the infatuation of absolute power. In words that recall Marvell's references to Caesar in "An Horatian Ode," he notes that he who would kill a traitor may himself fall in love with treason "when he may be honoured or lifted up by it." With a vivid personification Winstanley sums up: "where Tyrannie sits, he is an enemy to Christ, the spreading spirit of righteousnesse: He wil use the bare name, Christ, that he may the more secretly persecute, and kil his power. Tyrannie is a subtile, proud and envious Beast; his nature is selfish, and ful of murder; he promises fair things for the publique; but all must be made to center within self, or self interest."

Now the visionary energy slowly subsides. The first half of *The New Law* contains a mythologized moral history from the old Adam to the new; the second half recapitulates this phylogeny ontogenically; that is, having told how people arrived at their present state, Winstanley shows the effect of that state on each person. Running after others for knowledge and comfort, the buying and selling of land, and the dominion of one over another bring on every social ill. Private property and unjust punishment "tempts people to doe an evil action, and then kils them for doing of it." Under the present state "Adam is the commer in of bondage, and is the curse that hath taken hold of the Creation." Again a pun gets

128

the meaning across: "And he may wel be called A-dam, for indeed he does dam and stop up the streams of the waters of life and libertie. When slaverie began to creep in upon the Creation, the Spirit might wel cry out in Lamentation, Ah-dam, A-dam." Chafing against the confines of language, Winstanley strains the credibility of his metaphors: "The seed from whence the Creation sprang, shall bruise that Serpents head, and open the dam againe, and cause the waters . . . to run free againe without any stoppage." Yet the dam metaphor effectively explains neurotic tendencies. While in place this dam ties up humanity "in chains of darknesse within it self" and stops "the free running streams of the Spirit of life." By causing people to live covetously "this A-dam hath lifted up mountaines and hils of oppressing powers" to dam up the "universal communitie." Therefore this "serpentine power" enslaving humanity "might wel be declared by way of Lamentation, A-dam Adam." Elaborating this false etymology, he explains that "covetousnesse, or selflove; is the dam; the letter A: before, declares, that he is a preparer to miserie . . . The imagination arising from that covetous power is the woman, or Eve, which like the Ivie, clings about the tree." By telescoping the serpent and the tree into one image, this concupiscent tableau, reminiscent of Raphael's and Dürer's iconographic renderings of the Fall, suggests a libidinous relationship between Eve and the serpent.

The union begets "a supposed joy, pleasure and delight; but it proves a lie." For the offspring of this mating are pride, envy, hypocrisy, cruelty, and lust. Adam and Eve fail to beget joyous children because "the damhead is made up strong, to stop the streams of waters of life." With Adam's lifegiving seed blocked up, Eve produces deformed monsters of the imagination in the same way that Milton's Satan begets Sin. Yet "in the fulnesse of time, the Spirit wil break down this dam-head againe, and cause the waters of the Spirit of life to flow again plentifully." Turning on the metaphor of restricted sexuality, Winstanley explains, "herein you may see, how the publique Preachers have cheated the whole world, by telling us of a single man, called Adam, that kiled us al by eating a single fruit, called an Apple." Preachers typify this Adam. While inhibited by covetousness, their sexuality is unfulfilling because they have "no community with the spirit within . . . nor community of love with fellow creatures." This constriction "does so puff them up with covetousnesse" that they desire only to "rule one over another." As first Adams they see each other as imaginary extensions of themselves: "tel me whether the first Adam be one single man, as the publique Preachers tel you; or is not more truly that covetous, proud and imaginary power in flesh, that hath dammed and stopped up the way of the spirit of life." Yet just as Dürer used the same model to depict Adam and *sol Apollo*, Winstanley wants to transform all people, now reflections of the first Adam, into fertile suns of righteousness. For though Satan "holds the Creation under bondage," the Son, "which is the light in the Creation," will shine forth and set "us at libertie: And if the Son set you free, you are free indeed."

Winstanley's bold imagery shows his contemporaneity with the metaphysical poets, but *The New Law* also suggests another quality he shares with Donne, Herbert, Marvell, Vaughan, and Traherne—the ability to be transformed by experience and to transform the experience of others. "What I have spoken," he announces, "I have not received from books, nor study, but freely I have received, and freely I have declared what I have received." Unafraid of the egotism implicit in such statements, he believes "the Declarations of the Lord through his servant shal not be in vain." He is sure the revolutionary transformation will soon come. "Then there shall be no begger, no tears, no complaining, no oppression." Swords will be beaten into plowshares and spears into pruning hooks. Like all utopians he looks back obliquely to a lost Golden Age and simultaneously projects that age into the near future. After Christ's disciples laid his body in the earth, the spirit of communal love spread among all; "they did not rule in slavery one over another; neither did the rich suffer the poor to beg and starve, and imprison them as now they do . . . for they had all things common." Then Esau rose up again and "strove to suppresse this community." But now his reign is expiring. Soon the sun of righteousness will rise in all sons and daughters; his light will break forth and "none shal say, this is mine, but every one shal preserve each other in love." As this spirit spreads, the rich will voluntarily give up their treasures. If they do not, "they shal be stripped naked of all, and shal either be destroyed by plagues," or "they shal be servants . . . till the Spirit of the Son rise up in them, and make them free." This transformation will not take place "by wars, councels, or hands of men, for I abhor it." Those who live by the government of Esau will destroy one another. The poor despised "fools of the world" will "rise out of the dust" to declare this new law just as the word of "the Son of Man was first declared by . . . men that the learned, covetous Scholars despised." Focusing his wrath on the ministers who extract tithes from working people and, in return, mislead them into submission with spiritual mumbo-jumbo, Winstanley notes that they "are *Iudas*." And Judgment Day will occur when they are overthrown. King Esau is merely a paper tiger, a "Gaffer Dragon."

> Do what thou wilt, speak what thou wilt against Christ the Anointing, thou shalt come off a loser: threaten, reproach, imprison, whip, work hypocritically, oppresse, kil and slay, fawn and frown, do things out of fear, or do things out of heavy rashnesse, or out of a

watchful moderation, as thou thinks, stil thou shalt lose ground; for all thou doest, is to advance self, and thou must perish . . . now it is done, it is done, it is done.

Then comes the release. With a trumpet call up in the sunlight, Winstanley bids the people rise and kneel no more. The "salt-mines" are opened; the streams of love "over-run the banks of rotten stinking oppressing injustice . . . The windows of heaven are opening, and the light of the Son of Righteousnes, sends forth . . . delightful beams, and sweet discoveries of truth that wil quite put out the covetous traditional bleareyes . . . Light must put out darknesse; the warm Sun wil thaw the frost, and make the sap to bud out of every tender plant, that hath been hid within, and lain like dead trees all the dark cold cloudy daies." The preachers of covetousness, isolated from the people's growing misery, have sowed the seeds of their own destruction. Centralization of education and pauperization of working people at last reach a point where they become incompatible with their integument. This integument is burst asunder. "Now the tender grasse wil cover the earth, the Spirit wil cover al places *with the abundance of fruit* . . . the wheat fields which is the best grain (the Fathers own people) shal flourish abundantly; the bondage of beastly Ceremonies, forms, customs, abominable actings in unrighteousnesse shal cease, there shall be lesse talking, preaching and prating, and more righteous acting." Like birds singing merrily on every bough, people will rejoice, "for the time that the Lord God omnipotent wil raign in al the earth is beginning, and he wil be servant to the Dragon, Beast, and man of the flesh no longer, but wil tread down that murdering power, and make him his footstool."

This last sentence epitomizes Winstanley's style. The imperfect "is beginning" indicates his sense of history, for while it deliberately avoids naming the agent of change, it encourages the reader to take part in the process of change. The statement, at the same time emphatic and indefinite, allows for open-ended interpretation. Similarly, the withholding of the negative in the second clause forces the reader to suspend judgment; the "no longer," serving as a contradiction to the entire clause, also characterizes the dialectical way history moves and the way change will take place. The next clause, with its active "wil tread" reminds the reader of the frequently cited passage from Genesis 3:15, and the Saxon "murdering" icily heightens the effect of the innocuous but nevertheless apt "footstool." How like Winstanley to follow the emphatic "murdering" with such a homey yet biblical word to suggest that the punishment for the most heinous crime should be so mild and still so humbling. This too represents his philosophical direction. He does not want revenge, supremacy, or even retribution. He wants equal justice. It is quite sufficient for an omnipotent God, who could easily destroy the Dragon, simply to make the beast his footstool.

The revelation projects inner experience into the external world, and the act of seeing denotes this process. Illuminated by the inner light of the sun of righteousness, people will see the need for outward reformation. Hearsay preachers must be made to see "they speak they know not what," for when they "see they speak other mens words (like Parots)," they will know "they have had neither voice, vision, nor revelation to warrant their words." Words shall grow fewer and fewer, and actions will become more righteous and reasonable. For even though the civil wars signify the last gasp of Esau's reign, kings, rich men, and gentry will not give up their hegemony without a fight. They will violently oppress the poor, "treading them like mire in the street." The internal war between light and darkness is reflected in the external war between rich and poor. "The worshipping of God in types, ceremonies, formes and customs, in set times and places" is part of buying and selling, and the rich "cannot indure" to trade with righteous men and women, for it frightens them to know others are less deceitful and pleases them to know others are less fortunate than themselves. Therefore, the rich escape into forms and customs to defend their selfishness; they hire teachers, professors, and lawyers who are "blind guides and poor hearts" to defend their privileges. But "both shall fall into the ditch, and be mired in their own inventions most pittifully." So when people come to see themselves stuck in confusion and disorder and know that their teachers have deceived them they will remember "That the first must be last." Zeal to make money and advance self is "zeal without knowledge," and experience teaches those who are earnest not to be offended at being told this but ashamed, for shame is a revolutionary emotion.

Playing on the word "seer" as a synonym for prophet, Winstanley explains that "that man or woman that sees the Spirit, within themselves . . . is able to make a Sermon, because they can speak by experience of the light . . . within them." Since those who see and speak from experience are true prophets, Adam, "that they say lived on earth about 6000 years ago," cannot be blamed for bringing misery, for he is an inward impulse "which kils or surpresses *Abel*," who is a type of Jacob, who is a type of Christ, who is a type of all free people. Cain said, "Thou hast set a mark upon me, and every one that sees me, wil kil me," and yet there were no other people in the world except Adam and Eve. Cain's reference to sight shows the Genesis story as a parable of an inner conflict. Therefore this figurative Adam is "the causer of all your sorrow and tears," not the supposed historical first man. All men and women "hath eaten the *forbidden fruit*, by delighting . . . more in the objects of the

Creation, then in the Spirit; for the Spirit is the seed, the Creation is the fruit." If people delight more in the objects of the earth, to please themselves than in feelings of love for others, then they eat of the forbidden fruit; they "take the Apple, and become naked and ashamed." Such feelings of shame create sorrow and trouble in their hearts; they run and hide themselves, and run preaching and praying and sheltering themselves in a congregation, and so "sow the figge-leaves" of their own observing forms, for the sight of themselves is their hell.

By turning the story of the Fall into what we might call a contemporary psychodrama, Winstanley distances the reader from historical illusion and shocks him into new awareness. As a true poet he understands the Bible as a metaphorical history, not as a literal record. So to him "*Adams* innocency is the time of child-hood," but soon each person reaches a point where, like Adam, he must choose between light and darkness, reason and selfishness. Everyone, at first, chooses selfishly, but sooner or later the sun of righteousness rises within, "and as the curse is seen and felt within, so the blessing of freedom and life, must rise up, and be seen and felt within." Knowledge is a matter of perception, of having the veils of selfishness stripped away until people see things clearly, wholly, rationally. "Therefore let not your blind guides deceive you any longer; Doe not look beyond your selves to *Adam,* a man that died 6000 years agoe, though they bid you; but look upon *Adam* within your self." In stressing that people are what they see, Winstanley exemplifies the "new man" of seventeenth-century England. As a non-university-educated tradesman gone bankrupt, he offers a representative picture of the effects of literacy on the unschooled. He perfectly encapsulates the way literacy bestowed on the autodidact the ability to extend one of his senses, sight, which in turn enabled him to develop "perspective" in both the literal and figurative sense. His works offer a McLuhanish example of the change from aural to typographical culture, but this involves much more than the passive reflection of a message in an existing medium.[1] To understand Winstanley's pamphlets is to understand the transformation of the social relations between the artist and his audience that takes place when people become readers rather than listeners.

John Foxe taught that printing was miraculously invented to consummate the reformation of the church.[2] Winstanley is the first "hired laborer" to communicate his ideas to other working people through the printed page. No non-university-educated Englishman before him published as much as he did under his own name. His pamphlets are not just transcribed speeches or sermons; they are written with full consciousness that they are to be read in private. This drastically affects the way Winstanley writes. His emphasis on the act of seeing, for example, continually calls attention to the words on the page. His images repeatedly force the reader to visualize, in his mind's eye, the object of his thoughts. When he writes: "And here you may see the deceit of imagination and fleshly wisdom and learning; it teaches you to look altogether upon a history without you, of things that were done 6000 years agoe, and of things that were done 1649 years agoe," the words "see" and "look," drawing attention to the act of perception, lead inevitably to the inner light: to study one age and then another in search of truth is the same as traveling from one land to another in search of peace, for truth and peace are to be found "within the heart, not without . . . *The Kingdome of heaven . . . is within you*"; therefore, people may "Goe read all the books in your Universitie, that tels you what hath been formerly, and though you can make speeches of a day long from these readings yet you shall . . . encrease in sorrow till your eyes return into your selves, and the spirit come from on high to make you read in your own book your heart." A frightening ambivalence about typographic culture underlies these lines. Moving from the aural medium of the sermon to the visual one of print, Winstanley tries to make the printed page convey a message in a way most people had not yet internalized. Repetitions and circumlocutions, though quite effective and even necessary in the sermon, are distracting and annoying in print. Just as Dürer saw that the woodcut had a different effect on the viewer than the painting, Winstanley realizes that the printed word's power to focus on discursive thought differs from the sermon's static reaffirmation of existing ideas and institutions and enables the writer to point up the need for change. But he also understands that the book gains its ability to telescope space and increase the possibility for innovative thought by sacrificing the social cohesiveness of the sermon. Caught in this ambiguity, he sees that the book changes the way people think, the way they look at the world, and with his rhetorical questions and vivid visual images he attempts to use this chief tool of typographic culture to further the quest for a new social order.

Why are poor despised men and women afraid to deal with middleclass tradesmen? "Because these single hearted ones are made to look into themselves, wherein they can read the work of the whole Creation, and see that History seated within themselves; they can see the mystery of Righteousnesse." The analogue here is Revelation 10:9-11 where the seer eats the book given him by the mighty angel whose face was like the sun, the *sol iustitiae*. In Winstanley's prophetic world everything would be turned right side up again. As it is, "now those that are called Preachers, and great professours that runs a hearing, seeks for knowledge abroad in Sermons, in books and Universities, and buyes it for money . . . and then delivers it out again for money . . . And those men that speak from an inward testimony of what they have seen . . . are called by these buyers and sellers, Locusts, factious, blasphemers, and what not." Now "the whole world wanders after the Beast, and though the people . . . doe see that their Preachers are blinde guides . . . yet they are ashamed and afraid to disown them, O great bondage under the devils." Thus the division between rich and poor, educated and uneducated, is also a division between those who read books and those who read the book within them in light of the book of nature, between those who live by intellectualization, the letter, and those who live by feeling, the spirit: "Nay let me tel you, That the poorest man, that sees his maker, and lives in the light, though he could never read a letter in the book, dares throw the glove to al the humane learning in the world, and declare the deceit of it." Using their own means of disseminating knowledge, Winstanley turns the tables on the university-trained ministers and writes an anti-book, a book to destroy exclusive reliance on humane learning, on tradition, formal logic, and discursive reason. Book learning "doth bewitch & delude man-kinde in spiritual things, yet it is that great Dragon, that hath deceived all the world, for it draws men from knowing the Spirit, to own bare letters, words and histories for spirit." Like many other middle-class renegades, Winstanley objectifies and universalizes his ambivalence about his class betrayal. Living in the middle-class entrepreneurial society of the freehold farmer in his native Wigan, then in the overwhelmingly literate society of London tradesmen, and now in the marginally literate agricultural society of Kingston-on-Thames, brought home to him the contradictions in his own class background. It was one thing to be able to read and write in urban London; it was quite another in rural Wigan and Kingston where people marveled that a literate man guilty of murder could get off with a small brand on the hand.[3]

As one of the first to see the relationship between capitalist economic relations and typographic culture, Winstanley understands the objectification that occurs when people rely on print as the main source of information, and he directly relates this to the alienation (Blake calls it Urizen), that takes place between buyer and seller in the marketplace and worker and employer in the shop. Since the scriptures are not a literal history of events but a metaphorical record of experience, the Bible is a parable of the conflicts seen and felt within. The phrase "seen within" is used sixteen times in two pages to invoke inner conflicts. The sun of righteousness, who draws all things into himself, reconciles these conflicts. And since the seed of this sun is (like Blake's Los), found within everyone, there is no need to look to heaven for their resolution, "for what glory soever you shal be capable of to see with your eyes . . . is but the breakings forth of that glorious power that is seated within for the glory of the Father is not without him, but it is all within . . . All that glory which declares heaven, is seen within." And hell and sorrow are seen within. The sunny seed of Abraham within will "burn up that serpent, and deliver the Creation from that burden."

Having established that heaven and hell are inner states, Winstanley examines that alienation everyone experiences. In a state of "troubled conscience," each man is an island, alone unto himself, turning "every thing into gall and worm-wood to terrifie himself, thinking every bush to be a devil to torment him, he saies, he sees fearfull shapes without; but they arise from the anguish of his tormenting conscience within." This transformational experience, primarily internal, may not be apparent to others: "Let a man lie upon his sick bed, and to the view of others the chamber is quiet, yet he saith, he seeth devils, and flames, and misery, and torments." These may be figments of the imagination, but they are real nonetheless. For the appearance of these visions signifies the desire to be released from inner conflict, and while the expunging of these demons may not be pleasant, it is better than allowing the conflicts to remain hidden. The important thing is to bring "the appearance or risings up of unrighteous flesh to its own view," to make what is hidden and latent visible and active. In the "dark condition" a man is "tormented by visible bodies of fury, and ugly shapes," which are "all the creatures of his own making." So he sees "snakes, scorpions, toads, devils in bodily shapes, and flames of fire," but these apparitions are of his own making—"and this is hell." Therefore, after death it is senseless to say a person is in heaven or hell, for "the senses of the body are not sensible of either such," and if there is no sense experience there can be no awareness of pleasure or pain. If there is "a local place of hell, as the Preachers say there is . . . time will make it manifest but as yet none ever came from the dead to tell men on earth, and till then, men ought to speak no more than they know." "What I speak," Winstanley assures his readers, "I speak from what I have in some measure seen within me."

And he now exhibits the maturation of the seed of the sun of righteousness he has seen within him. To do this he poses the following conundrum: "is not hell the execution of Justice? And is not God the Authour of that wrath?" And if these things are true, is not evil part of God's nature since he created all things and has the power to control them? To answer these questions Winstanley chastizes a "Universitie man" who preached that God is the author of human misery and punishes people for their sins. This man, with a "multitude of words, darkened knowledge mightily," but the true answer is simple. In the Bible the name of God is a synonym for the magistrate, the devil, and the sun of righteousness. Only the last truly describes God. The first merely refers to the government or ruling power at any given time; the second is simply a rationalization for unreasonable deeds people are made to see "by the light of the Sun of Righteousnesse . . . for all mens sorrows are but the risings up of their own works against themselves." The sun of righteousness is truly just, for he gives man free will, and he "arises up, and lets man in his light to see himself to be a devil." The illustration is emblematic: "If a man have sore eyes, and look in the Sun, his eyes smart; now that smart comes not from the Sun, but from the venome of the eyes rises up & torments it self, when the Sun causes it to see or feel it self." The alchemical sun of righteousness, by shining forth and burning in his brightness, consumes the dross of the flesh. Like Blake's little black boy, those purged by the cleansing sun learn to bear the beams of love and "stand before the righteous Law" to accept this justice from the righteous judge.[4] As he often does, Winstanley breathes new life into an old image. Following the Song of Solomon ("I *am* black, but comely," 1:5), Francis Quarles asked in 1635: "Who can indure the fierce rayes of the Sunne of Justice? Who shall not be consumed by his beames?" Far from being a "solemn recognition of the futility of man's struggle against nature,"[5] such questions imply a recognition of nature's cleansing and purifying power, for Quarles, like Winstanley, knew the answer to these rhetorical questions: one who has renounced wickedness and accepted Christ as his savior. Yet the curse of the Fall, that man must earn his bread by the sweat of his brow, suggests work performed under the skin-blackening sun, work to be avoided if possible. Winstanley turns this image right side up again by glorifying the tilling of the soil under the soul-cleansing midday sun. The class-consciousness implicit in such an inversion needs no explanation.

What of the deluge and the burning of Sodom? Were these mere accidents? Surely God did more than let humanity see its unrighteousness. Winstanley is undaunted. These calamities were caused by elemental upheavals, by nature's revulsion at man's inhuman treatment of man. "So that the risings up of waters, and the breakings forth of fire to waste and destroy, are but that curse, or the works of mans own hands." The purpose of water and fire is to preserve humanity, but if humanity misuses these elements they will rise up and destroy it. One who looks at the sun of his own free will cannot say the sun forced his eyes to smart. So, too, water and fire are not in themselves destructive; they are but the instruments of destruction caused by humanity's wanton heedlessness of nature's laws. Like Marvell, Winstanley inverts the idea that the civil wars represent the wrath of God visited upon the English people.[6] Although he does not suggest that Cromwell himself is the sun of righteousness, he sees that "when the Sun of Righteousness begins to shine into this earth, the venimous parts rise up to kill and destroy light, but in the end the flesh destroyes it self." Like Lucifer, the angel of light, a proud, unrighteous, covetous man rises up to make war on the sun of righteousness, but because of dissension in the ranks of selfish people, because they "cannot yield one to another, to preserve one another, but rise up to destroy each other in the light of the Sun: The Sun shines, and the dunghill casts up his stinking smell: The Lord he shines, and proud flesh kils one another; flesh kils but it self." The story of Job exemplifies how the sun of righteousness allows the angel of light to affect the body but not the spirit until the body is finally purged of covetousness. In this way the *sol iustitiae* will make all flesh "see it self in its own colours," and when this happens, "when the flesh doth see it self in his own beastly shapes, he will appear so deformed, so piteous a confused Chaos of miserie and shame, that the sight thereof shall be a great torment to himself." The "self-satisfying glory" in which covetous men and women now live "and seem to have rest" will become a "hell-torment." They will then see they are "not men, not Saints, but Devils and cursed enemies, even the Serpents power, that must be burned."

Winstanley never tires of stating his reliance on experience as the source of knowledge and reaffirming the need to purify language of tradition-bound constructions. The prime metaphor, the act of seeing within, enables him to stud his prose with images of sunlight and darkness, starlight and dimness. But another metaphor introduces the notion that poor people must rely on inner experience, the subconscious, an oceanlike vessel upon which one may draw buckets of perfect water forever without running dry. In the external world, wars and rumors of war will multiply; father will be against son and son against father until "zealous professours . . . wear out every one that seeks to advance Christ, by their bitternesse and oppression." Inner experience guides the poor to reject the allurements of middle-class life. The first Adam seeks "peace from wife, children, friends, riches, places of dominion over others, and from such like: But that peace that is built upon such hay and stubble-foundations, will fall and come to nothing." This first Adam seeks "peace from Sermons, Prayers, Studies, Books, Church-fellowship, and from outward Forms and Customs in Divine Worship: But that peace that is built upon this foundation of gold, silver and pretious stones, will fall and come to nothing." To be reborn one must experience total despair and return to infantile helplessness: "All creatures teats are to be dried up, that the soul can suck no refreshing milk from them, before the Lord teach it knowledge." Everyone at one time "wonders after the Beast," seeking "for new *Jerusalem*, the City of *Sion*, or Heaven, to be above the skies, in a locall place," but, in a strikingly apt simile, Winstanley notes that this is "like the seeing of a show or a mask." It is "a strange conceit" that would have people believe they can "see" something after death. "This is a fancy which your false Teachers put into your heads to please you with, while they pick your purses." People obtain knowledge of the outer world only through the five senses; out of this experience they may create a heaven within. Hypocrites resent being told these things; they grow angry and rage against those who expose them. Failing to look within, they think whatever they do is good and whoever crosses them crosses the Lord. But the sun of righteousness takes revenge on covetous pride, the serpent and dragon, and casts him out. Having seen within, one may then "look abroad with the eie of pitty and compassion." And though this inner combat causes trouble and torment for a while, when the battle between the serpent and the sun ends, everyone will enjoy the benefits of creation.

This inner battle unfolds "in a three-fold posture of war." First, "the Sacrifices under the Law" made by the spirit in types and shadows "is a distance of Cannon-shot." Second, the Father's killing of the Beast or Dragon "In the prison of Jesus Christ" is "at a closer distance closing in the Front." Third, the hand-to-hand encounter of the serpent and the sun ends by the bruising of the serpent's head "in the whole body of his Army." Before the battle is over the sun will "fire all the strong-holds of this murderer, so that he shall not have a place to keep garrison in." All will then be filled with "holy breathing," an inspiration which will take away the weariness of all external forms of religion and government so people "may find rest for the soles of their feet." The present confusion shows the dividing of times is near. Torment will end; the inner bondage of "confusion and losse" and the outer bondage of tyrannical government will expire. "Many have attained to inward freedom already, they wait upon the Lord for outward freedom, that the yoke may be taken off their backs." Opposed to these Foxean waiters are those living in comfort, deaf to the warning. "The proud and covetous hearts cry, what slavery is this? we know not what he speaks." To this he can only reply, "It is true you do not know; but they who have lesse or more attained to the resurrection of the dead know what I say; and shall rejoyce in the declaration of this power, waiting the Lords leisure with a calm silence, til he hath gathered together our brethren." The gathering together of such brethren initiated the Digger community.

The prospective members of that community must see their inner light reflected in nature, and by seeing the light in nature they will learn to see it in themselves: "To see the Divine power in the Creation-objects is sweet; but to see him ruling in the heart is sweeter." First they see the sun of righteousness "at a distance far off, as to see him in meat, drink, cloaths, friends, victories, riches, prosperity, to see him in the Sun, Moon, Stars, Clouds, Grasse, Trees, Cattle, and all the Earth." Yet this is but "to see and meet him from home." The sexual imagery of the Song of Solomon expresses the relationship best. For just as the lover needs the beloved, a man needs to be fed, and to see the sun of righteousness "in his banqueting-house," the heart, is "to be refreshed with those sweet-smelling spices . . . sweeter then the honey or the honey-comb" (cf. Psalms 19:10). Such a man, though he "be in prison, be in straits, be forsaken of all his friends in the flesh, none wil buy nor sell with him, because they count him a man of strange opinions and blasphemies, call him an Atheist . . . because he wil neither preach nor pray . . . Yet this man is not alone." He is "secret and silent" and "slow of speech . . . yet quick-sighted and Eagle-eyed" and not a sottish drone. Above all else he is able to "discern and judge others righteously, for "those that are drawn up to wait upon the Lord" are not dependent upon "outward preaching, praying, observation of forms and customs". Their eyes are turned inward.

Forging group consciousness with his readers, Winstanley knows those who see the divine power within them will understand him; to others his words will sound strangely and "draw words of reproach and slander . . . but it matters not, they cannot hurt." Those in whom the sun of righteousness rises submit patiently and quietly to his will, for those who see this sun, this "antient of daies" from Daniel's vision (7:9-14), where the original sun of righteousness sits on a fiery throne clothed in white, do not chafe "when nothing can be done abroad, either in adversity or prosperity." They know that the inner strength of the sun of righteousness "lies not in the strength of memory, calling to mind what a man hath read and heard, being able by a humane capacity to joyn things together into a method; & through the power of free utterance, to hold it forth before others, as the fashion of Students is." Like Langland, Winstanley believes "a plough man that was never bred in their Universities may do as much," and do it better than those who "take Tythes to tell a story." But the sight of the inner sun "lies in the beholding of light arising up from an inward power of feeling experience" that "continues like the Sunne in the firmament shining forth," for the feeling of joy within may as soon be separated from the law of righteousness "as the heat and light of the Sunne, can be seperated from the Sunne." The words such a person speaks are, as foretold, "good seed; wheresoever they are sown, they will spring up and bring forth fruit."[7]

Winstanley recalls his anguish and notes that what especially held him down was "the enthraldome to my own lusts." Under such bondage he could not act reasonably. Then he heard the words of one that had passed through the same condition. This sounded liberty and life to his weary soul. "I speak what I have felt in this particular," he assures his readers. So strong was his "delight . . . of the flesh" that he sought satisfaction of his envy, self-will and lust, but "in the midst of this my folly" he heard "the words of experience from some other," possibly John Everard who preached in the parish where Winstanley was married and at Putney Church, a short distance from Kingston-on-Thames. Forsaking "anger, distemper, grudging, and torment," he emerged from his trial led by "pure language," which purges the mind of illness; its operation is like "a launcing of the dead flesh that the disease may be cured." This mental "wounding is not to the ruine of the creature, but it is a medicine sent . . . to heal him." Such an operation takes away "the evil peace from the flesh, that so the created part may lie down in rest." Self-knowledge can be terrifying. One who does not know of the evil within him is placid and arrogant; one aware of the inner battle between good and evil suffers the torment of self-revelation. But once the sun of righteousness wins, a "man is carried on with much joy and sweet calmness, meeknesse and moderation, and is full of glory."

The divine power emanating from the sun of righteousness "is called a tree or a vine, because he doth not lie in one single person, but spreads himself in mankind, and every single body in whom he breaths, is but a bough or bud of the vine." This Tree of Life symbolizes the diachronic and synchronic unity of mankind. The "learned University men that despise the unlearned, are pricks of the thorn-bush, not branches of the vine." But "every single one alone in whom Christ breaths, is but a parcel of the vine . . . Even as every branch of an Apple-tree, is filled with the sap, which is the life of the whole tree." The sun of righteousness "is said to be divine, because he grows and flourishes in the time of light . . . Trees that grow in the heat of the Sun bring forth pleasant fruit . . . Therefore the Saints are called, Children of the day." Enjoying the playfulness of his imagery, Winstanley contrasts this "day-vine" with a "night-vine, which is the power of selfishnesse, or the bottomlesse pit . . . And this night-vine which I called Lord *Esau*, or fleshly man, hath filled the whole earth with darknesse (under pretense of his learning . . .) so that he is a spread tree. But he is called by the Spirit, the Thorn-bush." As may be expected, the fruit of the night-vine is "sour and bitter, and good for nothing but the dunghill . . . every bud from it, is a sharp prickle: treacherous & covetous *Judas*, is one branch from that root, and he hath risen up to a mighty great tree; for every treacherous and covetous heart, is but the buddings forth of *Judas*." The "envious Scribes & Pharisees, are other branches from the same root, & these have risen up into mighty spreading trees." Such trees "are all buddings forth of the thorn-bush, and have covered the earth with their branches, to keep it in darknesse, and to hide the Sun of Righteousnesse from it." And all this centers on the ministers, who, supported by "the standing ponds of stinking waters," the universities, spread ignorance, confusion, and bondage over all nations. By corrupting the scriptures ministers perpetuate the greatest oppression, tithe-gathering. "By the one they deceive the souls of people . . . and by the other they pick their purses." Those writings that they live by did not come from "any Schollars, according to humane art, but from Fishermen, Shepherds, Husbandmen, and the Carpenters son."

Knowing that literacy is the key to intellectual liberation, Winstanley accuses the "learned schollars" of trampling laypeople under foot so that "trades-men, and such as are not bred in schools, may have no liberty to speak or write." Eschewing self-pity, he established a rapport with "these despised ones" who "speak from experience" until they were "made to see the Father face to face in his own light." Such people, tradesmen and laborers, "shall encrease, let the Universitie men do the worst they can." And "the light of truth that springs up out of this earth, which the schollars tread under feet, will shine so clear, as it will put out the candle of those wicked learned deceivers." For "many of them that are more ingenious or subtile then the rest, seeing light arises much amongst the people, begin to comply with the people, and give people their liberty to speak as well as they, and denie the tithes," upon the condition that "people will give them a free contribution." Winstanley will have none of it. He sees this liberalism as a sham, a "deceit of the flesh, to draw people under a new bondage, and to uphold the hearsay-preaching, that in time matters may be wheeled about again, to advance the schollars, and give them the supremacy in teaching."

For all his sincere insistence on moderation and waiting upon the Lord, Winstanley's metaphoric use of the ancient wheel of fortune indicates his revolutionary leanings. As long as common people look to the ministers for truth, they will "be wrapped up in confusion and bondage." And this is why people are so ignorant and cold-spirited. "The night-Vine, or branches of the Thorn-bush, are so mighty great and thick, that they hide the light and heat of the Sun of Righteousnesse . . . This Thorn-bush or night-Vine, grows in the cold time of night, while the Sun of Righteousnesse is under the Clouds . . . and they that act from this Vine, are called children of the night." Therefore the light of the ministers, who call themselves divines, "is but a candle stoln from the Apostles and Prophets writings, it is not their own light." These "branches of the Thorn-bush, that are full of sharp pricks," bind people to them. And the corrupt magistrates crush them "if they oppose these Preachers." Yet shame will defeat the ministers, for they will find "that poor despised ones of the world . . . are the labourers that are sent forth" to tend the vineyard. The ministers have "had warning enough" and are "left without excuse; you are the men whose mouths must be stopped; not by the hand of Tyrannicall, humane power, as you have stopped the mouths of others, I abhor it." But their mouths will be stopped by "shame and sorrow."

Ever alive to the nuances of words, Winstanley looks at the meaning of "divine." Ministers "are as bad under this description, of Divines, or Diviners, witches, sorcerers, deceivers, as Balaam was." They pick the purses of the poor "by this divination and sorcerie," this skillful manipulation of language. Ministers have learned to make people believe their "words of hear-say are the testimony and experience of the spirit," but their words darken knowledge. With their "fine language" they fool some people, "but when it comes to triall, it is but a husk without the kernall; words without life."[8] If the ministers "go on selling words for money to the blind people whom" they have deceived, they will fall. For the people "have prophesies and promises in the writings of Prophets and Apostles"; they will "wait upon the Lord" until they see the fulfilling of them within themselves. Calling for "all mouths to be silent, that speak from hear-say," and for ministers to leave off their "talk about words and sillables," he closes with the injunction that what he can speak from his own experience is

that while I was a blind Professour and strict goer to Church, as they call it, and a hearer of Sermons, and never questioned what they spake, but believed as the learned Clergy (the Church) believed; and still forgot what I heard; though the words they spake were like a pleasant song to me, while I was hearing: And this I know is the condition of all your publique zealous Professours, let them say what they will, for they live in confusion, ignorance and bondage to the fleshly man.

The line about the words of the clergy being like a pleasant song indicates the ambivalence underlying Winstanley's radical quest. His concern for language is the lynch-pin of his philosophy, for once he comes to see the sun of righteousness in himself, once he comes to feel the power of life within his own breast, he becomes an heroic outcast: "my former acquaintance now begin to be afraid of me, and call me blasphemer, and a man of errors, and look upon me as a man of another world; for my own particular, my portion is fallen to me in a good ground; I have the Lord, I have enough." Having found this new freedom in the truth at the expense of his own alienation, he wishes to unite with others: "O my dear friends," he pleads, "despise not this word I speak; wait upon the Lord for teaching; you will never have rest in your souls, till he speak in you."

He asks only that his followers discover the truth within themselves; some, he knows, will be offended at his words, but "if they be, I care not." Others "may have their joy fullfilled in seeing a conjuncture of experience between me and them . . . So I rest."

In December Lilburne and Ireton resumed their debates at Whitehall. On 30 January 1649 Charles I was beheaded. Lilburne, Walwyn, Overton, and Prince were imprisoned in the Tower on 28 March. It began to appear that the revolution had been aborted by a coup d'etat. Two days later the Buckinghamshire writer published *More Light Shining in Buckingham-shire*, which uses Winstanley's device of comparing the extremism of the rich to the moderation of the poor, but lacks his subtlety and constraint. In comparison to Winstanley, the writer shows genuine power but no restraint. The style, precisely because it is so forceful and biting, emphasizes, by way of contrast, what can only be called Winstanley's poetic sensibility, evidenced in his greater depth, his ability to suggest several shades of meaning simultaneously. Winstanley's love of words highlights his moderate and in fact scholarly temperament. No one can doubt the Buckinghamshire writer's intelligence; one who perceives the economic framework of society and explains it clearly cannot be dismissed as a malcontent. But he cannot sustain an analysis. He lacks ability to gauge reader reaction to his argument, and his prose is shallow and mechanical. The reader misses the sense of being in touch with a personality that truly knows itself. The emphasis, however wellmeaning, is entirely negative and the writer's gift is for vituperation, not persuasion. Winstanley's pamphlets, on the other hand, force the reader into new awareness, and the moderation of his appeal always allows the reader room to reassess his own position. The Buckinghamshire writer's prose, although impersonal, is self-centered and alienating.

On 1 April 1649, along with William Everard and three others, Winstanley began to dig and sow the commons on St. George's Hill, seven or eight miles southwest of Kingston, Surrey, with parsnips, carrots, and beans. By 23 April the colony's number had risen to fifty, and they planned for an expansion to five thousand. Having prepared seed corn, they intended to plow up the ground in Oatland's Park, Windsor Park, and other places, and invited all to join them, promising meat, drink, and clothes for their labor. They also warned that if local people let cattle destroy their crops they would "cut off their usurping heads, and the four-footed legs." They drove this point home by reciting a jingle:

> Our thoughts are lofty, proud, and full of ire,
> We can be good, or bad, as times require.[9]

On 16 April Henry Sanders filed an alarmist complaint against the colony with the Council of State. John Bradshaw, head of the Council, forwarded Sanders' letter to General Fairfax and requested that he send troops to disperse the colony. The Council directed the Cobham Justices of the Peace to do whatever necessary to destroy the colony. On 19 April Captain John Gladman told Fairfax he found the Diggers unworthy of notice—but he asked Winstanley and Everard to report to Fairfax at Whitehall the next day. The press avidly reported the proceedings of that meeting.

Six days later, on the day the Leveller mutineer Robert Lockier was sentenced to death, the Diggers published their first manifesto: *The True Levellers Standard ADVANCED: OR, The State of Community opened, and Presented to the Sons of Men.* The main text, obviously by Winstanley, opens auspiciously with "A DECLARATION TO THE POWERS OF ENGLAND, AND TO ALL THE POWERS OF THE WORLD, shewing the cause why the common people of England have begun, and gives consent to digge up, manure, and sowe corn upon George-Hill in Surrey." Reiterating the recently published Buckinghamshire writer, Winstanley reminds his readers of the original state of perfection: "Every single man, Male and Female, is a perfect Creature of himself." Therefore if people subject their flesh to reason, they need "not run abroad after any Teacher and Ruler." Summarizing his basic epistemology, that the Spirit Reason dwells in the five senses but was corrupted and distorted by selfishness until mankind "fell into blindness of mind and weakness of heart," he tells how "selfish imagination taking possession of the Five Senses, and ruling as King in the room of Reason therein, and working with Covetousnesse, did set up one man to teach and rule over another; and thereby the Spirit was killed, and man was brought into bondage, and became a greater Slave to such of his own kind, then the Beasts of the field were to him." Nothing could more graphically prove the mastery Winstanley gained over his material than this swift and sure opening. Immediately he moves to the heart of the matter, plunging into narration with no hesitation, no maneuvering for position, no empty rhetoric, no murky meandering or self-indulgent puffery. The reader is at once drawn into an epic account of his present predicament, and like all good stories the pamphlet creates its own sense of time and space within the reader's mind. Borrowing heavily from the majestic opening of Genesis, the next sentence clears away the fog and states the essential principle:

And hereupon, The Earth (which was made to be a Common Treasury of relief for all, both Beasts and Men) was hedged in to Inclosures by the teachers and rulers, and the others were made Servants and Slaves: And that Earth that is within this Creation, made a Common Store-house for all, is bought and sold, and kept in the hands of a few, whereby the great Creator is mightily dishonored, as if he were a respector of persons, delighting in the comfortable Livelihood of some, and rejoycing in the miserable povertie and straits of others.[10]

Having firmly established this guiding principle in his earlier pamphlets, Winstanley adds depth and character to his writing by a symbolic shorthand referring back to previously developed ideas and images. For example, the pun on Adam as a dam introduces the concept of constricted freedom acting both inwardly and outwardly to fill the heart with "slavish fears of others" and to allow the body "to be imprisoned, punished and oppressed." This spiritual blinding reduces mankind to helpless dependence on external authority. The Foxean analogy between England and biblical Israel points up the fatal dependence on kingship. But just as Jeremiah prophesied liberation for the people of Israel when they renounced outward teachers and rulers, Winstanley marks that "the present state of the old World that is running up like parchment in the fire" heralds the destruction of "proud Imaginary flesh, which is the wise Serpent." Yet, though the Esau's now rule the Jacob's, the Spirit Reason promised: "The Seed out of whom the Creation did proceed, which is my Self, shall bruise this Serpents head, and restore my Creation again from this curse and bondage."

The story of Esau and Jacob typologically explains the restoration of mankind. For while Esau counts himself to be "an Angel of Light," in the light of the sun of righteousness he appears as a devil, as "*A-dam.*" Winstanley increases this dramatic effect when he challenges Esau with having oppressed the seed of Jacob throughout the three Joachite ages of mankind's birth, infancy, and childhood. Yet like watchmen in the nighttime of the world, some few have been guided by the light within them. The "Powers of *England*," have brought the common people "to a morsel of Bread" and have confounded all people by their government. In the end, just as the biblical rulers "were continually the Ocean-head, out of whose power, Burdens, Oppressions, and Poverty did flow out," the Esaus will be "drowned in the Sea of Covetousnesse." The Diggers who rise from the dust are willing to shed their blood for their cause, not "by force of Arms . . . But by obeying the Lord of Hosts, who hath Revealed himself in us, and to us, by labouring the Earth in righteousness together, to eate our bread with the sweat of our brows, neither giving hire, nor taking hire."

Winstanley asks the General Council and the New Model Army either to join the Diggers or to let them go peacefully about their work: "making the Earth a Common Treasury for All, both Rich and Poor, That every one that is born in the Land, may be fed by the Earth his Mother that brought him forth." They will provide the seed to glorify all creation and bruise the heel of "the Serpent, which is Covetousness." "Civil Propriety [private property] is the Curse" because those who have it "got it either by Oppression, or Murther, or Theft." Winstanley's language and imagery flow directly from his discovery of what is called the labor theory of value. That working people produce profit for those who do no work so outrages him that he repeatedly emphasizes the injustice inherent in a system that perpetuates it. The system itself, not the people who use it or who are used by it, is at fault. This radically affects the way he presents his argument. For example, he blames the poor almost as much for allowing themselves to be oppressed as he does the rich for oppressing them. The system engenders such inequality and hypocrisy, for "by subtile wit and power" the rich pretend to keep people safe from oppression, but in so doing, through taxes, tithes, "and other Booties, which they call their own, they get much Monies, and with this they buy Land, and become landlords; and if once Landlords, then they rise to be Justices, Rulers, and State Governours, as experience shewes."

And what is this system but "the Babylonish yoke laid upon Israel of old, under *Nebuchadnezzar*," which is analogous to the Norman Conquest.[11] The present "Kings, Lords, Judges, Justices, Bayliffs, and the violent bitter people that are Free-holders, are and have been Successively" the descendents of "The *Norman* Bastard *William* himself . . . who still are from that time to this day in pursuite of that victory, Imprisoning, Robbing, and killing the poor enslaved *English* Israelites." Here, even at his most imitative, Winstanley injects the Norman Yoke theory with a metaphoric and practical significance that the Levellers neglected. For he notes that not only do the Freeholders and Landlords choose "some very rich man, who is the Successor of the *Norman* Colonels or high Officers . . . to Establish that *Norman* power the more forcibly over the enslaved *English*, and to beat them down again, when as they gather heart to seek for Liberty," not only do they make laws that are "Cords, Bands, Manacles, and Yokes that the enslaved *English*, like *Newgate* Prisoners, wears upon their hands and legs as they walk the streets," and not only do "the powers of *England* . . . pretend to throw down that *Norman* yoke, and . . . yet . . . hold the People as much in bondage, as the Bastard Conquerour himself," but they do not see "it was not thus from the Beginning." Taking the present state of things as somehow "natural" and unchangeable, they refuse to acknowledge the possibility of returning to a previous Edenic life where private property did not exist. Winstanley understands that language presupposes a mythology, that words are meant to relate experience, not just convey information. And while the Norman Yoke theory may be doubtful history, its use shows he understands the need to explain the past and to make it meaningful.

Just how powerfully this idea motivates Winstanley's radicalism is evident from his insistence that "It was shewed us by Vision in Dreams, and out of Dreams, That [St. George's Hill] should be the Place we should begin upon." As Christopher Hill points out, had the Diggers simply wished to start a commune, to live together as a family and grow their own food, they could have picked arable land in a remote area; there they could have gone about their business unmolested. Instead they picked a spot near London with a long radical tradition where they had access to the publishing industry. They knew they would attract the attention of the press, and they intended to use that press themselves. Second, they were "within easy reach of any poor man there who might be interested in the colony."[12] And third, they deliberately chose land that was "very barren" to emphasize "That all the Prophecies, Visions, and Revelations of Scriptures, of Prophets, and Apostles, concerning the calling of the Jews, the Restauration of Israel; and making of that People, the Inheritors of the whole Earth; doth all seat themselves in this Work." In other words, they did everything they could to play up the symbolic aspects of the experiment. Winstanley knew the increasingly oppressive and intolerable conditions surrounding the civil wars called for a reinterpretation of history—for a "new" mythology, which is always a return to the "old" mythology of man's relationship to nature. Unwilling to live in a world of war, poverty, and degradation, he understood that people's desire to escape to a time and place where life is simpler and safer—a desire to look at the past as an oblique utopia—also represents the need to believe in the future. Therefore, seeing the setting up of the Digger community as a symbolic act does not imply that it represented a childish wish to evade real responsibilities or escape into a fantasy world of the past.

Unlike Hobbes, Winstanley was not interested in writing a philosophical treatise on the causes and consequences of the civil wars; he wanted, rather, to revitalize what scientist Jacques Monod calls "the ancient animist covenant between man and nature.[13] Using key biblical texts, he revives the theory of a communistic community "supprest by covetous proud flesh . . . the powers that ruled the world." He looks forward to the day when the "pure waters of *Shiloe*, the Well Springs of Life and Liberty" will "over-run *A-dam*, and drown those banks of Bondage, Curse, and Slavery." This, he believes, is the meaning of the voice that spoke to him when he was in a trance. This, more than anything else, gives him the audacity to act on his belief that "The Earth is the Lords, that is, Mans, who is Lord of the Creation." And like all those who believe they act not out of personal motives but out of unselfish universal need, Winstanley says he has the right to enforce his vision for the good of all. His newly discovered sense of shared suffering supports his belief: "we have peace in our hearts, and quiet rejoycing in our work, and filled with sweet content, though we have but a dish of roots and bread for our food."

Resolved to give all he has "to buy this Pearl which we see in the Field," reason assures him "that Bondage shall be removed, Tears wiped away, and all poor People by their righteous Labours shall be relieved, and freed from Poverty and Straits." Moreover, "if there was no Begger in literal Israel, there shall be no Begger in Spiritual Israel the Anti-type." He insists that, as in the time of Christ, priests and professors lead people away from their natural worship by substituting "Sacrifices and Types . . . Forms and Customs" for true spontaneous exaltation of man and nature. Everyone now "Preacheth for money, Counsels for money, and fights for money to maintain particular Interests . . . So that the earth stinks with their Hypocrisie, Covetousness, Envie, sottish Ignorance, and Pride." They observe the letter but not the spirit of scripture; they obey the form but not the substance of the law; they pay attention to the outer shell of words but know nothing of their inner kernel because they completely divorce words from deeds. The people therefore "wait and wait for good, and for deliverances, but none comes." While waiting they are whipped with "old Popish weather-beaten Laws . . . to be standing pricks in our eys,.and thorns in our side." Were taxes distributed to the soldiers instead of being "too much bagd up in the hands of particular Officers and Trustees, there would be less complaining." Yet Winstanley knows this will be rejected; the "A-dams of the Earth," who have "rich Clothing, full Bellies . . . Honors and Ease . . . puffe at this," but "the day of Judgement is begun, and it will reach to thee ere long . . . the poor people whom thou oppresses, shall be the Saviours of the land."

This first Digger pamphlet concludes with two key tropes: the Foxean analogy between biblical Israel and contemporary England and the ancient alchemical doctrine of the marriage between Mother Earth and the sun. To honor them, people must first respect the seed of the sun of righteousness in every living person, "which is the Spirit of Community," and second, they must not "hinder the Mother Earth, from giving all her Children suck, by thy Inclosing it into particular hands." The rich may best obey all the commandments by letting Israel go free so "the poor may labour the Waste land, and suck the Breasts of their mother Earth, that they starve not." Winstanley does not entreat the rich to do this, for they "art not to be intreated." Instead he commands them and warns against continued oppression, not because the poor will resist them by force of arms, but because they will "make thee weary, and miserably ashamed." The Diggers have "no intent of Tumult or Fighting, but only to get Bread to eat." And if any of "the great Ones of the Earth" are unable to work but are willing to turn their private property over to the Diggers, Winstanley promises "we will work for you, and you shall receive as we receive." But if they "endeavour to Oppose," then "this Conquest over thee shall be got, *not by Sword or Weapon, but by my Spirit saith the Lord of Hosts.*"

This was wise advice indeed, for after Cromwell and Fairfax defeated the Leveller regiments at Burford on 14 May, poor people had no chance of winning a stronger voice in the government by force of arms. The fact that Winstanley's pamphlets show no sudden shift from mysticism to materialism or from millenarianism to communism testifies to his political acumen. Digger pamphlets such as *A Declaration from the Poor Oppressed People of England*, published just five days after Fairfax visited the colony on 26 May, show no break in either continuity or style. For although this pamphlet may not be entirely by Winstanley, it illustrates how he sharpened his words and refined his message while working with the Diggers so that key motifs could get iconoclastic ideas across swiftly and surely. The Digger colonists have now become suns of righteousness, representatives of their Father, Reason, the sun-god. The mound of St. George's Hill has become the breast of the great Mother who suckles her young with the fruits of the earth. Obeying "the inward law of Love," the colonists challenge the landlords to give up private property: "for though you and your Ancestors got your Propriety by murther and theft, and you keep it by the same power from us . . . yet we shall have no occasion of quarreling." Reaching back to More's *Utopia* and popular alchemical lore, and anticipating Marx's famous comment on Shakespeare's *Timon of Athens*, Winstanley argues that since "Money is but part of the Earth," it belongs equally to all as part of the "common treasury" that Mother Earth was made to be.[14]

The King's image on money symbolizes the tyranny of private property, the desire of his class to have exclusive rights to Mother Earth. The rich, like selfish children jealous of their mother's milk, wish to keep their childish satisfactions well into adulthood. The desire for private property is an extension of the childhood wish to monopolize the mother. Therefore Winstanley's wish that all "people shall live freely in the enjoyment of the Earth" is a desire for psychological as well as economic liberation. All men and women may become suns of righteousness and have equal rights to enjoy Mother Earth: "they shall buy Wine and Milk, without Money, or without price, as *Isaiah* speaks. For after our work of the Earthly community is advanced, we must make use of Gold and Silver, as we do of other mettals, but not to buy and sell." When all "have food and rayment from the Earth, their Mother," all will be equal. In Winstanley's poetic history, "since the power of the Sword began to rule," men set themselves up as gods; they usurped the role of the Father and took control of the Mother, but "that Government that is got over people by the Sword, and kept by the Sword, is not set up by the King of Righteousness to be his Law, but by Covetousness." This impotent sword may kill but not nurture. It has no seed. But the Diggers "labor the Earth, to cast in Seed" and bring forth abundance to be shared equally by all. Therefore if those who live by the sword will not join them, the Diggers wish to be left alone and allowed to use the trees growing on the commons. These trees stand in opposition to the landlords' swords. The swords destroy; the trees save. The swords are individually owned and kept; the trees are communally owned and shared. The jealous swords hinder the poor; the fruitful trees help them. The swords are artificial and subject to rust; the trees reproduce themselves naturally and provide shade in the summer and warmth in the winter. The sword, like the land, "is kept in your hands by murder, and theft." But the Diggers mean to take land by moving the spirit within, "and not from our Swords, which is an abominable, and unrighteous power, and a destroyer of the Creation." Since "*England*, the land of our Nativity, is to be a common Treasury," the trees should belong to the people, not be cut and sold "by the murdering and cheating law of the sword." Such is the drama Winstanley sees being enacted on St. George's Hill, a drama that shows no break between pre- and post-Digger activities. For the colony is not just an attempt to put preconceived principles into action; it is an experiment in living, an effort to reach back to the origins of consciousness and forward to the frontiers of knowledge.

On 9 June, Winstanley sent Fairfax a thirteen-page letter. Believing he has found a kindred spirit of "mildnesse and moderation," he lays bare his belief that the Digger community is playing out its role as protagonist in the "pitched battaile between the Lamb and the Dragon." The Dragon strives to lock and hide the glory of creation from mankind while the Lamb labors to unfold its secrets. The enclosing landlords represent elder brothers; the Diggers, as younger brothers, wish only for the elder brothers to become moderate. They are not against obeying the law, but they find no use for it in their commune. They ask only to be left alone to live in peace: "we shall honor our Father, the Spirit that gave us our being. And we shall honor our Mother the earth, by labouring her in righteousnesse, and leaving her free from oppression and bondage." A further difference between the left-hand man and the right-hand man is represented by the higher powers of the five senses as opposed to the five "well springs of life . . . understanding, will, affections, joy, and peace." By obeying the left-hand man, people may "walk in the light of reason," the *sol iustitiae*, who "sits upon this five cornered Throne." Then people may be strengthened by the five well-springs represented by the right-hand man so they may feel "the light and power of the Son of righteousnesse within"; with "the righteous Law written in our hearts" the Diggers need no other. Winstanley asks not for protection but for understanding. Some soldiers quartered near St. George's Hill mercilessly beat a man and boy and took their clothes. For this he asks not that the soldiers be punished—only that the Diggers be left in peace "according to the Law of contract between you and us, That we that are younger brothers, may live comfortably in the Land of our Nativity, with you the elder brothers." Since the Diggers do not attempt to take private property by force, they wish for nothing more than to be left alone while they "indeavour to hold forth the Sun of righteousnesse in their actions." They ask only that the rulers live up to their bargain and submit to the sun of righteousness "in whose name you have made all your Covenants, Oaths, and promises to us: I say unto him we appeal, who is and will be our righteous Judge." To support his case Winstanley lists ten questions challenging the supposed historical and political basis of the Norman Yoke. In short, he asks why the civil wars were fought and the king executed if not "to return into freedom again, without respecting persons, or els what benefit shall the common people have (that have suffered most in these wars) by the victory that is got over the King?" He suggests it would have been better had the common people not fought to free themselves than to live impoverished and made worse than they were before. If common people are only free to work for hire, "what freedom then have they in England, more than we can have in Turkie or France?"

Finally Winstanley addresses seven questions to the ministers to show that the Diggers speak for moderation and that the ministers "are rebells to their Maker, and enemies to the Creation." Here, for the first time, he explicitly equates the Fall with private property: when Adam "consented to that serpent covetousnesse, then he fell from righteousnesse, was cursed, and was sent into the earth to eat his bread in sorrow: And from that time began particular propriety." Using the typological example of Cain and Abel, he demands to know "whether all wars, blood-shed, and misery came not upon the Creation, when one man indeavoured to be a lord over another?" Does not the work of restoration lie in casting the serpent, covetousness, out of heaven (mankind), so people may live in the light of the sun of righteousness? Is the sun of righteousness a *"re-specter of persons,* yea, or no?" It was covetousness since the Fall, not the Fall itself, "that made that difference"; therefore, covetousness is not part of an unchangeable human nature, and there will be no true peace until everyone acts upon "the Law of universall righteousnesse." Human laws give the gentry and the ministers the right to rule over the common people, but Winstanley asks only that "all of you seriously in love and humility . . . consider of this businesse of publike community, which I am carried forth in the power of love . . . to advance as much as I can." Knowing he is "called fool, mad man, and have many slanderous reports cast upon me, and meet with much fury from some covetous people," he remains patient and feels guarded by joy and peace. "I hate none," he dis-armingly declares; "I love all, I delight to see every one live comfortably. I would have none live in poverty, straits or sorrows." His final task is not just to restore the pre-Norman state, "No, that is not it"; rather, he expects that a restoration of the pristine state of nature that existed before the Fall, when mankind lived in the light of the sun of righteousness, will hasten the coming of the New Jerusalem.

On 11 June a pack of men dressed in women's clothing beat four Diggers senseless; one nearly died. On the same day Winstanley dashed off an account of this brutal attack: *A Declaration of the Bloudie and Un-christian Acting of William Star and John Taylor of Walton.* The at-tackers' assumption of women's dress justifies his earlier distinction between masculine and feminine powers. The townsmen could not attack as men because that would have been a tacit admission of their own fear and the Diggers' equality. Assuming the dress of women disguised their individual identities but allowed them to act out their true group identity as men who corrupt and hold the feminine side of human nature in bon-dage, men who must destroy any attempt to show equality with women. The Diggers, after all, presented a potential threat to male-dominated society. Recognition of that threat was tantamount to agreement that masculine aggressiveness, selfishness, egocentricity, belligerance, ac-quisitiveness, toughmindedness, and ruthlessness were necessary for capitalist survival and that feminine sharing, loving, giving, yielding, helping, caring, and nurturing were in need of subjection. The towns-men's assumption of women's clothing was a cowardly refusal to deal with the Diggers on their own terms. "Every one," Winstanley notes, "that seems to prevaile over another, saies, God gave him the victory, though his conquest be tyranny over his brother."

Exactly a month later, on 11 July, the Diggers published *AN APPEAL to the House of COMMONS, Desiring their ANSWER; Whether the*

Common-People shall have the quiet enjoyment of the Commons *and* Waste Lands; *Or whether they shall be under the will of* Lords *of* Mannors *still.* The lines on the title page state:

> Unrighteous Oppression kindles a flame;
> but Love, Righteousness and
> Tenderness of heart quenches it again.[15]

The pamphlet, written after Winstanley and two others were arrested for trespassing, reiterates the Norman Yoke theory, declaring that "since the fall of man" the land has been fought over until "the teeth of all Nations hath been set on edge by this sour grape, the covetous murdering sword." Even the best of laws, the Magna Charta, "are yoaks and manicles, tying one sort of people to be slaves to another."[16] The ministers and gentry are free, but common people are still "like the *Israelites* under the *Egyptian* Task-masters." Since Charles has been cast out, Parliament should "cast out all those enslaving laws, which was the Tyrannical power that the Kings prest us down by." As a skillful debater, Winstanley shifts the burden of proof upon his opponents, but instead of berating and angering them, he allows them a way out. He asks Parliament not to shut its "eyes against the light, darken not knowledg, by dispute about particular mens priviledges, when universal freedom is brought to be tried before you, dispute no further when truth appears, but be silent, and practise it." Courageously, he pleads, "stop not your ears against the secret mourning of the oppressed, under these expressions, lest the Lord see it, and be offended, and shut his ears against your cries, and work a deliverance for his waiting people some other way then by you." This is brilliant rhetorical strategy. Understanding the importance of Foxe, Winstanley knows how preciously the members of the Rump hold the belief that they are God's instruments. He merely asks them to live up to their promises. "You swore in your National Covenant to endevour a Reformation according to the Word of God." And what does this mean if not "to restore us to that Primitive freedom in the earth . . . for this is the Reformation according to the Word of God before the fall of man." Are they just interested in manipulating symbols and covering their greed with vague rhetoric? Are things really going to change, or have the common people, for all their sacrifices, merely substituted one set of rulers for another? If Parliament will not grant common people freedom to work the land, "you will pull the blood and cries of the poor oppressed upon your heads." The poor will never trust their words again, for just as Parliament did not trust the King because he failed to keep his word, poor people will not trust Parliament if it fails to restore the common land.

"For our parts," Winstanley ironically adds, "we are sorry to hear the muttering of the people against you."

Winstanley reveals his passionate concern for language in his final paragraphs. First, he laments: "O that there were a heart in you to consider of these things, and act righteousnesse, how sweetly might you and the people live together: If you grant this freedom we speak of, you gain the hearts of the Nation; if you neglect this, you will fall as fast in their affections as ever you rise: I speak what I see, and do you observe; slight not that love that speaks feelingly, from the sence of the Nations burdens." Here the desire to convince, to win over, is everywhere apparent. "Surely," he pleads, "if these Lords and Free-holders have their Inclosures established to them in peace, is not that freedom enough? Must they needs have the Common-land likewise?" Do the members of Parliament wish to be like Ahab and "eat the bread out of the poores mouthes?" If they maintain that the lords of manors will be lords of the common land, then they "pull the guilt of King *Charles* his blood upon their own heads; for then it will appear to the view of all men, That you cut off the Kings head, that you might establish your selves in his Chair of Government, and that your aym was not to throw down Tyranny, but the Tyrant."[17] In a dexterous argumental ploy, Winstanley begs: "Let it not be said . . . , That the Gentry of England assembled in Parliament, proved Covenant-breakers . . . to God, and the Common people, after their own turn was served; and killed the King for his power and government, as a thief kils a true man for his money." But he immediately adds: "I do not say you have done so." The restoration of the common land to the people will ensure peace because private property can be held only by the sword: "Here we see who are thieves and murderers; even the buyers and sellers of land, with her fruits, these are they that take away another mans right from him; and that overthrowes righteous propriety, to uphold particular property." The Norman laws William the Conqueror brought into England robbed people of their land. And those very laws were "written in the *Norman* and *French* tongue"; then the Kings appointed Normans to expound and interpret those laws, "and appointed the *English* people to pay them a Fee for their paines, and from hence came in the trade of Lawyers" who created a closed legal system so that "no man should plead his own cause, but those Lawyers should do it for them." Controversies could no longer be settled locally and quietly, but had to be tried at Westminster. Thus, just as the ministers distort scripture to control man spiritually, the lawyers concoct laws to control him materially. Language is the tool by which the ruling class manipulates the poor.[18]

After moving from St. George's Hill to Cobham Heath, Winstanley prefaced *A WATCH-WORD to the City of London and the ARMIE,* dated 26 August, with his best lines to date:

> When these clay-bodies are in grave, and children
>   stand in place,
> This shews we stood for truth and peace and
>   freedom in our days;
> And true born sons we shall appear of England
>   that's our mother,
> No Priests nor Lawyers wiles t'embrace, their
>   slavery we'll discover.[19]

A heartrending address to the City of London declares: "I am one of thy sons by freedome" who, "by thy cheating sons in the theeving art of buying and selling . . . was beaten out both of estate and trade, and forced to accept of the good will of friends." And because of taxes and the free-quartering of soldiers, "my weak back found the burthen heavier then I could bear." Even though during the last eight years he has "been willing to lay out what my Talent was, to procure Englands peace inward and outward," he found, even among those with whom he worked, only enemies. Although his heart was filled with sweet thoughts, some people could not bear his words. But a "voice within" bade him declare his revelation, "That the earth shall be made a common Treasury of livelihood to whole mankind, without respect of persons." And he "was made to write a little book called, *The new Law of righteousnesse.*" Even though he obeyed this divine afflatus, his mind was not at rest "because nothing was acted, and thoughts run in me, that words and writings were all nothing, and must die, for action is the life of all, and if thou dost not act, thou dost nothing." With this leap, equal to the original revelation itself, Winstanley took his "spade and went and broke the ground upon *George-hill* in Surrey."

As soon as he had done this, he was arrested. And, like Bunyan's imprisonment and Blake's trial for sedition, Winstanley's confrontation with the Kingston authorities heightened his awareness of the meaning of freedom; it also affected his style. Ever aware of linguistic manipulation, he knows the question is: freedom for whom to do what? Promises were made of freedom, but with the common enemy gone,

> you are all like men in a mist, seeking for freedom, and know not where, nor what it is: and those of the richer sort of you that see it, are ashamed and afraid to owne it, because it comes clothed in a clownish garment, and open to the best language that scoffing *Ishmael* can afford, or that railing *Rabsheka* can speak, or furious

Pharaoh can act against him; for freedom is the man that will turn the world upside downe, therefore no wonder he hath enemies.

The men of the City may assure themselves that if they do not begin to act upon "the right point of freedome . . . you will wrap up your children in greater slavery then ever you were in." As long as the poor are enslaved the rich will never be free. Since he no longer defines himself by the needs and desires of civil society, since he has rejected the ruling class's ideology, Winstanley freely defines his relationship to it and to others on his own terms. He knows "every one talks of freedome, but there are but few that act for freedome, and the actors for freedome are oppressed by the talkers and verball professors of freedome." For true freedom "lies in the community in spirit, and community in the earthly treasury." Citing, as Lilburne often did, Coke's *Institutes*, he prints the defense he was not allowed to present when he refused to hire a lawyer: "Mr. *Drake* [Winstanley's accuser] . . . is a Parliament man, therefore a man counted able to speak rationally." As such, he should understand that "the plain truth is, theeves and murderers, upheld by preaching witches and deceivers, rule the Nations: and for the present, the Laws and Government of the world, are Laws of darknesse, and the divells Kingdome, for covetousnesse rules all."

Here Winstanley reaches a watershed. Now that he has passed from thought to action, from theory to practice, he sees he has been naive. Priests, lawyers, and bailiffs are "servants to *Belzebub*," for even though the King has been cast out, they will never willingly forsake their privileges: "their Prisons, Whips, and Gallows are the torments of this Hell." Having felt the naked sword of ruling power upon his neck, having exposed the hypocrisy of the new government, and having stripped away the veil of false promises, he freely chastises the living embodiment of this covetous power that countenances "murder and theft in them that maintaines his Kingdom by the sword of Iron, and punishes it in others: and so that which is called a sin in the Common people, if they act such things, is counted no sin in the action of Kings, because they have the power of the sword in their hands." Though the king is dead, kingly power is still abroad in the land, "and those that doe imprison, oppresse and take away the livelihood of those that rise up to take Possession of this purchased freedome, are Traitors to this Nation, and Enemies to righteousnesse: And of this number are those men that have arrested, or that may arrest the Diggers." Still willing to "waite with patience on the Lord, to see who he blesses," he concludes:

> Covetous might may overcome rationall right for a time,
> But rationall right must conquer covetous might,

> and that's the life of mine
> The Law is righteous, just and good,
>   when Reason is the rule,
> But who so rules by the fleshly will,
>   declares himself a foole.

The fate of the four cows he was hired to tend dramatizes his persecution and directs the reader's attention toward those issues Winstanley
wants him to consider. When the bailiff's men came to arrest him he was
not at home so they took what they thought were his cows; "strangers"
eventually "rescued" the cows and returned them. But before they did,
Winstanley, hearing of the lost cows, turned himself over to the bailiff
and asked him to release the cows. The bailiff said he did not want his
body but his property. Winstanley said the cows were not his property,
but he was turned away. As he walked home he pondered his predicament and addressed his thoughts to the sun of righteousness. He decided
to live on bread and beer until his innocence was proven and poor people
set free. He recalled his earlier revelation and reassured himself that he
never read it or heard it anywhere, that he did not try to bring it about or
imagine it; he knows he is incapable of such self-delusion. He still feels
the power of love between people attracting him to them and them to
him, even his enemies—those who try to make him a beggar. He wonders
why since his revelation, as he has spoken and acted the truth, he is
hated, reproached, and oppressed at every turn, especially by the clergy.
He laments that England would rather fight with the "Sword of Iron"
than the "Sword of the Spirit." He does not pretend to understand all that
has happened, is happening, or will happen; as he walked along he says
he felt like a man caught in a storm who stands under a shelter upon a hill
waiting for the torrent to subside.

Abruptly he breaks off and returns to "the Dragons Den, or Hornets
nest, the selfish murdering fleshly Lawes of this Nation, which hangs
some for stealing, and protects others in stealing." But again the cows are
the objective correlative: "they took away the Cowes which were my
livelyhood, and beat them with their clubs, that the Cowes heads and
sides did swell, which grieved tender hearts to see: and yet these Cowes
never were upon *George* Hill, nor never digged upon that ground, and
yet the poore beasts must suffer because they gave milk to feed me." Yet
the cows were delivered out of the devil's hands and spared the torments
of hell. In contrast to the cows, the bailiffs in the "*Norman* Camp,"
depicted as "snapsack boyes" and "ammunition sluts," secretly try to unseat the New Model Army and "get the foot fast in the stirrup" to "lift
themselves again into the *Norman* saddle." They intend to sell the cows
to pay his fine and to "victuall the Camp" and pay for the sack and to-
bacco the officers bought at the White Lion tavern on 24 August while

plotting the Diggers' destruction. The freeholders own words condemn them: "if the cause of the diggers stand, we shall lose all our honour and titles, and we that have had the glory of the earth shall be of no more account then those slaves our servants and younger brothers that have been footstools to us . . . ever since the *Norman William* . . . took this land (not by love) but by a sharp sword." Grasping the importance of dramatization, Winstanley invents a dialogue between him and the freeholders. The freeholders naively ask: "do we not deserve the price of some of the diggers Cows to pay us for this our good service?" Winstanley asks in return: "doth the murderers sword make any man to be Gods anointed?" The sun of righteousness within each man and woman judges this debate and rules that the gentry cannot win, for "though you should kill my body or starve me in prison, yet know, that the more you strive, the more troubles your hearts shall be filled with." They will lose their "Kingdome of darknesse" even though they destroy "the poor Cowes that is my living," and throw him in prison:

Alas! you poor blind earth mouls, you strive to take away my livelihood, and the liberty of this poor weak frame my body of flesh, which is my house I dwell in for a time; but I strive to cast down your kingdom of darknesse, and to open Hell gates, and to break the Devils bands asunder, wherewith you are tied, that you my Enemies may live in peace, and that is all the harm I would have you to have.

Winstanley will let all this go if the lords of manors, freeholders, ministers, tithe-gatherers, and gentry will "pluck up bondage; and sinne no more."

But the cows still bother him. After he was tried and found guilty, he was condemned to pay £11 5s. 1d. without being allowed to speak and the cows were "rescued" from the court "by strangers, not by me," men came to his house at night and drove away seven cows and a bull. Thus he has been "executed" twice, "that they might be sure to kill me." But yet a second time the cows were "brought home againe," much to the vexation of the local gentry, which has grown so hungry "that they will eat poor lean Cowes that are little better then skin & bone." Though the cows were thin, the lawyers would sell them, for the main intent is to destroy the Diggers. Their fury is so great that they drove hogs and cows into the Diggers' barley and "went hollowing and shouting, as if they were dancing at a whitson Ale." But the Diggers will continue "to plant the plesant fruit trees of freedom, in the room of that cursed thornbush," the Norman camp. Parliament's victory has proved to be but the killing of him "that rid upon you, that you may get up into his saddle to ride upon others." England, now blindfolded and drowsy, "sleps and snorts in the bed of covetousnesse"; it will not awake though the enemy be upon its back "ready to scale the walls and enter Possession." The Norman "streames of bondage," running in the same river as before, now grow bigger "so that if you awaken not betimes, the flood of the Norman Prerogative power, will drown you all; here's more rivers comes into the maine stream, since the storm fell and the waters of fury rises very high, banked in by Laws."

England's battles are now spiritual, the lamb against the dragon, love against covetousness, younger brother against elder, and these two armies are led by two great generals, Christ and Beelzebub. Winstanley willingly waits to see the outcome: "I see the poore must first be picked out . . . , but the rich generally are enemies to true freedome."

> The work of digging still goes on,
>   and stops not for a rest:
> The Cowes were gone, but are return'd,
>   and we are all at rest.
> No money's paid, nor never shall,
>   to a Lawyer or his man
> To plead our cause, for therein wee'll do
>   the best we can.
> In *Cobham* on the little Heath our digging
>   there goes on.
> And all our friends they live in love,
>   as if they were but one.

Warning the City merchants that the Diggers will be "thorns in your eyes, and pricks in your sides" until they have a "fair open triall," he asks not to be treated like a beast. If reason and equity, instead of money, stand for justice, peace will reign; "otherwise both you with the corrupt Clergy will be cast out as unsavoury salt."

In December, after two more letters to Lord Fairfax, pleading for the "freedome to worke," failed to summon relief from physical abuse, Winstanley reissued his five earliest tracts in one volume. A note of pathos creeps into the Lear-like opening epistle.[20] Having shunned madness and found solace among the poor naked wretches that bide the pelting of pitiless storms, he considered how to defend the houseless heads and unfed sides from seasons such as these. Having exposed himself to feel what wretches feel, he unbuttoned his soul to nature. At the point of farthest extremity he saw the bond between all unaccommodated men;[21] therefore, he does not set himself up as an extraordinary man but as a typical man. With nothing but what he has received from within, he writes only to cast a word of comfort into a broken and empty heart that was full of deadness as he waded through dark and gloomy weather.

Finding peace, light, life, and fullness among the poor, his heart overflowed with such abundance of joy and rest that he forsook his ordinary food for days. When he did eat he rose immediately to return to his work. Neglecting menial tasks and friends, he felt best when alone. He was so filled with love and delight that he wrote whole winter days, never feeling the cold except when forced to rise by degrees and grasp the table till strength and heat returned to his legs. Secretly, he was sorry when night forced him to leave off. Yet this did not last. His heart was shut up again, and he laid aside his pen and could not bear to sit in the cold. His flesh rebelled against his spirit, and he was willing to be at ease. The worldly opposition he met with because of what he wrote or said caused fear and trembling in his soul, and he vowed never to write or speak openly again. But this too passed away, and he immediately became another man. His heart opened like a door; light flooded in. The power of love, joy, peace, and life overpowered him, and he had to write and speak again. And when he did he rested quietly; when he kept the light to himself he was troubled. Trying to recall neglected things was as difficult as carrying a steeple on his back, but he learned to wait upon the spirit and to write what it dictated. Though some friends told him he should have stopped writing after completing *The Saints Paradise,* they knew little of the spirit's inward workings. The works written since then are of the same order and spring from the same source, the spirit within. And though he has since met others who have experienced inner illumination, he never heard or read of it before he saw the light rise within himself. Others may cast dirt upon his flesh, but this light of life is inviolable.

The first tangible sign of this renewal is the two delightful poems the Diggers wrote. In twenty-five six-line stanzas, the Diggers' Christmas carol, addressed to those who are wise because they have experienced slavery, ironically states the position of the poor during the past eight years:

> When great Men disagree
> About Supremacy,
> Then doe they warn poor men
> To aid and assist them
> In setting up their self-will power,
> And thus they doe the poor devour.

Pretending they have no other end but to set the poor free, the great men's "blinde Guides," "finely fed" priests, will be cast out when the poor open their eyes. The leaders of the Parliamentary Army took a covenant to liberate the poor, but, in league with priests,

> They neither plow nor sow,
> Nor do they reap or mow,
> Nor any seed do finde,

Lawyers also trick the nation into slavery to gain money and suck the blood of the poor. Lords of manors, following William the Conqueror, hold people down. The answer to breaking this tyranny is for each man and woman "To Till each Heath and Plain":

> For we do plainly see,
> The Sword will not set's free,
> But bondage is increased;
> > By paying Taxes and Free-quarter,
> > Expecting Freedom would com after.

> But Freedom is not wonn,
> Neither by Sword nor Gun:
> Though we have eight years stay'd,
> And have our Moneys pay'd:
> > Then Clubs and Diamonds cast away,
> > For Harts & Spades must win the day.

"A Hint of That Freedom Which Shall Come, When the Father Shal Reign Alone in His Son," a more meditative and lyrical poem, opens with a declaration of God's omniscience. Through a skillful control of verb tenses, the poem manages to telescope past, present, and future time, which, blended with ordinary typological allusions, creates a sense of historical simultaneity. The light of life, from which both tyrant and slave "have their increase," will in his own time take

> . . . away the tyrants food,
> and gives it to the Son.
> Then *Esau's* potage shall be eat,
> for which he sold his right;
> The blessing *Jacob* shall obtain,
> which *Esau* once did slight.

The root of the tree of Jesse, Christ as the seed or logos, will rise and set the oppressed free; Esau will tearfully seek blessing from the once meek slave. An abrupt shift in tense at the midpoint of the poem declares the Son has already judged Esau and removed him from the worldly stage:

> For when thou think'st thy self most safe
> and riches thou hast got;
> Then in the middest of thy peace,
> torment shall be thy lot.

The poor must now be bold and claim their birthright.

> For now the Father's pointed time,
> which he did fore-intend

> To set up Freedom, and pull down
> the Man which did offend.

When the sun of righteousness takes power all tyrants will be made to serve him, and worldly strength will prove "but as a broken reed." The mighty stone cut without hand will rise to break Kingly power:

> The first that which this Stone shall smite
> shall be the head of Gold;
> A mortal wound he shall them give
> now minde thou hast been told.[22]

Winstanley further demonstrates his renewed vigor in his longest pamphlet since the founding of the Digger colony, *A New-Yeers Gift for the PARLIAMENT and ARMIE* (1 January 1650). The subtitle frankly says that the Diggers represent the life and marrow of the cause for which Parliament and the Army fought and calls for England to forsake the "Babilonian Beast":

> Die Pride and Envy; Flesh, take the poor's advice
> Covetousness be gone: Come, Truth and Love arise.
> Patience take the Crown; throw Anger out of doors:
> Cast out Hypocrisy and Lust, which follows whores:
> Then England sit in rest; Thy sorrows will have end;
> Thy Sons will live in peace, and each will be a friend.[23]

This pamphlet represents a new beginning, evidenced throughout by straightforward, crisp, clear narration, which merges with biblical metaphors taken over and made personal. With energy and insight, Winstanley, having forsaken accumulated continuous knowledge for ecstatic discontinuous wisdom, strips away literary conventions and speaks as a prophet. He had never written for money, but to inform others. Now, having obeyed his vision, the act of writing becomes a means of self-liberation, part of his being, his purpose in life. Possessed by a power greater than his individual will, he is in touch with a wellspring of energy, light, and life. Surrendering to this vital life-force, he becomes its instrument. Parliament and the Army ought to be the implements of the common people because they gave money and blood to deliver "this distressed bleeding dying nation out of bondage." Yet they wait in vain for their freedom. "Kingly power is like a great spread tree, if you lop the head or top-bow, and let the other Branches and root stand, it will grow again and recover fresher strength."

But there are two kingly powers, the sun of righteousness, embodying love, truth, and unity, and the prince of darkness, standing for covetousness, pride, and self-seeking. Parliament and the Army have pretended to set up the former and cast out the latter, but the sun of righteousness, embodied within each reborn "saint," looks upon all their actions, "and truly there is abundance of Rust about your Actings, which makes them that they do not shine bright." The dark kingly power sits in "the Chair of Government, under the name of Prerogative . . . And under the name of State Priviledge of Parliament . . . he is called the Murderer, or the great red Dragon." On the stage of history the rulers of England must "play the men, and be valiant for the Truth"; neither God nor the Devil will be mocked. For just as God waits to see them put their words into actions, the Devil waits to "maule both you and yours to purpose." His dark power "lies within the iron chest of cursed Covetousness" ready to devour all, and the key to this iron chest is private property, "fruit of War from the beginning." For "when Covetousness sheaths his Sword, and ceases to rage in the field, he first makes sharp Laws of Bondage" dictating that the conquered are "not to enjoy the Earth" but be "turned out" to become "Servants, Slaves, and Vassals to the Conquerers party: so those Laws that upholds Whips, Prisons, Gallows is but the same power of the Sword that raged, and that was drunk with Blood in the field."

Winstanley assures England's rulers that if "Parliament, Army, and rich People, would cheerfully give consent that those we call Poor should Dig and freely Plant the Waste and Common Land for a livelihood" unemployment would cease, scarcity of food would stop, crime would be halted, and people would be "knit together in love . . . so that if this Freedom be quietly granted to us, you grant it but to your selves, to En-glish-men, to your own flesh and blood." The gentry, with the aid of the common people, destroyed Charles I, so the "top-bow is lopped off the tree of Tyrannie . . . but alas oppression is a great tree still, and keeps off the sun of freedome from the poor Commons still, he hath many branches and great roots which must be grub'd up, before every one can sing Sions songs in peace." Three branches of kingly power remain: the tithing priests, the lords of manors, and the "bad Laws, or . . . bad Judges corrupting good Laws." Ministers will do or say anything to get money; "they will turn as the Ruling power turns . . . they cry who bids most wages." Just as "whorish Laws" pretend to love everyone and are "faithful to none," lawyers are "old Whores" who pick men's pockets. Referring to Cromwell's "mission" in Ireland (15 August 1649 to 26 May 1650), Winstanley notes that "as your Government must be new, so let the Laws be new, or else you will run farther into the Mud, where you stick already, as though you were fast in an *Irish* Bogge." But if they "do not stick in the Bogge of covetousness," and "Let not self-love so be-muddy your brain, that you should lose your selves in the thicket of bramblebush-words, and set never a strong Oak of some stable Action for the Freedome of the poor Oppressed," they may prove good servants. The lords of manors, thieving, murdering descendants of William the Conqueror's soldiers, hire lawyers who "love Mony as deerly as a poor mans dog do his breakfast in a cold morning" and cheat the lords who pay them and the poor they prosecute. "For truly Attourneys are such neat workmen, that they can turn a Cause which way those that have the biggest purse will have them."[24]

"Do these men," Winstanley rhetorically asks, "throw down Kinglie power? O no . . . Monies will buy and sell Justice still." Deftly moving from metaphor to metaphor, he laments that the civil wars have left the people lying "in the kennel of injustice as much or more then before." Chiding the rulers as schoolboys, he asks whether the wars have taught them anything: "O ye Rulers of *England*, when must we turn over a new leaf? will you alwayes hold us in one Lesson? surely you will make Dunces of us; then all the Boyes in other Lands will laugh at us: come, I pray let us take forth, and go forward in our learning." Clearly enjoying what he is doing, he comments on what he has witnessed and distances himself from it. The ceaseless tropes and plays on words are his way of stepping outside the experience and forcing the reader to do the same. He cajoles, pleads, warns, promises, threatens; in short he does everything verbally possible to get the reader to agree with him and follow his argument. This constant word play, the repeated puns and mock metaphors, are meant to shock the reader into objectivity. By treating serious subjects trivially and trivial subjects seriously, Winstanley hopes to so disorient the reader's "normal" view of things that he will see the falsity of accepting the present state as "natural" and recognize the need for change. The ruling class says the common people want anarchy, but the law gives land to those who got it by conquest and denies it to those who work. Under the rule of "the great Red Dragon . . . *England* is a Prison; the variety of subtilties in the Laws preserved by the Sword, are bolts, bars, and doors of the prison; the Lawyers are the Jaylors, and poor men are the prisoners; for let a man fall into the hands of any from the Bailiffe to the Judge, and he is either undone, or wearie of his life." The law, "a Nurserie of Idleness, luxurie, and cheating," pretends justice, "yet the Judges and Law-Officers, buy and sell Justice for money, and wipes their mouths like *Solomons* whore, and says it is my calling, and never are troubled at it."[25]

Lawyers are "false Prophets" who say, "Lo here is Christ, Ile save you in this Court, and lo there is Christ, Ile save you in that Court: but when we have tried all, we are lost . . . for we are either utterly made Beggars by this Saviour, the Law, or else we are nursed up in hardnesse of heart."

Winstanley shifts to the second person to hurl his charges and pounds his points home by reasserting the interdependency of gentry and working people:

> My Advice to you Gentlemen is this, Hereafter to lie still and cherish the Diggers, for they love you . . . why should you be so bitter against them? . . . will you now destroy part of them that have preserved your lives? . . . let not the Atturneyes or Lawyers neatly councel your Money out of your purses, and stir you up to beat and abuse the Diggers, to make all rational men laugh at your folly . . . If you have yet so much Money . . . give it to some poor . . . this will be your honour, and your comfort; assure your selves you never must have true comfort tell you be friends with the poor . . . make restitution of their Land you hold from them; for what would you do if you had not such labouring men to work for you?

Shifting back to the first-person plural he asserts: "We that are the poor commons, that paid our Money . . . have as much Right in those crown Lands and Lands of the spoil as you; therefore we give no consent That you should buy and sell our crown Lands and waste Lands." The land "is our joynt purchased inheritance; we paid you your wages to help us to recover it, but not to take it to your selves, and turn us out." For forty weeks the Diggers have withstood beatings, imprisonments, torture, and wanton destruction, but they have waited upon the sun of righteousness within them, struggling to return the precious seed of the sun to the soil, the Mother Earth. All they desire is to live quietly "in the land of our nativity, by our righteous labour, upon the common Land." Is it not tyranny to deny then that right? "In that which follows I shall cleerly prove it is, for it appears so cleer that the understanding of a child does say, It is Tyranny, it is the Kingly power of darkness."

Since "bare talking of righteousnesse, and not acting" causes "immoderate confusion and ignorance," writing becomes an eschatological exercise. Winstanley's polemical manipulation of personal pronouns, the movement back and forth from "we" to "you," is not an attempt to alienate an opposition, to draw a line between "us" and "them"; it is rather a dialectical thrust and parry whereby the union of opposites is continually reasserted by encouraging the opposition to forsake irrational positions and join the other side. Winstanley constantly leaves this choice open to his readers, whom he treats as deceived and misled fellow human beings rather than willful sinners or malicious evildoers. He feels he can make people receptive to change if he can show them it is for their own good. Believing that "a man knowes no more of righteousness than he hath power to act," he attempts to put theory into practice, and he enjoins Parliament to do the same. In his detailed recounting of the destruction of the Diggers' fields and huts by soldiers paid by the lords of manors, he carefully points out that the soldiers are "fearfull, like a dog that is kept in awe, when his Master gives him a bone, and stands over him with a whip; he will eat, and look up, and twinch his tail; for they durst not laugh out, lest their Lords should hear they jeer'd them openly; for in their hearts they are Diggers." One soldier, feeling pity and guilt, gave the Diggers twelve pence to buy drink. The rendering of such precise details, like Robinson Crusoe's and Moll Flanders' careful reckoning of their accounts, comes to stand for the inner development of the colony members. The recounting of the Diggers' persecutions exaggerates them, emphasizes them, until their pains become purges, their troubles a war, their sufferings a holocaust. Winstanley knows that to elicit the reader's sympathy he must put him in the picture, make him *see* so he can *feel*.

While the King was the tallest oak in the royal forest the lords, landlords, corrupt judges and lawyers were his boughs: "he was the head, and they, with the Tything-priests are the branches of that Tyrannical Kingly power; and all the several limbs and members must be cast out, before Kingly power can be pulled up root and branch." But Winstanley quickly adds, "mistake me not, I do not say, Cast out the persons of men: No, I do not desire their fingers to ake: but I say, Cast out their power." The land "is every ones, but not one single ones."

Daemona non Armis, sed Morte subegit Iesus.

Which Winstanley translates:

> By patient Sufferings, not by Death,
>   Christ did the Devil kill;
> And by the same, still to this day,
>   his Foes he conquers still.

Connecting his longing for truth with his desire for social justice, he remarks that "true Religion, and undefiled, is this, To make restitution of the Earth, which hath been taken and held from the Common people, by the power of Conquests formerly, and so *set the oppressed free*." The key to both transcendental peace and political equality is rooted in the land. And since "Buying and Selling is an Art, whereby people endeavour to cheat one another of the Land," communal sharing of it is the answer.

The second part of *A New-Yeers Gift*, entitled THE CURSE AND BLESSING THAT IS IN MANKINDE, is a mythopoeic exposition of human history. "In the beginning of Time, the Spirit of Universal Love appeared to be the father of all things: The Creation of Fire, Water, Earth, and Air, came out of him, and is his clothing." Love is the logos, and the creation is "the House or Garden, in which this one Spirit hath taken up his seat." For love can be seen or known only by "the inward feeling" or by the outward expression of love by someone else. Within creation there are two earths. "The Living Earth, called *Mankinde*," is at peace as long as love is universal, but when love is selfish, "then this Earth is brought into Bondage, and Sorrow fills all places." The other is "the great Body of Earth in which all creatures subsist." This earth, the soil, since it provides food, shelter, and clothing for all, unites everyone "into a sweet harmony of willingness to preserve Mankinde." But when covetousness, the murderer, appeared, "all creatures were divided, and enmity rose up amongst them." Now the process is reversed; people begin life under the rule of self-love and have to work their way back to universal love; likewise, the earth, now divided, must be restored to the common treasury it originally was. Mankind, the "Lord of all the Earth . . . unfolds himself in Light and Darkness: his face is called the universal power of Love: his back parts is called the selfish power." These two primordial powers, also called "the Son of Bondage" and "the Son of Freedom," "strive in the womb of the Earth which shal come forth first; and which shall rule; the fleshy man hath got the start; but the other will prove the stronger, and cast him out with honour."[26] Before the Fall, in the morning of mankind, "every thing was in peace, and there was a sweet communion of Love in the creation." Mother Earth belonged to everyone; she "was a common Treasurie of delight for the preservation of their bodies." After the Fall it was night. Isaiah lived "about midnight" when he cried, "Watchman, What of the night?" (Isaiah 21:11). But a new era is dawning; the sun of righteousness, now called "the Son of universal Love," is rising to disperse the darkness; "for as the night and day, Sun and Moon, hath their exchanges, so hath these Two powers, called Sons of God in mankind." "Like lightning from east to west," this new power casts out "the Mysterie of Iniquitie . . . by the word of his mouth, and by the brightness of his comming."

The creation works by a dialectical interplay of opposites. And just as the sun completes its seasonal cycle, making what seemed dead fruitful, "the Son of universal Love . . . moves upon the living waters mankind" and enlightens those in confusion, "lying under Types, Shadows, Ceremonies, Forms, Customes, Ordinances, and heaps of waste words." For this "Son of universal Love" is the seed "out of which the creation sprung forth," and when he shines mankind "stumbles not, he walks in the light, because the light is in him." When the light within withdraws, man tries to "be a God, and calls his weakness strength." Yet he is tormented "because his inward power is not sutable to his outward profession . . . he is a Saint without, but a Devil within." To have peace people must act in accordance with their inner selves. Contentment cannot be feigned, for "hypocritical self invention" destroys happiness and tears mankind in pieces.

An Army colonel said the Diggers wished only "to draw a company of People into Arms." This shows how "knavish imagination" deceitfully hinders the establishment of freedom. Through such vain slanders, "imagination studies how to keep himself up and keep others down." The battle is greater than Winstanley thought. He has indeed awakened "all the powers of darknesse" that "come forth and help to set the Crown upon the head of Self." Now he sees how "imagination begets Covetousnesse after pleasure, honour, and riches: Covetousnesse begets Fear, least others should crosse them in their Design; or else begets a Fear of want, and this makes a man to draw the creatures to him by hook or crook, and to please the strongest side, looking what others do, not minding what himself doth." Other officers said the Diggers "took away other mens Propriety," but the truth, to Winstanley's mind, is quite the opposite. Fear begets hypocrisy, subtlety, envy, and hardness of heart, causing people to seek to save themselves by ruining others and to suppress and oppress all who speak and act differently. This, in turn, causes people, through pride, to seek security, and this begets luxury and lust, and this leads to greed and discontentment until people's hearts become "fully like the heart of a Beast." By such excess the power of darkness rises to perfection until one branch tears and devours another "by divisions, evill surmisings, envious fightings, and killing." And all this quarreling is "about the earth who shall, and who shall not enjoy it." Judges and lawyers take bribes and clients' money but neglect their cases. "Parliament and Army lives in Theft" because they take money from the poor and promise freedom, but they only give freedom to the gentry. Now, with his prophetic voice waining, Winstanley once more gathers his strength to warn that the earth was made for all and that the sun of righteousness rising within poor men and women "will set us free though you will not: when will the Vail of darknes be drawn off your faces? will you not be wise O yee Rulers?"

When indeed? Winstanley reluctantly concedes: "for the present in outward view there is nothing but darkness and confusion upon the face of the earth." It seems "the clouds that hide the Son of righteousness from man" may not pass away. At first the dark power, Adam, was small, "but he is risen to great strength, and the whole Earth is now filled with him, as *Isaiah* saith, *Darknes hath covered the Earth*, mankind. For let any that hath eyes look either to them above or them below, and they see darknes or the Devil rule." As eloquent in defeat as others in victory, Winstanley notes how "the Creation sits like *Rachel* sighing, mourning, and groaning under his oppressing power." In such a state there are many "saviours in word, but none in deed, and these great false Christs and false Prophets" destroy creation under pretense of saving it. Now all these saviors are linked together; if one falls all must fall. Winstanley turns on them: "you are all selfish, you are afraid to own publike spirited men, nay you are ashamed some of you to be seen walking or talking with true publike spirited men, called *Levellers.*" Though defeated for now, he remains convinced that "if ever the creation be wholly saved," it will be through "the true seed with us" who will "bruise the Serpents head in every one . . . This is the Sun of righteousness. When he ariseth, he disperseth darkness, and will make all ashamed that had hands in promoting of the other false saviours power." Inwardly this false power is covetousness that makes one want to rule another. This is what some call "The power and Ordinance of God, which is true: It is God indeed, but it is the god of the world," the god of smugness, conventionality, and hypocrisy. The thing this god hates most is community, and those who serve him stop at nothing to destroy it. Outwardly this power manifests itself in the gentry, which rules by the sword. The only way to fight it is to withdraw, to refuse to participate in its doings. Christ, the sun of righteousness, is none other than "the universal Love or Free community" manifest in two ways: "*Community of Mankind . . .* which is called Christ in you, or the Law writen in the heart," and "*Community of the Earth,*" which is communal ownership of land. Therefore, "Jesus Christ the Saviour of all men, is the greatest, first, and truest Leveller that ever was spoke of in the world."

If the sun of righteousness is not recognized he will, like the *sol iustitiae,* rise up and "shew himself a Lion, and tear you in pieces for your most abominable dissembling Hypocrisie." It comes back once again to the relationship between words and deeds. Because of the "confederacie between the Clergy and the great red Dragon: the Sheep of Christ shall never fare well so long as the wolf or red Dragon payes the Shepherd their wages." And to ensure the payment of these wages they have the law, built to uphold private property, enforced by "Prisons, Whips, and Gallows" so "We that work most have least comfort in the earth, and they that work not at all, enjoy all." And if a poor man says the meek shall inherit the earth "the tithing Priest stops his mouth with a slam and tels him that is meant of the inward satisfaction of mind." Such twisting of words is most abominable. By such shows "the Kingly power swims in fulness, and laughs at the others miserie." Concluding on an ironical note, Winstanley scoffs at "these men that will enjoy the earth in realitie, and tell others they must enjoy it in conceit." But in the end "the people shall all fall off from you, and you shall fall on a sudden like a great tree that is undermined at the root . . . this falling off is begun already, divisions shall tear and torter you, till you submit to Communitie . . . Jesus Christ . . . the head *Leveller* . . . *will draw all men after him,* and leave you naked." For this great Leveller is not a single man but the sun of righteousness in us.

An appendix lists fifteen OF THE MOST REMARKABLE SUFFERINGS THAT THE DIGGERS HAVE MET WITH FROM THE GREAT RED DRAGONS POWER SINCE APRIL 1, 1649. A pathetic note again appears in the concluding lines:

> You Lordly Foes, you will rejoyce
>   this newes to hear and see;
> Do so, go on; but wee'l rejoyce
>   much more the Truth to see:
> For by our hands truth is declar'd,
>   and nothing is kept back;
> Our faithfulness much joy doth bring,
>   though victuals we may lack.

Now they must take refuge in time, put off the revolution, and look for the day when

> . . . all shall see,
> And verbal talk it will appear
>   a Devil for to be:
> For actions pure, holds forth the life
>   of God and Christ most dear:

Then preachers will see truth acted and false promises put to the test. The scribes, pharisees, and Judas himself

> Great preachers were, but for no deeds,
>   the Truth they much did stain:

Their deeds were

> . . . but stinking weed:
> For Persecution ever was
>   the Work that came from them.

Having put his arm as far as his strength will go, Winstanley ends: "I have Writ, I have Acted, I have Peace." He knows defeat is imminent; "yet there is hope." But his words belie him. "My Spirit," he laments, "shall strive no longer with Flesh."

Late in 1649 a group of Ranters, under the leadership of Laurence Clarkson, tried to infiltrate the Digger colony.[27] The resulting clash between the leaders of the two groups highlights an essential difference between two forms of radicalism. Clarkson, a libertine, practiced "free love" and saw the family as tyrannical and restrictive. Winstanley, a utopian, saw the tightly knit family as paradigmatic of a more egalitarian state. Viewed in this context, Winstanley's remarks on the Ranters point up the consistency of his moderate communistic ideal. As with other communist groups, from the Taborites and Waldenses to the Babouvists and early Marxists, the Diggers found some naively or disingenuously misunderstood the distinction between property and people and believed they held women to be common.[28]

In *A New-Yeers Gift* Winstanley paused to disown "some come among the Diggers that have caused scandall." In *A VINDICATION OF THOSE, WHOSE ENDEAVORS IS ONLY TO MAKE THE EARTH A COMMON TREASURY, CALLED DIGGERS*, he explains how these Ranters believe only "in the outward enjoyment of meat, drinke, pleasures, and women; so that the man within can have no quiet rest." Like the landlords who want to own and use all the land, the Ranters simply want to possess and violate all women. But, like the young lady in Milton's *Comus*, Winstanley believes overindulgence stultifies rather than stimulates sensual pleasure: "abundant eating and drinking, and actuall community with variety of women . . . fights against reason, who is the seed or tree of life, or the righteous man . . . within." Negating the whole man in favor of one aspect, the Ranters overemphasize sensuality in reaction to the ministers' hypocritical denial of sensual pleasure. Winstanley wants a balance between sensual pleasure and intellectual delight: "when Reason rules in the house or heart not suffering the sences to runne into excesse in any action: then the whole body enjoyes quiet rest and peace." Painting a lurid picture of where the "immoderate ranting practise of the Sences" leads, he explains that just as general envy is the disguise of individual greed, "the Ranting practise is the proper Kingdome of Covetousnesse, or King Lust of the flesh, which is the Kingdome of darknesse, full of unreasonablenesse, madnesse and confusion." True to the ideal of moderation espoused in *Piers Plowman*, he explains that this "land of darknesse" brings misery to its inhabitants because "it is destructive to the body, house, or Temple, wherein Reason . . . dwells; it brings diseases infirmenesse, weaknesses and rottennesse upon the body, and so ruines the house about the mans eares, that he cannot live in quiet peace; for diseases of body causes sorrow of mind." Even greater than the destruction of venereal disease is the "vexation to the mind" brought about by "excessive copolation with Women, and . . . superabundant eating and drinking." Treating a woman as property, "as the spoil and handmaid of communal list," degrades human nature, for not only does it lead "to quarrelling, killing, burning houses or Corne, or to such like distructivenesse," it destroys families and "rents in peeces mankind, For where true Love hath united a man and woman to be Husband and Wife, and they live in peace, when this Ranting power or king lust of the flesh comes in, he seperates those very friends, causing both sides to run into the Sea of confusion, madnesse and distruction, to leave each other, to leave their Children, and to live in discontent each with other."

The Ranter pretends to love all, but loves only himself. His crude reaction to middle-class society merely universalizes the vileness of private property, reduces the five senses to the bestial level, and denies the socially acquired characteristics of thinking, observing, reflecting, caring, and nurturing. It "hinders the pure and naturall Generation of man, and spills the seed in vaine, and instead of a healthfull groth of mankind it produces weaknesse and much infirmnesse." Children of such unions, lacking familial ties, become Esaus; like William the Conqueror they prove "furious and full of rage." Since the Ranters simply represent the obverse of middle-class values, they "neither can nor will work, but live idle, like wandring bussy bodies, expressing and cheating others, that are simple and of a civill flexible nature, so that by seeking their owne freedom they imbondage others." And since they treat everything, including each other, as objects, as means rather than ends, they are estranged from their own needs and desires. To "say nothing against this ranting practise," is sheer hypocrisy, maintained only by the economically secure who find them amusing aberrations. But Winstanley cautions, "see thou be without sinne thy selfe, and then cast the first Stone at the Ranter." Left to their own devices, the Ranters will perish through inanition. Moderate work, like moderate sex, builds the bond of love between man and nature and men and women.

V

THE IMPRISONED EARTH

PATIENT BUT undaunted, Winstanley entered the last phase of his defense of the Digger colony with an investigation of the meaning of freedom. In *ENGLANDS SPIRIT UNfoulded. OR AN INCOURAGEMENT TO TAKE THE ENGAGEMENT*, published in late February or early March 1650, he invents a dramatic dialogue "between two Friends," which opens with a brief poem addressed to the point that freedom is the reflection of the inner light in the outer world:

> Freedom is the mark, at which all men should aime
> But what true freedom is, few men doth know by name,
> But now a light is rise, and nere shall fall
> How every man by name, shall freedom call.[1]

In essence, this short pamphlet explains why the establishment of communal property is a moderate and rational alternative to Cavalier greed on the one hand and Ranter wantonness on the other. The Engagement is a means to this end.[2] By abolishing kingship, parliament has declared that "the Land of *England* shall be a common Treasury to all *English* men without respect of persons . . . and those that hinder this freedom, do begin to set themselves down in that *Kingly* and *Lordly* conquering chaire, out of which they have cast King *Charles* and House of *Lords* . . . because the people now do generally understand their freedom" there is no denying them. "Some," Winstanley declares, "are troubled how to live, their poverty is so great, and this is a great burden among our friends, who have lost all in the time of the Warres." The question, as he sees it, is one of choosing between "great men" who wish to "make their wills a Law" and those who wish "reason the spirit of burning" to cast out the "corrupt bloud, that runs in every man, and womans vaines, more or lesse." With his inner and outer dialectic, Winstanley attempts to persuade his readers that "these that would enslave others, are slaves themselves, to the Kingly Power within themselves." For if the rich "would give the poor their freedom . . . they would win the peoples hearts, and free themselves from that trouble. And if this they do not do

174

quickly, that which they fear will come upon them, for they will be left naked." On the other side he cautions that the Ranter practice of mimicking the behavior of the rich also corrupts the meaning of freedom:

> BEware you Women of the ranting crew
> And call not freedom those things that are vaine,
> For if a child you get, by ranting deeds
> The man is gone and leaves the child your gaine,
> Then you and yours are left by such free-men,
> For other women are as free for them.

Winstanley's next pamphlet was published unfinished on 19 March 1650. *FIRE IN THE BUSH. THE SPIRIT BURNING, NOT CONSuming, but purging Mankinde. OR, The great Battell of God Almighty, between* Michaell *the Seed of Life, and the great red Dragon, the Curse fought within the Spirit of Man* is neither a desperate attempt to save the colony, an admission of defeat, nor a return to pre-Digger positions; it is the culmination of Winstanley's visionary, which is to say poetic, experience. Like Milton's *Paradise Lost* and Blake's *Jerusalem*, it sets out to explain how the bond between man and nature was destroyed, what that destruction means in modern life, and how it may be repaired:

> The righteous Law a government will give to whole
> mankinde,
> How he should governe all the Earth, and therein
> true peace finde;
> This government is Reason pure, who will fill man
> with Love,
> And wording Justice; without deeds, is judged by
> this Dove.[3]

Much that appears obscure about this pamphlet becomes clear if the reader keeps in mind that Winstanley specifically addresses it "TO ALL THE SEVERALL SOCIETIES OF PEOPLE, CALLED CHURCHES, IN THE PRESBYTERIAN, INDEPENDENT, OR ANY OTHER FORME OF PROFESSION." The churches' garbling of typology incenses him even more than the lawyers' manipulation of legal terminology and the landlords' control of the land. In the hands of the ministers, the fourfold method handed down from Tertullian and Pope Gregory had been corrupted beyond recognition. But Winstanley perceives that the study of the methodological principles underlying scriptural interpretation, hermeneutics, attempts to maintain contact with the sources of revolutionary energy, to preserve the concept of freedom itself. Images from Genesis, Ezekiel, Daniel, Malachi, and Revelation burn in his brain because he sees in them analogies to his own day. Moreover the yearning for freedom he finds in these books stirs awareness of his longing for utopian future. Freedom, in this sense, is, in Fredric Jameson's words, "never a state that is enjoyed, or a mental structure that is contemplated, but rather an ontological impatience in which the constraining situation itself is for the first time perceived in the very moment in which it is refused . . . Thus the idea of freedom involves a kind of perceptual superposition; it is a way of reading the present, but it is a reading that looks more like the reconstruction of an extinct language."[4] At the very time when the promise of the English Revolution is rapidly evolving toward counter-revolution, Winstanley reassesses the way the prophetic impulse relates to the realistic expectation of change. This is not a diversion from politics but a transvaluation of political ideas resting on the premise that by returning to point zero, by casting off the accretion of over 4000 years of linguistic rationalization, a rational base for social progress may be reached. For the practice of hermeneutics itself, the very act of attempting to recover the vitality of the original scripture, implies that the possibility of an ideal society lies within the future.

On one level *Fire in the Bush* merely states, in the allusive language of the mechanic preacher, that the common people have nothing to fear from the establishment's ministers, lawyers, and landlords if they only look within. Second, after discovering the paradise in their hearts, they must eschew the selfish temptation of getting and spending and set about creating a new Garden of Eden in the real world. On a more complex third level, by interpreting two of his favorite biblical passages, the dream of the four beasts from Daniel 7 and the beast from the sea in Revelation 13, Winstanley tries to show the practicality of his vision of a New Jerusalem based on the common ownership of land. He conveys this message through the dialectical interaction of the sets of contraries found in earlier works: spirit and flesh, light and darkness, Christ and Adam, Michael and the Dragon, and Jacob and Esau. The fourth level of interpretation, the anagogic, discloses the dialectic of inner and outer transformation that first looks back into pre-history, then is brought forward into the present state of England, and is finally projected into a utopian future. The development of each person retraces the moral evolution of the human race; in everyone primitive, infantile, and archaic consciousness exists side by side with progressive, civilized, and humane impulses. This rudimentary version of the ontogeny-re-capitulates-phylogeny theorem demonstrates Winstanley's belief that everyone has the potential for saintliness, and this is neither accidental nor a sign of Calvinistic election but is the result of a delicate balance of forces that, under different circumstances, might produce purposeless-ness or selfishness.

Winstanley grounds his thought in "the word of Life," the direct and pure apprehension of the logos uncontaminated by second-hand interpretation. Having committed the word to paper he delayed publication "by almost a fortnight, and thought not of it." But one night he woke and felt a voice in his heart and mouth urging him to "send it to the Churches." A great feeling of love made his heart pound with pity for their great striving for life, and he saw the great confusion of words among them. They "speake and preach of the life of Love; But . . . have not the power of it." Their "verball profession," resulting in no righteous action, shows they are "outlandish men, of severall Nations, under the government of darknesse." They "are not yet the true Inhabitants of the Land of Love" because they do not understand that "before you live you must die, and before you be bound up into one universall body, all your particular bodies and societies must be torne to pieces." This principle subverts the basis of church authority, the allegorical method. To restore the legitimacy of scriptural typology one must go back to the direct apprehension of the word so he may declare "the true Light is comming now once more, not onely to shake the Earth, that is, *Moses* worship, but Heaven also; That which you call Gospell-worship, and the Kingdome without shall fall, that so the Kingdome within may be established." An apt simile gets the point across swiftly and directly: "all your particular Churches are like the inclosures of Land which hedges in some to be heires of Life, and hedges out others; one saying Christ is here with them; Another saying no: but he is there with them."

Prepared for battle, Winstanley knows to some his book "will be refreshing, but others will storme, and prepare warre against it; And the *Ishmaelites* they will scoffe; but be it so: yet my Armour is tryed, I am sure it will keep off the blow." For over a century the theological dispute in England involved the relationship between the order of nature and the order of grace, the physical and the spiritual worlds, which Puritans tended to segregate. This issue threatened to destroy the validity of scriptural exegesis. Historical hindsight shows why; a radical movement acting against the religious and political establishment had to make a distinction between the spiritual and the secular and so drive a wedge between church and state. In practical terms Puritans argued that thoughts and beliefs were autonomous, and as long as a person went about his business without harming anyone the government should leave him alone. This, of course, is the basis for Puritan tolerationist arguments. But there is another side of the issue, for by separating the monolithic secular structure of church and state and the unified spiritual edifice of grace and nature, Puritans created a fractured world order they did not know how to heal. As A. S. P. Woodhouse points out, "when the order of nature and the order of grace are considered together, the superiority of the latter will always assert itself."[5] The Calvinistic tendency to exalt the order of grace and denigrate the order of nature is always in opposition to the tolerationist tendency in Puritan thought. The great stress orthodox Puritans such as Thomas Hooker put on innate human depravity led them to emphasize man's fall from grace.[6] The story of Adam and Eve is the key biblical text because it dramatizes the eternal conflict between nature and grace. Winstanley, like Milton, reinterprets the Fall as a means of asserting his position in relation to Puritan thinking. "You shall finde I speake of the Garden of *Eden*," he writes, "which is the spirit of man, not the spirit of Beasts. And in that Garden there are weeds and hearbs. The weeds are these. Selfe-Love, Pride, Envie; Covetousnesse after riches, honours, pleasures, Imagination, thinking he cannot live in peace, unlesse he enjoy this or that outward object . . . And the stinking weeds over-spreads the sweet flowers and hearbs, which are the lights of the spirit of truth."

Thrusting himself into the controversy, he attacks tyranny and hypocrisy by personifying them as venomous weeds in the Garden of Eden "attended with evill surmising, grudgings, speaking and promising, nay, swearing one thing, yet doing another, inventing much shew of holinesse to compasse his selfish ends; and while he rules King, as he doth rule at this day; he is assisted with vain glory, feare of being disthroned, oppressing others, unmercifull; carelesse of former promises and engagements; persecuting those who doth such things as he promised and vowed to doe." Looking back to the ancient Stoic belief that the natural world is a metaphor of God, Winstanley shows his agreement with the attempts of Richard Overton and William Walwyn to draw nature and grace together.[7] However, in adopting Neo-Stoic doctrines, the Levellers, for the most part, avoid theological issues and ignore divine law in favor of pragmatic politics.[8] At the conclusion of *Legall Fundamentall Liberties* (June 1649), Lilburne repudiates any relationship with "all the erronious tenents of the poor Diggers at George hill in Surrey, laid down in their late two avowed Books, called *The true Levellers Standard,* and *The new law of Righteousnesse."*[9] In their desire to break from Anglican dogma the Levellers reject theology and shut themselves off from the radical metaphysical tradition. Their language shows this; nowhere in Lilburne's writings do we find the free-play of metaphors drawn from the Bible and alchemy so evident in Winstanley's prose. Most Levellers seem to draw no sustenance from nature and refer to it in only the most mechanical terms. And lyrical appreciation of the English countryside, so crucial to Winstanley, appears totally foreign to the Leveller imagination.

Of course Winstanley's idea of man's intimate relationship with nature is not unique. In translating works of Nicholas of Cusa and Sebastian Franck, John Everard rediscovers and reworks the Neo-Stoic doctrine, stemming from a recondite mixture of Ciceronian and Pauline ideas going back to Zeno and Origen, that the divinity is infused in astral bodies and natural forces, and that God is a symbol for cosmic or natural law.[10] When revived by the Florentine Neoplatonists, this method, on a broader scale, led Erasmus to suggest that the sun is a natural metaphor for God: "As the sun is the source of light and warmth," he wrote, "so the Father is the source of the Son, who is 'Light from Light.' And as warmth comes from sun and rays together, so the Holy Spirit proceeds from Father and Son."[11] As Everard explains, "God himself is nothing to us without Christ: As every Jubar and Beam of light that comes from the Sun, they are all included in the body of the Sun, but they are not communicated to us but by those Jubars and beans that come from the Sun: so God is like the Sun."[12] Such analogies enable Winstanley to call those who insist on keeping the order of nature and the order of grace separate "outlandish men; for they are not the true native Inhabitants of the heart, but strangers to the righteous spirit . . . And this power is the night time of mankinde, or the absence of the Sonne of righteousnesse from the heart." To him, as to the German reformers, those unwilling (all were able) to read the book of nature as the word made material are reprobates who will never enter into true rest. Such separation, which inevitably leads to covetousness, "is the wicked man, or Dragon in you, which causes all warres and sorrowes." And as long as people lie under this "selfish, darke, imaginary power," they are "strangers to the Sonne of righteousnesse." The contrasting powers, light and darkness, are not merely separate, equal forces battling for supremacy in the heart of each individual and in the world. They are personifications like those Milton conjures up in *Areopagitica* (November 1644), where Truth and Falsehood grapple in an unequal battle, unequal because "when the new light which we beg for shines in upon us" we scatter and defeat all objections.[13] So too to Winstanley the "wicked man" and Dragon in people is but an "imaginary power," which, like falsehood, like evil itself, is self-created, an absence, a void, a negative unilluminated by truth.

The thread linking Everard and Winstanley is stronger, however, than the congruence of the sun image to represent the divine spark reflected within man and nature. In his translation of a 1561 Latin edition of Franck's *Of the Tree of Knowledge of Good and Evil*, Everard encapsulates the inner and outer dialectic by which all things operate. The Genesis account of the Fall, he says, is a parable, an allegory of human development. The Tree of Knowledge was both an outward "Natural

Tree Planted by God in Paradise" and also an inward tree "in the heart of Adam, That he was there Tempted by the SEED of the Serpent; To make some Account and Reckoning of his own Wisdom[,] Will and Nature, and not to Submit Himself unto God, As Void of all Name, Knowledge, or Work; But to be SOMETHING of himself." Two "causes" moved Franck to believe this. "The First is this, Because the Promise is, That the seed of the Woman should Bruise the Head of the Serpent; Now, We read of no Natural or Living Serpent whose head was so Bruised, by that Seed; Therefore say I, As the Spiritual Seed of the Woman was in Adams Heart, So likewise was the Serpents Seed, For Man indeed was made Good, Not of the Substance of God, But out of Nothing." The second reason is the scriptural indication that the City of God and the New Jerusalem are to be extensions of the paradise within since the word of God, the logos, is life itself, and this "Almighty Word, is our Paradise, The Tree of Life, The Temple Where we Dwell, Walk, Sacrifice and Pray; As we likewise are His Temple and Paradise." But the Tree of Knowledge, which is evil, is also in us, and the eating of its fruit turns men to worship the Beast of Revelation 13. Since the outer world reflects the inner world, this "Figure and Fashion . . . must pass away and Perish, As being Nothing else but a certain Imaginary world." Then man can set about recreating the outer world in correspondence with the purified inner world. But this requires a complete recapitulation of mankind's psychological history: "all things, which in the Bible were done Externally and Signifyingly, must again be done and again, brought to pass After their Manner; And, All the History of the Bible . . . Whose Scriptures Do, To this Day, Stand in Force, And are Continually Accomplished and Fulfilled, Internally, and Spiritually. All things are By Christ Translated, into the Truth, And it must needs be, That All the Prophesies which God spake, From the beginning of the world, by the Mouth of his Holy Ones must still be Called back, Reiterated, or Done over again."[14]

Winstanley writes that the Garden of Eden, containing both "weeds and hearbs," is in "mans heart." The weeds are the Tree of Knowledge; the herbs are the Tree of Life, "the daytime of Mankinde, or the presence of the Sonne of righteousnesse in the heart." As Franck wrote, and as Everard stresses in his sermons, the Tree of Knowledge represents second hand knowledge that prevents people from returning to childlike innocence and receptivity. So also, to Winstanley, "Babes and sucklings doe see, and can say, that in your established formes you worship, and professe you know not what; you say one thing and doe another; you make God and Christ a very cheat to the world, as if he were all words and no deeds." Like Franck, Winstanley maintains that hypocrites "all must and shall be torne in pieces, and scattered, and shamed." Their "verball profession shall be loathed by all, and be cast out, as stinking, imaginary dung of false-hearted ones, who professes Love in words, and in actions deny Love." The restorative sun of righteousness "comes to set all free," he "comes not to put sackcloth and mourning weeds upon mankinde, but to pull them off and wipe away all teares." But as long as Mother Earth "is intangled, and appropriated into particular hands, and kept there by the power of the sword"; and as long as ministers support such bondage, words and deeds are separated, "and so hypocrisie reignes King in the Earth at this very day." But all is not lost. For if people share the fruits of the earth and act "not like the Rats and Mice, that drawes the treasures of the Earth into . . . holes to looke upon" while others "starve for want," then "the Sonne within . . . will set you free." This inner sun-son is coming "to breake down all your pinfoulds, and to lay all open to the Common; the rough wayes he will make smooth, and crooked wayes strait; and levell mountaines and valleys . . . for the voyce is gone out, freedome, freedome, freedome: he that hath eares to heare, let him heare, he that is filthie, let him be filthy still, till he be cast out as dung." Thus purified by "the Sunne within," Winstanley has earned the right to sign his opening epistle as *a friend to Love, wading through the bondage of the world.*"

Originally he intended to write thirteen chapters, but he published only seven. A noticeable break occurs between the brief headings of the seven completed chapters and the long headings for the six unpublished ones; possibly these were never attempted. The first chapter, *"What the Garden of Eden is,"* opens with a restatement of Bonaventure's adaptation of the Stoic idea that nature is the *vestigium Dei*: "The whole Creation of fire, water, Earth and Aire; and all the varieties of bodies made up thereof, is the cloathing of God." Observing the usual distinction between God in nature and God as nature, Winstanley notes that all things "looked upon in the lump" are filled with God but are not synonymous with God, the spirit of "universall Love, strength and life." As often, he explains radical ideas in deceptively simple language. His definition of God appears conventional, but careful examination shows he is saying something quite unorthodox. By using plain words and by briefly withholding his assumptions, he moves the reader along until, enmeshed in the argument, "assent" is taken by fiat. If the reader agrees God is universal love, strength, and life, he must agree God "begets and brings forth every thing," and if he agrees with this he must also find "he is the Restorer of all things," and if he agrees with this he must admit God is the "deliverer from the oppressing power, preserving every one in peace," and if he follows this logic he sees that "Therefore he is called

Lord God, Almighty; for he is the onely, and alone living spirit, which dwells every where, and can doe, what he will." The impression is that the argument is circular, but this is not the case. Winstanley is temporizing. For the reader who grants this definition sees that "of all those bodies, that are called Creatures; or the cloathing of God, Mankind is the chief." And if God manifests himself in mankind "more then in any other creature, therefore mankinde is made the Lord of all; And the whole Earth is this: The Lords." And if man is lord of the earth, then the earth belongs to everyone "(not to one or a few single branches of mankinde)," and everyone has a right to "till the Earth; and . . . multiplie and fill the Earth: And no part or branch of mankind is shut out by him from this imployment."

Following his usual practice of stating the second half of a thesis before the first, Winstanley gives the reader no choice but to agree that just as "the great Earth, and the inferiour creatures therein are as the Commons, Forrests, and delights of God in the out Coasts of the Creation; Even so Mankind, The living Earth is the very Garden of *Eden*." Again, while the argument appears circular, actually Winstanley has made a dazzling dialectical leap from metaphorical to literal truth, and in so doing has moved the reader from comfortable orthodoxy to dangerous heterodoxy without so much as a scholastic quibble. At the same time, he has also broken down the historical distance that allows the reader to push the Fall into the distant past. Displacing the Garden of Eden into the psychological here and now heightens the dramatic effect and lets Winstanley challenge the reader's unconscious assumptions.

Moving from the figuratively abstract to the politically specific, Winstanley freely develops his controlling metaphor. The inner Garden contains "five Rivers. Hearing, Seeing, Tasting, Smelling, Feeling, which we in our age of the world, call five Senses; And these five water springs, doe refresh and preserve the whole Creation, both of the out coasts, and of the Garden." Here the reference to "our age" again calls attention to contemporary degeneration and insensitivity, and the contrast between "out Coasts" and the inner Garden shows Winstanley's awareness of the historically conditioned alienation between outer and inner worlds, between body and soul, flesh and spirit. Also the notion of the senses refreshing and preserving all creation has direct affinities with the Stoic pneumatic theory, derived from Grecian medical schools, that Descartes called "animal spirits." But if Augustine's mistakes confirmed his existence and Descartes's thoughts asserted his identity, Winstanley's senses establish his humanity; his motto is *Sentio, ergo sum*. The Garden is simultaneously internal psychological existence and external material existence, and the senses are the streams of communication between

them. The Tree of Knowledge is "called Imagination," and the Tree of
Life is "called universall Love, or pure knowledge." When mankind feeds
upon the first, "which is his weaknesse and disease: then he looses his
honour and strength, and falls from his dominion, Lordship, and becomes like the Beasts of the field, void of understanding." What Winstanley calls "Imagination," then, is neither instinctive nor uninhibited
behavior but a stultifying combination of morose introspection and
sottish overindulgence. Blind imagination may sometimes lead the right
way, but just as often it leads mankind astray, for to oversee the creation
people "must know all things cleerely, as they be." One who eats of the
Tree of Knowledge is "driven out of the Garden, that is, out of himselfe, he enjoys not himselfe, he knowes not himselfe" and only delights
in external "objects." Turning to personification, Winstanley vivifies the
horror of this self-alienated state: he "fills you with feares, doubts,
troubles, evill surmisings and grudges, he . . . stirs up warrs and divisions; he makes you lust after every thing you see, or heare of, and
promises delight to you," such as "riches, places of Government, pleasures, societie of strange women: and when you have all these . . .
troubles follow the heeles thereof; and you see your selfe naked and are
ashamed." Now, in the twilight of the Beast's reign, all the nations of the
world eat of the Tree of Knowledge and are "cast out of themselves, and
knowe not the power that rules in them."

To eat of the Tree of Life is to experience undefiled delight. "Then man
is drawne up into himselfe againe; or new *Ierusalem*, which is the spirit of
truth, comes downe to Earth . . . This is the life, that will bring in true
community; and destroy murdering propriety." This "true community,"
where material existence is "drawne up" and the spiritual kingdom
"comes downe," this perfect reciprocation between outer and inner
worlds, results from a recognition of "the word within." Aware of his
place in time, Winstanley notes that his age calls this word "righteous
Conscience, or pure Reason; or the Seed of life that lies under the clods of
Earth, which in his time is now rising up to bruise the Serpents head, and
to cast that imaginary murderer out of the Creation." These linked
analogies move the reader from literal to moral to figurative interpretation before plunging him into the deep waters of anagogic truth. Such
rhetorical strategies prepare the reader to entertain a point of view,
which, stated baldly, he would thoughtlessly spurn: "This Seed . . . leads
mankinde into Truth, making every one to seeke the preservation and
peace of others, as of themselves; This teaches man inwardly to know the
nature and necessity of every body, and to administer to every body accordingly." Ultimately, the meaning of the Tree of Life is that society
should be governed, as the Geneva Bible's gloss on Acts 4:32 indicates, by

the axiom: from each according to his ability, to each according to his need. "This is the Kingdome of Heaven within, and the white stone, with the new name written therein, which no man knowes the glory, beauty, life, peace and largenesse of, but they which have it" (cf. Revelation 2:17).

When this kingdom becomes a reality, all will be saved; that is, all will "live in peace and rest." Therefore, this inner word or seed "is called the restorer, Saviour, Redeemer, yea and the true and Faithfull Leveller." And this kingdom is not an imaginary metaphysical place in the hereafter; it is experienced "by the five Sences, which is the Creation, Mankind, or the living Soule." Once cleansed of selfishness, the senses "are called pure Rivers of the waters of life," for then they convey the waters of life "from one to another through the whole body: and so bringing all into a onenes, to be of one heart and one minde." Then the whole creation "will laugh in righteousnesse, for there will be no murmuring or complaining . . . the heart shall sit singing, where are all my enemies . . . ? they are sunk, they are gone, as if I never had any." And just as this jubilant transformation takes place within "a particular body," so too will it take place without, in society. This "restoring spirit" or "vine" spreads until "the whole creation is brought into the unity of himselfe." When this "spirit of Love" rules, "then that great reformation, and restauration spoken of, shall be made manifest in the Nations of the world." All external rule, power, and authority will be destroyed, and "Mankinde every where, shall be made to speake and act purely according to the life and necessity of every body."

Having set forth his ideal and raised the reader, by degrees, to a higher level of consciousness, Winstanley returns to his controlling metaphor, the Garden of Eden, to explain more fully "What the Tree of Knowledge of Good and evill is." Simply stated, it is the corruption of the five senses by the imagination. To dramatize this point Winstanley personifies imagination as a Grendel-like beast who tears and devours "members of his owne kinde." And, like all beasts, this one has no sense of time, of history, and cannot prepare for the future, cannot conserve the fruits of the earth or believe in progress. Therefore it wantonly murders and destroys until, brought to where it began, it must die, not by "sword or weapons" but "by the word" of the sun of righteousness "and by the brightnesse of his comming." The logos, the word made flesh, brings together lower and higher worlds, the abstract and the concrete, general and particular, nature and grace. The divine seed of the sun of righteousness mates with "the mother Earth[,] mankinde" and completes the union betwen God and all creation. The history of this "copulative theology"[15] clarifies Winstanley's position. The basic image of the sun as the embodiment of divine knowledge, already ancient by the time of Plato's *Republic* (Book VI, 508e-519c), passed to the Romans and appears most notably in Cicero's *Timaeus ex Platone* where it implies that the empirical world is a "simulacrum" of the divine one.[16] However, while Neoplatonists—Bonaventure, Pico della Mirandola, Ficino, and Nicholas of Cusa—may have used this analogy to escape from history and confused biblical typology by taking such metaphors literally, they also provided the means by which radical reformers could reunite the creator and creation. In seeking to reconcile the Platonic distinction between mind and matter, idea and thing, they drew attention to the need to reassert the Thomistic synthesis between the order of grace and the order of nature in a way that was acceptable to the "new" philosophy.[17] For as Bacon explains in discussing medicine in *The Advancement of Learning* (1605), the poets knew what they were doing when they made Aesculapius "the son of the sun, the one being the fountain of life, the other as the second stream: but infinitely more honoured by the example of our Saviour, who made the body of man the object of His miracles, as the soul was the object of His doctrine."[18]

As Winstanley explains it, the battle between the forces of light and darkness is not an abstract Neoplatonic notion but a metaphor of real political significance. For while man "would be as God, knowing good and evill . . . he fills all creatures with sorrow and slavery, and so in the end . . . he is proved a Devill, and not the true God, the destroyer and murderer, and not the Saviour. The curse and not the blessing of the Creation, the power of darknesse, and not the power of Light." Those who call light darknesse, and darknesse light, good evill, and evill good" place mankind "in prison and bondage within himselfe." Men have built "the whole government of the world" upon this topsy turvy foundation; "all Nations are under this Kingdome of darknesse," and this power cannot be overthrown by the sword because it must be defeated by its opposite, by "a power contrary" to the devil's, "And that is, Love and patience." To bring down the evil kingdom about the ears of the devilish imagination, the power of love and patience must be "acted with a cheerefull life." Imaginary, conceited, intellectual knowledge, which makes a man envious and destructive, creates "feares where no feare is" and "rises up to destroy others, for feare, least others destroy him: he will oppresse others, least others oppresse him; and he fears he shall be in want hereafter; therefore he takes by violence, that which others have laboured for." Such a person is "like a blinde man" who beats the ground imagining "that hill or block lies in his way." Therefore Winstanley reinvests the Platonic seed, which Neoplatonists from Bonaventure to Eckhart saw as representative of the seed of Adam and Abraham embodied in Christ, which Cusanus metamorphosized into a metaphoric link between microcosm and macrocosm, and which Franck recombined with the logos concept, with something of its original meaning. As a true poet he sees that moving into the future often requires reaching into the past. This is not just a facile understanding of previous events or historical currents. It is an attempt to regain contact with that point in consciousness where words were united with deeds, thoughts with actions.

As Winstanley comes to know and understand that connection, as he pushes back further and further toward primitive cognizance of cosmic unity, he achieves a more clear-sighted view of his own day and time. When he personifies the contradiction between imagination and truth as a battle between the forces of darkness and light he regains some of the primal power found in the most ancient poetry: "as soone as Imagination began to sit upon the throne (Mans heart), The seed of Life began to cast him out, and to take his Kingdome from him; So that this is the great battaile of God Almighty; Light fights against darknesse, universall Love fights against selfish power; Life against death; True knowledge against imaginary thoughts." These two powers may also be personified as Michael and the Dragon. The battle fought between them in heaven is emblematic of the struggle within each human breast, the Garden of Eden, "where God principally resolves to set up his throne of righteous government." With this simple inversion of the Neoplatonic hierarchy, the world of the senses becomes the "real" world and the world of divine essences becomes a metaphor of it. The world is turned right side up, and the veil of obscurity is torn away.

When "every thing shall appeare naked, and bare before the Lord of the whole Earth, and all Imaginary coverings shall be taken off every where," people will see that the power of universal love comes from within. In this Lear-like divestiture of external dependence, Winstanley moves to the first person, becoming, in words much like Traherne's, the concrete universal of his experience:

Oh that I could see and feele Love, humility, chastity, sincerity, truth, wisdome, contentednesse, and peace live and rule in power in me: Then I should rejoyce abundantly, in the enjoyment of my selfe, within my selfe; though all other outward contentments in objects were taken away; though I were poore without, yet if I were rich within, I could rejoyce: if I were in prison, without, If I were in freedome within, I could rejoyce; if all my outward friends and objects forsooke me; yet if I had familiar friendship, with that sweet Spirit within, I should have peace enough.

Expounding on the inner kingdom's excellence, he explains how dependence on the outer kingdom (by which he means personal possessions, not the natural material world), is deceptive because "it forsakes a man in his misery; but the inward Kingdome never failes a man, in life nor death." Emphasizing the imminence of spectacular change, he counsels that "now is the coole of the day; And the heate of opposition betweene flesh and Spirit begins to decline." And, as in Marvell's "A Dialogue between the Soul and Body," he draws out his description by personifying Flesh and Spirit as distinct characters acting out this inner moral drama: "flesh sees his folly, and growes very weary." He honors the feminine Spirit, and the sun of righteousness, "The Seed and tree of Life, begins to walke in this coole of the day, with delight, in the middle of the garden (Mans heart)." The sweet breath of the Spirit is "now entertained, and falne Earth begins to see himselfe naked, and to acknowledge his nakednesse before the spirit, and is ashamed."

As a hush falls over the scene, the sanctified union approaches. "Falne Earth," symbol of the fleshly imagination, "declares how he came by his nakednesse; Even by embracing objects, and seeking a Kingdome without himselfe; his covetous heart closing with that imaginary conceit, promised him much delight," but this romance proved barren. Now, in union with Spirit, "the Seed begins to worke, to bruise the Serpents head." As he looks up, Spirit answers: "Thou seest thy selfe naked, and thou seest the Serpent that deceived thee; and thou art now separated from me . . . Thou art afraid to look within, because thy conscience, the Light, that is within thee, which is my selfe, condemns thee; And this feare is the fruit of thy Imagination; thou fearst where there is no cause of feare; Thou lookedst for good to come from objects without, but behold sorrow." Spirit is able to see Flesh's innermost thoughts and tells him how he thought that if he lost his possessions he could have no joy—but he now sees how the serpent, imagination, has deceived him. "Oh thou living soule," Spirit cries, "how art thou falne? Flesh argues that if Spirit does not enjoy "fulnes of all objects" it will "starve for food, and so presently feare of poverty takes the throne and reignes; and feare bids thee goe, get what thou canst, by hooke or by crooke, least thou want, and perish, and die miserably." But universal love and inner life, Flesh reminds Spirit, "will not preserve thy body from misery." Indeed, Flesh argues, though getting and spending is a hard life, to forsake it is to die alone and in want. Spirit, undaunted, agrees "this is an evill time"; and sees that the battle is "of another nature, then the former was." At first "Imaginary flesh was lofty and stout, and full of presumption . . . laughing in his sleave as we say, at the wayes of the Spirit of Life." Now his weapons are "slavish feare, evill surmising, sense of misery," anger, and despair. But Spirit's weapon, "consuming fire," will "come and fire Imagination out of all his strong holds, and with a strong power redeeme the imprisoned Earth from his presumptuous and dispairing bondage."

This second battle is the topic of the rest of *Fire in the Bush*, for "though there was a parley before, between flesh and spirit . . . yet the Serpent (Imagination) is not conquered by a sleight parley; but by a stronger contest." Therefore, before Flesh is reconciled to Spirit, before the consummation of the marriage within the heart, the battle must be fought out to the end. It is not enough simply to tell people they must forsake their attachment to objects and their dependence on external laws. It must be shown that "after this parley within himselfe, man is cast out of himselfe, that is, out of the garden," and the battle rages to show that "the Kingdome of Heaven is within you; and the word is nigh you, even in your mouth and in your heart . . . the Spirit is within; for the Creation is his clothing." And, true to the Neoplatonic principle set down by pseudo-Dionysius, Bonaventure, Eckhart, and Cusanus, Winstanley concludes that everything the imagination holds "to be without us, as *Adam*; the Serpent, the Garden, the Tree of Knowledge, of Good and evill; and the Tree of Life; and the fall of Man, and promise of redemption . . . are within the heart of man clearly." Whether these things actually existed outwardly in historical time "matters not much." What does matter is that they be seen within and that the natural soul, the imaginary serpent, and the restoring seed be recognized as essential parts of each person.

When recognized, this seed planted within grows to fruition and becomes the Tree of Life, the resurrection of Christ; "then woe, woe, woe, to the imaginary power, that rules the world, he shall be shaken with terror, and fall, and burst asunder . . . whatsoever government is set up by Imagination, shall be throwne downe." This government is fourfold. First, there is "the Imaginary, teaching power, called hear-say, booke-studying." Second, there is "The Imaginary Kingly power," by which one part of mankind rules another "By murder and theft." Third, "the imaginary Judicature, called the Law of Justice," upholds the Norman Yoke of the ruling class through the courts. And the fourth aspect is the "buying and selling of the Earth, with the fruits of the Earth." So, at the time of revolution, clergy, nobles, lawyers, and landlords—the entire ruling class—will "be shaken to pieces . . . by the brightnesse of his comming, and by the word of his mouth . . . These foure powers," Winstanley explains, "are the foure Beasts, which *Daniel* saw rise up out of the Sea . . . And this Sea is the bulke and body of mankinde, which is that Sea, and waters, upon which the Spirit of God is said sometimes to move; for out of Mankinde arises all that darknesse and Tyranny that oppresses it selfe; And though these Beasts appeare divers, one from another, yet they are all one in their power." This is typology with a vengeance; reaching back to the Book of Daniel, Winstanley reinvigorates the eschatological metaphors with contemporary significance. And, true to the fourfold method, he uses those metaphors to assert the relevance of prophecy in an historical perspective. First there is the literal dream itself; second, the dream's moral significance is the perpetual injustice inherent in the idea of a ruling class; third, this ruling class corresponds allegorically to contemporary institutions, and fourth, anagogically, the dream illustrates the persistence of these images in the human imagination. Moreover, by insisting that these "Beasts" are not coeternal but imaginary creatures of human origin, he opposes Gnostic dualism, avoids the Manichaean heresy, and reaffirms the total goodness of God's power. His point by point exegesis of Daniel's dream, in which the four beasts—the lion with eagle's wings, the bear with three ribs in its mouth, the leopard with four heads, and the beast with ten horns—are respectively identified with the nobility, the lawyers, the landlords, and the clergy ("the Father, that begot the other"), asserts the essential unity and interdependence of the ruling class. "All these Beasts, they differ in shape, and yet they agree all in one oppressing power, supporting one another; one cannot live without another; and yet they seem to persecute one another; and if one truly die, all dies."

The civil wars are cleansing plagues that will end when "that curse which hath destroyed the Earth, shall now in the period of time destroy himselfe." Then the sun of righteousness, the spirit of love within each man and woman, will take "dominion of the whole Earth," supplanting the aggressive masculinity dominated by the body. This new sexual identity represents a higher, more progressive, unified stage of consciousness, aware of its own responsibility for self-preservation, and, shared by all, this new consciousness maintains a sense of superiority over the body by rising above petty pains, fears, and lusts. Members of this community will be illuminated by a higher principle, the good of the collective whole. The microcosmic transformation each man and woman must undergo joins them to the macrocosm. The sun of righteousness mediates between spiritual and material worlds.[19] Democratizing this process, instead of seeing himself as a classical hero who will liberate his people, a Promethean figure like Marvell's Cromwell, Winstanley sees an entire class—the preindustrial proletariat—as attaining the distinctive consciousness that will give it the power to transform Babylon into the New Jerusalem. They will collectively see and know the truth, and the inner seed (or light) and the outer sun will combine to conquer the fear of returning Mother Earth to Edenic purity and apostolic communism. But the defeat of this fear entails giving up the aggressive masculine possession of Mother Earth, the basis of private property. Only those with stable egos dare surrender domination of Mother Earth and take the revolutionary leap to the next stage. For by this act alone, by overcoming the old phase of self-aggrandizement and selfishness, people successfully cast out fear and achieve lasting joy.

The end of the soldier's trade is to destroy itself, thus destroying kingly power. But the other three beasts, the clergy, the lawyers, and the landlords, still retain their power. Of these the clergy is most insidious because "he bred all the other; He is a King, understanding darke sayings, and he shall by craft deceive many." This beast first taught people to look outside themselves for justice and contentment, and in so doing created conditions favorable for setting up private property. "And so by that meanes the Creation is divided and Mankinde is put upon an Art to cheat, and burden himselfe." Next, this beastly clergy called up "the Law of Justice; a very good name, to cover his knavery; for he is a mighty Beast with great teeth, and is a mighty devourer of men; he eates up all that comes within his power . . . goe to Law, and none shall get but the Lawyer. The Law is the Fox, poore men are the geesse; he pulls of[f] their feathers, and feeds upon them." The clergy differs from the other beasts because it holds the others under its foot and gives them strength by its teaching. Out of its ten horns rise "ten particulars" that fight against the five senses and against understanding, will, affection, joy, and peace, which together form the seed of the new man. The clerical beast thus makes war against the new man and darkens heaven and earth by restraining "the liberty of the outward man, not suffering him to have a free enjoyment of his portion in the Earth; making such actions to be sinne, which the righteous creating Spirit made not a sinne." This, in turn, restrains "the liberty of the inward man, not suffering him to act in the liberty of himselfe; for he makes a man a sinner for a word, and so he sweeps the Stars of Heaven downe with his tayle . . . and defiles body and mind." The clergy's dominance of teaching causes spiritual blindness. For so long as he may not act according to his own inner needs, "but must be guided by others without me, and punished for such actions, which others in the ruling Chaire doe, in a higher nature then I doe; I am then in bondage, and my eyes are put out."

The clergy's usurpation of consciousness is an attempt to wrest the hero's role from the people, to turn altruism and self-sacrifice into selfishness and aggression. To do this the clergy must "blind" the people because the act of seeing represents self-consciousness just as light represents knowledge. The loss of intellectual creation by the hero, the working class, Winstanley represents as a spiritual blinding and regression to simple physical creativity—procreation and farming—which the clergy denegrates as lust and gluttony. Working people must take higher consciousness away from the clergy and reunite it with physical creativity. The clergy, by its "outward teaching power" formed a covenant with "the branches of Mankinde, to put out their owne eyes, to see by others; telling them none can see, but schollars." And now that kingly power has been destroyed, the clergy, "the extract of selfish righteousnesse," rules unabated and sets itself up as "a King of a fierce countenance." Spiritually blind people "easily receive him to be the outward ruler over their soules; for now the Sea being bemuddied, that is, mankinde being mightily deceived, he by his learned policy, riseth up out of that deceived Sea, for all the people wandered after him, though he sore oppressed them."

The sword of this clerical beast "is not his power," but it "lifted him up and supports him, by forcing the people to pay tithes; for the Law of the Magistrate forces the people to pay them." And this erect sword makes war with the heroic saints, the working people, and overcomes them "for a time, times, and dividing of time." Since it was not lifted up by its own power, it will be destroyed, not by the sword but "by the light and wisdome of the Spirit of Truth, that shall rise up out of the Sea of mankinde likewise, appearing in sonnes and daughters of righteousnesse, in the latter dayes." This sun of righteousness will destroy the clerical beast "by the word of his mouth, and by the brightnesse of his comming." Enlightened men and women will "see the deceit and falshood of this Beast, that hath deceived all the world; and shall fall off from him, and leave him naked and bare." By a chain reaction the beasts will be destroyed, "for they all depend one upon another." Therefore, far from representing anarchistic, wanton force, an instinctive animal passion wanting to destroy everything, the Christ-Levellers or Diggers express the idea embodied in the sun of righteousness. For just as this sun-son stands for the spiritual father, and just as he possesses the power of eternal rejuvenation through his sunny beams, he incestuously mates with Mother Earth to bring forth man. There is no reason to give examples drawn from pagan, Jewish, and Christian sources. The important thing for an understanding of Winstanley's use of this mystical pattern is to see how he explains that just as the first Adam broke God's law by eating of the Tree of Knowledge, the second Adam, Christ, breaks man's law, private property, to return to the original sharing of the Tree of Life, the great mother symbol.

If the reader thinks of the microcosmic spiritual seed uniting with bodily instinct in relation to the macrocosmic idea of the sun impregnating the earth, he will grasp the controlling metaphorical conception underlying *Fire in the Bush.* The reclamation of the body by the spirit corresponds to the reclamation of the earth by the sun. And by arrogating to themselves the strength of the sun, working people will become lords of the earth. They will conquer their animal instincts, subject the body to the spirit, and this conquest of instinct will no longer take the archaic form of possessing Mother Earth as private property, but will be manifest in the act of renouncing this instinctive desire and also of renouncing the desire to wreak revenge on the ruling class. Adam's sin, unbridled instinctuality, is attoned for by Christ's sacrifice, the conquest of instinct—the cross being the perfect symbol of the Tree of Life. By taking "the Iron sword" the New Model Army has reverted to Adamic or instinctive behavior; they slaughter their "owne sonnes" like an enraged father. But Christ, the sun of righteousness, "came not to destroy, but to save . . . Therefore, if there be any amongst you, that count truth and peace precious, take the Spirits advice, and come out of Babylon, dwell no longer in the Courts and wayes of Imaginarie confusion; come into truth, Light, and Liberty, and be at peace." By taking the spirit's advice (subjection of the body to the spirit, of animal instinct to conscious choice) the aggressive and destructive tendencies of the unconscious are assimilated and turned to constructing a new society. The old kingly power is destroyed by the unchecked anger of the New Model Army that rises against the King like adolescent sons against a harsh father. These "sons" represent an unleashing of instinctive power long kept down forcibly by kingly power. Now, having spent their passion, they too are ready to be superseded and absorbed into adult consciousness. Thesis, antithesis, synthesis—childhood, adolescence, adulthood; this is the inevitable pattern Winstanley sees behind the English Revolution. Now the blood-dimmed tide is loosed; it is time to move to a new stage of history. Instead of simply taking back Mother Earth from the kingly father, Winstanley asks the Puritans to conquer and sacrifice their base tendencies for the good of the community. So "when Christ comes, and is glorified with thousand thousands attending upon him, they shall not be cloathed with devouring instruments, like Dragons, but be cloathed with Love, Righteousnesse and Peace, like Lambs." The reign of the beasts ends, as the Book of Daniel indicates, in a fiery *lux in tenebris,* for just as the beasts' bodies were "given to the burning flame . . . all the Imaginary selfish Power, that made people run abroad for a Teacher, and a Ruler, was all cast into the fire of pure Light, and was consumed in that unquenchable flame; Even destroyed by the brightnesse of Christs comming, as darknesse vanisheth when Light comes in."

Having lifted the reader to a new level of consciousness through the exegesis of Daniel's dream, the Spirit affirmatively answers the question of whether all government and ministry created by the imagination will be destroyed. Every government stands only for a limited time, and when it proves to be "a Devill, a destroyer, and waster" it is "throne down." This will continue until the Spirit rules within each man and woman. The oppressing Puritans who think God has blessed them because they "sit downe in that Chaire of Government, out of which the former Tyrants are gone," should remember that their "overturning, overturning, overturning" will come to them as well as to their enemies; "You that pretend to be saviours of the people . . . and yet serve your selves upon the peoples ruines, not regarding the crie of the poore, surely you must have your overturnings too." Again the crucial point is the destruction of private property; equal access to Mother Earth must be ensured: "That Government that gives liberty to the Gentry to have all the Earth, and shuts out the poore Commoners from enjoying any part . . . is the Government of imaginarie, selfe-seeking Antichrist." Ministers have so debased and distorted language to make it seem as though the word "magistracie" is synonymous with both judicial power and divine power. Actually the two should be synonymous, but now they are diametrically opposed: "Magistracie is a good name, and the mystery of iniquity, hath not only got this name, but many other excellent names: to be set upon the head of his blacknes of darknesse, that under a good name he may goe undiscovered, and he puts bad names upon things that are excellent." If we submit the present "imaginary government" to the empirical test to see whether it deserves the name of magistracy, we see that a power "that divides part of mankinde to enjoy the Earth, and the other part not to enjoy the Earth" is unworthy of that name and "is an enemie to Magistracie." For "Magistracie signifies a great Light," which is the sun of righteousness, representing love, humility, reason, truth, and peace. And second, "Magistracie signifies the greatest Band, that ties the Creation together in peace, and this band is universall Love." True magistracy would be a government where internal love constrains all to act for the benefit of each other: if any say the present government is a band of peace, then he'll answer "What meanes then the lowing of the Oxen, and bleating of the Sheep? what meanes such complaints, that those that sit in the Chaire of Magistracie, are covenant, promise, and oathesbreakers, and are selfe-Lovers; Lovers of honour, money and ease, and regard not the cries of the oppressed? They favour the rich for reward, and despise and sleight the poore. They give the Earth to some, and denie the Earth to others . . . Now judge," Winstanley asks his righteous reader, "Is such a Magistracie as this the greatest Light?"

Like the child who announces the emperor's nakedness, "the babes and sucklings will draw off his vaile, and shew all his nakednesse and shame him." True majesty is found among the poor despised ones of the earth; "there you shall see Light and Love shine in Majestie indeed." The rich "are too stately houses for Christ to dwell in; he takes up his abode in a manger, Inne, and amongst the poore in spirit." And just as Christ rejects the rich, he also rejects "the learned publick Ministrie . . . set up by craft and covetousnesse." Such as serve this lord study only "how to draw the Earth, and the labours of men into the Clergies hands; These men make themselves ministers, as a man teaches birds to speake; But they doe not stay till Christ make them, for that will be too long for them to wait, the rich Benefices will all be taken up." Ministers take it upon themselves "to interpret other mens words and writings." Their arrogance in calling their interpretations "pure Doctrine," their audacity in telling people it is "pure Religion," and their venality in demanding tithes for such practices, show them to be false prophets who preach by imagination and hearsay evidence, not, as Christ taught, but what they "have heard and seen." They should preach the truth "purely and experimentally . . . The Scriptures . . . were written by the experimentall hand of Shepherds, Husbandmen, Fishermen, and such inferiour men of the world; And the Universitie learned ones have got these mens writings; and flourishes their plaine language over with their darke interpretation, and glosses, as if it were too hard for ordinary men now to understand them; and thereby they deceive the simple, and makes a prey of the poore, and cosens them of the Earth, and of the tenth of their labors."

This succinct statement of literary principle further illustrates Winstanley's concern for clarity and precision and his hostility toward obscurantism and pedantry. What is more, in perceiving that the ministers' dominance of scriptural exegesis is linked to political conditions, he sees that such hegemony keeps working people from achieving intellectual maturity. The clergy "shuts out the true Penmen in whom the Spirit dwells, and saith now, such Mechanicks must not meddle with spirituall things; and so by covetous policie, in opposition to the righteous spirit, they engrosse other mens experimentall spirituall teachings to themselves; as if it were their owne by University or Schoole learning succession. Pope like, Nay just the Pope." Worst of all, "by their blacknesse or darknesse, in their Schoole-learning, they have drawne a veyle over the truth; And Light by them is hid from the world" (cf. 2 Corinthians 3:14-18, which the Geneva Bible glosses in Malachi 4:2, the sun of righteousness passage). Winstanley wants nothing less than full and complete democratization of learning, "for the plaine truth is, this Imaginary ministrie is neither better nor worse, but plaine unmasked *Iudas*. And the snappish bitter profession, that cries it up, is the unmasked murdering Scribes, and Pharisees."

This far surpasses clever rhetoric; Winstanley is not merely summing up a point with a commonplace allusion. The reference itself concretely illustrates how the clergy tries to keep working people in ignorance. When he says the clergy has hidden the light from the world, he means just that, that ministers obscure the seed of the sun of righteousness within every man and woman by their control of language and culture. The reference to Judas precisely describes how the ministers betray the seed of God within them and within others. Therefore, Winstanley is not just relating the clergy's treachery to an abstract principle or to a personal sense of piety; he openly attacks the ministers for "preaching and praying, to a God without, they know not where, nor what he is" and for calling "every thing blasphemie, unlesse they approve of it, still tying the Spirit to themselves; saying Loe, here is Christ in this man, and loe, there is Christ in that man," when Christ is in everyone. He is "the Light of Life, spread abroad, and he is now rising in Husbandmen, Shepherds, Fishermen." The light within these unaffected working people "takes off the black interpretation, that the imaginary learned Scholars by their studies have defiled the Scriptures of old with, and restores them to their owne genuine and pure Light." For working people are "the vine that shall overspread the Earth" (cf. John 15:1-5); scriptures will no longer be confined "within a Colledge, or private University Chamber, or under a covetous, proud, black gowne, that would alwayes be speaking words: but fall off when people begins to act their words."

When the historical Jesus Christ, "the Sonne of man," walked the earth, the "hypocriticall snappish Pharisees" tried to "trap him in his speech . . . or else . . . they cryed out, he is a blasphemer, a Devill, and a friend of Publicans and sinners, condemning him, because he was no scholar." And just as the pharisees persecuted the historical Christ, ministers now "endeavour to suppresse him, and will not suffer him to arise in sonnes and daughters." They restrain and confine Christ to a limited historical phenomenon. "They owne him in words, but they denie him in power . . . And they call this blasphemie, to say Christ is in you, though the Scriptures which they professe say the same." This brings Winstanley to his most complex theological point, his explanation of "What the living Soule (Man) is." In the macrocosmic body of mankind and in the microcosmic body of each individual are "three particulars" that must "be knowne, without which no man can know himselfe . . . The first is the Creature, or the living Soule, which before the curse defiles it, is very good." This is the "Image of God (or of the righteous spirit) in flesh, or first *Adam*." Within this living soul is a heaven where Michael and the Dragon battle. "And this living soule is the wax fitted to receive, either the impression of the curse . . . or the impression of the blessing." The second particular is "the mysterie of iniquitie, or the power of deceit," also known as "the God of the world, or Prince of darknesse," or the devil "that deceives the living soule first, and takes possession, and this in one man is the Image . . . that is spread abroad through the Creation, to cover over, or keep downe the blessing, or Seed of Life from rising. The third particular is the rising of "the second *Adam*" within the living soul to cast out the curse or power of darkness. Only then may body and soul be united. In John 14:20 Christ prayed that his disciples would be united in body and soul, for "they were not united yet."

With this image of the seed of the sun of righteousness rising in the flesh, Winstanley moves toward completion of his organic metaphorical system. The spiraling reconciliation of opposites now approaches its consummation in the full maturity of the Tree of Life. The reader, if he has followed closely, has been led through a process of microcosmic self-preservation that at all times has maintained contact with nature, the macrocosmic world of things. Now he draws near the final step when the inner image of his own transformation is projected back out onto nature. The salvation of humanity entails the redemption of nature, and the Tree of Life perfectly symbolizes this conjunctive transformation. Descending into Mother Earth and reaching upward toward Father Sun, the Tree of Life, which is Christ, represents the union of body and soul within the individual and throughout history. Like the Fountain of Life, the Tree of Life is an image of the endless cosmic renewal:

> you that say you know but one power, be not deceived; for if this one power of righteousnesse, which is the tree of Life rule in you, then you are new creatures indeed, you are one with the Father and the Sonne; And then you shall know death no more: that is, you shall not live in opposition to the spirit of righteousnesse no more, neither in thought, word, nor deed; And then all sorrow and teares shall flie away likewise, and you shall be at rest, which is the day of the Lord, or the Light or day time of Mankinde. Darknesse is now swallowed up and gone.

Microcosmically, the divine seed planted within each human breast since Adam's time cannot grow until the dark cloud of covetousness vanishes and the sun of righteousness rises within. Then the seed sprouts and flourishes until the Tree of Life reaches out from the individual and bears fruit in the world in the form of giving and receiving love. Simultaneously, the seed of love within the world, hidden since the Fall, cannot gestate until mankind is freed from selfishness, especially private property; then when Mother Earth is restored to her primal condition of universal sharing, her son, Christ, the Tree of Life, nourished by the water of the fountain and the sunny beams of the Father, will germinate and burst into bloom. Everyone will eat from this tree, and the world will become an earthly paradise, matching, in reciprocation, the paradise within. The relationship between microcosm and macrocosm is dialectical. To speak of obtaining individual internal perfection without, at the same time, seeking universal external betterment is nonsense. Neither can be achieved alone. Therefore Winstanley, as before, enjoins the Ranters to pause and think whether they have truly achieved internal perfection and whether the world is actually prepared for universal peace.

The Ranters say those who see two powers contending within each person and within the cosmos see with two eyes, and they themselves, "see every thing and power with a single eye," and they therefore see no evil and declare "all things and actions are good, and as they must be."[20] If they are right and honestly strive to make this metaphysical truth a reality and "to eat of that Tree of Life," Winstanley will not condemn them. But if their actions show they are hypocrites and self-seekers, "if your owne eye be darke, that is, if darknesse rule your whole body; then all the actions of your body towards others are in darknesse, and builders up of selfishnesse, which is the one power you yet live in." If their "eye be truly single, and full of Light, then the Light power wholly rules in" them. To avoid simpleminded solipsism they must understand that each individual passes through the "three particulars" of mankind corresponding to the three stages in the development of the race. "The first particular is the living Soule, or that estate of simple plaine heartednesse, which hath the Life of the five Sences only." One living in this particular is devoid of "the Life of the Spirit," for "sound reason lives not yet in the Sences; for pure Reason lives like a corne or wheate, under the clods of Earth." In this state one "is set in the midst of many objects, tempting him like the Serpent"; and is susceptible to many injuries "like the tender grasse, that is soone bruised by the foot of the oxe." In this state, though there is self-love, "there is no hatred towards others." One is "as a childe," who, "though he love himselfe . . . yet he envies not others." Such a person may be compared to "plaine, honest hearted, even Innocent *Adam*"; he is "like wax, prepared for any stamp." But just as "*Judas* the twelfth man was a Devill" who followed Christ for selfish ends, so most ministers strive to advance themselves. The two powers— Christ and the Devil, light and darkness, Jacob and Esau, Flesh and Spirit—struggle with each person and "within the wombe of the living Earth, who shall rule first." At first darkness "prevailes, and rules within," drawing one "to seeke content in objects without." Then the restoring power "delivers the living soule againe from that bondage, and sets him downe in himselfe," and he becomes, as Vaughan wished to be, like "a little child." This is the meaning of the phrase "born again" from John 3:3-7 and 1 Peter 1:23, and is what Mark 10:15 and Luke 18:17 mean when they speak of the need to become childlike to enter heaven. This is also what St. Paul means when he says a man must become a fool to be wise (1 Corinthians 3:18). "This plaine heartednesse without envie or guile, is the Virgine-state of Mankinde; And this Virgine is she that must beare a sonne, and call his name *Emanuell*, God with us."

Drawing upon his familiarity with alchemical imagery, Winstanley explains that once one regains this chaste, childlike, androgenous state, "that hath no outward Lover, and that is not defiled, but cleansed from deformity . . . the Sonne of righteousnesse will arise, and take the man into union with himselfe; he rules as King, and Mankinde, the living soule, is freely subject with delight."[21] With a stroke he consummates the union of Flesh and Spirit by projecting the conventional androgyny of Christ into each breast. And he immediately follows this potent image with his most profound psychological insight: "this Innocencie, or plaine heartednesse in man, was not an estate 6000. yeare agoe onely; But every Branch of mankinde passes through it, & first is defiled by imaginary covetousnesse, and thereby is made a Devill; and then he is delivered from that darknesse, by Christ the restorer, and by him made one with the Father and the Son." Suddenly, in a burst of creative energy, he sees how the vital union of opposites must take place; in a flash the perfect synthesis of nature and grace springs to mind.

By seeing the world in a grain of sand and heaven in a wild flower, Blake and Darwin perceived that the specific implies the general, that the microcosm is analogous to the macrocosm, and they knew

> Many Sorrows and dismal throes
> Many forms of fish, bird & beast,
> Brought forth an Infant form
> Where was a worm before.[22]

This epigenetic metaphor, as Stephen Jay Gould writes, "may be the most durable analogy in the history of biology."[23] Because of the special role Aristotle's philosophy played in the Middle Ages, his idea of the relationship between ontogeny and phylogeny achieved something approaching universality. And his comparison of the threefold sequence of souls to adult organisms—nutritive to plants, sensitive to animals, and rational to humans—is, as Sir Thomas Browne notes, something more than a figure of speech to the seventeenth-century mind:

> first wee are a rude masse, and in the ranke of creatures which only are, and have a dull kinde of being not yet priviledged with life, or

preferred to sense or reason; next we live the life of plants, the life of animals, the life of men, and at last the life of spirits . . . thus is man that great and true *Amphibium* . . . and truely for the first chapters of *Genesis*, I must confesse a great deale of obscurity; though Divines have to the power of humane reason endeavoured to make all goe in a literall meaning, yet those allegoricall interpretations are also probable.[24]

Like Browne's "true *Amphibium*," Winstanley's new man is at once more limited and more progressive than the biological model. For to Browne and Winstanley the correspondence between microcosmic and macrocosmic evolution reveals the actual connection between the emotional development of each individual and the psychological history of the human race. From the time of Augustine Christian thinkers maintained a belief in some form of spiritual evolution; and just as William Harvey anticipates the "biogenetic law" that Charles Bonnet and Ernst Haeckel formulate into the ontogeny recapitulates phylogeny theorem, Winstanley's use of the three Joachite ages as a paradigm of psychological development anticipates Freud's expropriation of Haechel's theorem for his theory of psychosexual stages.[25]

However, Winstanley's true descendents in relating personal psychological recapitulation to the restoration of social equality are Marx and Engels. And this is no accident, for by converting the Tree of Life into the Tree of History, Joachim established the belief that history is a continuum, an unfolding process, in which the fruits of the past contain the seeds of the future. Joachim's idea of three successive, historical stages implies that the future will supersede the present and return to a pristine state of innocence, peace, and happiness here on earth. Changing economic circumstances in fourteenth-century Europe made this idea volatile. It passed into the mass millennial movements that culminated in the Peasant War in Germany, hastening the Reformation. And Joachim's three-part periodization of history still occasionally emerges as part of revolutionary rhetoric. Thus, just as Winstanley sees the civil wars as an opportunity to restore "the innocencie of mankinde," Marx and Engels look upon the upheavals of mid-nineteenth-century Europe as heralding a return to classless communism. As early as 1844 Marx connected historical change to the idea of returning man to himself. This concept, more fully developed in *The German Ideology* (1846), finds its way into *The Communist Manifesto* (1848), is present in the famous preface to the *Critique of Political Economy* (1859), and culminates in a passage near the end of the first volume of *Capital* (1867) where Marx writes that the part primitive accumulation plays in political economy is the same "as original sin in theology."[26] And in *The Dialectics of Nature* (1876),

Engels explains the "scientific" basis for the connection between social and biological evolution: "just as the developmental history of the human embryo in the mother's womb is only an abbreviated repetition of the history, extending over millions of years, of the bodily evolution of our animal ancestors, beginning from the worm, so the mental development of the human child is only a still more abbreviated repetition of the intellectual development of these same ancestors, at least of the later ones."[27]

But while Winstanley's ideas may be traced backward and forward, he should not be made to appear an anomaly. His ideas, like his images, are firmly rooted in his age. When he writes: "many men live in their innocencie longer then others, some are tempted sooner than others, but all must be tempted, and tried by the evill one," he expresses the seventeenth-century equivalent of the theory of neurosis in prose rhythms totally foreign to Freud. And in the following passage the delicate modulation of tone and voice, the extended balance and dialectical symmetry deftly broken at the end, catches the eye and ear in a way that Marx and Engels' ironic turns of Hegelian logic seldom do: "this innocent estate is the Image of God, but not the strength and life of God; It is wise, but not wisdome it selfe; it is just but not Justice; it is loving, but not Love it selfe. It rejoyces, but it is not Joy it selfe; it is patient, but not Patience it selfe; It is chaste, yet not Chastity; it is plaine hearted without guile, yet not sincerity it selfe; It is filled with rest and peace, while he injoyes himselfe within, and doth not make a league with Satan, or outward objects." And the circular movement of the lines on the fortunate fall motif synopsize the entire process of birth, death, and rebirth, which, like history, completes the circle on a higher level.

As men and women pass through this cycle they move from innocence to conflict to peace. The second estate, the "time of the curse" is most difficult. Here "lust of the Eye," "lust of the Flesh," and "pride of Life" struggle to dominate the spirit. "Lust of the Eye," caused by self-estrangement, is what Marx describes as the commodity fetishism resulting from alienation:[28] "The lust of the eye is covetousnesse, after any object the man sees, thinking within himselfe, that if he can obtaine such and such objects, he shall be at rest and filled with delight." Yet lust is never satisfied. When he cannot enjoy objects, envy and anger arise, and even when he can joy is fleeting "and ends in vexation." Similarly, "Lust of the flesh" looks upon others as sexual objects to be wasted and consumed, not cherished and preserved. In this state there is no healthy enjoyment of mutual pleasure between man and woman, only the urge "to satisfie excessive Beastly desire," which carries over into immoderate eating, drinking, and dress where such a person, "by his excesse, destroyes himselfe." In "the pride of Life" man becomes a devil; "he is a prisoner to his lusts, and is in bondage within himselfe," hating himself and all others. "Discontent dwells in his heart" and he "feeds upon husks like the swyne: that is, his delight reaches to outward things only; to riches, honours, pleasures, and women, they are the husks he feeds on, which dies and rots." But "the third estate of Mankinde" when the sun rises up within "is the restoring power." All things are made new, and man is brought "back againe, to his estate of Innocencie and plaine heartednesse." Thus a man must be made a fool in the eye of the world before he is made wise and sits down in rest never to fall again. And while all people do not move through these three estates at the same rate, everyone sooner or later sees the two powers oppose each other within and casts the murderer out before eating of the Tree of Life and entering into the New Jerusalem. As it is now, "the Devill rules the world; Imaginary selfe-loving Covetous-nesse rules the King in the Earth." Yet the promised third age of the spirit is coming. The ages of the Pharaoh and the Pope are past. Now is the dividing of times; "reformed Episcopacy" has been overthrown; the "variety of Independent and Presbyterian Churches, or State-Govern-ment" has come in. This dividing of times is reflected "within the heart of man, which is the occasion of that outward division of times."

Winstanley divides the transition from innocence to full maturity into five separate "times." The first stage, innocence, is one of free, sim-ple, sensuous pleasure when the senses discover the world of enjoy-ment. During this stage one "knowes not the power of the Seed, or of the creating spirit"; he is "wise, and loving and just; but not Wisdome, Love, and Justice it selfe." One tempted "breaks out into folly, envie, and un-justice." The second stage is when "the pleasure of sinne enters . . . and the man being deceived, lookes altogether without him for good, for pleasure and for content." Greed begins, and there is no guilt: "he can lie, and cheat, and whore, and oppresse others, and thinks all is good." This stage corresponds to the first step of the Fall, "eating the Aple." Next comes "a time of trouble of minde" when his crimes begin to catch up to him. Friends desert him, his health deteriorates, and guilt reigns in his heart. The fourth stage is "the dividing of time, within a man, and this is, when the Law in the members fights against the Law of the minde." In this most important stage, a man "sees himselfe a prisoner to his Lusts," and the light in him strives against the darkness. This battle between Michael and the red Dragon becomes unbearable, and the man cries out for deliverance. Finally, "the man enters into rest." The seed kills the serpent, casts him out, takes possession, and rules in righteousness and peace, transforming "the five living Sences" into a "living Soule, or Earth."

This process, recapitulated within each person, is not complete until it takes place in the external world. And while a few liberate themselves before the external world is liberated, most lie groaning under the darkness of the dividing of time within them because they are "mightily opprest." To them Winstanley counsels patience. As ever, he promises "the day of Sions glorie" draws near. To those who say that if universal love prevails all private property and trading for profit will be destroyed, he boldly answers, "it is true." To those who say the sword must be used "to restraine the unrulinesse of mankinde," he answers that such people intend to rule "and beat downe others . . . And indeed this power is the cause of all warres; for if this murdering selfe-honouring power were once cast out; Love would live in peace, and know warre . . . no more."

To complete the revolutionary transformation, people must understand how things have arrived at their present state. Since history is a shared view of the past, it must be reinterpreted to make the transformation seem necessary and the utopian future possible. In medieval miracle plays the Fall parodies courtly life; God is a manorial lord governing his estate with providential absolution. But in Sir Walter Ralegh's *History of the World* (1614), with its emphasis on free will, the determinent of middle-class ideology, the Fall becomes the *locus classicus* of history; it is at once "historical" in that it refers to events alleged to have taken place long ago and "timeless" in that it describes a recurring pattern.[29] It explains the present and the past as well as the future. During the civil war era this function of myth was replaced by a political ideology, a consciousness related to a class effective enough to make a practical difference. To understand how this ideology is redefined through the story of the Fall, the reader must see the story and the ideological implications attached to it, in Louis Althusser's words, "as a real whole, internally unified by its own *problematic*, so that it is impossible to extract one element without altering its meaning," and he must also see that "the meaning of this whole . . . depends not on its relation to a *truth* other than itself but on its relation to the existing *ideological field* and on the *social problems and social structure* which sustain the ideology and are reflected in it."[30] Finally, the reader must step outside the ideology to discover its motivating principle.

Just as Winstanley returns to simple Anglo-Saxon words, he returns also to the intense visual imagery of the Fall found in Caedmon's hymn and *Genesis B*. To clarify the reasons for rejection of middle-class ideology, he tries to force fallen words back to their prelapsarian state. First, "outward objects" such as riches and honors are "set before the living soule"; second, "Imaginary covetousnesse . . . moves the man to close with those objects and to seeke content without him"; third, "warres, divisions, and discontent" arise. "The misery of mankinde came in by these degrees." In the beginning "mankinde walked in singlenesse and simplicity each to other." Even though "Some bodies were more strong then others . . . the stronger did work for the weaker, and the whole Earth was common to all without exception." In time the stronger grew to resent the weaker and said, "why should I that doe all the worke, be such a servant to these . . . ? It is fit I should have some larger part of the Earth . . . and that they should acknowledge me in some degree above them." This is the original corrupting impulse, for it sets individual gain above public good. "Imagination is the Serpent that deceives the man." What was "an honour," the stronger helping the weaker, was perceived as a fetter. At first this envy was but a thought—"consent within being moved by outward objects of pleasure"—but it soon broke forth "into outward action." The stronger set out "to inclose parcells of the Earth into severall divisions, and calls those inclosures proper or peculiar to himselfe . . . and the younger brother lets it goe so; and presently their nakednesse appears." Note that the objects appear first as a temptation— an outward cause—and that the thought, which came second, gave birth to the deed. Moreover, and this is essential, even afterward the younger brother, by letting it "goe so," complies in the deed.

The creation of private property was neither natural nor easy: "this dividing of the Earth into parcells, was long before it grew a strong setled custome; for plaine heartednesse did much oppose the growth of this imaginary covetousnesse, or Serpent." The Fall constitutes the progessive destruction of innocence through the creation of private property. Desire for "outward objects" and "for one to be above another" precipitated the Fall; the actual act was the logical extension of the corrupted impulse. Corruption of humanity's relation to the real conditions of existence caused the Fall—"Imagination . . . deceives the man"—now the reader sees the importance of these words. Distortion of the real world by the imagination gave rise to original sin, which, in turn, precipitated the creation of an ideology. The *cause* arises *out of* the situation; it is not imposed *on it*. The distortion is an act as well as an idea. It has material existence in the form of private property, and although it originates in a distorted view of reality, it distorts reality itself and makes itself felt in concrete objective reality. The story of the Fall is the myth through which middle-class ideology is expressed. That is why it plays such a central role in seventeenth-century English thought and why Winstanley, by reinterpreting the Fall, attacks the central myth of middle-class society. Paralleling Freud's myth of the primal horde, he dramatizes the process of the Fall by depicting how private property, the possession of Mother Earth, gradually came to dominate the economic affairs of men until "divisions and wars begins to arise betweene the brothers." The younger brother rises up against the elder, but, as with Cain and Abel, the elder triumphs: "he kills his brother, and removes him out of the way, though Conscience tormented him afterwards for it." This continued until "at last *Moses* was raised," and while he justly endeavoured to keep peace and tried to limit each to his own property, he was "not he that shall restore you to your first singlenesse and Innocencie," but Moses "points out Christ," and declares all who will not hear "shall be cut off from amongst the people." Everything prior to Christ's coming "was part of the fall," and the earth degenerated until "now divisions and enmity is risen to the height, and the power of the Sword is the very strength of the curse . . . for this takes not away propriety from others, by labour, or by buying and selling; but by cruell violence and force." The Fall was a process, not a single act, taking place throughout history.

Emphasizing the imminence of the restoration of fallen mankind, *Fire in the Bush* closes by projecting the contradiction between spiritual nakedness and material covetousness resulting in man's alienation from himself and from others out into the world. Citing the parable of the rich man and Lazarus from Luke 16:19-31, Winstanley explains how hypocrites fare deliciously every day, go about dressed in silk and gold, and have "Chests full of silver, houses full of corne, and other fruits of the Earth," yet they see others starve for want before their faces and make a profession of Christ, as though they served him. All their power comes from "the title they have to their Land" got by the sword by which they not only kill and rob but make laws to keep themselves in power. A member of such a group "hedges the weake out of the Earth, and either starves them, or else forces them through poverty to take from others, and then hangs them for so doing." All working people want is to supply necessities, but a rich man calls this "unrighteous, and hangs them for it . . . the plaine truth is, the Law of propriety is the shamefull nakednesse of Mankinde." Having torn away the ideological veil masking such greed, Winstanley holds up the soldiers and lawyers who "would be called Saints and members of Christ" to ridicule and forces the ordinary reader to step back from beliefs that coincide with those of the ruling class. When Winstanley writes: "you are members and actors of the curse . . . you are that power that hedges some into the Earth, and hedges others out, and takes to your selves by the power of the killing sword," he expects the reader to be appalled by the shock of recognition.

Therefore it is not enough simply to say that he perceives the economic base of society or that he makes the formation of private property part of original sin; his major achievement is the objectification of middle-class ideology. Using his own experience as a concrete universal, he concludes that the "enmity that brought in this division; first of inclosing; then of buying and selling, then of killing one another for the Earth, is the curse within of imaginary covetousnesse, and it was bred by the presentment of outward objects, tempting the five Senses." Original sin, then, comes not from an inborn tendency toward evil; it arises not from a trivial single act in the past; it is a process growing out of particular economic conditions manifested in actual material existence. To Winstanley, the Fall is not an abstract, timeless generality, but a historical phenomenon originating with the creation of private property and the commodity character of the division of labor it produces.

Cutting through theological obscurantism, Winstanley sees "all the strivings that is in Mankinde, is for the Earth, who shall have it." The only real issue is "whether some particular persons shall have it, and the rest have none, or whether the Earth shall be a common treasury to all without respect of persons." All oppositions are reducible to this conflict between private property and community. Rejecting those, such as Hobbes, who hold that the power causing divisions and war is "the state of nature, which every man brings into the world with him," Winstanley wishes to return to single-heartedness so he may "walke in the light of pure Reason." For evil is not part of human nature; human nature is a potentiality in bondage. A newborn child "is innocent, harmelesse, humble, patient, gentle, easie to be entreated, not envious"; like Adam, such a child continues this way "till outward objects intice him to . . . seeke content without him; And when he . . . suffers the imaginary Covetousnesse within to close with the objects, Then he falls." So the Fall results from a reciprocation between "outward objects" and a Satanic inner impulse. This dialectic continues throughout the process of the Fall: first the "lusts within" enslave the man, then "inward torment" takes over until he "reject outward objects . . . preferring this Kingdome within." Christ had no "imaginary covetous power" within him so he was not tempted "to seeke a Kingdome, or happinesse without himselfe, in those objects of pleasure, riches, and honours." He "preferred the Kingdome within"; "there was nothing in him that consented to the temptation without." But Winstanley does not altogether reject material needs or pleasures. Christ "made use of outward objects in moderation, for the safety and peace of his body, but desired nothing in excesse." For just as the marriage between the inner seed of the sun of righteousness and the outer Mother Earth produces the fruit of spiritual and material abundance, the union of "The objects without" and "the curse within" brings forth enslavement of "the Earth, or the living Soule, which is the innocencie of the five Sences. While these two joyne together, and meet in consent, Mankinde enters into sorrow, and hath [no] true rest." Yet, true to the promise of Matthew 6:19, when the seed rises up and mankind "seeks for a Kingdome within, which moth and rust cannot corrupt" quietness and contentment will reign.

Pleading for people to "kill Covetousnesse, or that imaginary darknesse within." Winstanley closes with a paean to the rising seed of the sun. He looks for a return to "pure creation" so mankind may move on "into a better condition then he was in before" when the seed will be "seen within." For the two greatest sins are

> First for a man to lock up the treasuries of the Earth in Chests and houses; and suffer it to rust or moulder, while others starve for want to whom it belongs, and it belongs to all; This is the greatest sinne against universall Love; this is the destroying sinne, this is *Achans* sinne;[31] this is the action of Covetousnesse.
>
> The second sinne is like to this, and is the same in nature with the other; And this is for any man, or men, first to take the Earth by the power of the murdering sword from others; and then by the Lawes of their owne making, doe hang, or put to death any who takes the fruits of the Earth to supply his necessaries, from places or persons, where there is more then can be made use of by that particular family, where it is hoorded up.

Desperately trying to hold their small band together under continued legal and physical harrassment, on 26 March 1650 the Diggers published *AN APPEALE TO ALL ENGLISHMEN, to judge between Bondage and Freedome, sent from those that began to digge upon* George Hill *in* Surrey; *but now are carrying on, that publick work upon the little Heath in the Parish of* COBHAM, *neare unto* GEORGE Hill, *wherein it appeares, that the work of digging upon the Commons, is not onely warranted by Scripture, but by the Law of the* Common-wealth *of England likewise.* Focusing directly on the issue at hand, Winstanley calls once more for all Englishmen to "let not *Sottish* covetousnesse in the *Gentrey,* deny the poore or younger Brethren, their just Freedom to build and plant Corne upon the common wast Land: nor let slavish fear, possesse the hearts of the poor, to stand in awe of the *Norman* Yoake any longer, seeing it is broke." Paraphrasing Psalm 107, he rhetorically asks "what hinders you now? will you be slaves and beggars still, when you may be Freemen? will you live in straits, and die in poverty, when you may live comfortably? . . . wil you not rise up & act?" And building on the premise that "it is the badge of hypocrisie, for a man to say, and not to do," he attacks the clergy for compelling the poor who make 12 pence a day to pay them as much as £ 100 to £ 200 yearly and at the same time preaching that the poor "must be content with their Poverty, and they shall have their Heaven hereafter. But why," he asks, "may we not have our Heaven here (that is, a comfortable livelihood in the Earth) And Heaven hereafter too?"

Overturning the Neoplatonic notion that the body must be mortified to elevate the spirit, he pleads: "while we have bodies that must be fed and cloathed, let us have Earth to plant, to raise food and rayment by our labours, according to the Law of Creation, and let us live like men." To those who say the old Adam looked after the earth and the new Adam looks to heaven, he answers that if this were true the old Adam would be "more rational and tender over our bodies; then the second *Adam, Christ,* who brings in the blessing to all Nations." If ministers really expect heaven in the hereafter they should give up their livings and beg instead of living in comfort on working people's tithes. The old Adam represents bondage and straits, but the second Adam stands for "Freedom, plenty and peace, here in this Earth." With King Charles dead, clerical and legal power revert to the people. The land now belongs to all, for with Parliament's victory *"England* is made a free *Common-wealth.* And the common Land belongs to the younger Brother, as the Enclosures to the elder Brother." Those who refuse to subscribe to the Engagement "shall have no priviledge in the *Common-wealth* of *England,* nor protection from the Law." The poor are now free to "build upon, and plant the Commons," and tenant farmers are freed from paying rents.

By seeing the hostile tenant farmers as vulnerable and manipulatable Winstanley shows understanding for the very people who have injured him most and tries to build a coalition between the poor and the lower-middle-class strong enough to withstand the increasing pressure from the gentry who control Parliament. "You *Englishmen,*" he exhorts, "whether Tenants or labouring men, do not enter into a new bond of slavery, now you are come to the point that you may be free, if you will stand up for freedom." Assuring his readers that "nothing is wanting on your part, but courage and faithfulness," he asks them to take possession of their own land, "which the *Norman* Power took from you, and hath kept from you about 600. yeares." This coalition between tenant farmers and laborers will solidify an attack on the gentry and clergy. People should "stand up for your freedom in the Land, by acting with *Plow* and *Spade* upon the *Commons.*" By so doing begging will be abolished; production will rise; England will fulfill its destiny as the first nation to overthrow Babylon and establish the New Jerusalem; hearts will be united against any foreign invader; crime will be prevented, and the earth will be restored to its original position as a common treasury.

In April 1650 Giles Calvert published the last Digger pamphlet. *An Humble Request to the Ministers of both Universities and to all Lawyers in every Inns-a-court* resulted from "*a discourse between Parson* Plat *Lord of the mannor* of Cobham, *and* Gerard Winstanley." Platt promised to cease molesting the Diggers and even join them if Winstanley "could prove by Scriptures, the lawfulnesse of the work." Since "this difference between Lords of Mannours and the poor, about the common Land, is the greatest controversie that hath rise up this 600. yeares past," Winstanley will show that "the whole Earth: By the Law of Creation, is the Common treasury of free Livelyhood, to whole Mankind." Epitomizing the arguments of *Fire in the Bush,* the pamphlet succinctly outlines the typological approach to history that produced Winstanley's political philosophy. Christ's bidding the young man to give all he had to the poor (Luke 3:5-6) shows mankind will be restored "to the law of righteousness, from whence he fell; for when once the Law of Love and truth is written in the heart of Man-kinde, they will never quarrell one with another about the earth, who shall have it, and who not, for it is the birth-right and Inheritance of all." These scriptures, "being but a gleaning of the Bible, gives a full warrant to all poore men, to build them houses, and plant corne upon the Commons . . . [for] true Religion, and unde-filed, is to let every one quietly have earth to manure, that they may live in freedome by their labours; for it is earth that every one seekes after, that they may live in peace, let them say what they will." The abolition of private property and the setting up of a communist state will destroy covetousness. And since scripture confirms the right of all to enjoy the earth, it follows that all laws and customs upholding private property are null and void, especially now that kingship is overthrown. People must not just be declared free however, "for our freedome must not lye within the clasps of a Booke, in words that may be read; nor in the bare title of a Victory; but it must be freedome really enjoyed, or else it will do us no good." If England is truly a free commonwealth, the Norman Yoke is broken, and if "all the old ancient fundamentall lawes" are re-established then "*Salus populi,* the safety, peace, and preservation of the whole body of the people, excepting none," is the law of the land.[32] This "fundamentall law," Winstanley reminds his readers, gave "life and strength to the Parliament and Army to take up Armes against the King; for they had not the least letter of any written law." Finally, the Engage-ment confirms the people's freedom under the commonwealth: "for if I have not freedom to live in peace, and enjoy food and rayment by my Labors freely, it is no *Commonwealth* at all." What is more, this freedom has been purchased by money and blood in the civil wars.

In spite of repeated prosecutions and persecutions, the Diggers broke no Laws: "if idle persons, who wander up and down idly" should be punished, "Then judge whether it be not the idle Gentry, rather then the laborious poor man." Assured of the righteousness of his cause, Winstanley only regrets he can "set no time" for its success, "but I wait for the consolation of *Israel* to arise up, and break forth in others, as I have a taste of him in my self." Seizing the offensive, he declares the lawyers and clergy "are put upon the tryal" to be saved or damned in the eyes of the poor. Parson Platt and a gang attacked a Digger family, beat the wife so that she miscarried, and destroyed their house. And after the Diggers agreed, in exchange for peace, "to let the wood alone till people did understand their freedom a little more," Platt and fifty men burned the colony to the ground, showing "they will not suffer the poor to have either earth or freedom, but what they hire of them." Left with nothing but the hope that "though the Devill be let loose to swell against us, in these Gentry that rule over us . . . yet his time to be chained up drawes nigh: and then we are assured this righteous work of earthly community, shall have a most glorious resurrection out of his ashes," Winstanley closes with a prophecy that "your name shall rot, and your own power shall destroy you." He retreats to the paradise within, leaving the "work of digging, being freedom, or the appearance of Christ in the earth" to another day. He knows he has "ripped up the bottom of their Religion," has proven it to be "meere witchcraft, and cosonage," yet, for the present, he admits that the gentry has "trod our weak flesh down." The battle between "freedom and bondage" still rages over "who shall rule in Mankind."

The colony's destruction dimmed, but did not destroy, Winstanley's desire to create a better world. After some Diggers threshed wheat on Lady Eleanor Douglas' estate in Pirton, Hertfordshire, this notorious prophetess accused Winstanley of cheating her. In a long letter Winstanley, who acted as steward, says she calls him to judgment "like a theeff in the night" to pick a hole in his coat. He punningly prays for her to moderate her jealousy until they "have threshed all out," and he chastises her for calling herself "the prophettesse Melchisedecke," and reminds her that true prophets "delayed not to keep covenant . . . They were noe taxmasters . . . They did worke with there owne handes . . . They would not eate others' labors and live att ease themselves." He assures her, "it is the convertion of your spirit to true Nobilitie . . . not the weight of your purse that I looke after." And he reminds her he was her "Saviour in this last Somer's crop in getting the sequestracon taken of[f] your estate." The letter concludes by accusing the lady of having "lost the Breeches, which is indeed true Reason . . . and you must ware the long coates still, tell you know yourself."[33] Clearly Winstanley lost neither his wit nor his ire after the Digger defeat.

Sometime before 20 February 1652 he published his last and

best-known work, *THE Law of Freedom IN A PLATFORM: Or, True Magistracy Restored*, with a dedicatory letter to Cromwell dated 5 November 1651. Although this platform has obvious similarities to More's *Utopia*, Bacon's *New Atlantis*, and Gabriel Plattes' *Marcaria*,[34] it differs from these abstract programs in that it is meant to be put into effect immediately. In this sense its predecessor is the Levellers' *Agreement of the People*, and its descendents are James Harrington's *Oceana* (1656) and Milton's *Readie and Easie Way to Establish a Free Commonwealth* (1660). Winstanley nowhere suggests his platform is permanent or perfect. It is rather a device for ensuring that the *opportunity* for England to develop into a utopian society be kept open. The title-page poem makes the provisional nature of what follows clear.[35]

> In thee, O England, is the Law arising up to shine,
> If thou receive and practise it, the crown it will
> be thine.
> If thou reject, and still remain a froward Son to be,
> Another Land will it receive, and take the crown from
> thee. (Revel. 11:15, Dan. 7:27)

With an extended metaphor from Jonah 4:6, Winstanley tells Cromwell "*Jonah's* Gourd is a remembrancer to men in high places," and asks him to recall that "the worm in the Earth gnawed the root, and the Gourd dyed, and *Jonah* was offended." Begging Cromwell to bear with him while he speaks plainly, he explains that "the Earth wherein your Gourd grows is the Commoners of *England*. The Gourd is that Power which covers you, which will be established to you by giving the People their true Freedoms, and not otherwise. The root of your Gourd is the heart of the People, groaning under Kingly Bondage, and desiring a *Commonwealths* Freedom in their English Earth. The worm in the Earth, now gnawing at the root of your Gourd, is Discontents." The three heads of this worm are opportunism, time-serving, and plain-dealing. The last is the only one Cromwell should heed. For if he is to have his gourd "stand for ever," he must "cherish the root in the Earth; that is, the heart of your friends, the oppressed *Commoners* of *England*, by killing the Worm. And nothing will kill this worm, but performance of professions, words, and promises, that they may be made free men from Tyranny." Winstanley takes up the metaphor again when he explains that he laid his platform aside two years earlier "in silence, and said, I would not make it publick," but after the New Model Army chaplain Hugh Peters published *Good Work for a Good Magistrate*, Christ's warning not to "bury thy talent in the earth" burned like fire in his bones: "I was stirred up to give it a resurrection, and to pick together as many of my scattered papers as I could finde, and to compile them into this method." Since the only choice is either to be governed by rule of law or by the arbitrary wills of rulers, he sets the candle at Cromwell's door, "for you have power in your hand . . . to Act for Common Freedome if you will; I have no power." And, he asks Cromwell to emulate the "industrious Bee," and "suck out the honey and cast away the weeds" from his treatise. "Though this Platform be like a peece of Timber rough hewd, yet the discreet workmen may take it, and frame a handsome building out of it."

Winstanley's program "is like a poor man that comes cloathed to [Cromwell's] door in a torn country garment, who is unacquainted with the learned Citizens unsetled forms and fashions," and he asks the leader of the Commonwealth to "take off the clownish language, for under that you may see beauty." Indeed, in this final pamphlet Winstanley is all too conscious of his "clownish language," for while there are flashes of brilliance, the work's choppiness disconcerts the reader, and the artificially imposed structure of the platform lends the ideas a rigidity not seen previously. The awkward method of composition, the throwing together of bits and pieces of "scattered papers," the deliberate, almost obsessive, outlining and categorization shows Winstanley tried to force his material into a shape it would not willingly take. This validates Jameson's point that when the utopian longing concealed behind prophetic language or displaced in the Golden Age enters a work "directly, as content, in secular fashion, as in the various literary Utopias themselves, there results an impoverishment which is due to the reduction of the multiple levels of the Utopian idea to the single, relatively abstract field of social planning."[36] To the degree that Winstanley maintains contact with the prophetic tradition through typological exegesis he succeeds in pointing up the need for social reform, but the adaptation of his material to the secular realities of a workable political system causes a falling off of linguistic intensity and nuance. The dialectical interplay of opposites so evident in earlier works is altogether lacking here. The lack of inherent form indicates Winstanley's failure to organize his utopian plan into a coherent whole and seriously inhibits the practicality of his agrarian scheme.

A brief epistle "TO THE FRIENDLY AND UNBYASSED READER," giving "a short Compendium of the whole," skillfully anticipates the general reader's objections to a communistic state:

Every Family shall live apart, as now they do; every man shall enjoy his own wife, and every woman her own husband, as now they do; every Trade shall be improved to more excellency then now it is; all children shall be educated, and be trained up in subjection to parents and elder people more then now they are: The Earth shall be planted, and the fruits reaped, and carried into Store-houses by common assistance of every Family: The riches of the Store-houses shall be the Common Stock of every Family: There shall be no idle person nor Begger in the Land.

The law of freedom is the necessary assurance of restraint on those who, out of "unreasonable ignorance," would hinder the "common Freedom" of others. This is in complete accord with Winstanley's previous explanations of the consequences of the Fall.[37] The platform defines the conditions that make true freedom possible. Rejecting free trade, free preaching, free sex, and the freedom of one person to oppress another as freedoms that "lead to Bondage," Winstanley asserts the materialistic basis of his utopia:

> true *Freedom* lies where a man receives his nourishment and preservation, and that is in the use of the Earth: For as Man is compounded of the four Materials of the Creation, *Fire, Water, Earth,* and *Ayr;* so is he preserved by the compounded bodies of these four, which are the fruits of the Earth; and he cannot live without them: for take away the free use of these, and the body languishes, the spirit is brought into bondage, and at length departs, and ceaseth his motional action in the body.

To him "a man had better to have had no body, then to have no food for it." Psychological bondage, such as "covetousness, pride, hypocrisie, envy, sorrow, fears, desperation, and madness, are all occasioned by the outward bondage." Therefore, by "natural experience" he believes "true Freedom lies in the free enjoyment of the Earth."

History records the attempts by a few to wrest freedom from many. The rich live in a heaven on earth and the poor live in hell; the rich enjoy the fruits of other's labor while they hire ministers to tell the poor of a heaven and hell after death. They blind the reason of the poor so they believe every doctrine preached by the rich ministers and never question anything because they are told "The Doctrine of Faith must not be tryed by Reason," for if it were "their Mystery of Iniquity will be discovered, and they would lose their Tythes." The rich thus count the freedom of others their bondage and enjoy great possessions while others who have worked harder have little and are "made slaves to their brethren." As the example of Esther shows, "common Freedom was that which men of righteous spirits always fought after." To insure this "common Freedom" against transgressions that "may arise from ignorant and rude fancy in man," "Laws of moderate diligence, and purity of Manners" should be made. But these will be few for under "Common Freedom" murmurings, grudges, troubles, and quarrels seldom arise as they do among oppressed peoples. When there is "freedom in the Land" no "Club Law" is necessary. But under kingly government there is no order "because it is the covetous and proud will of a Conqueror, enslaving a conquered people . . . Indeed this Government may well be called the Government of high-way men, who hath stoln the Earth from the younger brethren by force, and holds it from them by force."

Kingly government "makes one brother a Lord, and another a servant, while they are in their Mothers womb, before they have done either good or evil." This "Machavilian spirit" hypocritically tells people, "Well, I'le ease you, and I'le set things to rights," and proceeds to set up capitalism. When people begin fighting it says, "*Come follow me, to one sort of people that are oppressed, and stick to me, and we will fight with those who wrong you; and if we conquer them, then we will govern the Earth as we please, and they shall be our servants, and we will make them work for us.*" Thus mankind falls from innocence "and from the glory of the spirit of common Freedom . . . every one striving to be King one over another; every one striving to be a Landlord of the Earth, and to make his brother his servant." The evil spirit then says, "*You must make one man King over you all, and let him make Laws, and let every one be obedient thereunto:* And when the people consented thereunto, they gave away their Freedom, and they set up Oppression over them selves." This "Monarchial spirit is the power of darkness, for it is the great thick Cloud, that hath hid the light of the Sun of Righteousness from shining in his full strength a long time." But now, as in Milton's description in *Eikonoklastes* (October 1649) of Charles I as a false sun who darkens the true sun of the Reformation embodied in parliament,[38] Winstanley's sun assumes his rightful throne:

> The Winter's past, the Spring time now appears,
>   Be gone thou Kingly Tyrant, with all thy Cavaliers.
> Thy day is past, and sure thou dost appear
>   To be the bond-mans son, and not the free-born Heir.

The cloak hiding subtle covetousness, pride, and oppression will be stripped off; commonwealth government will "arise from under the clods, under which it is buryed, and covered with deformity." For this spirit of mankind "called the *light*, or *son of righteousness and peace*" whose name tyrants have used "while he hath lien buryed, to cover their cheating mystery of Iniquity" so the people would "dance after the pipe of self seeking wits," is none other than the "antient of days" who ruled before "oppressing government crept in." This healing and caring "spirit of universal Righteousness dwelling in Mankinde, now rising up" will draw all to him. But since this spirit does not rise at the same rate in everyone, law is necessary "to preserve common Peace and Freedom."

A couplet sums up the opportunity that must be seized:

> The Haven gates are now set ope for English Man to enter:
> The Freedoms of the Earth's hid due, if he will make adventure.

Here the key phase, "make adventure," looks back to both "Man to enter" and "The Haven gates" waiting to receive him like the prodigal son's father's arms. Through such metaphors, in line with Milton's view in *The Tenure of Kings and Magistrates* (February 1649) that government rests upon a mixture of Aristotelian and Augustinian principles, Winstanley ground his program on a combination of the classical view of the state as a natural development from the family and the medieval theory that government is based on a provisional contract set up to stem the appetites of the unregenerate and attain a better correspondence with nature. "The Law of Necessity, that the Earth should be planted for the common preservation and peace of his household, was the righteous Rule and Law to *Adam*, and this Law was so clearly written in the hearts of his people, that they all consented quietly to any counsel he gave them for that end."[39] It was therefore not just Adam's will but the will of his people "that governed both Adam and his houshould." Two roots of law spring from the extension of the familial relationship, the root of "common Preservation" attached to "the tree of Magistracy" whose boughs and branches are the laws of righteousness and peace and the root of "Self perservation" attached to "the Tree Tyranny" whose boughs and branches are "all particular Kingly Laws found out by covetous Policy to enslave one brother to another." Since "in the first Family, which is the Foundation from whence all Families sprang," the father, the first link of the chain of magistracy, taught his sons and daughters "how to plant the Earth" and live in peace, all succeeding magistrates, chosen as father surrogates, must oversee the government: "And thus a Father in a Family is a Commonwealths Officer, because the Necessity of the young children choose him by a joynt consent, and not otherwise." These commonwealth officers, elected annually from those over forty years old, like good fathers, cherish their children until they grow wise and strong.

From family to town, from town to county, from county to nation, everything in Winstanley's commonwealth is organized "according to Reason and skill." There is no luxury, idleness, or ease; all must work to support themselves and to "learn the inward knowledg of the things which are, and find out the secrets of Nature." There is forced labor for idleness and execution for major crimes, but no prisons; there are judges who "pronounce the bare Letter of the Law," but no lawyers because "the good Laws made by an industrious Parliament, are like good Eggs layd by a silly Goose, and as soon as she hath layd them, she goes her way, and lets others take them, and never looks after them more, so that if you lay a stone in her nest, she will sit upon it, as if it were an Egg." Now that England is a "free Commonwealth" Winstanley hopes Parliament will "not only dandle us upon the knee with good words and promises till particular mens turns be served, but will fill our bellies, and clothe our backs with good actions of Freedom."

To this end the commonwealth's function, in conjunction with feeding, clothing, and sheltering its inhabitants, is the investigation of man and nature. Yearly elected ministers will read the law and instruct the young. Speeches on "all Arts and Sciences" will be made often. "And in these Speeches may be unfolded the nature of all herbs and plants from the Hysop to the Cedar, as *Solomon* writ of. Likewise men may come to see into the nature of the fixed and wandring stars, those great powers of God in the heavens above; and hereby men will come to know the secrets of Nature and Creation, within which all true knowledg is wrapped up, and the light in man must arise to search it out." All knowledge is to be made public and none kept "secret to get a living by." Indeed, knowledge will "cover the Earth, as the waters cover the Seas" when everyone speaks freely from experience "what he hath found out by his own industry and observation in tryal," for "thus to speak, or thus to read the *Law* of Nature (or God) as he hath written his name in every body, is to speak a pure language." Once the material conditions to free people's minds and bodies are provided they may discover God's secrets in nature. In what J. Max Patrick calls "the finest passage in all his works,"[40] Winstanley reveals the final stage of his material pantheism:

> To know the secrets of nature, is to know the works of God; And to know the works of God within the Creation, is to know God himself, for God dwels in every visible work or body.
>
> And indeed if you would know spiritual things, it is to know how the spirit or power of wisdom and life, causing motion, or growth, dwels within, and governs both the several bodies of the stars and planets in the heavens above; and the several bodies of the earth below; as grass, plants, fishes, beasts, birds, and mankinde; for to reach God beyond the Creation, or to know what he will be to a man, after the man is dead, if any otherwise, then to scatter him into his Essences of fire, water, earth and air, of which he is compounded, is a knowledge beyond the line, or capacity of man to attain to while he lives in his compounded body.

To spin speculative fancies out of the imagination is to "build castles in the air" and to tell "of a world beyond the Moon, and beyond the Sun, meerly to blinde the reason of man . . . God manifests himself in actual knowledge, not in imagination; he is still in motion, either in bodies upon earth, or in the bodies in the heavens, or in both; in the night and in the day, in Winter, in Summer, in cold, in heat, in growth, or not in growth."

Experience proves that the only truth is knowledge of the material world and the only peace is enjoyment here on earth. All else is obscurantism and hypocrisy covered over with corrupt language. Theology does not speak of the truth within each human heart; it speaks "words to deceive the simple, that he may make them work for him, and maintain him, but he never comes to action himself to do as he would be done by; for he is a monster who is all tongue and no hand." This monster "takes upon him to tell you the meaning of other mens words . . . and by thus doing darkens knowledge, and wrongs the spirit of the Authors." And if anyone objects he says, "you must not judge of heavenly and spiritual things by reason, but you must believe what is told you, whether it be reason or no." This specious doctrine assails the sickly and weak spirit of the poor and maddens the spirit of the wise. "For my own part," Winstanley says in evidence of his knowledge of biblical hermeneutics, "my spirit hath waded deep to finde the bottom of this divining spiritual Doctrine: and the more I searched, the more I was at a loss; and I never came to quiet rest, and to know God in my spirit, till I came to the knowledg of the things in this Book." He knows enough of the methods of biblical exegesis to see that those who "preach this divining Doctrine are the murtherers of many a poor heart, who is bashful and simple, and that cannot speak for himself, but that keeps his thoughts to himself." Such language "is made a cloke of policy by the subtil elder Brother, to cheat his simple younger Brother of the Freedoms of the Earth."

Warning poor people not to have their eyes put out and their reason blinded so "they see not what is their birthrights, and what is to be done by them here on Earth" by this "filthy Dreamer" and "Cloud without rain," the "divining spiritual Doctrine," he attempts one final time to revive the living ideas beneath the layers of dead language. He attacks theological mystification as a practice that "came in after Christ to darken his Knowledg; and it is the language of the Mystery of Iniquity and Antichrist, whereby the covetous, ambitious and serpentine spirit cozens the plain-hearted of his portions in the Earth" by being made to "bazle" his estate away to the priests in hope of a heavenly reward or by "running to hear Divinity Sermons, and dancing after his charming pipe." To avoid such casuistry and hasten the day when light will cover the earth, he advocates concentration on discovering the "secret in Nature." In this way he hopes to ensure freedom and avoid returning to "Kingly Oppression," for he reminds his readers there is no difference between "a professed Tyrant, that declares himself a Tyrant in words, Laws and deeds . . . and him who promises to free me from the Power of the Tyrant if I'le assist him; and when I have spent my estate and blood, and the health of my body . . . sits himself down in the Tyrants Chair, and takes the possession of the Land himself, and calls it his, and none of mine."

His own fate illustrates what all poor people may expect if England remains a capitalistic society:

> now my health and estate is decayed, and I grow in age, I must either beg or work for day wages, which I was never brought up to, for another; when as the Earth is as freely my Inheritance and birth-right, as his whom I must work for; and if I cannot live by my weak labors but take where I need, as Christ sent and took the *Asse colt* in his need, there is no dispute, but by the Kings and Laws, he will hang me for a thief.

Neither mute nor inglorious, he asks the "Righteous Spirit of the whole Creation" to "judg, who is the thief. Him who takes away the freedom of the *common-earth* from me, which is my Creation rights . . . Or I, who takes the *Common-earth* to plant upon for my free livelyhood, endeavouring to live as a free *Commoner*, in a free *Commonwealth*, in righteousness and peace." He calls upon the "Prophets of old" to speak "if this be not true" and asks once more for the "right ordering of Land, to make it fit to receive seed" and the exercise of reason "to finde out the Secrets of Nature" so "the Spirit of Knowledg" may flourish. Only then will the serpent's head be bruised and "the power of Life (called the Law of Nature within the creatures) which does move both man and beasts" be guided by an inner law and governed by a spirit of "moderate watchfulness [that] is still the law of Nature in a higher resurrection." Now, having achieved this state, Winstanley closes his career as poet, prophet, and utopian with his finest poem. He asks the key question and supplies the pathetic answer:

> Here is the righteous Law, Man, wilt thou it maintain?
> It may be, is, as hath still, in this world been slain.

The next line summarizes the contradiction he cannot accept:

> Truth appears in Light, Falshood rules in Power;
> To see these things to be, is cause of grief each hour.

He calls out to Apollo, in Faustian anguish:

> Knowledg, why didst thou come, to wound, and not to cure?
> I sent not for thee, thou didst me inlure.
> Where knowledge does increase, there sorrows multiply,

To see the great deceit which in the World doth lie.
Man saying one thing now, unsaying it anon,
Breaking all's Engagements, when deeds for him are done.

All passion spent, he invokes one final time the prophetic spirit connecting him with eternity, and reaffirms the vital link between man and nature:

O power where art thou, that must mend things amiss?
Come change the heart of Man, and make him truth to kiss:
O death where art thou? wilt thou not tidings send?
I fear thee not, thou art my loving friend.
Come take this body, and scatter it in the Four,
That I may dwell in One, and rest in peace once more.

LITTLE IS known for sure of Winstanley's life after 1652. In October 1660, the executors of the estate of the cloth-merchant Richard Aldworth had him arrested and put under subpoena in chancery, claiming that he owed £114 15s. 3d on a bill of £331 left over from his bankruptcy in 1643. Winstanley said he had paid the debt but had no receipt and therefore filed a complaint asking that Aldworth's books be examined for record of payment.[41] Fifteen years later, in June 1675, a corn-dealer living in Bloomsbury named Gerrard Winstanley filed suit claiming that one Ferdinando Georges owed him £1850 by an indenture of 10 April 1666 and had promised to pay his wife, Elizabeth, and her two sisters, an annuity of £200. If this is the former Digger, his first wife, Susan, must have died before 1664, for according to records of the Westminster Monthly Meeting of the Quakers, the older of his two sons by Elizabeth was born about 1665. There was no settlement on the suit because Winstanley died on 10 September 1676.[42]

Such matters, however, are of little consequence in assessing the literary merit of Winstanley's pamphlets. For when viewed in its entirety the body of work he created forms an overarching pattern of completion. The progressive development of theme and structure from *The Mystery of God* to *The Breaking of the Day of God* to *The Saints Paradise* finds its most lucid expression in the visionary outburst at the center of *The New Law of Righteousnes*. And, after the founding of the Digger colony, a gradual lessening of prophetic excitement and literary control in subsequent works is momentarily regained in the incomplete *Fire in the Bush* but irredeemably lost in the diffuse *Law of Freedom*. This suggests that the silence of his later years is a sign of wisdom. His refusal to call upon the gods with vulgar spite testifies to his sanity and his perspicacity. The fall of the Barebones Parliament and the establishment of the Protectorate in December 1653 rendered his moderate millenarianism untenable. "The Revolution," as Christopher Hill aptly remarks, "was over."[43] From that point on the choice for people like Winstanley was either to support the champions of propertied society or join with the fanatical Fifth Monarchists in attempting to establish the millennium by violence.[44] Clearly Winstanley could accept neither of these tyrannical alternatives. He had spoken; he had acted. No more could be expected of him. Not until Blake raised his fierce prophetic voice a century later did England see his like again.

But while Winstanley failed to build a New Jerusalem, his career as a radical pamphleteer was not futile. Like all true poets who live in tumultuous times his ideas developed and changed in response to experience, but where there is change there is also continuity. For underlying Winstanley's vigorous attempt to seize the day, a strong and powerful intellect is at work that insists upon rising to the occasion with firm principles in mind. The first of these, which he articulated from the beginning of his career, is that a just government must be based on impartial laws and run in the best interests of ordinary working people. A second principle is that the dialectical interplay of opposites observable in nature requires a reasonable moderation in all things. And a third principle, the one this study has emphasized, is that the restoration of political vitality proceeds hand in hand with the development of linguistic accuracy. Clear thinking and plain speaking lead the solitary way through Eden. With these political, natural, and literary principles, Winstanley reached back to the origins of consciousness and looked forward to the day when the earth shall all be paradise and not for ourselves but for the eternal family we live.

NOTES

I. THE RISING SUN

1. Thomas Carlyle, ed., *Oliver Cromwell's Letters and Speeches* (1845; rpt. New York, n.d.), I, 427-434.

2. Charles H. Firth comments on Winstanley's works in *The Clarke Papers* (London, 1894), II, 215-221. G. P. Gooch brought him to a wider audience in *English Democratic Ideas in the Seventeenth Century* (1898); 2nd ed. (1927; rpt. New York, 1959), pp. 182-191. Edward Bernstein discusses him in *Sozialismus und Demokratie in der grossen Englischen Revolution* (Stuttgart, 1895), translated by H. J. Stenning as *Cromwell and Communism: Socialism and Democracy in the Great English Revolution* (1930; rpt. New York, 1963), see pp. 105-131. Perez Zagorin sees Winstanley as a transitional figure between Anabaptism and socialism in *A History of Political Thought in the English Revolution* (London, 1954), pp. 43-57; C. H. George argues for a rationalist view in "Gerrard Winstanley, a Critical Retrospect," in *The Dissenting Tradition: Essays for Leland H. Carlson*, ed. C. Robert Cole and Michael E. Moody (Athens, Ohio, 1975), pp. 191-225; and George Juretic gives a mechanistic interpretation in "Digger No Millenarian: the Revolutionizing of Gerrard Winstanley," *JHI*, 36 (1975), 263-280.

An opposing view emerges from Lewis H. Berens, *The Digger Movement in the Days of the Commonwealth* (1906; rpt. London, 1961); and from Rufus M. Jones, *Studies in Mystical Religion* (London, 1909), and *Spiritual Reformers in the Sixteenth and Seventeenth Centuries* (1914; rpt. Gloucester, Mass., 1917), where Winstanley's similarity to Traherne is first noted (p. 334). This view is taken up by Winthrop S. Hudson in "Gerrard Winstanley and the Early Quakers," *Church History*, 12 (1943), 177-194, and "Economic and Social Thought of Gerrard Winstanley: Was He a Seventeenth-Century Marxist?" *Journal of Modern History*, 18 (1946), 1-21; and by Paul Elmen in "The Theological Basis of Digger Communism," *Church History*, 23 (1954), 207-218. A recent work in French is Olivier Lutaud's *Winstanley, socialisme et christianisme sous Cromwell* (Paris, 1976).

3. David W. Petegorsky, *Left-Wing Democracy in the English Civil War, a Study of the Social Philosophy of Gerrard Winstanley* (London, 1940), p. 178.

4. George H. Sabine, ed., *The Works of Gerrard Winstanley* (1941; rpt. New York, 1965), p. 5.

5. J. Max Patrick, "The Literature of the Diggers," *UTQ*, 12 (1942), 95-110.

6. Christopher Hill, ed., *Winstanley, The Law of Freedom and Other Writings* (Harmondsworth, 1973), p. 54. Hill's view is discussed by Lotte Mulligan, John K. Graham, and Judith Richards in "Winstanley, a Case for the Man as He Said He Was," *Journal of Ecclesiastical History*, 28 (1977), 57-75.

7. Franklin H. Littell, *The Origins of Sectarian Protestantism, a Study of the Anabaptist View of the Church* (1952; rpt. New York, 1964), p. 21; also Stephen E. Ozment, *Mysticism and Dissent, Religious Ideology and Social Protest in the Sixteenth Century* (New Haven, 1973), pp. 1-13.

8. Christopher Hill, *The World Turned Upside Down, Radical Ideas During the English Revolution* (London, 1972), pp. 121-147.

9. John Passmore, *The Perfectibility of Man* (New York, 1970), p. 213.

10. K. B. McFarlane, *John Wycliffe and the Beginnings of English Nonconformity* (London, 1952), pp. 90-91.

11. Hill, *World Turned*, p. 27; also William Haller, *Foxe's "Book of Martyrs" and the Elect Nation* (London, 1963).

12. Stanley Edgar Hyman, *The Tangled Bank: Darwin, Marx, Frazer, and Freud as Imaginative Writers* (New York, 1962), p. x.

13. Petegorsky, pp. 121-122. Sabine mistakenly gives the date of Winstanley's baptism as 10 July.

14. Hill, *Winstanley*, p. 11.

15. Petegorsky, p. 122. It was not unusual for boys to be apprenticed to widows; see Stephen R. Smith, "The London Apprentices as Seventeenth-Century Adolescents," *Past & Present*, No. 61 (November 1973), p. 158.

16. Alfred P. Wadsworth and Julia DeLacy Mann, *The Cotton Trade and Industrial Lancashire, 1600-1780* (1931; rpt. Manchester, 1965), pp. 26-27.

17. Petegorsky, p. 123; Sabine, p. 6.

18. Quotations in this paragraph are from William Haller, *The Rise of Puritanism, or, The Way to the New Jerusalem as Set Forth in Pulpit and Press from Thomas Cartwright to John Lilburne and John Milton, 1570-1643* (1938; rpt. New York, 1957), pp. 261, 267. On Everard's and Randall's probable influence on Winstanley see Sabine, pp. 29-31; and also Robert W. Kenny, ed., *The Law of Freedom in a Platform* (New York, 1973), p. 23.

19. Haller, *Rise of Puritanism*, p. 269; see also Katherine Koller, "The Puritan Preacher's Contribution to Fiction," *HLQ*, 11 (1948), 321-340.

20. John F. Wilson, "A Glimpse of Syon's Glory," *Church History*, 31 (1962), 66-73; and A. R. Dallison, "The Authorship of *A Glimpse of Sions Glory*," in *Puritans, the Millennium and the Future of Israel: Puritan Eschatology 1600 to 1660*, ed. Peter Toon (London, 1970), pp. 131-136.

21. In *Puritanism and Liberty, Being the Army Debates (1647-9) from the Clarke Manuscripts with Supplementary Documents*, ed. A.S.P. Woodhouse, 2nd ed. (1951; rpt. Chicago, 1974), pp. 234-237.

22. Woodhouse, pp. 239-241.

23. Wadsworth and Mann, pp. 57, 63.

24. Petegorsky, p. 123.

25. Christopher Hill, *God's Englishman, Oliver Cromwell and the English Revolution* (London, 1970), p. 98.

26. According to Gregory King's 1699 estimate, the population of London was 530,000; towns contained 870,000 inhabitants, and small villages housed 4,100,000. He further estimated that 246,000 people earned their living from commerce, 240,000 from trades and industries, and some 4,265,000 from agriculture; M. A. Gibb, *John Lilburne the Leveller, a Christian Democrat* (London, 1947), p. 208.

27. Michael Walzer, *The Revolution of the Saints, a Study in the Origins of Radical Politics* (1965; rpt. New York, 1973), p. 216.

28. Hill, *World Turned*, p. 126.

29. In Hill, *World Turned*, p. 128.

30. I have used the copy in the British Library, shelfmark 4377. a51. (1).

31. William Haller, *Liberty and Reformation in the Puritan Revolution* (1955; rpt. New York, 1963), p. 85.

32. Erich Auerbach, "Figura," in *Scenes From the Drama of European Literature*, trans. Ralph Manheim (New York, 1959), pp. 42, 52. On the distinction between typological and allegorical interpretations see Thomas M. Davis, "The Traditions of Puritan Typology," in *Typology and Early American Literature*, ed. Sacvan Bercovitch (Amherst, 1972), pp. 11-45; and Karlfried Froehlich, " 'Always To Keep the Literal Sense in Holy Scripture Means To Kill One's Soul,' the State of Biblical Hermeneutics at the Beginning of the Fifteenth Century," in *Literary Uses of Typology from the Late Middle Ages to the Present*, ed. Earl Miner (Princeton, 1977), pp. 20-48.

33. William M. Lamont, *Godly Rule: Politics and Religion, 1603-1660* (London, 1969); see also the debate between Lamont and Bernard Capp from *Past & Present* reprinted in *The Intellectual Revolution of the Seventeenth Century*, ed. Charles Webster (London, 1974), pp. 386-434.

34. Auerbach, pp. 53, 57. I disagree with William G. Madsen's view that "unlike Everard, Winstanley explicitly denies the literal-historical reality of the biblical narratives"; *From Shadowy Types to Truth, Studies in Milton's Symbolism* (New Haven, 1968), p. 45. In my judgment both Everard and Winstanley deny the literal but accept the historical reality of the biblical narratives.

35. John Everard, *The Gospel-Treasury Opened*, ed. Rapha Hartford (London, 1657), I, 94. The first edition (1653) is entitled *SOME Gospel-Treasures Opened*; another edition was published in 1659.

36. [Giles Randall], *Divinity and Philosophy Dissected and Set Forth by a mad man* (Amsterdam, 1644), p. 13.

37. John Saltmarsh, *Sparkles of Glory* (London, 1647), pp. 20-22.

38. Woodhouse, p. 390. Collier believed that "the kingdom of God is within you" and, like Winstanley, held that heaven and hell were mental states. The opposing view—that Christ would literally come and swiftly create a utopia—came, as John F. Wilson shows, almost exclusively from university-trained divines; *Pulpit in Parliament: Puritanism During the English Civil Wars, 1640-1648* (Princeton, 1969), pp. 222ff.

Marjorie Reeves explains that a belief in the Second Coming as the final historical event with a millennium to follow as an extrahistorical state "runs counter to the Joachimist philosophy of history. The true mark of a Protestant

Joachimism is the third historical *status*, with its assignation of historical roles matching those of the Old and New Testaments which represent the first and second *status*" ushered in by an outpouring of the spirit; *Joachim of Fiore and the Prophetic Future* (1976; rpt. New York, 1977), pp. 142-143.

39. Haller, *Rise of Puritanism*, pp. 153-154.

40. In *A Preface to Chaucer: Studies in Medieval Perspective* (Princeton, 1962), D. W. Robertson, Jr., explains that "the Old Testament 'types' are more than foreshadowings of the Gospels; they are historical manifestations of principles set forth in the New Law . . . In technical language, typology employs allegory to imply tropology, which is its ultimate aim . . . The relationship between the two elements, old and new, is implied rather than stated, but the spiritual meaning for the individual which arises from their combination is something which can result only from the intellectual effort of the observer" (pp. 189-190).

In *Sparkles of Glory* John Saltmarsh says that the idea that humanity will be restored to a purely spiritual existence results from "a mistake of the *type* of the Jewish Apostacy and captivity which figured out the *Spirituall* Church or new *Jerusalem* in *Babylon*, or Captivity to the flesh" (p. 117). The destruction of Antichrist, he notes, is "the sum and substance of all types" (p. 120).

41. In "Upon Appleton House, to my Lord Fairfax," "ev'ry Thing does answer Use" (1. 62); *The Poems and Letters of Andrew Marvell*, ed. H. M. Margoliouth, 2nd ed. (Oxford, 1952), I, 60; and in *Paradise Lost* (IV, 691-692), "the sovran Planter . . . fram'd/ All things to mans delightful use"; *The Complete Poetry of John Milton*, ed. John T. Shawcross, rev. ed. (Garden City, N.Y., 1971), p. 334.

42. G. E. Aylmer, *The State's Servants: The Civil Service of the English Republic, 1649-1660* (London, 1973), p. 292.

43. A. L. Morton, *The World of the Ranters, Religious Radicalism in the English Revolution* (London, 1970), p. 49.

44. Hill, *World Turned*, p. 301.

45. Petegorsky, page 126. Calvert began publishing Boehme in 1647; like Serge Hutin, I am unable to find concrete evidence of Boehme's influence in Winstanley's works; see *Les Disciples anglais De Jacob Boehme aux XVIIe et XVIIIe siècles* (Paris, 1960), pp. 54-58.

46. I have used the British Library copy, shelfmark 4377. a51. (2).

47. Since the publication of C. B. MacPherson's *The Political Theory of Possessive Individualism, Hobbes to Locke* (Oxford, 1962), the extent to which the Levellers wished to widen the franchise has provoked much debate. Key points are summarized in Morton, pp. 197-219; see also Keith Thomas, "The Levellers and the Franchise," in *The Interregnum: The Quest for Settlement, 1646-1660*, ed. G. E. Aylmer (London, 1972), pp. 57-78.

48. On the metaphorical basis of utopian thought see Mircea Eliade, *Cosmos and History, the Myth of the Eternal Return*, trans. Willard R. Trask (1954; rpt. New York, 1959); and Ernst Topitsch, "World Interpretations and Self-Interpretations: Some Basic Patterns," in *Myth and Mythmaking*, ed. Henry A. Murray (Boston, 1968), pp. 157-173.

49. H. N. Brailsford, *The Levellers and the English Revolution*, ed. Christopher Hill (London, 1961), pp. 47-48.

50. Traditionally, Norman Cohn explains, "popular eschatology had identified these witnesses as Elijah and Enoch, the two personages in the Old Testament who were 'translated' to heaven without undergoing death in the body"; *The Pursuit of the Millennium, Revolutionary Millenarians and Mystical Anarchists of the Middle Ages*, rev. ed. (New York, 1970), p. 145.

51. John F. Danby, *Shakespeare's Doctrine of Nature, a Study of King Lear* (1948; rpt. London, 1961), p. 113. In addition to 1 Cor. 3:18, John Everard preached that St. John "was counted a *madman* or a *fool*," but he "was content to be accounted a *Fool*" (I, 40, 42).

52. Cf. Thomas Goodwin's sermon *Zerubbabels Encouragement to Finish the Temple* (1642), discussed by Paul Christianson in "From Expectation to Militance, Reformers and Babylon in the First Two Years of the Long Parliament," *Journal of Ecclesiastical History*, 24 (1973), 225-249.

53. Explaining why he is not a Seeker, Saltmarsh notes in *Sparkles of Glory* "that to wait in any such way of seeking or expectation, is Antichristian, because there is no Scriptures to warrent any such restauration, or expectation of such administrations: and that all such waiting is, that desert, wilderness-condition prophesied on by Christ," in Matt. 24 (pp. 294-295).

54. Following Foxe, Puritan preachers taught, using Isaiah 66:11 and Luke 23:29, that it was sinful for women not to nurse their babies; see *The Acts and Monuments of John Foxe*, ed. George Townsend (New York, 1965), I, ii, 334; and Haller, *Rise of Puritanism*, p. 30.

55. Winstanley earlier notes: "when Christ comes in his brightnes; in glory light and beauty as the Sonne that shines from East to West, enlighting the whole earth. Then will this Beast or wisdome of the flesh be distroyed, in all her shapes and disguises, first in the flesh and hearts of Saints, And afterward through the multitude of Saints, and their manifold discoveries from God all her confusion shall be thrown down in the world and she shal reign no more." For further discussion of this important image see below Chapter II, n. 62.

56. Roger Sharrock summarizes the principles of seventeenth-century spiritual autobiography in his edition of Bunyan's *Grace Abounding to the Chief of Sinners* (Oxford, 1962), where he notes that Puritan autobiographies "tend to conform to a standard pattern. The authors share a common method of introspection." But between 1640 and 1660 "Baptists, Quakers, and Seekers injected fresh vitality into the form and applied it to new purposes" (pp. xxviii-xxix). See also Owen C. Watkins, *The Puritan Experience, Studies in Spiritual Autobiography* (New York, 1972).

57. Frank E. Manuel, *Shapes of Philosophical History* (London, 1965), p. 37. Wilhelm Schenk notes the similarity in the way Saltmarsh and Winstanley connect unlimited spiritual power with a Joachite conception of the millennium in *The Concern for Social Justice in the Puritan Revolution* (London, 1948), pp. 98-99. A clear statement of the Joachite concept is found in Collier's Putney sermon: "first, in the times of the Law, God made himself known to his people under dark shadows and types . . . Secondly, in the days [of] Christ . . . there

was a higher manifestation of light and glory . . . which was the young or middle age. But thirdly, in this last time . . . [it] will be much more glorious . . . and therefore called a new heaven" (Woodhouse, pp. 390-391).

58. Karl Marx, *Capital, a Critique of Political Economy*, trans. Samuel Moore and Edward Aveling, ed. Frederick Engels (1887; rpt. New York, 1967), I, 20. For discussion of Marx's "inversion" of Hegel's kernel image see Louis Althusser, *For Marx*, trans. Ben Brewster (New York, 1970), pp. 89-94.

In *Englands Birth Right Justified* (1645) Lilburne wrote: "the Law taken abstract from its originall reason and end, is made a shell without a kernel"; in J. C. Davis, "The Levellers and Christianity," in *Politics, Religion and the English Civil War*, ed. Brian Manning (London, 1973), p. 227. Cf. also John Everard's expression: "we cannot have the *kernel* without the *shell*" (I, 46-47); and Giles Randall's translation of *Theologia Germanica* (London, 1648), maintains: "thou shall find some kernels herein with their shell ready broken to thine hand" (sig. A3v). See below Chapter IV, n. 8.

59. Cf. the famous Theses on Feuerbach: "social life is essentially *practical*. All mysteries which mislead theory to mysticism find their rational solution in human practice and in the comprehension of this practice . . . The philosophers have only *interpreted* the world, in various ways; the point, however, is to *change it*"; *Karl Marx and Frederick Engels, Selected Works* (New York, 1968), pp. 29-30. Roger Garaudy remarks in *Karl Marx, the Evolution of His Thought*, trans. Nan Apotheker (New York, 1967), "the Hegelian system, to be sure, winds up in an eventual reconciliation with the world as it is, giving its 'rational' blessing to the bourgeois order, as in other days the theory of 'divine right' gave its blessing to the feudal order and to absolute monarchs" (p. 21).

60. *The Poetry and Prose of William Blake*, ed. David V. Erdman, rev. ed. (Garden City, N. Y., 1970), p. 601.

61. In *Of Christian Doctrine* Milton writes: "the light of the gospel . . . is . . . in our hearts just as much as in written records . . . There is the external scripture of the written word and the internal scripture of the Holy Spirit which he, according to God's promise, has engraved upon the hearts of believers . . . the scriptures . . . is the authority of which we first have experience. The pre-eminent and supreme authority, however, is the authority of the Spirit, which is internal, and the individual possession of each man . . . scripture, particularly the New Testament, has often been liable to corruption and is, in fact, corrupt . . . But no one can corrupt the Spirit which guides man to truth"; *Complete Prose Works of John Milton*, VI, trans. John Carey, ed. Maurice Kelley (New Haven, 1973), 586-588. Everard and Saltmarsh make similar comments.

62. In Walzer, p. 145; Perry Miller analyzes Perkins' book in *The New England Mind, the Seventeenth Century* (Cambridge, Mass., 1939), pp. 331-361; rpt. in *Seventeenth-Century Prose, Modern Essays in Criticism*, ed. Stanley E. Fish (New York, 1971), pp. 147-186.

63. The following pages are based on my "Gerrard Winstanley and Foxe's 'Book of Martyrs,' " *N&Q*, 222 (1977), 209-212.

64. Haller, *Elect Nation*, pp. 13-14, 183; *Liberty and Reformation*, p. 47; and "John Foxe and the Puritan Revolution," in *Seventeenth Century, Studies in*

the History of English Thought and Literature from Bacon to Pope (1951; rpt. Stanford, 1969), pp. 75-160. For a defense of Haller's controversial interpretation of Foxe see John T. McNeill, "John Foxe, Historiographer, Disciplinarian, Tolerationist," *Church History*, 43 (1974), 216-229.

65. Haller, *Elect Nation*, p. 242. In *John Foxe and the Elizabethan Church* (Berkeley, 1973), V. Norskov Olsen questions whether Foxe meant the English people or the Protestant church as his elect group. The controversy, of course, was over what a truly Protestant church was—whether the people belonged to the church or the church to the people.

66. Foxe exhorted his countrymen to "wait patiently upon the Lord and edify one another in all humility . . . 'They that be in error, let them not disdain to learn. They which have greater talents of knowledge committed, instruct in simplicity them that be simple. No man liveth in that commonwealth where nothing is amiss. But yet because God hath so placed us Englishmen here in one commonwealth, also in one Church, as in one ship together, let us not mangle or divide the ship' " (in Haller, *Elect Nation*, p. 250).

67. Haller, *Elect Nation*, p. 243.

68. Lamont, pp. 23-26ff. Christopher Hill's *Milton and the English Revolution* (London, 1977) came to my hands after the present study was completed; his remarks on Winstanley's literary merit (p. 266), his idea of a "third force" of radical Arminianism (p. 272), and his analysis of "radical millenarianism" (pp. 279-284) all lend support to my thesis.

II. THE DARKENING CLOUD

1. Karl Mannheim, *Ideology and Utopia, an Introduction to the Sociology of Knowledge*, trans. Louis Wirth and Edward Shils (1936; rpt. New York, n.d.), p. 39.

2. Quoted from the copy in the British Library; shelfmark E. 2137.

3. Mannheim, p. 41.

4. Mannheim, pp. 192-193.

5. Mannheim, p. 211.

6. Robert Baillie, *Anabaptism, the True Fountaine of Independency, Antinomy, Brownisme, Familisme* (London, 1646), p. 32; and also Thomas Edwards, *Gangraena* (London, 1646), p. 15; and Samuel Rutherford, *A Survey of the Spiritual Antichrist* (London, 1647).

7. *The Good Old Cause: The English Revolution of 1640-1660, Its Causes, Course and Consequences*, ed. Christopher Hill and Edmund Dell, 2nd ed. (London, 1969), p. 320.

8. Mannheim, p. 214; also H.-J. Goertz, *Innere und aussere Ordung in der Theologie Thomas Müntzers* (Leiden, 1967), one of the indispensable books on Münzer in German.

9. Mannheim, p. 216.

10. John Everard, *The Gospel-Treasury Opened*, ed. Rapha Harford (London, 1657), I, 79.

11. [Giles Randall], *Divinity and Philosophy Dissected and set forth by a mad man* (Amsterdam, 1644), p. 7.

12. Quoted in Leo F. Solt, *Saints in Arms, Puritanism and Democracy in Cromwell's Army* (1959; rpt. New York, 1971), p. 74; Solt points out that Saltmarsh was a firm believer in Joachim of Fiore's three ages of the world: law, grace, and the forthcoming age of the spirit. Erbury, unlike Saltmarsh and Winstanley, accepted the literal reign of Christ as a forthcoming historical event.

13. Christopher Hill notes that "opponents of tithes came from the middling and poorer sort; the rich suffered comparatively little, and might even be recipients of tithes"; *The Century of Revolution, 1603-1714* (1961; rpt. New York, 1966), p. 164.

14. "Salvation," Saltmarsh wrote, "is not made any puzzeling work in the Gospel; it is plainly, easily, and simply revealed; Jesus Christ was crucified for sinners; this is salvation, we need go no further; the work of salvation is past, and finished; sins are blotted out; sinners are justified by him that rose for justification. And now if you ask me what you must do to be saved, I answer Beleeve in the Lord Jesus Christ, and thou shalt be saved. All that is to be done in the work of salvation is to beleeve there is such a work, and that Christ died for thee, amongst all those other sinners he died for" (in Solt, p. 35).

15. Everard was fond of quoting Augustine's saying: "Love God absolutely and then you may do as you please." He also wrote: "turn the man loose who has found the living Guide within him, and then let him neglect the outward if he can"; quoted in Rufus M. Jones, *Spiritual Reformers in the Sixteenth and Seventeenth Centuries* (1914; rpt. Gloucester, Mass., 1971), p. 246. "No ordinance," Milton wrote in *Tetrachordon*, "human or from heav'n can binde against the good of man"; *Complete Prose Works of John Milton*, II, ed. Ernest Sirluck (New Haven, 1959), 588.

16. "We are sure," Foxe wrote, "these afflictions and persecutions of God's people in this world did not come by any chance or blind fortune, but by the provident appointment and forewarning of God"; *The Acts and Monuments of John Foxe*, ed. George Townsend (rpt. New York, 1965), I, ii, 288.

17. William G. Madsen, "From Shadowy Types to Truth," in *The Lyric and Dramatic Milton, Selected Papers from the English Institute*, ed. Joseph H. Summers (New York, 1965), p. 101.

18. Madsen, p. 105.

19. Erik Erikson, *Young Man Luther, a Study in Psychoanalysis and History* (1958; rpt. New York, 1962), pp. 254-263.

20. Stanley E. Fish, *Surprised by Sin: The Reader in Paradise Lost* (1967; rpt. Berkeley, 1971), p. 89.

21. G. A. Starr, *Defoe and Spiritual Autobiography* (1965; rpt. New York, 1971), p. 46.

22. *The Poems of George Herbert*, ed. Helen Gardner, 2nd ed. (London, 1961), p. 144.

23. *Poems*, p. 49.

24. F. E. Hutchinson, *Henry Vaughan, a Life and Interpretation* (Oxford, 1947), p. 99; and also E. L. Marilla, "The Religious Conversion of Henry Vaughan," *RES*, 21 (1945), 15-22, and "Henry Vaughan's Conversion, a Recent View," *MLN*, 63 (1948), 394-397.

25. *The Complete Poetry of Henry Vaughan*, ed. French Fogle (Garden City, N. Y., 1964), pp. 255-256.

26. *Complete Poetry*, pp. 257, 258, 259.

27. M. M. Mahood, *Poetry and Humanism* (1950; rpt. New York, 1970), p. 259. As Ross Garner explains, Vaughan rejects the Gnostic dualism implicit in Hermeticism and has affinities with the nonconformist "left" in seventeenth-century religious experience; *Henry Vaughan, Experience and Tradition* (Chicago, 1959), pp. 46-92, 99-101, 149-152.

28. Louis Martz, "Henry Vaughan, The Man Within," in *Seventeenth-Century English Poetry, Modern Essays in Criticism*, ed. William R. Keast, rev. ed. (New York, 1971), p. 410.

29. *Complete Poetry*, pp. 276-277. For a comprehensive analysis see Don Cameron Allen, "Vaughan's 'Cock-crowing,' " in *Image and Meaning, Metaphoric Traditions in Renaissance Poetry* (Baltimore, 1960), pp. 154-169.

30. Virgil connects the seed metaphor with millenarianism in *The Aeneid*, VI, 730-760; and Augustine relates this passage to Plato's teaching about the soul (see *Phaedrus*, 245e-250e) in *The City of God*, bk. XIV, ch. 3. On the seed as logos see William Foxwell Albright, *From the Stone Age to Christianity, Monotheism and the Historical Process*, 2nd ed. (New York, 1957), pp. 369-373; on the earth as womb see Mircea Eliade, *The Forge and the Crucible, Origins and Structures of Alchemy*, trans. Stephen Corrin (1962; rpt. New York, 1971), pp. 43-52. Seventeenth-century word play on the macrocosmic-microcosmic implications of the sun-seed earth-womb topoi is infinite; cf. Milton's description of "Volatil Hermes" and "Th' Arch-chimic Sun"; and his description of Eden as a "rural mound . . . whose hairie sides/ With thicket overgrown . . . On which the Sun more glad impress'd his beams" (*Paradise Lost*, III, 59-612; IV, 130-150; also V, 440-443). Bacon frequently refers to himself as a sower of seeds and to his sentences as seeds of thought; see Stanley E. Fish, *Self-Consuming Artifacts, The Experience of Seventeenth-Century Literature* (1972; rpt. Berkeley, 1974), pp. 88n11, 154. For further discussion see Brian Vickers, *Francis Bacon and Renaissance Prose* (Cambridge, 1968), pp. 193-198. The Cambridge Platonists, especially Henry More, were also fond of the seed metaphor; see C. A. Patrides, ed., *The Cambridge Platonists*, Stratford-Upon-Avon-Library 5 (1969; rpt. Cambridge, Mass., 1970), pp. 20, 208. See also R. A. Durr, *On the Mystical Poetry of Henry Vaughan* (Cambridge, Mass., 1962), pp. 125-130; and Wayne Shumaker, *The Occult Sciences in the Renaissance, a Study in Intellectual Patterns* (Berkeley, 1972), pp. 221-223.

31. "In every creature," John Everard paraphrased Plotinus, "there is an Angel, and this Angel is as the beam that comes from the Sun: and this beam goes directly in a strait line to the Sun: So that let a man, though he be in never so dark, stinking a dungeon, and never so deep, yet if any little beam of the Sun can but come in, though it be but a pinhole, yet go & lay your eye full in that beam, and you shall behold the Sun itself" (II, 56). "Christ comes into our barren ground," Randall wrote, "and by his mighty power maketh it fertill and fruitfull, bringing forth himselfe in us, to live of us, and we by him, for our barren ground is plowed up by the law of God, and all the thornes and thistles which is our

sinnes, is plucked up and throwne away that this holy seed may be sowed in our hearts in place of our sinnes, and this seed is a tender plant: wherefore, O man, look diligently to it, and weed up all things that is like to destroy the same in thee" (p. 51). Cf. Vaughan's "Joy of My Life" and "Psalm 104" (*Complete Poems*, pp. 174, 284).

32. Keith Thomas, *Religion and the Decline of Magic, Studies in Popular Beliefs in Sixteenth and Seventeenth Century England* (London, 1971), p. 227; see also P. M. Rattansi, "Paracelsus and the Puritan Revolution," *Ambix*, 11 (1963), 23-32.

33. Eliade, pp. 179-199; Shumaker, pp. 160-247; and William Haller, *Foxe's "Book of Martyrs" and the Elect Nation* (London, 1963), pp. 132-135.

34. A. L. Morton, *The World of the Ranters* (London, 1970), p. 127. Other works by Boehme began to appear in English in 1645, and they were still being published in 1659; see Jones, p. 213.

35. Blake comments on Paracelsus, Boehme, and Swedenborg in *The Marriage of Heaven and Hell; The Poetry and Prose of William Blake*, ed. David Erdman, rev. ed. (Garden City, N.Y., 1970), pp. 41-42; see Harold Bloom's commentary, p. 812. Blake's epistemology, which has striking resemblances to Winstanley's, is analyzed by Morton D. Paley in *Energy and the Imagination, a Study in the Development of Blake's Thought* (Oxford, 1970), pp. 99-109; and by Thomas R. Frosh in *The Awakening of Albion, the Renovation of the Body in the Poetry of William Blake* (Ithaca, 1974), pp. 17-32. On Blake and Newton see Mona Wilson, *The Life of William Blake*, ed. Geoffrey Keynes (London, 1971), pp. 56-58, 104; and Donald Ault, *Visionary Physics, Blake's Response to Newton* (Chicago, 1974), especially pp. 12-14. On Lord Herbert see Patrick Cruttwell, *The Shakespearean Moment and Its Place in the Poetry of the Seventeenth Century* (New York, 1960), pp. 166-184.

Woodhouse points out that the Diggers do not invoke the principle of segregation between nature and grace: "the ideal of the holy community, in the peculiar form which it takes in their minds, is not restricted to the order of grace but intrudes upon the order of nature" ([p. 99]). Cf. Marx's comments on the effect of private property on sense experience in "Private Property and Communism," in *The Economic and Philosophic Manuscripts of 1844*, ed. Dirk J. Struik, trans. Martin Milligan (New York, 1964), pp. 138-140.

36. Schumaker, pp. 223-224; also below, Chapter V, n. 20.

37. *Wonderful Predictions Declared in a Message, as From the Lord, to . . . Sir Thomas Fairfax* (28 October 1648), is in *Englands Friend raised from the Grave, giving seasonable Advice to the Lord Generall. Being the true copies of three Letters written by Mr. John Saltmarsh a little before his Death*, published by Giles Calvert. Excerpts are in Morton, pp. 66-69.

38. Christopher Hill, *The World Turned Upside Down* (London, 1972), p. 321. In *The Reason of Church-Government* (1642) Milton notes that "ease and leasure" were given him for his "retired thoughts out of the sweat of other men"; *The Complete Prose Works of John Milton*, I, ed. Don M. Wolfe (New Haven, 1953), 804; also *The Complete Prose Works of John Milton*, IV, ed. Don M. Wolfe (New Haven, 1966), 552-553.

39. The linking of *Utopia* and *The New Atlantis* is Miltonic; see *Complete Prose*, I, 881. For alchemical influences in *Utopia* see Frances A. Yates, *Giordano Bruno and the Hermetic Tradition* (Chicago, 1964), pp. 185-187. J. Max Patrick and C. H. George believe Winstanley was influenced by *Utopia* and may have read *The New Atlantis*; "The Literature of the Diggers," *UTQ*, 12 (1942), 95-110; and "Gerrard Winstanley, a Critical Retrospect," in *The Dissenting Tradition*, ed. C. Robert Cole and Michael E. Moody (Athens, Ohio, 1975), p. 219.

40. *The Complete Works of St. Thomas More*, IV, ed. Edward Surtz, S. J., and J. H. Hexter (New Haven, 1965), 103, 197. The Ralph Robinson translation, which Winstanley would have read, uses "affection" in place of "favoritism," the modern equivalent.

41. *The Complete Works of Christopher Marlowe*, ed. Fredson Bowers (Cambridge, 1973), II, 162.

42. The mocking "Communitie" is quoted below Chapter IV, n. 8. On Donne and alchemy, see my "Alchemical Imagery in John Donne's 'A Nocturnall upon S. Lucies day,' " *Ambix*, 24 (1977), 55-62.

43. *The Poems and Letters of Andrew Marvell*, ed. H. M. Margoliouth, 2nd ed. (Oxford, 1952), I, 40.

44. *Poems*, I, 41.

45. *Poems*, I, 49.

46. *Poems*, I, 76-79.

47. *The Prose of Sir Thomas Browne*, ed. Norman J. Endicott (Garden City, N. Y., 1967), pp. 20-23; Browne believed "there is a Nobility without Heraldry, a naturall dignity whereby one man is ranked with another . . . thus it was in the first and primitive Common-wealths, and is yet in the integrity and Cradle of well-order'd polities, till corruption getteth ground . . . every one having a liberty to amasse and heape up riches, and they a licence or faculty to doe or purchase any thing" (p. 68). He also believed in universal salvation.

48. *Complete Prose*, I, 874.

49. *Complete Poetry*, p. 150.

50. *Complete Poetry*, p. 169.

51. *English Literature in the Earlier Seventeenth Century, 1600-1660*, 2nd ed. (Oxford, 1962), p. 153.

52. R. G. Cox, "A Survey of Literature from Donne to Marvell," in *From Donne to Marvell*, ed. Boris Ford (1956; rpt. Baltimore 1963), p. 59.

53. Hill, *World Turned*, pp. 296-300.

54. Thomas Traherne, *Centuries, Poems and Thanksgivings*, ed. H. M. Margoliouth (Oxford, 1958), II, 39. Milton's use of the Gen. 3:15 passage is nearly as obsessive as Winstanley's; see, for example, *Paradise Lost*, XII, 125, 148, 233, 260, 273, 327, 379, 395, 600. This passage is also a favorite of the Cambridge Platonists.

55. *The Complete Poetry of John Milton*, ed. John T. Shawcross, rev. ed. (Garden City, N. Y., 1971), p. 618. Cf. Albert R. Cirillo, "Time, Light, and the Phoenix: The Design of *Samson Agonistes*," in *Calm of Mind*, ed. Joseph Anthony Wittreich, Jr. (Cleveland, 1971), pp. 219-226; and Don Parry Norford, "The Sacred Head: Milton's Solar Mysticism," *Milton Studies*, 9 (1976), 47-48.

56. *Centuries, Poems and Thanksgivings*, II, 60.

57. *The Works of Francis Bacon*, ed. James Spedding, Robert Leslie Ellis, and Douglas Denon Heath (London, 1870), III, 156.

58. *Complete Poetry*, p. 299.

59. James D. Simmonds, *Masques of God: Form and Theme in the Poetry of Henry Vaughan* (Pittsburgh, 1972), p. 147.

60. *The Works of Ben Jonson*, ed. C. H. Herford and Percy Simpson (Oxford, 1937), V, 325.

61. Eliade, pp. 51-52, 67, 75, 79.

62. *Winstanley*, p. 63. In his Christmas sermon of 1621 Donne explains "to you the *Day starre*, the *Sunne of Righteousnesse*, the Sonne of God is risen this day. The day is but a little longer now, then at *shortest*; but a *little* it is"; see *John Donne's Sermons on the Psalms & Gospels, with a Selection of Prayers and Meditations*, ed. Evelyn M. Simpson (Berkeley, 1967), p. 155. "As Christ is the sun in his heaven," wrote Thomas Goodwin in 1639, "so Satan . . . wasthe sun in this firmament"; quoted in Austin C. Dobbins, *Milton and the Book of Revelation, The Heavenly Cycle* (University, Ala., 1975), p. 49. In *Animadversions* (1641), Milton says "there is no imployment more honourable . . . then to be the messenger, and Herald of heavenly truth from God to man, and by the faithfull worke of holy doctrine, to procreate a number of faithfull men, making a kind of creation like to Gods, by infusing his spirit and likenesse into them, to their salvation, as God did into him; arising to what climat so ever he turne him, like that Sun of righteousnesse that sent him, with healing in his wings, and new light to break in upon the chill and gloomy hearts of his hearers" (*Complete Prose*, I, 721). In *Reasons for Unity, Peace, and Love* (1646) Saltmarsh notes: "some of you . . . bring Christ back again under the cool shadow of the *Law*, & make that *Sun of righteousness* that he warms not so many with the *love* of him as he would doe"; in Don M. Wolfe, *Milton in the Puritan Revolution* (1941; rpt. New York, 1963), p. 421. In *Sparkles of Glory* he says: "he who is the bright and morning Star is stil shining into the glory of the Sun of righteousness" (p. 72).

63. *Complete Poetry*, p. 210; Vaughan refers to the sun of righteousness again in "The Night" and "The Agreement."

64. Eliade, p. 101.

65. Fish, *Self-Consuming Artifacts*, p. 228.

66. Cf. *Measure for Measure*, III, ii, 232.

67. Norman O. Brown, *Life Against Death, the Psychoanalytical Meaning of History* (1951; rpt. New York, n.d.), p. 185.

68. Brown, p. 189.

69. Brown, p. 192; Empson, in *Some Versions of Pastoral* (New York, 1960), quotes "The Mechanical Operation of the Spirit," an appendix to *A Tale of a Tub*, and notes how Swift set out to defend "the Established Church against the reformers' Inner Light" and discovered " 'Hobbes and the scientists have proved this; all religion is really a perversion of sexuality.' The language plays into his hands here, because the spiritual words are all derived from physical metaphors" (p. 58).

70. Brown, p. 193.

71. Band-dogs were mastiffs or bloodhounds chained in front of a house as guards. Winstanley may have been familiar with Bishop James Ussher's *Body of Divinity* (London, 1647), where Satan lets loose "his band-dog, to . . . molest the godly" (p. 376).

72. An explanation of the political basis of Winstanley's anti-intellectualism may be extrapolated from Herbert Marcuse's "A Note on Dialectic," in *Reason and Revolution, Hegel and the Rise of Social Theory*, 2nd ed. (1954; rpt. Boston, 1960), pp. vii-xiv; also relevant is Fred Stripp, "The Anticlericalism of Gerrard Winstanley," *Historical Magazine of the Protestant Episcopal Church, 23* (1954), 188-201.

III. OIL IN HIS OWN LAMP

1. Quoted from *The Petition of the Lord Mayor and Common Council* (22 July 1648) in H. N. Brailsford, *The Levellers and the English Revolution,* ed. Christopher Hill (London, 1961), p. 339. Sir John Oglander noted that from May to mid-September there were "scarce three dry dayes together"; David Underdown, *Pride's Purge: Politics in the Puritan Revolution* (Oxford, 1971), p. 106.

2. In *The Large Petition of 11 September 1648*, after asking for the opening of "all late Inclosures of Fens, and other Commons, or have enclosed them onely or chiefly to the benefit of the poor," the Levellers request "that you would have bound your selves and all future Parliaments from abolishing propriety, levelling mens Estats, or making all things common"; *Leveller Manifestoes of the Puritan Revolution,* ed. Don M. Wolfe (1944; rpt. New York, 1967), p. 288.

3. George H. Sabine, ed., *The Works of Gerrard Winstanley* (1941; rpt. New York, 1965), pp. 103-104n1. David W. Petegorsky found no connection between William and John Everard; *Left-Wing Democracy in the English Civil War* (London, 1940), p. 134. Christopher Hill provides a full account of William Everard in *The World Turned Upside Down* (London, 1972), pp. 228-230.

4. The copy at Jesus College, Oxford, published by Giles Calvert and dated 1650, is entitled *TRUTH Lifting up his head above SCANDALS.* It has the following prolepsis based on the parable of the ten virgins (Matt. 25): "Professours of all forms, behold the Bridegroom is in comming; your profession will be tryed to purpose, your hypocricy shall be hid no longer. You shall feed no longer upon the Oyle that was in other mens Lamps (the Scriptures) for now it is required that every one have Oyle in his own Lamp, even the pure testimony of Truth within himself; for he that wants this, though he have the report of it in his Book, he shall not enter with the Bridegroom into the chamber of peace."

5. John Everard, *The Gospel-Treasury Opened,* ed. Rapha Hartford (London, 1657), sig. A18v.

6. Everard, I, 68. Both Langland and Chaucer noted that friars twisted scripture and contradicted established authority for their own ends; see *Piers Plowman,* C text, I: 56-65; and *The Summoner's Tale, CT,* III, 1788-1794. Similarly, Thomas Münzer traced the fall of the church to the corruption of scripture and maintained that the "new Scribes, like the Papists, are the perpetrators of this deception." He wrote that "if a man had neither seen nor heard the Bible all his

life, yet through the teaching of the Spirit he could have an undeceivable Christian faith, like all those who without books wrote the Holy Scriptures"; quoted in Gordon Rupp, *Patterns of Reformation* (Philadelphia, 1969), p. 273.

7. [Giles Randall], *Divinity and Philosophy Dissected and set forth by a mad man* (Amsterdam, 1644), p. 40.

8. John Saltmarsh, *Sparkles of Glory* (London, 1647), pp. 268-269.

9. Leo F. Solt, *Saints in Arms*, (1959; rpt. New York, 1971), p. 16.

10. Hill, *World Turned*, p. 242; see also Solt, pp. 93-95.

11. *Complete Prose Works of John Milton*, I, ed. Don M. Wolfe (New Haven, 1953), 677, 690, 720, 854-855. In Richard Overton's *The Araignment of Mr. Persecution* (1645), the Geneva-born, well-educated antagonist jumps "out of Scotland into England . . . and snatching a Rhetoricall Cassok he girt up his loynes with a Sophisticall Girdle, and ran into the wildernesse of Tropes, and Figures . . . [and] the briery thickets of Rhetoricall Glosses, Sophistications, and scholastick Interpretations . . . [skipping] from Pulpit to Pulpit, from Vniversity to Vniversity"; quoted in Richard L. Greaves, "The Ordination Controversy and the Spirit of Reform in Puritan England," *Journal of Ecclesiastical History*, 21 (1970), 231; see also Greaves, "Gerrard Winstanley and Educational Reform in Puritan England," *British Journal of Educational Studies*, 17 (1969), 166-176.

12. Hugh Kearney, *Scholars and Gentlemen: Universities and Society in Pre-Industrial Britain, 1500-1700* (London, 1970), p. 76; Kearney is quoting from William Dell's *The Right Reformation of Learning, Schools, and Universities* (1650).

13. Winstanley is paraphrasing the epigram attributed to Richard Rumbold who, according to Brailsford, was "condemned to a traitor's death, and on the scaffold gave posthumous fame to a Leveller commonplace by his last words: 'I am sure there was no man born marked of God above another; for none comes into the world with a saddle on his back, neither any booted and spurred to ride him' " (p. 624). Thomas Jefferson later quoted this epigram.

14. The inclusion of women here, as elsewhere in Winstanley's works, evidences his heartfelt and quite unusual feeling about the male-dominated educational system. Throughout his pamphlets Winstanley shows acute awareness of women's oppression. On feminism in the Civil Wars see Keith Thomas, "Women and the Civil War Sects," in *Crisis in Europe, 1560-1660*, ed. Trevor Aston (New York, 1967), pp. 332-357; and Patricia Higgins, "The Reactions of Women, with Special Reference to Women Petitioners," in *Politics, Religion and the English Civil War*, ed. Brian Manning (London, 1973), pp. 179-222.

15. "Our learned ones," Münzer wrote, "would like to bring the witness of the Spirit of Jesus into the university. But they will fail completely. For they have not taught in order that the common man, through their teaching, might be brought up to their level. No, they want to sit alone in judgment on faith with their stolen Scripture. They have no faith whatsoever . . . Everyone can see how they seek goods and honors. Listen, common man! You must teach yourself if you are to avoid deception!": quoted in Stephen E. Ozment, *Mysticism and Dissent* (New Haven, 1973), p. 80.

16. "With all their works and words," Münzer said, "the learned theolo-

gians have seen to it that the poor man may not learn to read because of his pre-occupation with making a living. And they preach unashamedly that the poor man should submit to the skinning and fleecing which the tyrants have prepared for him. When will the poor man learn to read the Scripture? . . . Oh yes there the theologians have found a fine trick . . . The people have always assumed . . . that the clergy are authorities in the faith because they have read so many great and beautiful books . . . no one attends to anything but creaturely goods. Hence each tarries outside the temple and cannot enter his heart because of his great unbelief, which he cannot even recognize because he is so busy trying to earn a living" (in Ozment, pp. 84-85).

17. Robert Hoopes, *Right Reason in the English Renaissance* (Cambridge, 1962), p. 161. Donne provides a perfect example of the subordination of scientific reason—which, he notes, discovered printing and artillery—to faith; *John Donne's Sermons on the Psalms & Gospels, with a Selection of Prayers and Meditations*, ed. Evelyn M. Simpson (Berkeley, 1967), pp. 140-143. Cf. Bacon's comment in *Novum Organum*, aphorism 129.

18. Christopher Hill, " 'Reason' and 'Reasonableness,' " in *Change and Continuity in Seventeenth-Century England* (London, 1974), p. 110.

19. Among many recent studies see Lotte Mulligan, "Civil War Politics, Religion and the Royal Society," *Past & Present*, no. 59 (May 1973), 92-116; and Barbara Shapiro, "Science, Politics and Religion," *Past & Present*, no. 66 (February 1975), 133-138.

20. *Complete Prose*, I, 548, 684-685, 707; also 625, 648-650, 664, 694-695, 700, 710, 714, and 727. Arthur E. Barker points out in *Milton and the Puritan Dilemma, 1641-1660* (1942; rpt. Toronto, 1971), that Milton's initial intention in *Of Reformation* was "to demonstrate the ineffectiveness of human reason and custom as opposed to divine prescript" (p. 50).

21. Stanley E. Fish, *Self-Consuming Artifacts*, (1972; rpt. Berkeley, 1974), p. 269.

22. *Complete Prose*, I, 782.

23. *An Apology Against a Pamphlet* (April 1642), in *Complete Prose*, I, 874.

24. *Complete Prose Works of John Milton*, II, ed. Ernest Sirluck, (New Haven, 1959), 223, 224. See my "Natural Law and Milton's Attack on Corruption," *Bucknell Review*, 23, no. 2 (1977), 13-32.

25. *Complete Prose*, II, 527; also 532, 543, 566-567, 582-584. Citing Gen. 2:18 Milton notes that "God heer presents himself like to a man deliberating . . . he intended to found it according to naturall reason, not implulsive command, but that the duty should arise from the reason of it, not the reason be swallow'd up in a reasonlesse duty" (*Complete Prose*, II, 595; cf. 621-622, 629-630, 632, 636, 648-651, 663, 692-693).

26. Quoted in M. A. Gibb, *John Lilburne the Leveller*, (London, 1947), p. 115; see also Norman T. Burns, *Christian Mortalism from Tyndale to Milton* (Cambridge, Mass., 1972); and Leonora Leet Brodwin, "The Dissolution of Satan in *Paradise Lost*, a Study of Milton's Heretical Eschatology," *Milton Studies*, 8 (1975), 198-199.

27. William Haller, *Liberty and Reformation in the Puritan Revolution* (1955; rpt. New York, 1963), pp. 170-175.

28. Gibb, p. 117.

29. *Leveller Manifestoes*, p. 124.

30. *Leveller Manifestoes*, pp. 3-4, 5.

31. *Leveller Manifestoes*, p. 158.

32. *Leveller Manifestoes*, pp. 158-160. A more conservative statement of the Puritan combination of God, reason, and natural law, is in William Ames's *Conscience* (1639); in *Puritanism and Liberty*, ed. A. S. P. Woodhouse, 2nd ed. (1951; rpt. Chicago, 1974), pp. 187-191.

33. As Gibb notes, others often bewilderingly obscure the clarity of Overton's presentation. "Worst offender in this respect . . . is Lilburne who, borrowing from the ideas of Overton and Walwyn, equates reason at his pleasure with natural law, fundamental law, or the Word of God. But it was by the interplay of all these diverse conceptions that there developed in the heart of Independency the sectarian theory of Church and State, and the naturalistic theory of human society, the one conditioning the other" (p. 117). Milton adopts something like Overton's theory in *The Tenure of Kings and Magistrates* (February 1649); see *Complete Prose Works of John Milton*, III, ed. Merritt Y. Hughes (New Haven, 1962), 197.

34. Morton W. Bloomfield, *Piers Plowman as a Fourteenth-Century Apocalypse* (New Brunswick, N. J., 1961), pp. 95-101ff.

35. J. Sears McGee, *The Godly Man in Stuart England: Anglicans, Puritans, and the Two Tables, 1620-1670* (New Haven, 1976), pp. 256-257.

36. Woodhouse, pp. [39-40, 57-60].

37. Underdown, pp. 143-163; and Gibb, p. 238.

38. *The Complete Works of St. Thomas More*, IV, ed. Edward Surtz, S. J., and J. H. Hexter (New Haven, 1965): "Utopian communism differs from previous conceptions in which community of possessions and living plays a role. Neither from one of these conceptions nor from a combination of them can it be deduced; it remains an integral whole, original—a new thing" (cxi-cxii).

39. The Thirty-Nine Articles of the Anglican Church maintain that original sin "is the fault and corruption of the Nature of every man . . . whereby man is very far gone from original righteousness, and is of his own nature inclined to evil," and lest there be any doubt about the consequences, "the Riches and Goods of Christians are not common, as touching the right, title, and possession of the same; as certain Anabaptists do falsely boast"; *The Book of Common Prayer and Administration of the Sacraments and Other Rites and Ceremonies of the Church* (New York, 1945), pp. 604, 610-611. More did not have to contend with the Thirty-Nine Articles, but he was familiar with the official view of the church that people were naturally sinful and in need of control.

40. *Complete Works*, IV, 163.

41. *Complete Works*, IV, 163.

42. *Complete Works*, IV, 165.

43. *Complete Works*, IV, 167.

44. *Complete Works*, IV, 167.

45. Herbert Weisinger, *Tragedy and the Paradox of the Fortunate Fall* (East Lansing, Mich., 1953), pp. 222-225; and D. P. Walker, *The Decline of Hell, Seventeenth-Century Discussions of Eternal Torment* (London, 1964), pp. 222-223.

46. *World Turned*, p. 114; Hill here perhaps suggests a connection between Winstanley and the Neo-Stoicism popularized by Walwyn and others; cf. Jean Seznec, *The Survival of the Pagan Gods, the Mythical Tradition and Its Place in Renaissance Humanism and Art*, trans. Barbara F. Sessions (1953; rpt. Princeton, 1972), p. 41.

47. Thomas Carlyle, ed., *Oliver Cromwell's Letters and Speeches with Elucidations* (1845; rpt. New York, n.d.), I, 390-395. In response to Hammond's advocacy of passive obedience to the powers that be, Cromwell responds that this is a "fleshly reasoned" position and argues that he must act for the good of the people because providence wills it.

48. Everard, I, 169 (actually 159).

49. Saltmarsh, p. 304. Cf. Aquinas' statement: "every law framed by man bears the character of a law exactly to that extent to which it is derived from the law of nature. But if on any point it is in conflict with the law of nature, it at once ceases to be a law; it is a mere perversion of law"; quoted in R. H. Tawney, *Religion and the Rise of Capitalism* (1926; rpt. New York, 1947), p. 41.

50. Saltmarsh says: "Christ is in all his spirit and truth, and as the eternal seed . . . he is in us . . . only we see him but in part." Christ will not appear again in the flesh but in us; "this is the Reformation to be expected" (pp. 296-297).

51. "There is not one Christ without us, and Another within us," John Everard explains; "Externall Jesus Christ is a shadow, a symbole, a figure of the Internal: viz. of him that is to be born within us, In our souls" (I, 54-55). Cf. also Everard's Neoplatonic parable of the two water drops, II, 401-406.

52. "All the Imaginations of mans heart," says Everard quoting Gen. 6:5, "are onely evil cóntinually." Comparing experimental knowledge to sunlight he says "when the Sun shines, you know it shews all things below it self, and darkens every thing above it self: for in the day ye can see nothing above the Sun; all the Stars, which are above the Sun, are obscured, and all things else: So while a man is in the state of unregeneration, he can see nothing above himself," but the "children of light" may see the truth, for "to see Christ to be all in all in us, this is to know him experimentally" (I, 60, 76-78).

53. Christopher Hill, ed., *Winstanley, the Law of Freedom and Other Writings* (Harmondsworth, 1973), p. 52. Also U. Milo Kaufmann, *The Pilgrim's Progress and Traditions in Puritan Meditation* (New Haven, 1966): "the Puritan union of exegesis and homelectics meant that approaches to Scripture were eminently rational and practical. The Word was consulted for clear authoritative instruction, and the imagination was irrelevant" (p. 23).

54. Bloomfield, p. 37; *Piers Plowman*, as Bloomfield notes (p. 39), is full of puns. Cf. Marshall McLuhan's remark that "puns condense ideas into single images," and "what we call 'acceptable prose' moves along on a single plane while puns do not. When you are dealing with a variety of facets simultaneously, you cannot use that kind of prose"; *McLuhan, Hot and Cool*, ed. Gerald Eman-

uel Stearn (New York, 1967), pp. 237, 285.

55. Arthur O. Lovejoy, "The Supposed Primitivism of Rousseau," in *Essays in the History of Ideas* (1948; rpt. New York, 1960), p. 19; and Michel de Montaigne, *Essays*, trans. J. M. Cohn (1958; rpt. Baltimore, 1963), p. 114. Overton's friend Walwyn was fond of quoting Montaigne, whose essays were available in John Florio's translation. Haller suggests Walwyn built his political ideas upon Montaigne's Neo-Stoic concept of reason and primitivistic idea of unspoiled nature (*Puritanism and Liberty*, pp. 170-172).

56. Cf. Traherne's statement that "there is no Salvage Nation under the Cope of Heaven, that is more absurdly Barbarous than the Christian World"; *Centuries, Poems and Thanksgivings*, ed. H. M. Margoliouth (Oxford, 1958), I, 117.

57. B. Evans, *The Early English Baptists* (London, 1862), I, 254; and Brailsford, pp. 49-57.

58. Petegorsky, p. 142.

59. Quoted from the copy in the library of Jesus College, Oxford.

60. Bloomfield, pp. 11-13; Barbara K. Lewalski's "*Samson Agonistes* and the 'Tragedy' of the Apocalypse," *PMLA*, 85 (1970), 1050-1062; is also pertinent to Winstanley's handling of Revelation in *The New Law*.

61. D. W. Robertson, Jr., *A Preface to Chaucer* (1962; rpt. Princeton, 1969), p. 301. Cf. H. D. F. Kitto's note on time in *Greek Tragedy, a Literary Study* (1939; rpt. Garden City, N. Y., 1954): "In view of the deeply rooted neoclassical misconceptions, it may not be out of place to say again that the Unities of Time and Place were accidental, not fundamental, in Greek drama . . . for a long time drama was not the presentation of action, but of thought and feeling about action . . . As for the unity of time, it would more closely correspond to the facts to say that time does not exist unless it is mentioned" (pp. 177-178).

62. Norman Cohn, *The Pursuit of the Millennium*, rev. ed. (New York, 1970), pp. 199, 202-203, 237.

63. Kenneth Clark, *Civilisation, a Personal View* (New York, 1969), p. 155.

64. Erwin Panofsky, *The Life and Art of Albrecht Dürer*, 4th ed. (1955; rpt. Princeton, 1971), pp. 55-57.

65. Cf. Bloomfield, p. 75; and *Piers Plowman*, C text, XV, 409-601; XIX, 202-330.

66. The correlation between moon-flesh-female and sun-spirit-male stems from the transference of prehistoric myths and rituals of the sacred marriage of the Sun God and the Earth Mother into the story of Diana as a goddess of fertility. The connection between moon-earth-female is still traceable in words like menstruation, just as the relationship between sun-seed-male is apparent in words like semen; Sir James Frazer, *The Golden Bough, a Study in Magic and Religion*, abridged ed. (1922; rpt. New York, 1963), pp. 161-169; and M. Esther Harding, *Women's Mysteries, Ancient and Modern; A Psychological Interpretation of the Feminine Principle as Portrayed in Myth, Story, and Dreams* (1971; rpt. New York, 1976), pp. 55-83.

67. Erwin Panofsky, "Albrecht Dürer and Classical Antiquity," in *Meaning in the Visual Arts* (Garden City, N. Y., 1955), pp. 258-259. For the accommoda-

tion of sun worship to Christianity see Helen Flanders Dunbar, *Symbolism in Medieval Thought and Its Consummation in the Divine Comedy* (1929; rpt. New York, 1961), pp. 104-154. D. H. Lawrence felt that Revelation originated from a pagan work on sun worship. In his *Apocalypse* (1931; rpt. New York, 1976), he writes: "I am part of the sun as my eye is part of me . . . What we want is to destroy our false, inorganic connections, especially those related to money, and re-establish the living organic connections, with the cosmos, the sun and earth, with mankind and nation and family. Start with the sun, and the rest will slowly, slowly happen" (p. 126).

68. Panofsky, *Meaning*, p. 260; also Seznec, pp. 42-43.

69. Panofsky, *Meaning*, p. 263.

70. Cf. *Paradise Lost*, III, 571-629.

71. *Complete Works*, IV, 219.

72. *Complete Prose*, I, 566.

73. *Centuries, Poems and Thanksgivings*, I, 47; in "A Vision of the Last Judgment" Blake makes a distinction between Vision and Fable analogous to Winstanley's between Reason and Imagination; *The Poetry and Prose of William Blake*, ed. David V. Erdman, rev. ed. (Garden City, N.Y., 1970), p. 55.

IV. THE SEED OF LIFE

1. Marshall McLuhan, *The Gutenberg Galaxy, the Making of Typographic Man* (Toronto, 1962), pp. 40-50, 159-166.

2. "The Lord began to work for His Church not with sword and target to subdue His exalted adversary, but with printing, writing and reading . . . How many printing presses there be in the world, so many block-houses there be against the high castle of St. Angelo, so that either the pope must abolish knowledge and printing or printing at length will root him out"; quoted in William Haller, *Foxe's "Book of Martyrs" and the Elect Nation* (London, 1963), p. 110.

3. Carl Bridenbaugh, *Vexed and Troubled Englishmen, 1590-1642* (1967; rpt. New York, 1976), pp. 57, 258-259; the rule excluding literate women from benefit of clergy caused even greater resentment.

4. I follow Harold Bloom's analysis of "The Little Black Boy" in *Blake's Apocalypse, a Study in Poetic Argument* (1963; rpt. Garden City, N. Y., 1965), pp. 43-46. The poem is a perfect emblem of Winstanley's explanation of the sun's purgative power.

5. Stanley Stewart, *The Enclosed Garden, the Tradition and the Image in Seventeenth-Century Poetry* (Madison, 1966), p. 61.

6. I discuss this point in "The Dialectic of History in Marvell's 'Horatian Ode,' " *Clio*, 1 (1971), 26-36.

7. In *Phaedrus* (277a) "the dialectician selects a soul of the right type, and in it he plants and sows his words founded on knowledge, words which can defend both themselves and him who planted them, words which instead of remaining barren contain a seed whence new words grow up in new characters, whereby the seed is vouchsafed immortality, and its possessor the fullest measure of blessedness"; *The Collected Dialogues of Plato*, trans. R. Hackforth, ed.

Edith Hamilton and Huntington Cairns (Princeton, 1961), p. 522. Stanley E. Fish comments on this passage in *Self-Consuming Artifacts* (1972; rpt. Berkeley, 1974), pp. 14-15.

8. In "Communitie" Donne notes that women

> . . . are ours as fruits are ours,
> He that but tasts, he that devours,
>   and he that leaves all, doth as well:
> Chang'd loves are but chang'd sorts of meat,
> And when hee hath the kernell eate,
>   Who doth not fling away the shell?

The Complete Poetry of John Donne, ed. John T. Shawcross (Garden City, N.Y., 1967), p. 120. Cf. Vaughan's "Religion" where he notes: "Nor must we for the Kernell crave/Because most voices like the *shell*"; *The Complete Poetry of Henry Vaughan*, ed. French Fogle (Garden City, N.Y., 1964), p. 150.

9. *The Declaration and Standard of the Levellers of England*, published 23 April 1649.

10. "If God had laid all common," George Herbert wrote in "The Church-Porch," "certainly

> Man would have been th' incloser: but since now
> God hath impal'd us, on the contrarie
> Man breaks the fence, and every ground will plough.

The Poems of George Herbert, ed. Helen Gardner, 2nd ed. (London, 1961), p. 4.

11. In his attack on Luther, Münzer notes that "just as King Nebuchadnezzar found that the Spirit-guided prophet Daniel could interpret his dreams and define the present course of history better than all his wise men, so the princes of Saxony should realize that [he] could better define and direct a godly transformation of the world with Saxon sword than 'Brother Fattened Swine' (Luther), who mocked the spirit of Christ and denied God's present revelations"; quoted in Stephen E. Ozment, *Mysticism and Dissent* (New Haven, 1973), p. 77.

12. Hill, *The World Turned Upside Down* (London, 1972), p. 89.

13. Jacques Monod, *Chance and Necessity, an Essay on the Natural Philosophy of Modern Biology*, trans. Austryn Wainhouse (1971; rpt. London, 1972), p. 158.

14. Marx, "The Power of Money in Bourgeois Society," in *The Economic and Philosophic Manuscripts of 1844*, trans. Martin Milligan, ed. Dirk J. Struik (New York, 1964), pp. 166-169; and *Capital, A Critical Analysis of Capitalist Production*, trans. Samuel Moore and Edward Aveling, ed. Frederick Engels (1887; rpt. New York, 1967), I, 132-133; Marx later relates the transformation of everything into money as an alchemical operation and documents the transformation of feudalism to capitalism with references to More's *Utopia*, I, 720, 736.

15. *Winstanley, The Law of Freedom and Other Writings* ed. Christopher Hill (Harmondsworth, 1973), p. 109.

16. William Walwyn, in *Englands Lamentable Slavery* (October 1645), points out that Lilburne lays too much stress on Magna Charta, "which was at best a concession wrung from an unwilling Conqueror: it was, in fact, the least

that could have been granted and in no way worthy to be regarded as the epitome of the people's liberties. The Charter had, he considered, been overestimated throughout the centuries"; M. A. Gibb, *John Lilburne the Leveller*, (London, 1947), p. 141. Overton followed Walwyn's dismissal of Magna Charta in *A Remonstrance of Many Thousand Citizens* (7 July 1646). Winstanley makes the same point in *The Law of Freedom*.

17. Milton makes similar comments in *The Digression to The History of Britain; Complete Prose Works of John Milton*, V, ed. French Fogle (New Haven, 1971), 441-451.

18. Like Winstanley, the anonymous author of *Tyranipocrit Discovered*, published before 14 August in Rotterdam, sees the connection between private property and language. The author notes that preachers and teachers are given a fine education so that they may become "humane Artists, good Gramarians, curious Linguist, such as can orderly speake Hebrew, Greeke, and Latine," but they "have no experience in that honest simple life, of tilling the land, nor keeping of sheepe, but some of them are good Sophisters, that can tell us that hote is cold and cold hote." Even though "God destroyed the ancient language, because of what proud Babilonian builder Nimrod . . . wee more impious then hee, learne strange languages to build Christ a Church withall, for in these dayes, hee that cannot speake strange languages, shall not bee thought fit to preach, nor to teach Christians, and are not such curious Artists and Linguists, worldly wise men? such as are not fit to preach the gospel of Christ, because arts and languages are enemies to humility"; in George Orwell and Reginald Reynolds, eds., *British Pamphleteers*, I (London, 1948), 97-98.

19. Hill, *Winstanley*, p. 125.

20. The rare "Preface to SEVERAL PIECES GATHERED INTO ONE VOLUME" is in Hill, *Winstanley*, pp. 155-157.

21. In *Shakespeare's Doctrine of Nature* (1948; rpt. London, 1961), John F. Danby points out that "Lear's prayer on the Heath (echoing the cry that Jack Kett had raised in 1549, and anticipating the cry to come in 1649 from Winstanley and the Diggers) is . . . central to Shakespeare's inspiration" (p. 223).

22. The story of the mighty stone cut without hand is from Daniel 2:31-45. The head of gold is Nebuchadnezzar's. In the alchemical tradition the stone was synonymous with the philosopher's stone and with Christ; C. G. Jung, "The Lapis-Christ Parallel," in *Psychology and Alchemy*, trans. R. F. C. Hull, 2nd ed. (Princeton, 1968), pp. 345-431.

23. In Hill, *Winstanley*, p. 159.

24. One of the officers of the Kingston court said "That if the Diggers cause was good, he would pick out such a Jurie as should overthrow him."

25. Marx quotes Shylock's "You take my life/When you do take the means whereby I live," in *Capital*, I, 487. And in *Henry IV, Pt. I*, I, ii, 101-102, Falstaff justifies his purse-taking by declaring: "Why, Hal, 'tis my vocation, Hal, 'tis no sin for a man to labour in his vocation."

26. The prevalence of hostile twins in Winstanley's work supports Erich Neumann's explanation that this trope represents the attainment of self-consciousness; *The Origins and History of Consciousness*, trans. R. F. C. Hull (1954; rpt. Princeton, 1970), pp. 95-101.

27. Clarkson, like Winstanley, was from Lancashire. In his autobiography, *The Lost Sheep FOUND* (London, 1660), he writes that "I made it appear to *Gerrard Winstanley* there was self-love and vain-glory nursed in his heart, that if possible, by digging to have gained people to him, by which his name might become great among the poor Commonalty of the Nation." After the destruction of the Digger colony, Clarkson says, Winstanley became "a real Tithe-gatherer of propriety." Disillusioned by his confrontation with the Diggers, Clarkson adds that he "saw all that men spake or acted was a lye and therefore my thought was, I had as good cheat for something among them" (p. 27).

28. Marx discusses this in "Private Property and Communism," in *Economic Manuscripts*, pp. 133-134; and Engels provides an extensive analysis in *The Origin of the Family, Private Property, and the State* (1884; rpt. New York, 1942), pp. 25-74.

V. THE IMPRISONED EARTH

1. G. E. Aylmer discovered this pamphlet and published it in *Past & Present*, No. 40 (July 1968), pp. 9-15; rpt. in Charles Webster, ed., *The Intellectual Revolution of the Seventeenth Century* (London, 1974), pp. 109-123.

2. On the Engagement see John M. Wallace, *Destiny His Choice, The Loyalism of Andrew Marvell* (Cambridge, 1968), pp. 43-68.

3. Quoted from the British Library copy, shelfmark C. 124 h.1 (1), which is discussed by Keith Thomas in "The Date of Gerrard Winstanley's *Fire in the Bush*," *Past & Present*, No. 42 (Feb. 1969), pp. 160-162; rpt. in Webster, pp. 138-142.

4. Frederic Jameson, *Marxism and Form, Twentieth-Century Dialectical Theories of Literature* (Princeton, 1971), pp. 84-85.

5. A. S. P. Woodhouse, ed., *Puritanism and Liberty*, 2nd ed. (1951; rpt. Chicago, 1974), p. [59].

6. J. Sears McGee, *The Godly Man in Stuart England* (New Haven, 1976), p. 108.

7. As Arthur O. Lovejoy shows, since the time of Tertullian Stoicism played an important role in the Christian view that in nature may be found valid norms of conduct; " 'Nature' as Norm in Tertullian," in *Essays in the History of Ideas* (1948; rpt. New York, 1960), pp. 308-338.

8. C. B. Macpherson, *The Political Theory of Possessive Individualism* (1962; rpt. London, 1964), pp. 154, 157-158; and J. C. Davies, "The Levellers and Christianity," in *Politics, Religion and the English Civil War*, ed. Brian Manning (London, 1973), p. 231.

9. *The Leveller Tracts*, ed. William Haller and Godfrey Davies (New York, 1944), p. 449.

10. Maren-Sofie Røstvig notes that "the close connection between typology and syncretism is illustrated by Dr. John Everard . . . whose published sermons . . . are full of typological expositions"; "Images of Perfection," in *Seventeenth-Century Imagery, Essays on Uses of Figurative Language from Donne to Farquhar*, ed. Earl Miner (Berkeley, 1971), p. 4n8. As Jean Seznec explains, "this

rationalist interpretation legitimized for most people the deification of the heavenly bodies"; *The Survival of the Pagan Gods*, trans. Barbara F. Sessions (1953; rpt. Princeton, 1972), p. 41.

11. In *The Complete Works of St. Thomas More*, IV, ed. Edward Surtz, S. J., and J. H. Hexter (New Haven, 1965), 517. Marsilio Ficino's *De sole* also stresses sun worship as does Tommaso Campanella's *Civitas solis*.

12. John Everard, *The Gospel-Treasury Opened* (London, 1657), II, 112.

13. *Complete Prose Works of John Milton*, II, ed. Ernest Sirluck, (New Haven, 1959), 562.

14. Everard, I, 379-381.

15. The phrase is from Ernst Cassirer, *The Individual and the Cosmos in Renaissance Philosophy*, trans. Mario Domandi (New York, 1963), p. 45.

16. William G. Madsen says "this interpretation is mistaken" when applied to biblical exegesis, for "there is a fundamental opposition between [Neoplatonic and Christian] world-views that is already apparent in Hebrews [10:1]. It is the opposition between the historical, eschatological spirit of Christianity implicit in the phrase 'shadows of good things to come,' and the nonhistorical, ontological spirit of Platonism"; *From Shadowy Types to Truth* (New Haven, 1968), pp. 88, 99. Jason P. Rosenblatt challenges the basis of Madsen's view in "The War in Heaven in *Paradise Lost*," *PMLA*, 87 (1972), 31-41.

17. Although Augustine attacks early Neoplatonists—Plotinus, Porphry, Iamblichus, Apuleius—in *The City of God* (bks. VIII-XI) for returning to "animism" and refusing to forsake Stoic pantheism, he also admits in his *Confessions* (bk. VIII) that they helped him to overcome Manichaeanism and enabled him to see the unity of material and spiritual worlds. Minucius Felix's *Octavius* (c. 200), cited by Sir Thomas Browne, epitomizes this point of view. Minucius employs the image of the *sol iustitiae* to represent Christ and insists that knowledge of God may be obtained from the natural world, especially from the sun.

18. Francis Bacon, *The Advancement of Learning*, ed. G. W. Kitchen (1915: rpt. London, 1962), p. 112. Paolo Rossi analyzes Bacon's relation to Hermeticism in *Francis Bacon, from Magic to Science*, trans. Sacha Rabinovitch (1968; rpt. Chicago, 1978).

19. Mircea Eliade points out in *Patterns in Comparative Religion*, trans. Rosemary Sheed (Cleveland, 1963), that the sun hero is not just a physical manifestation of the sun; he is connected with "the cult of sovereignty or of a demiurge. The hero 'saves' the world, renews it, opens a new era which sometimes even amounts to a new organization of the universe; in other words, he still preserves the qualities of the demiurge of the Supreme Being. A career like that of Mithra who was at first a sky god, later became a sun god and later still a saviour (as the Sol Invictus), can . . . be explained by this demiurgic function of ordering the world . . . The result is the hastening of the process of rationalization . . . Rationalization and syncretism advanced together" (pp. 150-151).

20. Cf. Matt. 6:22 and Luke 11:34. Christopher Hill says that this passage may refer to Laurence Clarkson's *A Single Eye, all Light, no Darkness*, published in October 1650, which Winstanley may have seen in manuscript; *Winstanley, The Law of Freedom and Other Writings* (Harmondsworth, 1973), p. 250. It also

seems likely that both Winstanley and Clarkson were familiar with John Everard's translation of Cusanus' *De visione dei*, published under Giles Randall's name in 1646 as *The Single Eye*. Norman T. Burns notes that "much of the Ranter teaching and behavior seems a vulgar parody of Everard's comparative sober experimentalism"; *Christian Mortalism from Tyndale to Milton* (Cambridge, Mass., 1972), p. 81. John Bunyan also may have quarreled with Clarkson, and *A Single Eye* may be one of the "Ranters books" referred to in his autobiography; *Grace Abounding to the Chief of Sinners*, ed. Roger Sharrock (Oxford, 1962), pp. xvii, 16-17, 137n44.

21. C. G. Jung examines androgeny in alchemy in *Alchemical Studies*, trans. R. F. C. Hull (Princeton, 1967), p. 219, and in *Psychology and Alchemy*, trans. R. F. C. Hull, 2nd ed. (Princeton, 1968), p. 161.

22. *The Poetry and Prose of William Blake*, ed. David V. Erdman, rev. ed. (Garden City, N.Y., 1970), p. 78.

23. Stephen Jay Gould, *Ontogeny and Phylogeny* (Cambridge, Mass., 1977), p. 13.

24. *The Prose of Sir Thomas Browne*, ed. Norman J. Endicott (Garden City, N.Y., 1967), pp. 41-42.

25. Gould, pp. 16, 156-157; Jung also believes in the biogenetic law, but, as Gould observes, his static concept of the collective unconscious denies him historical perspective (p. 162).

26. Karl Marx, *Capital, a Critique of Political Economy*, trans. Samuel Moore and Edward Aveling, ed. Frederick Engels (1887; rpt. New York, 1967), I, 713-714. "Adam bit the apple," Marx explains, "and thereupon sin fell on the human race. Its origin is supposed to be explained when it is told as an anecdote of the past. In times long gone by there were two sorts of people; one, the diligent, intelligent, and, above all, frugal elite; the other, lazy rascals, spending their substance, and more, in riotous living. The legend of theological original sin tells us certainly how man came to be condemned to eat his bread in the sweat of his brow; but the history of economic original sin reveals to us that there are people to whom this is by no means essential. Never mind! Thus it came to pass that the former sort accumulated wealth, and the latter sort had at last nothing to sell except their own skins. And from this original sin dates the poverty of the great majority that, despite all its labour, has up to now nothing to sell but itself, and the wealth of the few that increases constantly although they have long ceased to work. Such insipid childishness is every day preached to us in the defence of property."

27. Frederick Engels, *Dialectics of Nature*, trans. and ed. Clemens P. Dutt (New York, 1940), p. 291; Engels repeatedly states his intention to refute Haeckel's "nonsense" (see pp. 176ff). In *Anti-Dühring* (1878) he notes: "the philosophy of antiquity was primitive, natural materialism. As such, it was incapable of clearing up the relation between thought and matter. But the need to get clarity on this question led to the doctrine of a soul separable from the body, then to assertion of the immortality of this soul, and finally to monotheism. The old materialism was therefore negated by idealism. But in the course of the further development of philosophy, idealism too became untenable and was

negated by modern materialism. This modern materialism, the negation of the negation, is not the mere re-establishment of the old, but adds to the permanent foundations of this old materialism the whole thought content of two thousand years of development of philosophy and natural science"; *Herr Eugen Dühring's Revolution in Science*, trans. Emile Burns, ed. Clemens P. Dutt (New York, 1939), p. 152; also *The Origin of the Family* (1884; rpt. New York, 1942), pp. 162-163.

28. Karl Marx, "Estranged Labor," in *The Economic and Philosophic Manuscripts of 1844*, trans. Martin Milligen, ed. Dirk J. Struik (New York, 1964), pp. 107-119; the comments on *Robinson Crusoe* in *Capital*, I, 71-83, are especially relevant, as are Engel's views in *Socialism, Utopian and Scientific* (1892); *Karl Marx and Frederick Engels, Selected Works* (New York, 1968), pp. 421-434.

29. Christopher Hill analyzes the role of Ralegh's *History of the World* in *Intellectual Origins of the English Revolution* (Oxford, 1965), pp. 187-198.

30. Louis Althusser, *For Marx*, trans. Ben Brewster (New York, 1970), pp. 62-63; also pp. 231-232; and *Lenin and Philosophy*, trans. Ben Brewster (New York, 1971): "it is not their real conditions of existence, their real world, that 'men' 'represent to themselves' in ideology, but above all it is their relation to those conditions of existence which is represented to them there. It is this relation which is at the centre of every ideological, i.e. imaginary, representation of the real world" (p. 164).

31. Jos. 7:18-21. Achan's theft is a national disgrace for which the community, having created the moral climate that made such a crime possible, must suffer. Michael Fixler analyzes the story's popularity in *Milton and the Kingdoms of God* (Evanston, 1964), pp. 117-118.

32. Overton writes in *An Appeal from the Commons to the Free People* (1647): "*Salus populi est suprema lex:* the safety of the people is the supreme law of all commonwealths. Therefore it is in vain for our members in Parliament to think that we will justify or tolerate the same among them which we would not endure in the King—to pluck off the garments of royalty from oppression and tyranny, to dress up the same in Parliament-robes. No, no, that was ever, and is, far from our hearts, and we shall justify or allow the same no more in the one than in the other" (Woodhouse, p. 329; also p. 456).

33. Exod. 28:42; Winstanley's letter is in Paul Hardacre's "Gerrard Winstanley in 1650," *HLQ*, 22 (1959), 347-349. For "Breeches" see the Geneva Bible, Gen. 3:7. Winstanley so internalized scripture that it was part of his natural speech. C. H. George concludes that Winstanley "used the King James rather than the 'Puritan' Geneva Bible"; "Gerrard Winstanley, a Critical Retrospect," in *The Dissenting Tradition*, ed. C. Robert Cole and Michael E. Moody (Athens, Ohio, 1975), p. 211. My comparison of Winstanley's biblical quotations with texts of the Geneva and the 1611 King James versions indicates that he used neither consistently.

34. Charles Webster has established that Plattes, not Samuel Hartlib, wrote this utopian tract; "The Authorship and Significance of *Marcaria*," *Past & Present*, No. 56 (August 1972), pp. 34-48; rpt. in Webster, 369-385.

35. In Hill, *Winstanley*, p. 273.

36. Jameson, pp. 145-146; Geoffrey H. Hartman comments on the "hermeneutic character of art" in "Structuralism, the Anglo-American Adventure," in *Beyond Formalism, Literary Essays 1958-1970* (New Haven, 1970), pp. 20-21.

37. J. C. Davis argues, in opposition to Hill, that Winstanley changed his vision of ideal society from a moral commonwealth to an authoritarian utopia; "Gerrard Winstanley and the Restoration of True Magistracy," *Past & Present*, No. 70 (February 1976), pp. 76-93. My view is that the defeat of the Digger colony somewhat embittered Winstanley and caused him, in *The Law of Freedom*, to suggest a more rigidly appearing plan than he would have wished to see put into action.

38. *Complete Prose Works of John Milton*, III, ed. Merritt Y. Hughes (New Haven, 1962), 455, 467.

39. *Complete Prose*, III, 110-122. Milton employs this image extensively in other works; see *Complete Prose*, II, 198-199; III, 202, 206, 211-212; IV, 586-588; and Woodhouse, pp. 187-191.

40. J. Max Patrick, "The Literature of the Diggers," *UTQ*, 12 (1942), 110; Patrick relates *The Law of Freedom* to the utopian tradition in Glenn Negley and J. Max Patrick, eds., *The Quest for Utopia, an Anthology of Imaginary Societies* (New York, 1952), pp. 288-289.

41. David W. Petegorsky, *Left-Wing Democracy in the English Civil War* (London, 1940), p. 123. Aldworth's name is variously spelled Allsworth, Alsworth, and Aldsworth in other commentaries on the trial.

42. Richard T. Vann, "The Later Life of Gerrard Winstanley," *JHI*, 26 (1965), 135. Hill has serious reservations about whether Vann's findings refer to the former Digger; *Winstanley*, pp. 32-33. Even if this is the same man, there is little reason to assume, as does Vann, that Winstanley became a Quaker. There is no record that he ever attended a Quaker meeting, nor has any burial record of his first wife been found. It seems quite possible that upon his death his second wife, knowing of her husband's radical past, asked a group of local Quakers to provide a funeral service for him so he would not have to be buried under the auspices of the Anglican Church. Elizabeth subsequently married Giles Tutchbury, a cooper, at the famous Bull and Mouth meeting of London Friends in Aldersgate, the same meeting that had held funeral services for John Lilburne on 1 September 1657.

43. Christopher Hill, *God's Englishman* (London, 1970), p. 143.

44. Bernard S. Capp, *The Fifth Monarchy Men, a Study in Seventeenth-Century Millenarianism* (London, 1972), chap. 3.

BIBLIOGRAPHICAL NOTE

The most nearly complete edition of Winstanley's works is that edited by George H. Sabine, which was published by Cornell University Press in 1941 and reprinted by Russell and Russell in 1965. However, this edition contains only brief synopses of Winstanley's first three pamphlets and omits poems and introductory materials from other pamphlets. Christopher Hill's Pelican Classics edition of *The Law of Freedom and Other Works* (Harmondsworth, 1973) has an excellent introduction and reprints the poems and introductory materials not in Sabine's edition, but it does not include the early pamphlets. For these the reader must go to the best primary source for the history of the English Revolution, The British Library's Thomason Collection of some 22,000 tracts, now available from University Microfilms International, Ann Arbor, Michigan. The two-volume catalogue edited by G. K. Fortescue (London, 1908) is most helpful.

Of the important secondary sources, David W. Petegorsky's *Left-Wing Democracy in the English Civil War* (London, 1940) must be mentioned first, for although additional discoveries have been made since it was published, this book contains a balanced and informative assessment of Winstanley's career. Perez Zagorin's *A History of Political Thought in the English Revolution* (1954; rpt. New York, 1966) places Winstanley's ideas in a larger context, and Herschel Baker's *The Wars of Truth* (1952; rpt. Gloucester, Mass., 1969) covers the intellectual background. William York Tindall's *John Bunyan, Mechanick Preacher* (1934; rpt. New York, 1964) and A. L. Morton's *The World of the Ranters* (London, 1970) provide vivid pictures of Winstanley's milieu, and Christopher Hill's *The World Turned Upside Down* (London and New York, 1972), now available in Penguin Books, is indispensable for anyone desiring a greater understanding of seventeenth-century radicalism.

On the essential subject of millenarianism, in addition to the studies by Cohn, Hill, Toon, Lamont, and Capp cited in the notes, I have learned much from Charles Webster's *The Great Instauration* (London, 1975). Katherine R. Firth's *The Apocalyptic Tradition in Reformation Britain, 1530-1645* (Oxford, 1978) appeared too late for me to use in this study. In related fields, especially exciting are Carl Sagan's explanation of the Edenic myth as a metaphor of human intellectual evolution in *The Dragons of Eden* (New York, 1977) and Marvin Harris' theory of the origin of pristine states as the debasement of the many on behalf of the few in *Cannibals and Kings* (New York, 1977); both books point up Winstanley's literary and cultural sagacity.

Finally, I received special inspiration from a book only remotely related to Winstanley and his background, Steven Marcus' *Engels, Manchester and the English Working Class* (New York, 1974), which takes as its task "to see how far the intellectual discipline that begins with the work of close textual analysis can help us understand certain social, historical or theoretical documents." Like Marcus, I too hope that my study, if successful, may have some salutary effect on literary criticism in its present uneasy state.

INDEX

Abraham, 20, 69, 110-111, 136, 185-186

Achan's sin, 206, 245n31

Acts, 116, 183-184

Adam: represents all men, 13-16, 18-20, 65, 133; first and second, 14, 20, 26, 33, 57-59, 101-102, 114-116, 118, 120-122, 126, 128-130, 138, 149, 169, 176, 191, 195, 196-197, 207; pun on, 128-129, 146, 148; in man, 132, 188, 205; and Fall, 152; nature and grace, 178; seed of, 185-186; sin of, 192; law of necessity, 214

Aesculapius, 185

Agrippa, Henry Cornelius, 66

Alchemy: imagery of, 57, 63-80, 178; and H. Vaughan, 64, 77-79; and T. Vaughan, 66; and J. Everard, 66-67; and Jonson, 78; and creation, 104-106, 149-150; and sower, 110; and sun of righteousness, 117-119; and recapitulation, 198; and Marx, 240n14

Aldworth, Richard, 7, 218

Allegorical interpretation. *See* Typological method

Alienation, 135-136, 143-144, 182-183, 200, 204

Alsted, Johann Heinrich, 5, 12, 112

Althusser, Louis, 202

Anabaptists, 2, 37, 48, 55, 236n39

Androgeny, 69, 198

Angels: of light, 19, 20, 32, 120-122, 138, 146; four evil, 37, 85; nature of, 63-65, 69, 71; H. Vaughan on, 75; in Revelation, 82, 134; J. Everard on, 229n31

Anglicanism: popular opposition to, 4; corruption of, 32, 38-39; prose style of, 44; as common enemy, 49, 125; court system of, 53; opposes universal salvation and communism, 88, 236n39; conservatism, 94-95; as guardian of truth, 98; downfall, 108, 201; pessimism, 119; and Levellers, 178. *See also* Ministers; Innate depravity

Antichrist, 5, 30, 193, 216

Antinomianism, 20, 51, 52, 65, 106

Apocalyptic literature, 109ff

Apostles, 26, 53, 71, 102, 107, 116, 124, 142, 143, 148

Aquinas, St. Thomas: his synthesis, 92, 94, 101, 237n49

Archer, John, 6, 12

Aristotle, 198, 214

Ashmole, Elias, 66

Auerbach, Erich, 11

Augustine, St.: and inner light, 2; *The City of God*, 10; and typological compromise, 11; as "twice-born," 16; quietism, 35; anti-Manichaeanism, 70, 100; and sun-worship, 118; motto, 182; and spiritual evolution, 199; governmental principles, 214; and seed image, 229n30; and Neoplatonists, 243n17

Aylmer, G. E., 17

Babouvists, 172

Babylon: fall of, 25, 26, 30, 41, 123, 207; captivity in, 36, 147; Beast of, 163; transformation of, 189, 192

Bacon, Francis, as utopian thinker, 48, 73, 76-77, 94-95, 185, 210, 229n30

Bacon, Roger, 66

Baillie, Robert, 48

Bale, John, 5

Ball, John, 50, 110

Baptists, 8, 13, 90, 107

249

Baxter, Richard, 88

Bible, 1, 43, 111, 114, 178, 208; and Joachim, 2; and Blake, 38; and H. Vaughan, 64; and Winstanley, 71, 89, 116, 133; as metaphorical history, 135; God in, 136; and recapitulation, 180. *See also* Geneva Bible; Scriptures; Typological method

Blake, William: as model for reading Winstanley, 1; attraction to biblical prophecy, 26; defends Bible, 38; *Marriage of Heaven and Hell*, 46; relationship to Swedenborg, 68; and Winstanley, 68, 72, 101, 219; Albion, 102; prophetic books of, 109; and sun-god, 118; "madness," 120; Urizen and Los, 135; "Little Black Boy," 137; trial, 156; *Jerusalem*, 175; and recapitulation, 198

Blasphemy Ordinance, 28, 88-89

Bloomfield, Morton W., 105

Boehme, Jacob, 23-24, 67, 68, 88

Bonaventure, St., 181, 185, 188

Bonnet, Charles, 199

Bradshaw, John, 145

Brightman, Thomas, 5, 6, 12, 112

Brown, Norman O., 82

Browne, Sir Thomas, 73, 75, 198-199, 231n47

Bullinger, Henry, 5

Bunyan, John, 16, 33, 34, 70, 156, 243-244n20

Burroughs, Jeremiah, 112

Burton, Robert, 73

Burton, William, 5

Bush, Douglas, 75

Caedmon's hymn, 202

Cain and Abel, 132, 152, 204

Calvert, Giles, 23, 46, 207

Calvin, John, 10, 95

Calvinism, 2, 13, 17, 176, 178. *See also* Innate depravity; Sin

Cambridge Platonists, 93, 229n30

Capitalism: rise, 47, 69, 135, 153, 213, 217. *See also* Private property

Caryl, Joseph, 12

Castellio, Sebastian, 4

Cavalier Army, 37-38

Charles I: convenes Long Parliament, 4; denigrated, 13; punishment for, 30; as retributive angel, 70; treaty planned with, 88; beheading, 108, 144; image on money, 150; destroyed, 154, 164, 174, 207; as oak tree, 167; Milton's description of, 213

Chaucer, Geoffrey, 29, 233n6

Chiliasm, 48-49

Christ: Second Coming of, 6, 12-13, 16, 46, 48, 49, 71, 111, 119, 126-127; destroys serpent, 15, 101, 139; in history, 20, 38; atonement of, 21, 137, 192; indwelling of, 24, 28-32, 40, 50-51, 59, 61, 72, 86, 92, 101-102, 116, 117, 120, 141, 188, 195, 237n51, 237n52; as seed or logos, 25, 27-29, 31, 101, 162, 184-186, 237n50; Moses type of, 26, 34, 204; day of, 33; in scripture, 36; in church, 44; Jews did not recognize, 56; his mercy, 62; as alchemical hero, 67; and Gergesene demoniacs, 79-84; ministers deny, 93, 106, 130; first rational man, 105; Abraham type of, 111; as liberty, 114; and sun-god, 118, 179; Jacob type of, 122, 132; tyranny enemy of, 128; professors and, 138; as General, 160; used by lawyers, 165; true Leveller, 170-171; churches claim on, 177; translates truth, 180; and private property, 191; rejects the rich, 194-195; as Tree of Life, 196; and moderation, 122, 205; as second Adam, 207; mystification of, 216; and capitalism, 217

Cicero, 179, 185

Clark, Kenneth, 113

Clarkson, Laurence, 23, 34, 171-173, 242n27, 243-244n20. *See also* Ranters

Cobham, Surrey, 7, 145, 156, 160, 206-208

Coke, Sir Edward, 157

Collier, Thomas, 13, 223n38

Comenius, John Amos, 90

Communism: More's, 2, 124; Winstanley's, 17, 71, 98-99, 150, 167, 170-171, 174, 176, 189-190, 208; Levellers repudiate, 88; biblical, 127, 130, 148, 183-184; Marx's, 199; and Anglicanism, 236n39; Herbert on, 240n10

Conversion (metanoia), 33, 58ff, 61-63

Copernicus, Nicholas, 94

Coppe, Abiezer, 34
1 Corinthians, 18, 29, 52, 198
2 Corinthians, 18, 20, 194
Crab, Roger, 34
Crick, Francis H. C., 28
Cromwell, Oliver, 1; rejected by Levellers, 8; speaks against monarchy, 25; as leader of Army, 70; at Pontefract, 98; on "fleshly reason," 101; not sun of righteousness, 137; defeats Levellers, 150; in Ireland, 164; Marvell's view of, 189; *Law of Freedom* addressed to, 210-211

Danby, John, 29
Daniel, 5, 6, 25-27, 42, 97, 140, 176, 188-192
Darwin, Charles, 198
David, King, 9, 29, 125
Dee, John, 66
Defoe, Daniel, 60, 167
Dell, William, 23, 48, 50, 88, 90
della Porta, Giovanni Battista, 66
Denck, Hans, 4
Depravity. *See* Innate depravity
Descartes, René, 76, 182
Dialectic: Winstanley's inner and outer, 15-16, 20, 34, 49, 52, 68-69, 71, 81, 101, 110, 119, 121-122, 131, 166-167, 174, 176, 179, 183, 196-198, 205, 211, 219; Swift's 83; between idealistic and materialistic knowledge, 89; Hegel's, 99, 192
Digger colony: premonitions, 29, 71, 80, 139; investigated by Gladman, 88; Winstanley and, 89; principles, 108, 149; beginning, 144-145; peacefulness, 146-147, 150-152, 169; and press, 148; and land, 151; god of, 152; members beaten, 153; members arrested, 157; destruction, 159, 167; and gentry, 166; last phase, 174ff; Lilburne repudiates, 178; represents sun of righteousness, 191; *An Appeale*, 206; last pamphlet, 207-209; at Pirton, 209
Dionysius the Areopagite, 4, 188
Divine right, 19, 30, 70, 97, 226n59
Donne, John: contrasts with Herbert, 62; familiarity with Paracelsian texts, 66; effect of "new philosophy" on, 73-74;

social poetry of, 75; on nature, 76; and transformation, 130; and sun of righteousness, 232n62; and reason, 235n17; and kernel image, 240n8
Douglas, Lady Eleanor, 209
Downame, John, 13
Drake, Francis, 157
Dürer, Albrecht: *Apocalypse*, 112-114; *Sol iustitiae*, 117-119; engraving of the Fall (Adam and Eve), 129; woodcuts, 134
Dury, John, 90

Eckhart, Meister, 185-186, 188
Eden, Garden of: represents perfection, 13; made for use, 14; restoration of, 21, 33, 58, 71, 81, 84, 107-108, 147, 176, 190; devil in, 57; expulsion from, 99; as image of society, 103, 178, 219; in man, 180-182, 186, 188
Educational system, 50, 52-53, 86
Edwards, Thomas, 48
Elect, 8, 18, 22, 50. *See also* Saints
Eliade, Mircea, 78-79
Eliot, T. S., 55
Empson, William, 82-83
Engagement oath, 174, 207, 208, 218
Engels, Frederick, 199-200, 244-245n27
Ephesians, 116
Erasmus, Desiderius, 73, 179
Erickson, Erik, 58
Eve, 14, 129, 132; seed of, 33, 84; J. Everard on, 101; and nature and grace, 178
Everard, John: career of, 4; on Second Coming, 12; on corruption of clergy, 39; chiliasm, 48; on suffering, 49; and alchemy, 66; translation of *The Divine Pymander*, 67; on academic training, 90; on reason, 101; on sun and moon, 114; preaching of, 141, 225n51; and Neo-Stoicism, 179; and Tree of Knowledge, 180; and scripture, 223n34; and antinomianism, 228n15; on angels, 229n31; on indwelling of Christ, 237n51; on imagination, 237n52; and typology and syncretism, 242n10; and Cusanus, 243-244n20
Everard, William, 88, 92-93, 111, 144
Everlasting gospel, 90, 91

"Excremental Vision," 82-83
Ezekiel, 38, 56, 97, 175

Fairfax, Maria, 74-75
Fairfax, Thomas, 70, 75, 88, 98, 145, 150-153, 160
Fall, 9, 13, 15, 18, 21, 33, 129, 132-133, 137, 168, 182; recapitulates consciousness, 17, 179; and private property, 152, 154, 196, 203; and covetousness, 153; key biblical text, 178; in man, 188, 201; in Middle Ages, 202; in Ralegh, 202; as history until Christ, 204-205; cause, 205; consequences, 212-213; Marx on, 244n26
Familists, 2, 88
Family, ideal, 116, 172-173, 211-214
Ficino, Marsilio, 4, 185
Fifth Monarchists, 219
Fish, Stanley E., 59, 87
Foxe, John: accomplishment of, 2; *Actes and Monuments*, 5, 113, 119; influence on radical Independents, 12; cited by Winstanley, 42; millenarianism, 43, 97; influence on Winstanley, 44-45, 112, 154; on elect nation, 70, 55, 139, 146, 149; on printing, 133; and suffering, 228n16
Franck, Sebastian, 4, 179-181, 186
Frazer, James George, 31
Freud, Sigmund, 199, 200, 203

Galatians, 25
Galileo Galilei, 28, 92, 94
Gater, Sarah, 3
Genesis: *3:15*, 16, 20, 23, 25, 31, 76, 103, 126, 131; *18:18*, 20; *3:24*, 57; as myth, 58, 179; first and ninth chapters, 108; opening, 145; images from, 175. *See also* Images
Genesis B, 202
Geneva Bible, 113, 183-184, 194, 245n33
Gentry, 24, 132, 153-155, 164, 166, 169, 170, 193, 206-209
Georges, Ferdinando, 218
Gergesene demoniacs, 79-84
German reformers, 4, 179
Gilbert, William, 92
Gladman, John, 88, 145
Gnostic dualism. *See* Manichaean dualism

Golden Age, 6, 40, 99, 114, 130, 211
Golding, Arthur, 5
Goodwin, John, 12
Goodwin, Thomas, 6, 8, 12, 110-112, 232n62
Gouge, William, 13
Gould, Stephen Jay, 198
Gregory, St., 99, 175

Haeckel, Ernst, 199, 244n27
Haller, William, 4, 13-14, 42-43
Hammond, Robert, 101
Harrington, James, 1, 210
Hartford, Rapha, 12
Hartlib, Samuel, 50, 90, 245n34
Harvey, William, 92, 199
Hayne, Thomas, 12
Hebrews, 77
Hegel, G. W. F., 36, 37, 68, 99, 200
Herbert, George, 61-63, 75, 130, 240n10
Herbert, Lord, of Cherbery, 68
Hermeneutics, 111, 175-176, 216, 246n36
Hermes Trismegistus, 66, 67
Hermeticism, 66-69, 77. *See also* Alchemy
Herrick, Robert, 50
Hill, Christopher, 1, 8, 23, 94, 100, 104, 148, 219
Hobbes, Thomas, 1, 148, 205
Hobson, Paul, 18
Hooker, Richard, 94
Hooker, Thomas, 178
Hoopes, Robert, 94
Hosea, 21
Human nature, defined, 69-70, 100ff, 153, 205. *See also* Perfection; Reason
Hunter, William, 43
Hussites, 48
Hyman, Stanley Edgar, 3

Ideology, 17, 33, 47, 57, 86-87, 157, 202-204
Imagery: of Puritans, 4; literal interpretation, 12; as "shadows" of truth, 14, 40; familiarity, 27, 51, 77, 111, 118, 200; Frazer's, 31; organic, 33; logic, 49; alchemical, 64ff, 77, 117; playfulness, 70, 141; logic, 102-106; and symbolic thought, 110-112, 134, 146; boldness, 130, 175, 202; *specific:* prison, 15, 16, 54, 84, 125, 140, 165,

186; kernel, 36, 97, 143, 149, 226n58, 240n8; nursing, 32, 54, 106, 138, 149, 150; sword, 56, 57, 58, 59, 65, 85, 151-165, 170, 181, 191, 192, 206; riding, 91, 158-159, 234n13; candle, 93, 105, 142, 211; tree, 103, 151, 163, 164, 165, 167, 170-171; footstool, 115, 120, 131-132; storehouse, 115, 146, 211-212; wax, 195, 197. *See also* Metaphor; Seed image; Serpent image

Imagination: as begetter of covetousness, 47, 58-59, 84, 104, 112, 120, 129, 134, 136, 145, 146, 169, 178, 179, 185, 186, 187, 192-193, 215-216; as Tree of Knowledge, 183-184; as Serpent, 188, 197, 203; ministers preach by, 194-195

Independents, 37, 55; and franchise, 7; orthodox and radical, 12-13, 98; in Parliament, 25; corruption, 38; killed, 56; alarmed by radicals, 88; Saltmarsh on, 90; addressed, 175; rule of, 201

Innate depravity, 2, 4, 9, 14-15, 50, 178, 236n39. *See also* Calvinism; Sin

Inner light: history, 2; in everyone, 50, 65, 69, 104; sun of righteousness as, 72, 76, 114-117, 130-132, 135-136, 179, 196; Milton and, 127; reflected in nature, 139-140, 174; inviolability, 161

Inversion: of values, 24, 51-55, 58, 93, 119; in Marx, 36-37; and angels, 65; Calvinistic, 68; and work, 137; of Neoplatonic hierarchy, 186

Ireton, Henry, 98, 144

Isaiah, 27, 70, 97, 112, 151, 168, 169

Israel: biblical nation of, 9, 13, 26, 44, 54-56, 70-71, 74, 108, 110, 112, 125, 127, 209; Diggers as, 146-149, 154

Jacob and Esau, 110-111, 121-127, 130, 132, 146, 162, 173, 176, 197

James, 123

Jameson, Fredric, 176, 211

Jeremiah, 97, 146

Joachim of Fiore: and stages of history, 2, 35, 43, 48, 97, 146, 199, 223-224n38, 225n57, 228n12

Job, 58, 70, 138

John, 19-21, 66, 195, 196, 198

John the Apostle, 97, 113

John the Baptist, 21, 97

John of Leyden, 48

Jonah, 210

Jonson, Ben, 66, 78

Judas, 130, 141, 171, 194-195, 197

Judges, 70

Judgment Day, 21-23, 65-67, 130, 149

Kearney, Hugh, 91

Kepler, Johannes, 92

Kiffin, William, 6

Kings, 69

Kingston-on-Thames, Surrey, 88, 92, 135, 141, 144, 156

Lamont, William M., 12

Lancashire, 3, 7-9

Landlords, 24, 147, 175; swords, 151; will, 154; attack on, 155, 159, 162, 164-165; destroy Diggers, 167; compared to Ranters, 172; people should not fear, 176; fall, 188-189; as Beast, 190; appealed to, 208; as oppressors, 213

Langland, William, 89, 105, 109, 114, 120, 172, 233n6

Language: as abstraction, 26; prophetic, 31; corruption, 36, 70, 81-82, 93, 106, 143, 194-195; reformation, 63, 110-112, 121, 138, 141, 155, 215-216; repetitive, 89; of scriptures, 91; magic, 105; economic base, 147-148, 241n18; reconstruction, 176; Leveller, 178; simple, 181, 211. *See also* Imagery; Metaphor

Larner, William, 6

Laud, Archbishop, 5, 7, 89, 98

Laudians, 56

Lawrence, D. H., 238-239n67

Lawyers: not saints, 24; oppression, 89, 132, 159, 162, 165, 166-167; not needed, 124, 214; corruption, 155, 157, 169, 175-176; fall, 188-189; as Beast, 190; appeal to, 207-209

Levellers: and franchise, 7, 24, 224n47; and royalists, 8; in Parliament, 25; in Marvell's poetry, 74; *Humble Petition*, 88; repudiate communism, 88; adaptation of ideas, 97; program, 98; and Norman Yoke, 108, 147; mutineer Lockier, 145; defeated, 150; Christ truest of, 170-171, 184; avoid theology, 178; and nature, 178; *Agree-*

ment of the People, 210

Libertinism, 74, 172

Light Shining in Buckinghamshire, 108

Lilburne, John, 1; studied Foxe, 5; friend of Calvert, 23; and to Winstanley, 34; and John of Leyden, 48; and W. Everard, 88; debates Ireton, 144; cites Coke, 157; *Legall Fundamentall Liberties*, 178; repudiates Diggers, 178; and reason, 236n33; funeral, 246n42. *See also* Levellers

Literacy, 91, 135

Lockier, Robert, 145

Logos, 102, 167-168, 180, 184, 186, 229n30

Lollards, 2, 4, 42, 49-50

London, 3, 4, 7, 8, 34, 88, 135, 148, 156, 223n26

Luke, 198, 204, 208

Luther, Martin, 16, 34, 101, 240n11

McLuhan, Marshall, 133, 237n54

Madsen, William G., 56, 223n34, 243n16

Magistracy: out of joint, 38-39, 41; high power, 42; easy perversion, 119; defined, 193; in ideal commonwealth, 210; tree, 214

Magistrates: hope for, 25; and "two witnesses," 27; and truth, 29; and common people, 32; corruption, 38, 142, 167, 169; defense, 42-45, 53; protect ministers, 92; tyranny, 104, 115, 122, 164, 165, 191; in ideal commonwealth, 214

Magna Charta, 154, 240-241n16

Malachi, 79, 118, 175, 194. *See also* Sun of righteousness

Manichaean dualism, 56, 84, 88, 100, 189, 243n17

Mann, Julia DeLacy, 7

Mannheim, Karl, 47-48

Manuel, Frank E., 35

Mark, 82, 103, 198

Marlowe, Christopher, 73-74, 76

Marsh, George, 43

Marshall, Stephen, 12

Marvell, Andrew, 14, 73-74, 127, 128, 130, 137, 187, 189

Marx, Karl, 36-37, 99, 150, 199-200, 230n35, 240n14, 241n25, 244n26

Marxists, 172

Matthew, 63, 79, 82, 103, 206

Mechanic preachers, 1-2, 18, 34, 90, 94, 176

Mede, Joseph, 5, 12, 112

Merchant Taylors Company, 3

Metaphor: and vision of order, 3; heuristic use, 10, 26, 28, 47-48, 54-55, 77-78, 82, 85-86, 102-103, 105-106, 110-112, 126, 129, 142, 163-165, 191-192, 210, 214; and typology, 5, 6, 11, 14, 189; dialectical, 16; organic, 40-41, 196; and Satan, 56; alchemical, 63-77; heaven and hell as, 80-81, 136; and sun of righteousness, 118-119; and seeing inwardly, 120, 138; Bible as, 133, 135; and Norman Yoke, 147; and Stoicism, 178-179; and Neoplatonism, 184-186; epigenetic, 198. *See also* Imagery

Microcosm and macrocosm, 66-68, 72, 110, 186, 189, 191, 195-199, 229n30

Millenarianism: Puritans and, 5-6, 12-13, 112-113; Foxe and, 43-45, 97; and chiliasm, 48; Winstanley and, 85, 97, 117, 150, 199, 219; Virgil and, 229n30. *See also* Joachim of Fiore; Second Coming

Milton, John: Samson, 2, 76; and Eden, 14; and prophecy, 26; on corruption, 39; on reform, 50; and typology, 56; and disobedience, 58-59; privileged status, 73; on nature, 75; and inner light, 76, 127; on education, 90-91; on reason, 93-96; and primitive communism, 99; *The Tenure*, 108, 214; *Paradise Lost*, 110, 175; "L'Allegro," 118; Satan, 129; *Comus*, 172; and Fall, 178, 179; *Readie and Easie Way*, 210; *Eikonoklastes*, 213; *On Christian Doctrine*, 226n61; and seed image, 229n30; and sun of righteousness, 232n62

Ministers: appeal to poor, 4; and typology, 5, 36, 89-93, 106-107, 129, 130, 142, 143, 149, 155, 175, 193; not saints, 24; and Jews, 26; and "two witnesses," 27; and truth, 29; corruption, 21, 32, 38-42, 46, 50, 52, 53, 73, 134, 149, 160, 161, 190-191, 197, 206-207; in Foxe, 43; prose style, 44, 60; at Kingston, 88; slander, 92; worship devil, 119-120, 157; hypocrisy, 135-136, 172; as enemies, 152; and law, 153; freedom, 154; oppression, 158-159, 164, 167, 171; allied with gentry, 170, 212; fall, 188-189; rejected by Christ, 194-195; like Judas, 197; appeal to, 208-209

Minucius, Felix, 243n17

Mithras (sun-god), 117, 243n19

Moderation: advocation, 86-87, 89, 106, 119, 141, 142, 151; and reason, 100; Christ and, 122, 205; not to advance self, 131; of Diggers, 152, 172-174; of laws, 212; and millenarianism, 219

Monod, Jacques, 148

Montaigne, Michel de, 106, 238n55

More Light Shining in Buckinghamshire, 144

More, Richard, 5

More, Thomas, 2, 48, 73, 89, 98-100, 124, 150, 210

Morton, A. L., 23

Moses, 20, 76, 103, 107, 177; as type, 26, 27, 34, 204; covenant, 116

Mother Earth, 115, 149, 150-152, 166, 168, 181, 190-193, 196, 203, 205

Muggleton, Lodowick, 34

Münzer, Thomas, 48-49, 110, 233n6, 234n15, 234-235n16, 240n11

Murry, John Middleton, 82

Napier, John, 5

Natural law: reason and, 93-97; Milton and, 95; Overton and, 97; More and, 99-100; Saltmarsh on, 101; man heedless of, 137; God symbol of, 179; in ideal commonwealth, 214-217; Aquinas on, 237n49

Nature: pattern in, 3; and grace, 11-12, 55, 98, 101, 177-179, 184-185, 198, 230n35; images, 64, 93; perfection of, 67; poetic attitudes toward, 73-79; relationship to, 93, 100-102, 114, 116, 119, 137, 148, 160, 175, 178-179, 196, 205, 214, 216, 217, 219; Overton on, 96; Puritans on, 98; and More, 99-100; in Dürer, 118; book of, 134, 179; inner light in, 139; ministers ignore, 149; as clothing of God, 167, 181-182, 188

Naudé, Gabriel, 66

Nebuchadnezzar, 147, 240n11, 241n22

Neoplatonism, 4, 66, 74, 179, 184-188, 207, 243n16-17

Neo-Stoicism: material pantheism in, 67, 237n46; Walwyn's, 96, 238n55; Levellers and, 178; J. Everard and, 179; Montaigne's, 238n55

New Jerusalem, 9, 10, 12, 19, 41, 50, 71, 78, 111, 112, 124, 138, 189; coming of, 153, 207; communism in, 176; and paradise within, 180, 183, 201; failure to build, 219. *See also* Zion

New Model Army, 8-9, 24-25, 55, 105; chaplains, 8, 13; as destroyer, 55; represents Gideon's army, 70; Saltmarsh's warning to, 71; plan treaty with King, 88; and Pride's purge, 98; Winstanley warns leaders, 128, 156; asked to join Diggers, 146-147; bailiffs try to unseat, 158; do no work, 161; appeals to, 163ff; Adamic behavior of, 192; law and, 208

Newton, Isaac, 68

Nicholas of Cusa, 2, 4, 179, 185-186, 188, 243-244n20

Niclaes, Henrick, 24

Norman Yoke, 96, 108, 147-148, 152-165, 188, 206-208

Origen, 11, 179

Overton, Richard, 93, 96-97, 144, 178, 234n11, 245n32

Panofsky, Erwin, 113, 117-118

Pantheism, 67, 100, 215. *See also* Neo-Stoicism

Paracelsus (Theophrastus Bombastus von Hohenheim), 66, 77

Parliament: opening of, 4; loss of power, 9; conservatives in, 25; Saltmarsh warns, 71; Pride's purge, 98, 101; Winstanley's appeals to, 153-155, 163ff, 174; oppresses poor, 159; victory, 207; law and, 208

Patrick, J. Max, 1, 215

Paul St., 2, 10, 16, 34-35, 52, 60, 63, 179, 198

Perfection: idea of, 2; Eden and, 13; Augustine and, 35; J. Everard on, 49; human, 51, 72, 80, 101, 114, 118-119,

121, 124, 145, 176, 197; heavenly, 64; and hermeticism, 66-69; Browne on, 75; of Christ, 105

Perkins, William, 13, 40

Petegorsky, David W., 24, 108

Peter, 198

Peters, Hugh, 88, 210

Philo of Alexandria, 2

Pico della Mirandola, 185

"Plain style," 44

Plato, 28, 98, 185, 239n7

Platt, John, 208-209

Plattes, Gabriel, 210, 245n34

Plotinus, 4, 243n17

Pordage, John, 88

Presbyterians: in Parliament, 5; renege on promise, 7; loss of power, 9; pass Blasphemy Ordinance, 28, 88; corruption, 38; and chiliasm, 48; killing, 56; Saltmarsh on, 90; and nature and reason, 97-98; addressed, 175; rule, 201

Preston, John, 13

Pride, Thomas, 98, 101

Primitivism, 6, 106

Private property: transformation, 71; and money, 73, 82, 150; and selfishness, 99, 127, 128, 173; and law, 115, 170; curse, 147; Diggers and, 152; held by force, 155, 190; Christ and, 191; destruction, 192, 193, 196, 202, 208; creation, 203; and sin, 204-205

Proverbs, 77

Psalms, 9, 140, 206

Puns, 33, 82, 105, 115, 128-129, 141, 146, 165

Puritans: preaching, 4-5, 10, 60; attitude to poor, 8-9; reject Foxe, 12, 45; and spiritual autobiography, 34; attitude to church, 39, 98; hermenutics, 111; apocalyptic millenarianism, 112; attitude to New Testament, 42; prose style, 44; and individual heroism, 46; and spiritual combat, 54; and Calvinism, 68, 178; radical modes of thought, 76; fragmented sensibility, 82; Swift, 83; and spirit, 92; left-wing, 96; on nature and grace, 98, 177-178; base tendencies, 192; downfall, 193. See also Ministers

Quakers, 218

Quarles, Francis, 137

Ralegh, Walter, 202

Randall, Giles, 4, 12-13, 39, 48-49, 90, 229-230n31

Ranters, 171-175, 197, 243-244n20

Reason: respect for, 29; Marx on, 36; as guide, 69, 84, 89, 104-106, 111, 116, 126-127, 128, 145-146, 149, 157-158, 175, 183; Milton on, 75; God as, 80-81, 86-87, 93, 102, 108, 150, 152; faith and, 92, 212; empirical, 94-101; discursive, 121, 135; dialectical, 121-124, 197, 205; Ranters and, 172; communism and, 174; language and, 176; Browne on, 198-199; and nature, 214, 217

Recapitulation: and epistemology, 31; and hermeticism, 64-67; in *The New Law*, 128; in *The True Levellers Standard*, 146; in *Fire in the Bush*, 176; of psychological history, 180, 192, 197, 202; Engels on, 244-245n27. See also Gould

Reeve, John, 34

Revelation: in English, 5; and millenarianism, 6, 44; and orthodox Independents, 12; and universal salvation, 18, 19, 20, 23; as prophecy, 21, 22, 116; *16:10* and *11:6*, 30; *12:15-16*, 32; *11:7*, 35; *11:9*, 38; *21:23*, 52; *12:9-10*, 82, 124; and Norman Yoke, 108; and Dürer, 114; and sun of righteousness, 117-118; *5:13*, 120; *11:15*, 123; *10:9-11*, 134; images, 175; thirteenth chapter, 176, 180; *2:17*, 184. See also "Two witnesses"; Typological method

Robertson, D. W., Jr., 109, 224n40

Romans, 9, 18, 66, 116

Robins, John, 34

Royalists, 8, 30, 36, 37, 38, 97

St. George's Hill, 71, 144, 145, 148, 150, 151, 152, 156, 158, 178, 206

Saints: separation, 5, 138; suffering, 6, 11, 12, 24, 27-56; everyone a potential, 63-64; and earthly renewal, 67, 71, 110; paradise, 81, 84; words, 107; light

in, 141, 164; hypocrisy, 168-169, 204
Saltmarsh, John: as radical Independent, 12; his millenarianism, 13, 48-49, 225-226n57; and antinomianism, 20, 51, 65; works published, 23; and "wildernesse condition," 31; *Free Grace*, 33; on corrupt clergy, 39; and suffering, 49; *Sparkles of Glory*, 63, 90; warning to Army, 71; and W. Everard, 88; on everlasting gospel, 90; on law of nature and reason, 101; and typology, 224n40; and scripture, 225n53; and Joachim, 228n12; and salvation, 228n14; and sun of righteousness, 232n62; on Christ as seed, 237n50
Samson, 69, 76, 81
Sanders, Henry, 145
Satan, 32, 56, 70, 129, 130, 200, 205
Scriptures: interpretation, 5-6, 11-15, 29, 38, 40, 44, 53-54, 56, 80, 81, 85, 89-95, 102-108, 113, 116-117, 121, 125-127, 135, 149, 175; as evidence, 16; authority, 28; corrupted by ministers, 36-37, 194-195; corruption of text, 39, 142, 226n61, 223n6; and Digger principles, 148, 206, 208; vitality, 176-177. *See also* Bible; Gospel; Typological method
Second Coming: typical view, 6; literal and figurative, 12-13, 223-224n38; Augustine's view, 35; Winstanley's view, 45, 71, 111, 116, 126-127. *See also* Chiliasm; Millenarianism
Seed image (Gen. *3:15*): of mankind, 13, 129, 147, 170, 183, 186, 187, 196, 201; as dialectical metaphor, 16, 33, 110-111; and potency, 25; Christ as, 27, 28, 29, 30, 31, 168; of serpent, 56, 180; sun as, 64, 66, 166, 189-190, 191, 195, 205-206; Browne and, 75; Vaughan and, 76; and evil within, 84; and logos, 102-103; sensuous appeal, 105, 217; and apple, 121; words and, 126, 140, 184; spirit of reason as, 133, 146, 172; of Abraham, 136; sword and, 151; of life, 175; Platonic, 185, 229n30
Serpent, 10, 21; and selfishness, 15, 17, 19, 20, 32, 51, 65, 105, 152; and seed, 16, 33, 56, 76, 77, 84, 101, 129, 147, 180, 183, 187; rage, 22; punishment,

23, 78, 82; judging, 25; face, 31; let loose, 85; power, 138; battle with, 139; destruction, 146, 170, 201, 217; imagination as, 188, 197, 203
Shakespeare, William, 82, 150, 160, 186, 241n25
Sibbes, Richard, 13
Simmonds, James D., 76
Sin, 19-20, 84-85, 89; punishment, 29-30, 136; defeat, 46; freedom from, 51; temptation and, 53; man of, 77-78; curse, 86; Satan begets, 129; Adam's, 192; original, 203, 236n39; and private property, 204-205. *See also* Achan's sin
Skepticism, 47, 73
Skinner, B. F., 28
Sol iustitiae: and alchemy, 78-79; and sun worship, 117-119, 134, 138; and reason, 152; wrath, 170; use by Minucius Felix, 243n17
Song of Solomon, 33, 137, 140
Spenser, Edmund, 73
Spiritual autobiography, 16, 33-36, 54-61, 225n56
Starr, G. A., 59
Stoicism, 94, 178, 181, 182, 242n7, 243n17
Strafford, Earl of, 7, 89
Strong, William, 12
Sun of righteousness (Malachi *4:2*): as seed in everyone, 33, 36, 44, 47, 51, 69, 72, 77-79, 84, 86, 110, 117-122, 124, 127, 130-143, 146, 149-153, 158-159, 163, 166, 168-171, 180-181, 187, 205, 213; Christ as, 179, 192, 196, 198; word, 184; rule, 189; destroys Beast, 191; obscured by ministers, 195. *See also* Sol iustitiae
Swedenborg, Emanuel, 68
Swift, Jonathan, 82-83

Taborites, 172
Tauler, Johannes, 4
Taylor, Thomas, 13
Tertullian, 11, 175, 242n7
1 Thessalonians, 66
2 Thessalonians, 127
Theologia Germanica, 67
Thomas, Keith, 66

Tithes, 50, 104, 125, 130, 140, 142, 147, 167, 170, 191

Traherne, Thomas, 1, 75-76, 127, 130, 186, 238n56

Tree of Knowledge, 15, 19, 58, 129, 179-180; called "imagination," 183-184; in man, 188; and Adam, 191. *See also* Eden

Tree of Life, 20, 23, 57-58, 111, 141; reason as, 172; as logos, 180; called "love," 183; in everyone, 187, 188; mother symbol, 191; cross as, 103, 192; maturity, 196-197; and Joachim, 199; eating from, 201. *See also* Eden

Trinity, 2, 28, 35, 102-105

"Two witnesses," 24, 27, 28, 30, 36, 37, 40, 102

Typographic culture, 133-136

Typological method: Foxe's use, 5, 55; literal vs. allegorical, 11-13, 56, 121; and prophecy, 40-42, 211; and civil wars, 70-71, 139; and analogy, 102-103, 162; and time, 109; and Moses' covenant, 116; and Neoplatonism, 185; and history, 208

Tyranipocrit Discovered, 241n18

Universal salvation, 9, 16, 17, 18, 20-23, 67, 88

Universities, 3, 41, 86, 89-91, 93, 97, 134, 140, 142, 194-195, 207

Utopianism: revolutionary, 1; presbyterian, 5; and primitivism, 6; key to, 20; and "new vision," 28, 47-48, 81; communism and, 71, 98-99, 236n38; More's, 73, 124, 236n38; Diggers and, 128; oblique, 130, 148; and freedom, 172, 176, 202; in *The Law of Freedom*, 210-212

Vaughan, Henry, 130, 198; conversion, 62; *Silex Scintillans*, 62-63; and Winstanley, 63-64, 66, 77; "The Retreat," 64; "Cock-Crowing," 64; "Religion," 75; on nature, 75; "Angell-infancy," 75; thought, 76; and alchemy, 77; "Faith," 79

Vaughan, Thomas, 66

Wadsworth, Alfred P., 7

Waldenses, 172

Walwyn, William, 96, 144, 178, 237n46; 238n55, 240n16

Ware mutiny, 88

Watson, James D., 28

White, Rawlins, 43

Wigan, Lancashire, 3-4, 7, 135

"Wildernesse condition," 31, 54, 67

Winstanley, Edward, 3-4

Winstanley, Elizabeth, 218

Winstanley, Gerrard: early years, 3-7; *The Mysterie of God*, 9-23; *The Breaking of the Day of God*, 23-46; epistemology, 31, 72-73, 100-101, 104-105, 112, 127; *The Saints Paradise*, 46-87; *Truth Lifting Up Its Head*, 89-107; *The New Law of Righteousness*, 108-144; revelation, 126; *The True Levellers Standard Advanced*, 145-151; letters to Fairfax, 151-153, 160; *A Declaration*, 153; *An Appeal to the House of Commons*, 153-155; *A Watch-Word to the City of London*, 156-160; arrest and trial, 156ff; "The Diggers' Christmas Carol," 161-162; "A Hint of That Freedom Which Shall Come," 162-163; *A New-Yeers Gift to the Parliament and Army*, 163-171; *A Vindication of Those . . . Called Diggers*, 172-173; *Englands Spirit Unfoulded*, 174-175; *Fire in the Bush*, 175-206; *An Appeal to All Englishmen*, 206-207; *An Humble Request to the Ministers*, 207-209; letter to Lady Douglas, 209; *The Law of Freedom*, 210-218; last years, 218-219

Winstanley, Susan King, 4, 218

Wittenberg radicals, 2

Woodhouse, A. S. P., 98, 177-178

Wycliffe, John, 2, 42, 50, 89

Zechariah, 29

Zerubbabel, 29, 34

Zion, city of, 9, 10, 20-28, 63, 80, 110, 119, 138, 164, 202. *See also* Israel; New Jerusalem

Zosimos, 67

Zwickau prophets, 2